Continental
CHURCH FURNITURE
in England

A Traffic in Piety

CONTINENTAL CHURCH FURNITURE IN ENGLAND

A Traffic in Piety

Charles Tracy

ANTIQUE COLLECTORS' CLUB

ISBN 1 85149 376 X

British Library Cataloguing-in-Publication Data
A catalogue record for this book is available from the British Library

Printed in England
by the Antique Collectors' Club Ltd., Woodbridge, Suffolk
on Consort Royal Satin paper
supplied by the Donside Paper Company, Aberdeen, Scotland

FRONTISPIECE: *St. Mary, Harefield, Middlesex. Detail of high altar and Countess of Derby tomb (A/1 and B/7).*

Antique Collectors' Club

THE ANTIQUE COLLECTORS' CLUB was formed in 1966 and quickly grew to a five figure membership spread throughout the world. It publishes the only independently run monthly antiques magazine, *Antique Collecting*, which caters for those collectors who are interested in widening their knowledge of antiques, both by greater awareness of quality and by discussion of the factors which influence the price that is likely to be asked. The Antique Collectors' Club pioneered the provision of information on prices for collectors and the magazine still leads in the provision of detailed articles on a variety of subjects.

It was in response to the enormous demand for information on 'what to pay' that the price guide series was introduced in 1968 with the first edition of *The Price Guide to Antique Furniture* (completely revised 1978 and 1989), a book which broke new ground by illustrating the more common types of antique furniture, the sort that collectors could buy in shops and at auctions rather than the rare museum pieces which had previously been used (and still to a large extent are used) to make up the limited amount of illustrations in books published by commercial publishers. Many other price guides have followed, all copiously illustrated, and greatly appreciated by collectors for the valuable information they contain, quite apart from prices. The Price Guide Series heralded the publication of many standard works of reference on art and antiques. *The Dictionary of British Art* (now in six volumes), *The Pictorial Dictionary of British 19th Century Furniture Design*, *Oak Furniture* and *Early English Clocks* were followed by many deeply researched reference works such as *The Directory of Gold and Silversmiths*, providing new information. Many of these books are now accepted as the standard work of reference on their subject.

The Antique Collectors' Club has widened its list to include books on gardens and architecture. All the Club's publications are available through bookshops world wide and a full catalogue of all these titles is available free of charge from the addresses below.

Club membership, open to all collectors, costs little. Members receive free of charge *Antique Collecting*, the Club's magazine (published ten times a year), which contains well-illustrated articles dealing with the practical aspects of collecting not normally dealt with by magazines. Prices, features of value, investment potential, fakes and forgeries are all given prominence in the magazine.

Among other facilities available to members are private buying and selling facilities and the opportunity to meet other collectors at their local antique collectors' club. There are over eighty in Britain and more than a dozen overseas. Members may also buy the Club's publications at special pre-publication prices.

As its motto implies, the Club is an organisation designed to help collectors get the most out of their hobby: it is informal and friendly and gives enormous enjoyment to all concerned.

For Collectors — By Collectors — About Collecting

ANTIQUE COLLECTORS' CLUB
Sandy Lane, Old Martlesham, Woodbridge, Suffolk IP12 4SD, UK
Tel: 01394 389950 Fax: 01394 389999
Email: sales@antique-acc.com
Website: www.antique-acc.com
or
Market Street Industrial Park, Wappingers' Falls, NY 12590, USA
Tel: 845 297 0003 Fax: 845 297 0068
Email: info@antiquecc.com
Website: www.antiquecc.com

To
Clive Wainwright (1942-1999),
antiquary and scholar,
who gave me the idea for this book.

CONTENTS

ACKNOWLEDGEMENTS

It would not be possible to assemble all the information needed for a conspectus of this sort without the help and cooperation of many people and organisations. In particular, I would like to thank the many clergy who generously offered the interiors of their churches to my gaze, and allowed me to take photographs.

Also my thanks to the Bromley-Davenports at Capesthorne Hall, Hever Castle Limited, the Trustees of the Chatsworth Settlement, the National Trust at Oxburgh Hall, the various owners of Scarisbrick Hall, the Rector of Stonyhurst College, the Bowes Museum, the City of Manchester Art Gallery, and the Musée National du Moyen Âge (Musée de Cluny). The Churches Conservation Trust were kind enough to give me a free hand inside the redundant, and atmospheric, All Saints, Nuneham Courtenay, Oxfordshire. The Redundant Churches Fund allowed me to work at All Saints, Holdenby, Northamptonshire. Several objects from the Victoria and Albert Museum are included in Part II. I would like to thank James Yorke of the Department of Furniture and Woodwork for his help and patience. I hope that the many who have granted me small favours will accept my thanks non-specifically.

The necessary background research, both here and abroad, could not have been undertaken without the generous support of the British Academy. I have also received a welcome Small Research Grant from them towards the cost of black and white and colour photography and the preparation of text to camera-ready stage by the publishers.

I am grateful for the help and advice of colleagues, particularly the late Donald Findlay, who read and commented on some of the material. Simon Jervis' unwavering enthusiasm has lent encouragement, whilst Thomas Cocke and Peter Lasko have been supportive throughout. Such moral support has been invaluable through a gestation period of some seven years. It is evident just how much I have relied upon the various published and unpublished works of Clive Wainwright. I would also like to acknowledge a special debt to Kim Woods, whose dissertation on Flemish carved wooden altarpieces in England I have shamelessly mined. John A. Goodall has been uncomplainingly helpful in steering me clear of the treacherous reefs waiting to hole the novice in the murky waters of Continental heraldry. The following colleagues have been amongst those who have generously given me help and advice: Sarah Brown; Hugh Harrison; Christa Grössinger; Norbert Jopek; Sarah Medlam; Richard Palmer; Christopher Pickford; Anthony Rowland-Jones; Roy Thompson; Paul Williamson; The Reverend Canon David Weston; The Reverend Father Christopher Back; and The Reverend Prebendary Gerard Irvine. My thanks also to Timothy Shaw for suggesting that this study might be but a staging-post in a comprehensive study of European nostalgia.

For help on Part II I would particularly like to thank Stefaan Vandenberghe of the Stedelijke Museum, Bruges, who initially pointed me in the right directions for the Belgian material. The following Continental colleagues, have also given useful advice: Tim Graas; Georg Himmelheber; Ebbe Nyborg; Dirk Jonkanski; Martin Wenz; Christian Witt-Dörring; Jean-Claude Ghislain; and Robert Didier.

For permission to use archive material, I would like to thank James Yorke and my other colleagues at the Department of Furniture and Woodwork, the Victoria and Albert Museum; the Department of Prints and Drawings, the Victoria and Albert Museum; the Bristol Record Office; the archivists at the county record offices of Bedfordshire, Cheshire, Hampshire, Lancashire, Middlesex, and Warwickshire; Lambeth Palace Library; and the Council for the Care of Churches. Adrian Wilkinson of the Lincolnshire Archives deserves my undying gratitude for hitting the jackpot with the Rushbrooke letters. He has generously allowed me to publish extracts from the Cust journals and these letters.

To the Rector of Oscott College, I should express my gratitude for the help I received from that institution, and in particular for the memory of a very special day spent in the company of the late the Reverend Father Peter Dennison.

There are photographs used as illustrations from the collections of Batsford; the Caisse des Monuments Historiques et des Sites, Paris; the Bowes Museum; the Bristol Museum and Art Gallery; the Conway Library, Courtauld Institute of Art; the British Library; Country Life; the Gemeentearchief, Amsterdam; Harwood Church, Lancashire; Hugh Harrison; Institut Royal du Patrimoine Artistique, Brussels; A.F. Kersting; the National Monuments Record for England library; the Rijksdienst voor de Monumentenzorg, Zeist; the John Rylands University Library of Manchester; J.A.J.M. Verspaandonk; and the Victoria and Albert Museum picture library. I am grateful to the staff of these institutions for their help. An especial thank you, as usual, to Geoffrey Fisher at the Conway Library, Courtauld Institute of Art, who was unfailingly patient and helpful.

Bridget Cherry, and the publishers of the *Buildings of England Series,* have very generously allowed me to use their volumes as the basis for the Gazetteer.

Once again, I owe a special debt of gratitude to Yogish Sahota for processing and printing my photographs to such a high standard, and for creating such superb colour images under challenging conditions. And last, but not least, thanks to my editor, Prim Elliott, who has fielded my many corrections with cheerfulness.

PART I
INTRODUCTION
THE LATER MIDDLE AGES

In this wide-ranging conspectus of the importation of wooden church furniture into England from the continent of Europe between the later Middle Ages and the early twentieth century, it will be shown that motivations of different kinds, and even fashion, were important. Until the Reformation, commercial relations with our European neighbours, particularly Flanders, were intimate and England was importing a wide range of religious material.

Portable artifacts – such as plate, vestments, window glass, panel paintings and books – were imported into England from abroad throughout the Middle Ages and into the sixteenth century. Netherlandish manuscripts and printed books were acquired in large numbers, and there was even a specialised production in Flanders in Books of Hours for the English market, of which over two hundred still survive.[1] There was also a trade in Flemish painted panels. Petrus Christus of Bruges was commissioned by Edward Grimston to paint companion portraits of himself and his wife in 1446. In about 1480 the altarpiece, now in the National Gallery, London, by Hans Memlinc was ordered by Sir John Donne. In about 1510 the 'Master of the Magdalen Legend' was engaged to paint the 'Ashwellthorpe' triptych, now in the Castle Museum, Norwich. By the early sixteenth century several Netherlandish painters, not to mention artists from elsewhere in Europe, were being directly employed by the Tudor court. Indeed by that time there was a flourishing Flemish artists' colony established in Bermondsey.[2]

Before the sixteenth century, apart from the ubiquitous chest, we have only a little evidence for the direct importation of wooden furniture from abroad. The reason is most probably that oak choir-stalls, pews, lecterns and pulpits are cumbersome to transport and would have been of small intrinsic value compared to the more portable material. If furniture in a foreign style was required, it would have been much more rational to import the carpenter, as foreign wall painters, manuscript illuminators and goldsmiths are recorded as having been recruited throughout the period.[3]

It has often been suggested that certain church furniture, particularly in East Anglia, betrays a stylistic influence from Flanders. Indeed in 1931 Arnold Fleming put the case strongly when he said: 'The Church procured its wants chiefly from the Flemish craftsmen, who covered the altars with their finest Mechlin lace and linen, while the stalls, pulpits, and other pieces of furniture were not only made in Flanders, but were erected in various buildings by Flemings who crossed over to Britain for the express purpose'. He added: 'The history of Flemish wood-carving may be studied in the choir-stalls of many of our churches'.[4] Of course during the later Middle Ages, particularly in the south-east of England, contact with Flanders was close. But, *pace* Fleming, bulky wooden monuments, such as the screens at Lullingstone, Kent, and the Spring chantry at Lavenham, Suffolk, which are most often cited in this connection, are unlikely to have been fetched bodily from across the North Sea.[5]

The presence of an alien population in England was a fact of life, particularly from the late fourteenth century.[6] Indeed it has been estimated that by the early sixteenth century around 16,000 Flemish families were living in London.[7] However, in church furniture, apart from around twenty or so extant unambiguously foreign-made chests, it is most likely that a foreign stylistic influence is the mark of a resident alien or his son. The importance of the immigrant carvers and joiners in England is proved by the legislative means whereby it was deemed that they had to be controlled. In spite of the fact that many of them were encouraged to come to England in the first place, their conditions of work and domicile were closely supervised. A *Statute of the Realm* of 1483, which guaranteed that in the long run the English craft would benefit from the residence of the foreigners, insisted that foreign-born craftsmen could take only native-born Englishmen as apprentices.[8] This ordinance was regularly restated during Henry VIII's reign.

There are only a few tangible examples of the importation of metal and wooden church furniture of various kinds. The metalwork examples are prominent, such as the well-known bronze screen around the tomb of Henry VII at Westminster Abbey and its associated statuary. A Flemish example is the bronze grille, of about 1520, on the Earl of Worcester's tomb in St George's Chapel, Windsor.[9] A high proportion of the brass eagle lecterns in English parish churches and elsewhere are probably of Flemish manufacture. The iron gates of the Edward IV Chapel at St George's Chapel, Windsor, are of patently Flemish design, but according to Geddes are most likely to have been made in England.[10] There are also rare brass Continental candelabra in St John's Church, Perth, at Bristol Cathedral and another at Timberhill Church, near Norwich.[11] With the single exception of the canopies of the stalls at the Henry VII Chapel, Westminster Abbey, it is doubtful that Continental carvers played any significant part in the manufacture of the extant body of English Gothic choir-stalls. Certainly none of our choir-stalls was imported. It was also extremely rare for English screens to have been made by foreigners. The only safe exception to the rule is the mid-Devon group of parish church screens, which were almost certainly made by visiting French joiners (L/1, L/4 and L/5).

It is unlikely that any of the screenwork with strong Continental stylistic influence, such as the parclose screens commissioned by Prior Gondibour at Carlisle Cathedral (L/2), the lower part of the pulpitum and the parclose screen surrounding Prior Leschman's chantry at Hexham Abbey, or the French-influenced screens at Colebrooke, Coldridge and Brushford in Devon were imported.

In this connection the set of choir-stalls at King's College, Aberdeen, of 1506-09, should be mentioned.[12] Although the elaborate late Gothic tracery employed on the stall backs and stall ends has a Netherlandish appearance, the style is eclectic. It seems to be drawing on mid-fifteenth century Netherlandish exemplars as well as French Flamboyant ones of about the same period. Given that the quality is provincial, and the design sources heterogeneous and second-hand, it seems inevitable that the stalls would have been executed by the local craftsman, John Fendour, and his workshop. It is most unlikely that they were imported. The transportation over large distances of bulky items was generally avoided, and the exceptions to this rule were rare. One such is the canopywork for the St George's Chapel, Windsor, stalls, which was shipped by river from London. This was, of course, a relatively convenient domestic journey.

The only significant example of importation from abroad, in this case to Scotland, was the commissioning of a set of choir-stalls for Melrose Abbey, in about 1430, from Cornelius de Aeltre, a citizen and master of the carpenter's craft in Bruges.[13] The original contract stipulated that the stalls were to be made in the fashion of the furniture in the Cistercian church of Ter Duinen in West Flanders. Moreover they were to have as much carving on them as was to be found on the stalls of the sister church of Thosan, at Lisseweghe near Bruges. The reason that we know so much about this commission is that the details of a subsequent lawsuit have survived.[14] Legal proceedings were begun in 1441, probably some ten years after the drawing up of the original contract, which is lost. The master-carpenter had been paid in advance, but by 1441 the work was incomplete. The convent's claim for delivery of the furniture was brought before the Alderman of Bruges by Sir John Crawford, monk of Melrose, and Wiliam Carebis, a Scots merchant, both being procurators of the abbot and convent. Cornelius maintained that, shortly after he had been paid, there was a sharp drop in the value of the Flemish currency. Whilst he had been remunerated in debased coinage, he was still expected to purchase materials and pay his workmen in new coin. Furthermore he had discovered that the type of framing on the stalls at Ter Duinen was not robust enough for Melrose's requirements, so that he had to buy heavier and more expensive timber. Finally after a riot and a strike in Bruges, during which his carver was killed, his workmen had gone off with the advance he had paid them and he, his wife and children, were virtually penniless. At that time the choir-stalls were being stored in the refectory of the Franciscan friary in that city.

The case went in large measure against Melrose. It was found that the abbot and convent must compensate the friary for their trouble, pay for the woodwork to be transported to the port of Sluys and beyond to Scotland. In the meantime Cornelius was to receive an immediate lump sum to alleviate his condition and to pay for him to go to Scotland to set up the stalls. Cornelius was not to be molested or detained whilst abroad and, when his work was concluded, he should be fairly compensated for his losses. Apart from giving us a unique insight into the processes of a particular commission, the evidence shows not only that the choir-stalls were modelled on a Flemish design, but also that they were made in the master-carpenter's home town for shipment to Scotland. Both aspects of this commission are unique for Britain. The fraught circumstances of this enterprise demonstrate graphically why the direct importation of such material into England was never attempted. Special factors must have applied in this case to bring about such an unusual arrangement, over and above the flourishing Scottish wool trade with Flanders. If anything Melrose was more strongly connected with France than Flanders, through its relations with the Cistercian mother house of Cîteaux. One of the adjudicators in the case, John Cranach, Bishop of Brechlin, had been a student in the University of Paris. Also John Morrow, one of the master-masons at the abbey, is thought to have been a Frenchman.

It has been suggested that the choir-stalls at St Nicholas, Aberdeen, were also made in Flanders. The job of fitting up the choir was given to the John Fendour already mentioned, who was contracted to do the work on 20 December 1507. The proposition was that the stalls and canopywork were made in Flanders, and that the screen and chancel door were left to Fendour himself.[15] Fendour may have been a second generation denizened Fleming, who no doubt would have been ready to sub-contract the making of the stalls to a Netherlandish joiner. All we know for sure, however, is that he is unlikely to have had the time to carve the stalls himself, as he was employed at the same time to organise the King's

College, Aberdeen, workshop. Simpson states that the name Fendour might suggest a French origin, but in any case he was so deeply involved in organising joinery and structural carpentry commissions up and down Scotland, not to mention his forays into the Highlands to select timber, that he is most unlikely to have been a foreigner.[16] There is no documentary evidence for a Netherlandish commission at St Nicholas and the style of the canopywork fragments that have been published hardly betrays Flemish workmanship.

It is well established that the late medieval Scottish church was ready to commission and import foreign works of art for their use. Kinloss Abbey, Melrose's daughter church, is said to have bought vestments and silver plate from Flanders. In 1538 the French painter Andrew Bairhum was brought over to decorate the abbey's chapels and the abbot's lodgings.[17]

In 1508 the prior of Pluscarden Abbey issued a charter, dealing with imported tabernacled altar-pieces as follows: 'twa tabirnaclez in ye said abbay That is to say ane to yie alter and ane oyer to our lady alter to ye making in Flandris'.[18] Again, the accounts of Dunkeld Cathedral provide an idea of the cost of buying and shipping an altarpiece from Flanders. Two 'tabernacles' were ordered by Bishop George Brown of Dunkeld, arriving at the port of Dundee in 1505. One was placed in the parish kirk of Dundee and the other in Dunkeld Cathedral.[19] The accounts are specific about the cost of the altarpiece destined for Dundee parish kirk: 'Item ane tabirnacle to my Lordis altar in Dounde the price witht custum, fraucht and al uthir uncostis in Flaundris, thretty pundis and auchtene schilling greit'.[20] Another Continental altarpiece was collected for Paisley Abbey by Abbot Thomas Tervas. This is described in the *Auchinlech Chronicle* as 'the statliest tabernakle that was in all Scotland and the most costlie'.[21]

The Scottish medieval churches suffered a holocaust of iconoclastic destruction at the hands of the Calvinists.[22] However, if the only surviving painted panels from Holy Trinity Church, Edinburgh[23] are anything to go by, the quality of these Scottish imports was high. The intimacy of artistic links with Flanders is underlined by the fact that in 1468 a certain Alexander Bening, almost certainly a Scotsman, was admitted to the guild of painters in Ghent as an illuminator.[24] Indeed it has been suggested that the Holy Trinity panels may have been painted by Hugo van der Goes, who sponsored Bening and was most probably related to him by marriage.[25]

The traffic in carved Flemish late medieval altarpieces throughout northern Europe is well known. There was a vigorous dissemination to parish and greater churches from the Low Countries, particularly to the Rhineland, which was but a short journey away.[26] Several churches in that area owned more than one Flemish altarpiece. There is also a concentration of them in and around Stockholm in Sweden. The two altarpieces in the church of Ternant in France were ordered, probably in the 1440s and 1460s, by Philippe de Ternant, who was a councillor to Philip the Good, and his son Charles who served under Charles the Bold.[27] Claudio de Villa, an Italian banker, ordered an altarpiece in Brussels probably just before 1471.[28] In 1522 the Lübeck merchant, Johan Boenne, set up in the Marienkirche in that town the Brussels altarpiece dated 1518.[29]

Our knowledge of the export trade in Flemish altarpieces has increased enormously since the publications of Ewing and Jacobs in recent years. Formerly it was assumed that, in the medieval tradition, most altarpieces were especially commissioned. Although this continued to be the custom in Germany, Ewing's research into the operations of the markets, or *panden*, in Antwerp, from the mid-fifteenth century to the mid-sixteenth century, shows that the trade in 'off-the peg' altarpieces was predominant in Flanders. His work has provided a fascinating insight into the huge and flourishing export trade for Flemish luxury goods and religious artefacts over a very wide area of Europe and beyond.[30] The *panden* were specialist markets located in dedicated quarters of the city. The largest was 'Our Lady's *Pand'*, and is described by the author as 'the largest centralised art market in Europe'. Would-be patrons could travel to Antwerp from all over Europe and enjoy a wide selection of altarpieces to choose from. They could visit the *ateliers* of individual artists, or they could attend the auctions of the weekly free markets. In addition there were the two important international fairs in Antwerp, the St Bavo's Fair in October and the Pentecost fair. Brussels was also another important centre for this predominant 'ready-made' trade.[31]

The purchase of an altarpiece in 1524 from Our Lady's *Pand,* made directly by the patron for the Premonstratensian monastery of Averbode, Brabant is recorded as follows:

> 6 October 1524 (i.e. St Bavo's Fair): Gerart (van der Scaeft), abbot of Averbode, bought from Laureys Keldermans, alias the panel-maker, an altarpiece of eight feet, which stood in Antwerp in Our Lady's *Pand*, and is now on the altar of Our Lady and All the Virgins in the church of Averbode (for the price of) fourteen and a half Flemish pounds....[32]

On the other hand another kind of purchase is also recorded, probably by a dealer for resale in his own country. A Willem Knocx of Edinburgh bought a Mechelen-made altarpiece in Antwerp on 1 December 1439. He agreed with the Antwerp merchant, Wouter Michiels, to pay on delivery for '...a gilded altarpiece with sculptures that he bought in Antwerp from Hanne van Battele, van Mechelen'.[33]

Only two of the many painted altarpieces recorded in customs documents as having been brought over to England in the early sixteenth century have a secure provenance.[34] The so-called Ashwellthorpe Triptych was commissioned by Christopher Knyvet of Ashwellthorpe, Norfolk from a named Flemish artist.[35] We also know that in about 1478-80 Sir John Donne commissioned a triptych in Bruges from Hans Memlinc.[36] Another altarpiece which may have been in England since this period is the triptych in the Almshouse of St John the Baptist and St John the Evangelist, Sherborne, Dorset. It is thought to have been made in France under strong Flemish influence.[37]

There is plenty of evidence from wills and inventories for the importation of altarpieces into England. For instance a Kingston upon Hull will of the late fifteenth century records a bequest to the altar of Corpus Christi in the church of the Holy Trinity. In 1497 the merchant Thomas Dalton left £8 for the acquisition of a table of 'oversea work' to be placed at this altar.[38] Again in 1520 the sum of £10 was bequeathed by another merchant, Robert

Harryson, for a table of 'oversea work' to be set up in the same place.[39] Cardinal Wolsey was advised in 1515 by a letter from Brussels that the following would be sent to him: 'A table for an awter, which was made by the best master of all this land'.[40] It is safe to conclude that Flemish altarpieces must have been imported in significant numbers. However, as emblematic of the unreformed church in form and foreign in style, they have yielded up to the iconoclastic bonfires almost without exception.

A ship docking in London in 1509 had in its cargo three dozen painted tables (probably paintings), fifteen carved images, a basket containing fourteen wooden images, and an additional fifteen small wooden images.[41] The records of a trading dispute between Flemish and English merchants evidence that in 1512 at St Bavo's Fair in Antwerp, a Lysbette Lambrechts purchased two wooden altarpieces, polychromed and gilded, specifically for sale to England.[42] In 1523 the Mercer's Company, having appraised a *platt devised & drawn by oon Walter Vandale of Enderwerp karver*, commissioned from him a costly altarpiece for their new chapel in London.[43]

However, apart from altar tables, a trawl through the English medieval customs accounts turns up hardly any church furniture. Mention is made of lecterns (lectoria, letern, lettrone, letteron), an analogous entry for our purposes. None the less the importation of Continental secular furniture, particularly chests, is of interest. The very large quantities of chests involved indicate, of course, that the term in general must have denoted multi-purpose goods containers.[44] At the port of Southampton between 28 October 1308 and 17 August 1309 no fewer than 2,268 chests were conveyed on only four ships, probably of French origin. They were listed typically as 'xxxii duodenas arcarum'. The items that might be of interest come under many different names, chests being known as ciste, forcers, fortsiere, cof(f)ers, coffres, coffyns, trunces etc. Chests were sometimes listed on their own, such as '1 pruce cista', or in multiples, as in 'iii nests cistarum'. Often they were specified, sometimes as 'bankers', being filled with wool, textiles, soap etc. No doubt a few of the latter would have had an ecclesiastical application.[45]

The origins of the imported furniture varied from mainly France, Portugal and Italy, for ships arriving at Southampton and London, to the Low Countries, the Baltic and Rhineland Germany for ships docking at Kingston upon Hull and Newcastle upon Tyne.

The particular origins of some of the chests is indicated as Prussian, variously referred to as 'my pruce kyst', 'a chest del spruce', 'a sprosse chest', 'a spruce kyste', 'a spreuse kyste', 'my coffer of spruce', 'a spruse Kist', and 'Danske',[46] Flanders (Flaunders), or Portuguese (Portingall). The Books of Rates listing the import duty on different goods indicate that 'Danske' chests were made of pine.[47] The word 'spruce' is a corruption of 'Prussia', the lands south-east of the Baltic, whose port is Danzig ('Dantzic', 'Dainsiche', 'Dance', 'Danste' and 'Dansque').[48] Danske chests were probably always stained or painted.[49]

Wills and inventories are also a useful pointer to the origins of certain chests. They abound with such references to imported items. For instance, the inventory of William Melton, Chancellor of York, dated 1528 states: 'In the great chambre ... two Flaunders chistes, and ij other chistes vjs. viijd.' Robert Kyrkley, Rector of Loftus, in Cleveland, who died in 1468, left: 'a counter of Flanders warke'; and in 1552 Alice Maulever, a widow of Wothersome, left to Edmund her son: 'my great presses, my great cheiste carved upon the foreside and one counter of oversee work'.[50] Counters were tables or chests which had a special top marked out for making calculations. In an age before writing paper was freely available they were the principal means for bankers and merchants of carrying out business pricing and drawing up accounts.[51]

A group of surviving late-medieval chests in England has long been recognised as being of Continental origin, although as yet no detailed study has been made of them. They are nearly all secular in their decoration and so, with the exception of the one at Crediton, Devon (F/4) and the 'Cypress chests' (F/2, F/3, F/8, F/10, F/11 and F/12), have not been included in the highlights from the National Collection in Part II. A broad indication of their provenance is given below:

Low Countries: St Michael, Alnwick, Northumberland; St Brandon, Brancepeth, Co. Durham (now

destroyed); All Saints, Chevington, Norfolk; St Peter's, Derby; St Andrew, Hacconby, Lincolnshire; St Thomas, Harty, Kent ('Tilting' chest); St Mary, Northchurch, Hertfordshire; London, Victoria and Albert Museum, 'Tilting chest'; New College, Oxford ('Courtrai Chest'); St Mary, Wath, West Riding, Yorkshire.[52]
The so-called 'Courtrai Chest' is quite possibly a fake.[53]

France: Holy Cross, Crediton, Devon (F/4); St Elgin, North Frodingham, East Riding, Yorkshire; Christchurch Mansion, Ipswich, Suffolk; Romsey Abbey, Hampshire; St Edmund, Southwold, Suffolk.

Low Countries/Germany: All Saints, Hereford; Hereford Cathedral; St Mary Magdalen, Oxford; St Peter and St Paul, Saltwood, Kent.

The Cypress (or cipress) chests seem to have been imported mostly from Northern Italy, although they may have ultimately come from the island of Crete.[54] They were decorated on the front panel with cut-out designs, almost in the manner of a woodcut block. These panels were probably originally painted. On the inside of the lid were drawings in black penwork. They were probably made of both cypress and cedar wood, both of which are said to have moth-proofing qualities. The six ecclesiastical 'cypress' chests, or fragments of same, in the National Collection (Part II) were made on the cusp of the fifteenth and sixteenth centuries. They must have been either altar chests, or for storing vestments, or both.

The presence of 'cypress' chests in domestic settings is widely attested. In the early seventeenth century 'a sipresse cheaste' at Cockesden, Essex, in 1626 contained a full set of bed hangings and a 'popinjay green damask twillt'.[55] Some of them could be very large indeed, as the one at Walton in 1624, which contained a presumably dismantled loom.[56] Their function is graphically described in a passage from Shakespeare's *The Taming of the Shrew:*

> In ivory coffers I have stuff'd crowns;
> In cypress chests my arras, counterpoints,
> Costly apparel, tents, and canopies,
> Fine linen, Turkey cushions boss'd with pearl,
> Valance of Venice gold in needle-work,
> Pewter and brass, and all things that belong
> To house or house-keeping.[57]

Other kinds of secular furniture were imported in varying quantities. Wainscot panels were in considerable demand. In one year alone (1383-84) 6,260 panels were brought in via Kingston upon Hull. Various kinds of beds, including feather beds, and bed boards were imported, stools, chairs, 'cupbordes' and dressers. Tables were acquired from abroad, including '1 dossena writing tabularum' (1509), 1 'tabula plicante (covered)' (1392-93), 'vi pariis playing tabylles' (1420-21), and 'iii dossenis tabularum depictarum' (1420-21).

THE COLOUR PLATES

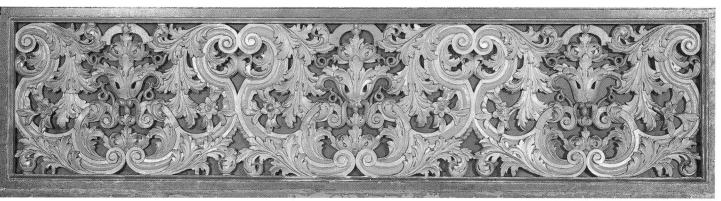

COLOUR PLATE 1. *All Saints, Tooting Graveney, London. Italian altar frontal. Late 17th century. (A/3)*

COLOUR PLATE 2. *St Mary's College, New Oscott, Sutton Coldfield. Flemish altar rails. Inscribed 1680. (B/13)*

COLOUR PLATE 3. *All Saints, Tooting Graveney, London. Italian high altar reredos. 18th century. (C/3)*

COLOUR PLATE 4. *All Saints, Tooting Graveney, London. Canopy. Probably Italian. 18th century. (C/4)*

COLOUR PLATE 5. *All Saints, Tooting Graveney, London. Florentine candle stand. 18th century. (D/1)*

COLOUR PLATE 6a. *St Mary and All Saints, Beaconsfield, Buckinghamshire. Italian ceremonial chair. Mid-18th century. Painted leather seat back (E/1)*

COLOUR PLATE 6. *St Mary and All Saints, Beaconsfield, Buckinghamshire. Italian ceremonial chair. Mid-18th century. (E/1)*

COLOUR PLATE 7. *The Deanery, Exeter Cathedral. Throne. One of a pair. Italian or Spanish. Second quarter 16th century. (E/3)*

COLOUR PLATE 7a. *The Deanery, Exeter Cathedral. Throne. One of a pair. Italian or Spanish. Second quarter 16th century. Detail of painted seat back. (E/3)* COPYRIGHT HUGH HARRISON

COLOUR PLATE 8. *All Saints, Tooting Graveney, London. Netherlandish bench. Mid-18th century. (E/6)*

Colour Plate 9. *All Saints, Tooting Graveney, London. Italian prie-dieu. Early 17th century. (H/3)*

COLOUR PLATE 10. *St Mary the Virgin, Buscot, Oxfordshire. Spanish lectern. 17th century. (I/2)*

COLOUR PLATE 11. *All Saints, Tooting Graveney, London. Italian lectern. Late 17th century. (I/7)*

COLOUR PLATE 12. *All Saints, Nuneham Courtenay, Oxfordshire. Italian lectern. Early 18th century. (I/8)*

COLOUR PLATE 13. *All Saints, Nuneham Courtenay, Oxfordshire. Italian font cover. 17th century. (J/11)*

COLOUR PLATE 14. *St Mary's College, New Oscott, Sutton Coldfield, Warwickshire. Reliquary coffer. Probably French. Late 15th century. (J/12)*

COLOUR PLATE 15. *St Mary's College, New Oscott, Sutton Coldfield, Warwickshire. Tabernacle. Probably French. Early 18th century. (J/13)*

COLOUR PLATE 16. *St Mary the Virgin, Buscot, Berkshire. Netherlandish choir-stall. Early 17th century. (M/6)*

COLOUR PLATE 17. *All Saints, Tooting Graveney, London. Italian choir-stalls. Third quarter 17th century. (M/17)*

COLOUR PLATE 18. *St Mary's College, New Oscott, Sutton Coldfield, Warwickshire. Flemish choir-stalls. Early 18th century. (M/31)*

COLOUR PLATE 19. *St Mary's College, New Oscott, Warwickshire. Confessional by A.W.N. Pugin.*

Chapter I

FROM THE REFORMATION TO 1700

From within a few years of the Reformation little church furniture was imported into England. There were even spells during this time when the political and trade relations with neighbouring countries was suspended altogether. On the other hand, the immigration of foreign craftsmen, and particularly joiners, increased very much during the sixteenth century, the seventeenth century up to the Civil War, and again from the restoration of the monarchy and into the eighteenth century.[1] We know that Henry VIII provided a stimulus to foreign craftsmen and painters, mainly from Burgundy.[2] The making of the windows for King's College chapel, Cambridge, in the second, third and fourth decades of the sixteenth century is a commission which exemplifies the phenomenon. Of the seven King's College glaziers identified by name in the contracts, one was German, three were Flemings, and the remaining three were probably English.[3] Two of the best known alien glaziers, Galyon Hone from Holland and Francis Williamson from Flanders, played an important part in the struggle of both provincial and immigrant glaziers to ward off the City of London's attempts to circumscribe them.[4] The choir-stalls at King's College, Cambridge, are another testament to Henry VIII's generous patronage of alien craftsmen.

During Queen Elizabeth's reign economic and artistic links with the North Netherlands became even stronger. In her 'Declaration' of 1585, the monarch commended the Dutch as England's 'most ancient and familiar neighbours', the nations 'by common language of long time resembled and termed man and wife'.[5] Indeed the late sixteenth century laid the basis for the close relationship with Holland which led eventually to the accession of William of Orange to the English throne. In parallel, relations of all kinds with the South Netherlands were very much reduced. In 1568 the Duke of Alva arrested the English merchants in Antwerp, and virtually all trade ceased between the two countries for five years. Whereas the Dutch gained economically from these developments, the English benefited from the immigration of skilled Protestant workers from Flanders and France. The suppression of the Protestants in the South Netherlands led to a fundamental change in English political and cultural allegiance in the Low Countries.

In the South Netherlands, during the persecutions, it is estimated that under the Duke of Alva (1667-73) some 60,000 people, some two percent of the population, emigrated. However, even before 1609, approximately 40,000 had already fled. Although many escaped to the Northern Provinces and Germany, a large number found shelter in England, in London, the south and East Anglia. Huguenot refugees flooded in from France, some 40,000 or 50,000 of them during the sixteenth century.[6] It was said of Norwich by a nineteenth century historian that 'in 1574 the town was so full of Protestant refugees from France and the Netherlands, that the bailiffs published an edict forbidding the influx of any more of these foreigners, many of whom were ingenious artisans, and by settling in Norwich and its neighbourhood, greatly improved the staple manufactures of this county.'[7] At that time 'strangers', principally from the Ypres area of western Flanders, made up approximately one third of the city's population.[8] At Canterbury in 1582 there were 1,679 members of the French-speaking Flemish and Norman immigrant congregation, amounting to nearly twenty percent of the total population of the city.[9]

With regard to the late sixteenth century and early seventeenth century, Wells-Cole has recently argued that most of the wood-carving workshops active in English country houses, churches and the metropolis seem to have been of native origin. On the other hand, he mentions the Exeter workshop where the joiners were probably members of the Garrett or Herman families who, to judge from their surnames, seem to have been immigrants from the Netherlands.[10] It must have been difficult for foreign joiners to work in some towns, as is shown, for instance, by the constitution of the Company of Joiners of Newcastle upon Tyne who banned any

Scots or aliens from being admitted as apprentices. Wells-Cole sensibly observes that much more research needs to be done on the regional workshops and 'the nature of foreign influence'.[11]

Large numbers of 'joiners', 'turners', 'scryn-makers', 'kistmakers', 'drayers', 'busmakers', 'arcularii', 'fabers', 'gilders', 'carvers' and 'carvers for joiners work'. 'virginal makers', 'cofer makers', 'boxe-makers' and 'stole makers' are recorded as living beyond the confines of the City of London.[12] The most important places of origin are Brabant, followed by Jülich (now part of North Rhine-Westphalia), Burgundy, Cologne and Antwerp.[13] Surprisingly few French craftsmen are listed. It is probable that these workmen specialized in the production of the kind of wares that they had made at home. The 'Offley' chest in Southwark Cathedral, for instance, and the many erroneously-called 'Nonsuch' chests, were probably made by denizened German joiners. However, it has not been possible as yet to distinguish between the output of native and immigrant craftsmen.[14]

From the first half of the sixteenth century, the Salkeld screen at Carlisle Cathedral and the choir-stalls at King's College Chapel, Cambridge, exemplify alien manufactures which must have been made here. They testify to the stylistic independence of their designers and confirm that the alien workshops of Southwark could command patronage from all over the country.

Apart from the fitting out of the Chapel Royal at St James's Palace, London, in 1535-40, and of several of the Oxford and Cambridge colleges, little new ecclesiastical building or renovation was carried out in England during the sixteenth century. At Cambridge, Clare College had a new chapel in 1535, and Corpus Christi College likewise in 1579. The choir of the chapel of King's College, Cambridge, was completed in the early 1540s and the chapel of Trinity Hall was renovated between 1560 and 1584. At Oxford the chapel of Balliol College was completed in 1529 and the chapel at Brasenose College consecrated in 1512. The chapel at Corpus Christi College was renovated between 1598 and 1607, the chapel of St John's College consecrated in 1530, and the chapel of Trinity College, Oxford, was renovated in the middle of the century and reopened for worship in 1556.[15]

By the early seventeenth century it becomes more difficult to differentiate between native and alien manufacture in woodwork. The problem is compounded by the fact that after the publication of books of plates with classical details, particularly Vredeman de Vries' *Architectura,* published in Antwerp in 1577, and Robert Peake's English edition of *Serlio,* in 1611, the stylistic repertory of this work on both sides of the North Sea becomes identical. The problem is particularly acute in East Anglia. Wells-Cole has said of the magnificent font cover at Walpole St Peter, Norfolk that, 'one may guess that he [the joiner] was either a foreigner, or a native joiner trained in a foreigner's workshop'.[16] Indeed he compares it with the pulpits at Ginneken and Beets in the South Netherlands (van Swigchem *et al.,* p.182). Writing about furniture made in Norfolk during the first three decades of the seventeenth century, he concludes that 'the printed page or the example of foreign craftsmen were the dominant influences in the county which had a long tradition of trade with the Low Countries and supported a substantial immigrant population'.[17]

The so-called 'Laudian Revival', with its interest not only in the reinstatement of altar rails and the re-introduction of a medieval form for the chalice, but also in the commissioning of completely new sets of chancel furniture, was a tentative but significant step on the long road back to self-confident ecclesiastical patronage in England.[18] This movement was, of course, anticipated in the building that Charles I commissioned for his Catholic queen in the mid-1620s, the Queen's Chapel. It was provided with altar rails, but, as far as we know, all the furniture was designed by the building's architect, Inigo Jones.

Only one Cambridge college chapel, that of Peterhouse, was renovated or rebuilt at this time.[19] There was more activity at Oxford, where the newly-founded Wadham College's chapel was dedicated in 1613, Lincoln College's new chapel dedicated in 1631, Balliol College's chapel provided with a new wooden screen in 1636, and Oriel College's chapel completed in 1642.[20] In London the furnishings at Lambeth Palace, which included stalls and an impressive western screen, were made by Adam Brown in 1633, at the specific direction of Archbishop Laud.[21] The most important commission of the Laudian era was the renovation of Old St Paul's Cathedral, which began in 1631. Unfortunately nothing is known of the wooden fittings.

There was, of course, a marked Continental influence visible in the best English furniture, secular and ecclesiastical, in the seventeenth century. The now destroyed pulpit of 1613, formerly at All Hallows, Barking, a prototype for the Restoration period pulpits, seems to derive from Italy.[22]

In general, the English learned about Renaissance and Mannerist Classicism through the medium of North European pattern books and with the participation of North European craftsmen. Although the executants of the Laudian commissions were most probably all native craftsmen, we do have evidence in 1636 for the involvement of a foreigner, the Fleming Thomas Caper, a resident of Salisbury, who is recorded as having made the pulpit at St Thomas's Church, Newport, on the Isle of Wight (Plate 1, K/10).[23] Unequivocal provenances like this are rare indeed. Unlike the Norfolk pulpits of this time, the monument is richly historiated and makes few concessions to English taste.

St Paul's Cathedral dominated ecclesiastical patronage again at the end of the seventeenth century, along with the rebuilding of the City churches. It seems that most of Wren's wood-working craftsmen, with the important exception of the Rotterdam born Grinling Gibbons, were native Englishmen. Gibbons' most important contribution to ecclesiastical furnishings was at St Paul's Cathedral, where, amongst other things, he designed and executed the organ case, and decorated the choir-stalls.[24] Apart from Gibbons there were two other outstanding foreigner craftsmen at the Restoration period – the Dane C.G. Cibber and the Fleming Arnold Quellin, the brother of Artus Quellinus who collaborated with the making of the choir-stalls at Hemiksem Abbey, Antwerp (page 100). Both were involved in church commissions. Cibber undertook the building of the Danish Church in Wellclose Square, London, which was consecrated in 1696.[25] Quellin, in partnership with Gibbons, made the altarpiece for James II's Roman Catholic Chapel at Whitehall.[26] A considerable portion of it, including Quellin's worshipping angels and Gibbons' cherubs, survives at St Andrew, Burnham-on-Sea, Somerset.[27]

PLATE 1. *St Thomas, Newport, Isle of Wight. Pulpit by Thomas Caper of Salisbury. Dated 1637. (K/10)*

In commenting on this work Pevsner drew attention to the French iconography of the angels adoring the sacrament.[28]

With these exceptions the introduction of foreign-influenced woodwork in English greater churches after the Civil War seems to have been limited to the altar rails of about 1700, in the style of Gibbons, at Winchester Cathedral,[29] and the choir-stalls erected by Bishop Hacket at Lichfield Cathedral around 1665,[30] although a few more examples could possibly be cited.

Whereas alien sculptors were active in England throughout the eighteenth century, their contribution is not recorded in the field of church furniture. Of foreign influence, Italianate reredoses proliferated, as for example at Canterbury Cathedral in 1732.[31] Surprisingly, the most uncompromisingly Continental Baroque pulpit and font cover were introduced at Beverley Minster in the early part of the century.[32]

Chapter II

THE BIRTH OF NOSTALGIA

The earliest instance of a self-consciously antiquarian-minded importation of alien church furniture may have been the acquisition of the Flemish pulpit for the chapel at Capesthorne Hall, Cheshire *c.*1722. We cannot be absolutely certain that the structure is contemporary with the new chapel, and was not introduced in the early nineteenth century, either by the picture collector Walter Davenport or subsequently by Edward Blore, who remodelled and enlarged the house. However, judging by the late nineteenth century arrangement, of which we have a record (Plate 2), the probability is that it is coeval. The Capesthorne pulpit was not an integral piece, being a fusion of Renaissance body on a Baroque base (K/3). None the less, its overall classical appearance suited perfectly the architecture of the enclosing space. The liturgical rationale for this centrally placed rostrum surely accords more nearly with an early Commissioners' church by Hawksmoor or Archer than with any scheme that the younger Pugin might have envisaged. In their furniture confections the Victorians tried as hard as possible to replicate authentic pieces. Whereas the Capesthorne conglomeration is blatantly unlearned, it is in keeping with the architecture, which is more than can be said for much of the Continental church furniture imported during the nineteenth century. The arrangement, if original, would predate any other such display of ecclesiastical antiquarianism by more than a hundred years.

The early nineteenth century passion for collecting European church furniture was not so much concerned with a new-found interest in medieval Gothic art so much as a manifestation of an appetite for bargain-hunting and an unashamed and enthusiastic curiosity. It was also a protest against the austerity of neo-Classical architecture. Horace Walpole collected Old Master paintings, as the monarchy and the Grand Tourists had always done, but little in the way of medieval Gothic. Walpole's eighteenth century Gothic revival was nostalgic, backward-looking and unfocused, on the one hand,

and ironical and witty on the other. His house provided whimsical 'sets' for 'medieval' fireplaces, plaster-vaulted ceilings and 'Gothick' doors. But the contents of Strawberry Hill were much less Gothic than has been supposed.[1] Amongst the objects sold in 1842 very few were medieval. As Reitlinger pointed out, the bulk of the stained glass windows were Renaissance, and Walpole had not acquired a single Gothic tapestry.[2] His medieval-style furniture was contemporary Gothic-Revival. Of the 'Gothic' furniture designed for the Great Parlour, according to Walpole's own *Description:* 'The chairs are black, of a gothic pattern, designed by Mr Bentley and Mr Walpole. The Table of Sicilian jasper on a black frame designed by Mr Bentley … over each a looking glass in a gothic frame of black and gold, designed by Mr Walpole'. About the table, Wainwright observes that: 'its style with its barley-sugar twist legs was Tudor or Elizabethan rather than Gothic …'.[3] Apart from the mantelpieces, which were inspired by Gothic tombs, there was a wooden screen in the Holbein Chamber, modelled on the late medieval choir-screen at Rouen Cathedral.[4] Walpole is supposed to have bought a medieval chair emanating from Glastonbury Abbey, which has since disappeared.[5]

His other medieval interests were manuscripts, coins, ivories, and metalwork. The chapel at Strawberry Hill contained some medieval English stained glass and an Italian Romanesque shrine, allegedly acquired from the church of Santa Maria Maggiore in Rome.[6] Also in the chapel were four panels, said to have come from Bury St Edmunds Abbey. They were described as the wings of an altarpiece. After he had bought them, Walpole 'had them sawed into four pictures'.[7]

The panels are considered in the *Description* in some detail. In the Oratory, attached to the house, there was, according to the *Description*, 'a saint of bronze'. This was a French fifteenth century figure of an angel, which has since been acquired by the Victoria and Albert Museum.[8]

The first category of church furnishings to be

PLATE 2. *Capesthorne Hall, Cheshire. Chapel. View looking east. Late 19th century photograph. (K/3)*

imported in any quantity before the French Revolution was stained and painted glass. Horace Walpole remarks that…

> About the year 1743 one Asciotti, an Italian, who had married a Flemish woman, brought a parcel of ancient glass from Flanders, and sold it for a very few guineas to the Hon. Mr Bateman of Old Windsor. Upon that I sent Asciotti again to Flanders, who brought me 450 pieces for which, including the expense of his journey, I paid him thirty-six guineas.[9]

In a letter to Sir Horace Mann, British Ambassador at the court of Florence, he requested some glass for his 'little gothic castle' at Strawberry Hill.[10] According to Walpole, 'in 1761 Paterson, an Auctioneer at Essex House in the Strand, opened the first Exhibition of painted glass, imported … from Flanders'.[11]

This trade in foreign glass began with secular material. It was not until after the Revolution that the English started to buy up ecclesiastical glass in any quantity, a preoccupation of the first four decades of the nineteenth century. None the less, as early as before 1775 the important glass by Arnold van Nijmegen came to England, to embellish the windows of St Mary and St Nicholas, Wilton, Lichfield Cathedral, and since 1840, St George's, Hanover Square. The Lichfield and London glass was acquired by Henry Loftus, later Marquess of Ely. In 1787 Lord Radnor purchased a Nativity at Angers which he placed in the east window of the church at Coleshill, Berkshire.[12]

Up to the French Revolution there would have been very little opportunity to bring church furniture in wood back to England. But the new-found interest in Gothic architecture, the burgeoning of archaeology, and the possibilities of fabricating a house interior that could recreate the past, produced the right climate to capitalise upon the buying opportunities offered by the upheaval in France when it came.

A rare example of the importation of a religious artifact before the French Revolution is the acquisition by Charles Towneley, of Towneley Hall, Lancashire, of an impressive carved Bruges altarpiece.[13] Towneley is much better known as an avid collector of Classical sculpture, and certainly most of his wanderings in Europe were in Italy. Although he is supposed to have bought the monument in Italy, it is far more likely that he acquired it on his way through to his preferred destination. As Woods has observed, the importation of the altarpiece anticipates by several decades the mania for collecting church furniture of all kinds in the early-Victorian period. The Towneleys were an old Catholic family, and Charles' immediate predecessors had rebuilt the old family chapel in a new position at Towneley Hall, being careful to preserve its seventeenth century wooden panelling. This was well before such families were officially given permission to reopen their chapels under the Catholic Relief Act of 1791. Like many of the prominent recusant families, the Towneleys had kept up a connection with Catholic Belgium and France. Charles himself studied at Douai College. During his later years he is reported as having become very religious.[14] He must have bought the altarpiece some time during his reign as head of the family, between 1772 and 1805, and possibly even earlier than this.

Chapter III

THE TRAFFIC IN CONTINENTAL CHURCH FURNITURE 1789-1860

Now commences the golden age for the transhipment of this material to our acquisitive shores. As Gustav Waagen in 1838 had observed:

> … when the storm of the French revolution burst over different countries of Europe … scarcely was a country overrun by the French, when Englishmen skilled in the arts were at hand with their guineas.[1]

Most of it was imported during the second, third and fourth decades of the nineteenth century because of the French Revolution, the revival of interest in medieval Gothic art, and the re-instatement of Roman Catholicism.

The Revolution was a catastrophe for French aristocrats, but it was to such portable possessions as paintings and movable furniture that they turned in order to raise cash in a hurry.[2] The process of secularisation in France, and later in the Belgian provinces, offered as prey, to anyone who would give even the slightest sum for them, the furnishings of probably thousands of greater, collegiate and parish churches. However, during the revolutionary and Napoleonic eras, the English grandees were understandably reluctant to travel abroad, particularly as a steady supply of paintings and small objects kept filtering through the salerooms in London. The preamble to a 'Catalogue of the Pictures, Drawings, Painted Glass etc., etc., … sold by private contract at the European Museum, King Street, St James's Square' in 1791 gives a graphic insight into the situation in France at the time:

> Wars and Commotions are seldom favourable to the fine Arts, the late Revolution in France and Flanders have deprived these Countries of many inestimable Productions which otherwise, could never have been removed; many of the Valuable pictures now consigned to the European Museum, but for this reason, would have always remained inalienable. The Demolition of the Convents and Religious Houses has also contributed towards the Enriching of this Collection, the curious painted Glass, several Pictures in the highest Preservation, and other Curiosities decorated for Ages the venerable Monastery of Carthusians at Louvain.

After the capture of Napoleon in 1815, and by the time that the Grand Tour was resumed by an, on the whole, wealthier and better informed class of traveller, most of the churches in France and Belgium had already been desecrated. In most cases the fitted furniture had been too unwieldy to be rescued, and had been cut up and used as firewood. In Belgium, where there seems to have been a greater determination amongst the population to preserve their patrimony, a proportion of wooden furnishings and sculpture was afforded limited protection by resourceful clerics and antique dealers. Not surprisingly, this proved to be a happier hunting ground for the English.

It would be an over-simplification to assume that the trade in Continental church furniture was simply due to the French Revolution, but this cataclysmic event certainly started the ball rolling. In fact, the number of French objects acquired was limited, the vast majority coming from Flanders and a few from Germany (see page 92). At first the main focus of interest amongst the English was stained glass. The earliest substantial purchases of church furniture seem to have been in the mid-1820s, as at Cockayne Hatley, Bedfordshire, but most was acquired in the 1830s.

This period of serious interest in acquiring Continental church furniture coincides with the Gothic Revival in England. But, perversely, most of the material brought over is post-medieval in origin. Much of the furniture at St Chad's Cathedral, Birmingham, and St Mary's College, New Oscott, chosen and installed by Augustus Welby Northmore Pugin, is of late medieval date. But at Oscott the magnificent altar rails are full-blooded Baroque and dated 1680 (Colour Plate 2), and the choir-stalls are of the early eighteenth century. Otherwise, practically all the Gothic-style furniture used in Pugin's churches was contemporary, much of it designed by himself.

The re-establishment of the Catholic Church in England was set in train by the Catholic Relief Act of 1791, which permitted the re-opening or building of family chapels. This was followed nearly forty years later by the Catholic Emancipation Act of 1829. One of the earliest public Catholic churches to be built was Bishop John Milner's, St Peter's Chapel, Winchester, in 1792. It was designed by John Carter, after a sketch by Milner, and was in some ways a prototype for the Catholic church of the nineteenth century, with its functional Georgian architectural proportions, Gothic decorative vocabulary and plain modern furnishings.[3] Milner resembled several other protagonists of the re-established church who followed him, in his profound knowledge of English ecclesiastical history and love of his native medieval architecture.[4] Nevertheless his chapel contained no ancient furniture except for a battered English fourteenth century statue of the Virgin and Child.

Whereas there are around 250 churches in England with at least one fragment of imported Continental woodwork, the number of Catholic institutions so endowed seems to be limited to five. The explanation is partly that the new Catholic churches were built to a budget from money raised by a small number of enthusiasts and, perhaps, a local patron. Foreign furniture would have been difficult and expensive to obtain. St Chad's Cathedral and Oscott College (the latter which has been characterised as the nerve centre of the Catholic Revival),[5] were wholly exceptional commissions, being prestige projects and the first two monumental Catholic buildings to be erected in England since the Reformation. In her parallel study of north European panel paintings in England, Grössinger similarly found that almost all of the churches containing such objects are Protestant.[6]

The furniture imported was mostly not French, Gothic or medieval. Unlike Lord Shrewsbury and Pugin's methodical combing of the Belgian antiques trade, much of the furniture was probably bought on the spur of the moment by travellers at the start or finish of the Grand Tour. Some of the purchasers were Low Church aristocratic patrons of livings, sometimes clerics themselves, for whom the utility of the objects was paramount. Such an outlook could not possibly be further from the religious and antiquarian high-mindedness of Pugin:

Now, however, when neither the terror of the rack nor any political restriction prevents them from celebrating the holy splendours of their ancient ritual, now is the time to direct the attention of all back to days of former glory, and from the inexhaustible source, which the talents of the middle ages furnish, draw the materials of all future works.[7]

Pugin gives us a vivid, if imaginary and substantially post-dated, account of the desecration of a French parish church.[8] More specifically, some records have been kept of the damage done to the furniture of some of the greater French churches. At Senlis Cathedral, Réau relates that 'In 1793 the portals were mutilated, the pavement taken up, the choir-screens taken away, the stalls and organ screen taken down, and the pulpitum of 1532 destroyed'. A Revolutionary club was established there, and a forage depot for the army.[9] At St Étienne, Dijon, the choir-stalls ordered in 1527 from a joiner in Troyes, Jean Boudrillet, and set up in 1535, were taken out by the Jacobins and sold at auction'.[10] 'At Vezelay in 1793, under the Terror, the furniture and stalls were sold'.[11] 'At Amiens Cathedral the stalls escaped destruction but the fleurs-de-lis were carefully removed from the superstructure'.[12] 'In Brittany, the cathedral of Saint-Brieue was turned by the Jacobins into a saltpetre factory, the ovens fed with wooden statues and the choir-stalls'.[13] Few Belgian churches escaped the attentions of the sans-culottes either, notably the collegiate church of St Gudule, Brussels (now the cathedral church of St Gudule and St Michael). In March 1795, at the cathedral in Geneva, the central window of the apse was covered over with a painting representing the Figure of the République. It was painted on twenty-one panels of chestnut wood and in oils. Some of these panels were the standards from discarded Gothic choir-stalls.[14]

The handful of instances of vandalism to the wooden furniture inside French churches could doubtless be multiplied many times for the immediate post-Revolutionary period, and under Napoleon and Louis-Philippe. It may have been possible to preserve some portable revered cult objects from the destructive fury of the mob, but the fitted furniture and much of the sculpture was an easy target. All things Gothic, or 'Teutonic', were anathema, as can be seen in a passage from the proposals of the architect Rousseau at Amiens for a re-ordering of the cathedral:

Il est temps de faire disparaître ces chapelles de goût tudesques, ces vieilles stalles gothiques et autres objets qui ont jusqu'ici défiguré une des plus belles basiliques de l'Europe. En déblayant ce beau temple des antiquailles dont je parle, on lui rendra toute sa beauté originelle.[15]

Such fragments of the former furnishings which it had been possible to rescue experienced a very indifferent fate. It was no use burying wooden furniture, as was done with some of the stone sculpture. Window glass could also be removed and stored safely. Some roving English antiquaries, and their commercial entrepreneur counterparts, were on the scene remarkably quickly, picking over the debris. Back in London the traffic that developed was shared by retail furniture dealers, or brokers, as they were known, and the wholesale auction houses. These scouts gave the English a bad reputation in France. Their activities were dubbed 'Elginism'. Baron Taylor (1789-1879), *Inspecteur de Beaux-Arts,* inveighed against them in no uncertain terms:

Toutes les figures qui décoraient le tympan du portail [at St Remi, Amiens] et qui réprésentaient le baptême de Clovis ont été achetées et emportées, ainsi que les vitraux et les portes en bois sculpté.

Nous n'exprimerions pas de regrets aussi amers si toutes des productions des arts avaient été transportées en Angleterre pour en former un musée où nous pourrions aller admirer et étudier nos Antiquités nationales; car enfin, les premiers coupables sont les gens qui les ont vendues, et le plus grand coupable le gouvernement qui ne les a pas achetées ou qui en a permis la vente.

Mais les oeuvres d'art sont allées orner quelques châteaux ou quelques parcs de lords où l'on joue au Moyen Age à la Walter Scott.

Arracher d'un monument des fragments qui souvent, loin de l'ensemble, perdent tout leur intérêt et leur valeur, pour embellir le jardin d'un cottage, c'est un déplorable folie.[16]

Until 1950 a set of carved wood panels, which probably came from the choir-stalls at Jumièges Abbey in Normandy, commissioned in 1501, was displayed in the entrance hall at Highcliffe Castle, Hampshire. This was one of the earliest instances of 'Elginism' in its most blatant form, involving the ransacking of the Abbey by the amateur architect and francophile, Charles Stuart, Lord Stuart de Rothesay (1779-1845). He had been the British ambassador to France in the early years of the nineteenth century. His new house was partly made up of fragments of both Jumièges and the 'Grande Maison des Andelys' in Normandy, both transported across the English Channel in specially constructed barges.[17]

The woodcarvings in the hall have always been said by the family to have come from Jumièges. Writing in 1885, the abbot Julien Loth notes that the cloister of Jumièges and 'other beautiful sculptures … were bought by an Englishman, and reconstructed in an English Park'.[18] Another writer in 1820 observed that 'the English carried away for cash the sculptured remains of Jumièges', stating that the cloister was thought to have 'departed … with the family of the ambassador'.[19]

By no means all of the imported stained glass was hidden away in country house chapels.[20] The incomparable collections from various parts now at St Mary's, Shrewsbury; the Guildhall, Canterbury; Wragby Church, Yorkshire; York Minster; the Victoria and Albert Museum; and formerly at Toddington Manor, Gloucestershire, are a testimony to the assiduity of both antiquarian collectors and freelance agents. Swiss, Flemish and German glass is prominent in these collections. Indeed, Italy and Spain are probably the only major countries of northern Europe not represented, having escaped the secularisation of their religious buildings.

After the Peace of Amiens in 1802 it seemed for a while that normal trading relations between France and England would be resumed. Indeed, even before the treaty was signed, at the end of 1801 or early in 1802, John Christopher Hampp and Seth William Stevenson travelled to Rouen to buy the windows of St John's Church in that city, which have since embellished the cathedrals of Wells and Ely.[21] Hampp, the best known of the two art entrepreneurs, travelled extensively on the Continent to sell his textiles, for he was a master-weaver and merchant. He was born at Marbach in Württemberg in 1750, migrated to England, and was living in Norwich in 1782. His partner, Seth William Stevenson, F.S.A., had been interested in saving threatened foreign glass for some time already, and in 1799 he presented a figure under a Gothic canopy of German origin to St

Stephen's Church, Norwich.[22] Wayment tells us that Stevenson was:

> …'a scholar and a gentleman'; he had been on the Grand Tour, and written books on his travels, as well as a dictionary of Roman coins which, with the additions by others, was published long after his death and became a standard work. But he was also 'in trade'. He was partner in a firm of printers, and part proprietor of the Norfolk Chronicle; he became a Freeman of the City of Norwich as a 'stationer'.[23]

His connection with Hampp was that he supplied designs for textiles. They bought quantities of ancient glass on the first trip, laying out the huge sum of around £20,000.[24] The account book, which almost certainly belonged to Hampp,[25] records the purchases of the two men's second trip in 1802-03. This shows that the glass came from Normandy, the Netherlands and Cologne, Aachen and Nüremburg.[26] The item, 'Donation to their church £25', testifies to the use of a monetary incentive. As Rackham pointed out, '…in 1797, during the French invasion, the windows [of the Chapel of the Holy Blood at Bruges] were sold for 14 francs apiece by the Communal Council of the day to a local *brocanteur,* from whom they were afterwards bought by an Englishman for shipment across the Channel'. Clearly, churches 'cashing in' on their art treasures was a commonplace.

Referring to Hampp and Stevenson, Alexandre Lenoir, the celebrated painter and antiquary (1762-1839) commented in 1803 that:

> About two years ago a foreigner bought a church in Rouen solely with the purpose of obtaining the stained glass which adorned it. After carefully taking this down, he transported it to London. He even sold the church at a profit![27]

Lenoir saved many works of art from destruction through his personal intervention. In 1821, writing to Hyacinthe Langlois and recalling the events of this time, he stated:

> Yes, the windows of the Chartreuse de Rouen representing subjects drawn from the life of St. Bruni were in my hands. I made friendly overtures with the object of obtaining the acquisition for the Museum but to my great regret I did not succeed. I believe that they passed into that absorbing gulf called England to which today all our art treasures are going.[28]

Stevenson and Hampp arranged exhibitions of their glass in London and Norwich, Stevenson being in charge of the former. Some of the glass went to private collectors in East Anglia, particularly Sir William Jerningham of Costessey Hall. On the whole the marketing seems not to have been a success. On 16 June 1808 a formal auction at Christie's was held, the glass being described as having been:

> collected, at a very great Expense, by a Gentleman of enlarged Information and fine Taste, during the early part of the French Revolution, from the suppressed Churches and Religious Houses, in Germany, France and the Netherlands.

The collection is now divided amongst churches, private holdings and museums in England, Scotland, the United States of America and Canada.[29]

The process of secularisation was also taking place in the Netherlands, Germany and Switzerland at the turn of the nineteenth century. About the glass in the east window of St Stephen's Church, Norwich, from Mariawald monastery, Heimbach, it was said that:

> Nach de Aussage alter Leute in Heimbach sind sie nach der Aufhebung des Klosters, 1802, für einen Spottkeis [trifle] nach England verkauft worden …[30]

At that time in the South Netherlands the contents of churches had been reasonably well preserved, in contrast to the North Netherlands, where the establishment of Protestantism ensured the neglect and removal of medieval church furnishings at a much earlier date. During the French occupation of Belgium (1794-1814) the convents were closed down and their furniture sold at auction. For example, much of the furniture and fittings at St Peter's, Leuven, was sold in 1798. Furthermore, in the mid-nineteenth century the churches of the South Netherlands underwent alterations similar to those initiated by the Ecclesiologists in England. Pulpitums were partially dismantled or removed, such as the one from Hertogenbosch now in the Victoria and Albert Museum.[31]

It will be recalled that Baron Taylor complained that so few of the threatened works of art had been rescued by the state. Yet, of course, at that time museums had hardly progressed beyond the stage of

Plate 3. *Hôtel de Cluny. View of the chapel. From A. de Sommerard,* Les Arts au Moyen Âge … Atlas, *Paris, 1838-46, Chapter xii, Pl.vi. BL 748.g.5.* By permission of The British Library

'Cabinets de curiosité'. One of the earliest such in England was John Tradescant's 'Musaeum Tradescantianum or a collection of rarities preserved at South Lambeth near London', to quote the title of the first catalogue, printed in 1656. It concerned itself mainly with natural history, but there were a few items of wood carving and furniture. Item VII lists 'Mechanick artificial Works in Carvings, Turnings, Sawings and Paintings'. Also, on page thirty-seven, there are two items, firstly, 'The story of the Prodigal son carved in wood: Antient', and 'A Deske of one entire piece of wood rarely carved'. Whether any of these were of Continental origin we cannot tell. A carved mid-sixteenth century panel, which is Anglo-Flemish in style, representing *Jacob at the Well,* has survived, but according to the cataloguer, might possibly be German.[32]

The only museum as such in France in 1800 was the *Musée des monuments Français,* founded by Alexandre Lenoir in 1795. With its proud chronological parade of French medieval art, displayed room by room, it heroically tried to stake a claim for Gothic in the face of the tidal wave of Classicism and secularisation engulfing France. Ironically, it was disbanded upon the restoration of the monarchy in 1816, on the basis that public displays of ecclesiastical artefacts were practically heretical. Happily, such an unreasonably violent reaction was quickly corrected. A *Musée de sculpture Française* was formed in 1817, to be opened in 1824 under the name of 'Galerie D'Angoulême'.[33] Even then there was still nowhere for secular furniture and room displays in general. This gap was eventually filled by Alexandre du Sommerard's *Musée de Cluny,* which opened in 1844.

Du Sommerard was the first to publish some of the church art to have escaped the depredations of the Revolution and after. In his magisterial five-volume *Les Arts au Moyen Age…,* published between 1838 and 1846, he illustrated a number of interesting items of wooden furniture. There is a three-seater stall in oak from the church at Bourgachard, in the Lower-Seine, said to be of the fifteenth century, still at the time *in situ.*[34] He shows a run of three fifteenth century stalls with a sixteenth century canopy, from an abbey in Picardy.[35] It was noted that this could be found in the chapel at the Cluny Museum, also illustrated in the book (Plate 3). There is a fine Mannerist stall with canopy, said to be at that time in the Musée Royal du Louvre.[36] There is also a rood screen from the church of Villemaur Aube, which is still there today.[37]

One of the most impressive illustrations in these volumes is the whole-page coloured engraving of a huge 'ecclesiastical' armoire (Plate 4). This is described as follows:

Grand-meuble de style gothique, ayant servi à la fois de Chappier (dans ses parties fermées) et de buffet ou dressoir pour l'exposition publique, à certaines époques des reliquaires et autres objets précieux du trésor d'une Cathédrale. Sur plusieurs des écussons, sont les armoiries de Charles VIII et d'Anne de Bretagne, etc.[38]

This Leviathan was said to have come from

PLATE 4. *Antiquarian sacristy cupboard. From A. du Sommerard,* Les Arts au Moyen Âge ... Album, *Paris, 1838-46, Chapter xii, Pl.xxxv. B.L. 748.g.1.*
BY PERMISSION OF THE BRITISH LIBRARY

PLATE 5. *Hever Castle, Kent. Antiquarian French Renaissance bishop's chair.*

Saint-Pol-de-Léon. In the interests of furniture archaeology it was taken to pieces in 1888 and found to consist of thirty-two re-used panels, uprights, canopy and dais. It is now thought that it was made up by du Sommerard to show off the precious exhibits in his collection.[39] It was probably not the first of the made-up 'medieval' pieces of furniture so typical of the Gothic Revival. So much of the genuine medieval material at this date, both secular and ecclesiastical, was in only fragmentary condition. Particularly in England, with the huge sudden demand for secular specimens to furnish the newly fashionable Romantic country-house interiors,[40] the supply of authentic pieces became wholly inadequate. Inevitably furniture dealers had recourse to making up pieces using modern materials and fragments of old furniture, particularly panels, of which there was a plentiful supply.

At Hever Castle there is a fine antiquarian French Renaissance bishop's chair of walnut which has been skilfully made up from different components (Plate 5 and Gazetteer). One could mention many more examples of the genre, in particular the throne in

PLATE 6. *Scarisbrick Hall, Lancashire. Great Hall. Made-up throne.*

PLATE 7. *St Chad's Cathedral, Birmingham. Made-up provost's chair on north side of choir-stalls. The outer wings are stall ends. Netherlandish c.1520 (M/3).*

the Great Hall at Scarisbrick Hall (Plate 6), the provost's chair at St Chad's, Birmingham (Plate 7 and M/3), the cupboard in Derby cathedral (Gazetteer) and the lectern at Pleasely in Nottinghamshire (Gazetteer).

At Scarisbrick Hall Pugin used all his ingenuity to accommodate fragments of Continental woodwork not only into seating, but panelling and doors, and even into a mantelpiece (Plate 8).

In the case of secular furniture, in 1836 Henry Shaw highlighted the dealer's predicament, when he declared:

> The painter, the sculptor, and the architect, when called upon to portray or imitate any article of early domestic furniture have been obliged to trust to imperfect descriptions or to their own imaginations.[41]

The 'dealer in curios' and auctioneer, Horatio Rodd, described in a letter to his client, G.W. Braikenridge, in 1827 how he intended to convert an oak cabinet that he had found into something peculiarly useful to himself. He writes:

> I have bought a very curious Cabinett carved in oak and very clean and perfect... [He then provides a rough sketch]. My idea has been to transform it to an Auctioneers Rostrum.[42]

Panels used in so-called 'antiquarian' furniture were shipped to England in their hundreds and adapted

PLATE 8. *Scarisbrick Hall, Lancashire. Red Drawing Room. Detail of panel of dying bishop on mantelpiece. South side. (Appendix, 3 August 1840.)*

to a multiplicity of purposes. Many of them would have come from modest early seventeenth century reredoses in the north Netherlands, like the one at Well Church, Yorkshire. Pugin got involved in the making-up process at Oscott and, as already mentioned, St Chad's Cathedral.[43] He also produced secular work of this kind, as is evidenced at Oscott.

At Scarisbrick Hall the doors leading from the King's Room into the Dining Room and the Red Drawing Room, which are made up from choir-stall ends, represent 'Wardour Street' workmanship at its very best (Plates 9a, 9b and 336-39). They were made by the London broker, Edward Hull. From the latter's accounts (Appendix 3), it seems that they cost the huge sum of more than £259. Interestingly, there are doors, also made from choir-stall ends, in the west of Ireland, at Adare Manor, Limerick, which used to be the home of the Earls of Dunraven and Mount Earl (Plate 11).

One of Pugin's most spectacular antiquarian specimens is the confessional in the chapel at Oscott (Colour Plate 19). It is in the form of a three-bay arcade, with the priest's seat in the centre. The pilastered uprights consist of terminal figures of the four Evangelists on deep plinths. These, the geometrical panelling behind, and the decorated arches above are seventeenth century Flemish. The massive decorated architrave above and the broken pediment with blank shield are Pugin's work. The additions are highly effective. Its maker would be pleased to know that his structure has been used by successive generations of Oscott seminarians for the last one hundred and fifty years. Yet Pugin is said to have disapproved of confessionals because they were not medieval. He explained:

> Even on the continent confessionals cannot be found older than the last century, and this is alone sufficient to place the extreme absurdity of the stories circulated by vergers and others, respecting confessionals in the ancient churches.[44]

Presumably, when asked to design a confessional for Oscott, he had to swallow his prejudices. He must have decided that, as he was going to have to supply one, the end-product should not disgrace his reputation.

A regular trade in made-up furniture was consistently promoted by the London furniture dealers from the 1830s. The fashion for these goods, as well as their dishonesty of craftsmanship, was attacked by H.N. Humphries in 1853:

> A variety of interesting publications have called public attention to the rich productions of medieval skill during the last twelve or fifteen years, causing the previous frigid attempts at reproducing a classical style in furniture to be completely abandoned for the

PLATE 9. *Scarisbrick Hall, Lancashire. Doors from King's Room to Dining Room. South side (M/28).*

PLATE 10. *Scarisbrick Hall, Lancashire. Doors from King's Room to Dining Room. South side:* 1. St Anthony being tempted by the Women; 2. Pilate's Wife urging him to abjure any part in Christ's Judgement, *whilst* Pilate washes his Hands, *and* Christ is led away to be scourged *(Plate 339, M/28).*

PLATE 11. *Adare Manor, Limerick. Double-doors, made up from early 16th century Brabantine choir-stall ends.*
© CHRISTIE'S IMAGES LIMITED, 2001

medieval styles. But in most cases those styles have been but imperfectly comprehended by the public at large, and a vast Wardour-Street commerce has been erected on the sure foundation of that ignorance, which is likely to last at least as long as the wretchedly cottered up specimens which minister to it.

These wretched patchwork combinations, consisting of every incongruous mixture, stuck together so as to form some article of furniture in common use, have hitherto found a ready sale, though without any pervading design, and the detached pieces themselves being generally fragments of the coarsest and most worthless specimens.[45]

Equivalent to the Romantic furnishings in country houses at this time,[46] were the theatrical interiors of a few rural churches. For an example of the 1830s

there is the small rebuilt medieval church at Gatton, Surrey (Plate 12) which was overloaded with the choir-stalls from two different churches in the South Netherlands (M/10 and M/11), altar rails probably taken from the top of a Flemish rood-screen (L/6), chancel wainscoting with Burgundian panels, a made-up pulpit decorated with historiated early sixteenth century panels, a made-up door from Rouen in the south transept and, as if that was not enough, a magnificent English West Country screen at the west end. Of about 1841 is the totally different and even more theatrical interior of Old Warden Church, Bedfordshire (Plate 13), by Robert Henley, Lord Ongley, characterised somewhat unkindly by Pevsner as a 'mass of woodwork indiscriminately got together'.[47] The main impression is of a sea of box pews, which seem to be modern, but which are heavily decorated with hundreds of fragments and around twenty good quality figurative panels of different origins. Lord Ongley is supposed to have obtained the material from France, Belgium and Italy. It was said that some of the carving comes from the private chapel of Anne of Cleves, at Bruges. These are panels with the initials AC prominent on them. They are of fine quality, but eighteenth century French work.

Another extraordinary interior of 1826 is that at Cockayne Hatley, in the same county (Plate 14). Baroque Flemish choir-stalls dominate the nave and chancel. Pevsner comments that: 'The backs (of these choir-stalls) abound with Catholic saints, looking very Catholic indeed'. The church has two sets of altar rails, one in the chancel said to come from Malines, and the other hoisted up on to the organ loft at the west end. There are also some genuine organ loft railings behind the instrument where they can never be seen. For good measure, a very large Flemish pulpit was manoeuvred into the church and put at the west end in front of the tower, the only place left for it.[48] The family pew in the north aisle has a delightful made-up frontispiece at the west end (Plate 15). Its woodwork is supposed to have come from the church of St Bavo at Ghent, but it is a confection of sixteenth and seventeenth century work.

St Wilfrid's Chapel, Brougham, Cumbria (Plate 16), has been described as 'one of the best early nineteenth century antiquarian ensembles in exist-

PLATE 12. *St Andrew, Gatton, Surrey. View of interior looking east.*

PLATE 13. *St Leonard, Old Warden, Bedfordshire. View of interior looking east.*

PLATE 14. *St John the Baptist, Cockayne Hatley, Bedfordshire. View of north side of chancel.*

ence'.[49] It is a small seventeenth century aisleless building, again, crammed with alien woodwork. The chapel was refurnished in the late 1830s, probably by William Brougham, the younger brother of Henry Peter, Lord Brougham, later Lord Chancellor.[50] With stallwork and benching along the sides and, originally, the pulpit in the middle, the climax was the fine Flemish carved altarpiece at the east end. As at Gatton, an English screen was installed at the west end. Disappointingly, apart from the altarpiece which is now at Carlisle Cathedral, there is not a single authentic piece of Continental church furniture in the chapel. As such it is another theatrical confection on the lines of Old Warden. There are choir-stalls made up from benches with reproduction stall ends. The stall canopies on the north side are a near copy of the Winchester Cathedral choir-stalls without the doubled bays. The major ancient component of the seating is the early

PLATE 15. *St John the Baptist, Cockayne Hatley, Bedfordshire. Frontispiece on family pew in north nave aisle. East side.*

PLATE 16. *St Wilfrid's Chapel, Brougham, Cumbria. View of interior looking east. Flemish altarpiece still* in situ *(now at Carlisle Cathedral).* COPYRIGHT A.F. KERSTING

sixteenth century Northern French panelling on the desk fronts, with Flamboyant tracery. They probably came from chests. In all there are just four ancient Flemish stall standards, one of which, a stall end, has the IHS symbol prominently displayed on the side (Plate 17). The present reredos, which has been moved from its original position at the back of the church, and the pulpit, incorporate some interesting low-relief sculptured panels.

Another important church interior of this period is the family chapel, and parish church at Charborough, Dorset, built by Thomas Erle Drax,

who died in 1790 (Plate 18). The building is late eighteenth century Gothick. As Pevsner said, from the outside you are led to expect 'a dainty white stucco interior. Instead one is stunned by big dark wooden spoils from Continental countries everywhere. They hardly leave you enough space to take them in individually'.[51] A plaque on the west wall reads:

In the year 1837 this chapel was fitted up for Divine Worship by Samuel Wanley Sawbridge Erle Drax Esq. who heightened the walls and put up the present oak panelled roof erected the stone spire and embellished the interior with oak carvings; comprising the pulpit altarpiece stalls and that elaborate work of art representing the life of Christ which was formerly the altarpiece in a church in Antwerp...

The two-decker pulpit is a showy mixture, containing decorative figures from the sixteenth to the eighteenth centuries, and some fine historiated Flemish Mannerist panels. The made-up stalls display two dates, 1626 and 1651. The altar rails are again very much made up, and secular in style. There are two Flemish altarpieces of the early sixteenth century, one of which is the best and most authentic item in the chapel.[52]

There exists a rare contemporary delineation of a pre-Ecclesiological church interior with Continental furnishings, in this case altar rails, in place. The ensemble at St Luke's, Brislington, near Bristol was the creation of the West Country collector, George Weare Braikenridge (1775-1856). The pencil and sepia drawing by W.W. Wheatley is of about 1830 (Plate 19).[53]

Braikenridge was perhaps the most eccentric of the Romantic antiquaries in his use of 'ancient' carvings in wood and stone to decorate external doorways in the grounds of his house, Broomwell House, Brislington (Plate 20). These amazing

Plate 17. *St Wilfrid's Chapel, Brougham, Cumbria. Flemish stall end on south side decorated with IHS symbol.*

PLATE 18. *St Mary, Charborough, Dorset. View of interior looking east.*

PLATE 19. *St Luke, Brislington, Bristol. View of chancel looking east. Pencil and sepia drawing by W.W. Wheatley, about 1830.* COPYRIGHT CONWAY LIBRARY, COURTAULD INSTITUTE OF ART

conceits either functioned as doors or were just ornamental. It seems that they were erected in the 1820s and 1830s as the collection burgeoned. We are told that:

> Saints stood on the top of walls, corbels peered out through the ivy and there was even a dovecote constructed in the same style.[54]

He also had some probably Flemish choir-stalls, as can be seen in the Wheatley drawing of the library at Broomwell House, inscribed 1829 (Plate 21).

A further example of the use of ecclesiastical material in a secular setting is provided by another West Country antiquary, George Matthew Fortescue, of Weare Giffard Hall, Devon. He placed any amount of ancient Continental panelling, as well as Flemish choir-stalls, in the great hall of his late medieval manor house in his 1832 restoration (Plate 22). They are identical to the choir-stalls at Oscott College, Sutton Coldfield, and must be from the same set of furniture. Such an incongruous placement can be paralleled by the three rows of seventeenth century Flemish stalls in the Music Gallery at Snelston Hall, Derbyshire, one of which was drawn by the architect L.N. Cottingham in about

PLATE 20. *Broomwell House, Brislington, Bristol. 'Emblems of the Passion' doorway, made up from stone and wood fragments of Continental church furniture. Photograph c.1860*
COPYRIGHT BRISTOL MUSEUMS AND ART GALLERY

PLATE 21. *Broomwell House, Brislington, Bristol. 'Library at Broomwell House'. Pencil and sepia drawing by W.W. Wheatley, inscribed 1829.* COPYRIGHT BRISTOL MUSEUM & ART GALLERY

1840 (Plate 23).[55]

Museums of the decorative arts were not set up in England until the 1850s with the establishment of the South Kensington Museum and the Royal Architectural Museum.[56] The early Victorian neo-Gothic architects had to form their own collections to provide the raw material for embellishing the interiors of their buildings.

It has been pointed out that Pugin 'by collecting antiquities and using them in his buildings, was following the eighteenth century tradition which had encouraged neo-classical architects to incorporate ancient Greek and Roman carvings into their buildings'.[57] When, in the late 1830s, Pugin had been appointed by Dr Henry Weedall 'Professor of Ecclesiastical Antiquities at St Mary's College', Oscott, 'to help instruct his pupils concerning mediaeval art and architecture he collected together ancient carvings, encaustic tiles, church plate and

vestments. These objects were housed in a special museum which still survives…'.[58] Indeed some of his original display cases with their Gothic fragments are still intact. The impressive French 'reliquary coffer' (J/12, Colour Plate 14) must have been considered one of the highlights of this collection.

The richness of the original collection of works of art at Oscott in 1839, mostly donated by John Talbot, 16th Earl of Shrewsbury and Waterford (1791-1852), the prominent Roman Catholic layman, cannot be overstressed. It was pointed out in 1899 that there were over eighty pieces of wood carving in the museum from many well-known English churches, as well as Amiens, Dieppe, Beauvais and Flanders. There was a 'triptych representing the Annunciation, the carved group representing the death of St Joseph, an Italian statuette of the Madonna and Child, in wood and ivory, [and] the Flemish statuette of the Madonna and Child by Van Weers

...'.[59] Of still greater value were the sculpture, furnishings, vestments and utensils of the chapel, the contents of the library and the large collection of old master paintings.

Pugin's fervent belief in the pedagogic importance of the collection is manifest in his reply to the students' address at the opening of the college:

> The ornaments used here in the celebration of the holy mysteries, and the sculptures which decorate our walls, were, for the most part executed by ancient artists in days of faith. Torn by heretical and revolutionary violence from their original position in the noble churches of France and Belgium, they have been, with infinite pains, collected on the spot, where, secure from further profanation, they once more fulfil the object for which they were designed, by increasing the glory and splendour of religion.[60]

Another well-known architect's museum was that of L.N. Cottingham (1789-1846). He crammed his house in Waterloo Bridge Road, Lambeth, with a horde of specimens of English and Continental Gothic art. The entire contents, arranged into nearly 1,500 lots, was put up for auction after his death. In the 1851 sale catalogue the auctioneers emphasise that the collection had been built up over a period of thirty-five years.[61] According to the catalogue, published in 1850, the Continental items

PLATE 22. *Weare Giffard Hall, Bideford, Devon. Flemish choir-stalls in Great Hall. Late 17th century.*

PLATE 23. *Snelston Hall, Derbyshire. Row of stalls placed in the Music Gallery. Pen and ink wash drawing by L.N. Cottingham. c.1840. Given to the Victoria and Albert Museum by Lt.-Col. J.P. Stanton, J.P. (E.527-1951)*
COPYRIGHT DEPARTMENT OF PRINTS AND DRAWINGS; VICTORIA AND ALBERT MUSEUM

of particular interest were as follows:

Flemish altar-screen, about 1490 (Formerly in the possession of the Duke of Orléans, Phillipe Egalité).

Fragments of choir-stall ends probably from St Mary in Capitol, Cologne, Thirteenth century.

Figures from a fifteenth century Flemish Crucifixion group.[62]

The altar-screen was probably a carved wooden altarpiece, but nothing more is known about it. The Crucifixion figures were probably a typical group wrested in a hurry from their context.

A little more is known about the choir-stalls from the sale catalogue.[63]

Lots 352-359
The following seven Lots consist of a set of ancient Stall seats, six in number, besides the return Standard Ends, and portions of the Throne with boldly carved groups of figures, etc., or rare 13th century work. They are of foreign manufacture, and afford the strongest evidence of being the production of the same Artist as the matchless Stalls of the Church of St. Gereon de Cologne.
352. One of the return standard ends – the end having for its termination a group of Sampson slaying the Lion; also, a smaller end to one of the seats, with the Lion of St Mark for its termination.

The provenance for the stalls has now changed from St Mary in Capitol to St Gereon, Cologne. The writer may have realised that the Flemish stalls placed by Pugin at St Chad's Cathedral, Birmingham, and supposed to have come from St Mary in Capitol, were early sixteenth century in date. If Cottingham's stalls were self-evidently German in character and as early as they were said to have been, they were probably similar to the ones given to Barming church, Kent, in 1871, which are of late thirteenth century date and probably Flemish in origin (M/1).

Another interesting collection of wood-carving was built up by the decorative sculptor W.G. Rogers. On his death, at the close of a career as a mainly ecclesiastical wood carver, his 'valuable assemblage of exquisite carvings in wood' was auctioned at Christie's on 17 June 1858. The catalogue included a reference to the owner of Charborough Park, Dorset:

136. Five boys, in oak, by Berger, the carver of the panels at the Abbey of Pare, near Louvain, now in the possession of G.H.S.C. Drax, Esq., M.P.

These panels are presumably some of those on the pulpit at Charborough.

The collecting of Continental church furniture in England seems to have been a somewhat haphazard affair, but in the case of the new Roman Catholic theological college at Oscott, and of the new Roman Catholic cathedral at St Chad's, Birmingham, the business was taken altogether more seriously. In both cases it was the architect and recent Catholic convert A.W.N. Pugin who was the inspiration and driving force behind the deliberate and costly introduction of ancient and exotic artefacts. If the Lichfield architect, Potter, had not been removed in 1838, Oscott would have got a utilitarian box-like chapel, furnished economically with modern materials.

The manner of Pugin's appointment to take over at Oscott is given in the diary of Dr Kerril Amherst, second Roman Catholic Bishop of Northampton (1819-1883), as follows:

The new College was then approaching completion, and Dr Weedall, recognising the talent of Pugin, placed the work of completion and adornment of the Chapel, Sacristies, the principal rooms of the house in Pugin's hands.[64]

Pugin had just become famous in 1837, in which year his *Contrasts* were read in the refectory during dinner, and in that year he made his first visit to Oscott, with an introduction from Lord Shrewsbury (this was Earl John), who had taken up his views with ardour. The New College was then approaching completion…

Dr Weedall was not slow in recognising the talent of Pugin, and the enthusiastic genius of the latter so won upon the president that he confided to that architect the completion and adornment of the chapel, and the furnishing of the sacristy and principal rooms. The great object of interest in the still incomplete building was a room, now the Vice-president's, in which what were called 'Pugin's things' were kept. These chiefly consisted of ancient carvings, statues and pieces of church and domestic furniture…. These things spoke directly of the faith that was in the man who designed and executed them; the 'Old Fellows' as Pugin was fond of calling them. Often as the time drew near for the occupation of the new house, we took delight in spending hours there in helping to distribute and arrange the various objects, and we used to hear Pugin's loud voice (a vast!) as he gave directions, sounding through the corridors, or his ringing laugh when he was struck by some ridiculous idea. He was then, quite a young man, not more than two or three and twenty, beardless, with long, thick, straight

Plate 24. *St Mary's College, New Oscott, Sutton Coldfield. Chapel interior, looking east. Late 19th century.*
COPYRIGHT OSCOTT COLLEGE

black hair, an eye that took in everything, and with genius and enthusiasm in every line of his face and play of his features.

...Pugin may have been eccentric, he may have been greatly carried away, or rather swept along by enthusiasm, but no reasonable man can doubt that what he did, wrote and said had an enormous effect upon the revival of Christian art here and abroad, helped to turn men's minds towards the Church, and awoke in numbers the slumbering love of the beauty of God's house. That beauty, and an intense aversion to the use of anything, whether in construction or ornament, of a purely pagan origin or significance in the service of the Church, were the main-springs of all his actions and ideas of an artistic character.

...He lectured to us in the exhibition-room, and we read with avidity his periodical and pungent little Articles in the *Orthodox Journal*. Catholics in England

had grown accustomed to holding a sort of inferior position ... and this feeling was very apparent in the retiring and modest character of their places of worship, and the services and devotions therein. Pugin certainly gave an impulse in the right direction in this matter....[65]

It is clear that Pugin's unique attribute was seen by the Catholic authorities as his ability to create through architecture, and more particularly neo-Gothic ecclesiastical interiors, a setting worthy of a re-established Church of Rome. As an anonymous writer put it at the time:

He has been actively employed amidst the edifices of Belgium, Germany, Switzerland and Normandy, ransacking ecclesiastical archives and storing his mind with facts, and his sketchbook with illustrations, to assist him in the noble, though somewhat arduous task, of re-Catholicising this once Catholic nation.[66]

The ancient components of the chapel furnishings were the fifteenth century Flemish reredos, bought from the London dealer Edward Hull for £600, the Baroque choir-stalls (M/31) (Colour Plate 18), purchased from Webb of Bond Street for £92, and the altar rails (B/13) (Colour Plate 2 and Plate 24).[67] The stone pulpit, originally in the north-east corner of the sanctuary, and the wooden altar frontal were designed by Pugin.[68] The total cost of the furniture at Oscott College is said to have come to the very large sum indeed of £3,576.13s.10d.

Thomas Walsh was Vicar Apostolic of the Midland District throughout the conception and construction of the new college, and the driving force behind it.[69] He must have been deeply impressed with Pugin's work there, because in 1838, when he had become Bishop of Birmingham, and immediately after the completion of the project, he commissioned the architect to design a new cathedral, without even consulting his rebuilding appeal committee.[70] As everyone knows, his judgement was fully justified. Pugin designed a fine building, and as at Oscott he took pains to create a homogeneous Catholic Gothic interior that was inhabited by suitable ancient and modern furniture. The Earl of Shrewsbury paid for most of the former, having played an active part in its collection abroad. His gifts included the canons' stalls said to come from St Mary in Capitol, Cologne (M/3), the pulpit from St Gertrude, Leuven (K/1),[71] the fifteenth century brass lectern from St Peter's, Leuven, a ciborium, a large ewer and basin, and a pair of brass candlesticks and six plates formerly the property of Cardinal Odescalchi in the seventeenth century. There were other prominent benefactors. Pugin himself gave a fifteenth century statue of the Virgin and Child, thought to have been the first such image to be displayed in England since the Reformation. Later, in 1846, he gave the organ. The high altar and the rood screen and loft were the gift of John Hardman, senior, of the Birmingham stained glass company. His son, John Hardman, junior, gave the bishop's throne, a made-up piece designed by Pugin, in 1854, presumably in memory of his father who died in the previous year. The cathedral cost nearly

£20,000, about £14,000 of which was paid by Bishop Walsh out of a legacy. His other gifts apart, the Earl of Shrewsbury gave £1,000, and the Hardmans, father and son contributed a total of £1,800.[72]

As has already been stressed, the furnishing of these important Catholic buildings is quite unrepresentative of what was going on elsewhere. It is true that at Stonyhurst College there were Continental choir-stalls at this early date. Moreover, the Dutch Baroque pulpit at St Elizabeth, Bescar, near Scarisbrick Hall may have been introduced into the earlier church there in the 1840s (K/12). But these comparisons are insignificant besides the prodigality of the Birmingham commissions. At Oscott and St Chad's it was the dynamic partnership of the enthusiastic Pugin and the wealthy and generous Lord Shrewsbury on the one hand, and the committed Dr Weedall and Bishop Walsh on the other, that has given currency to the idea that the Roman Catholics were principally responsible for the traffic in Continental church furniture in the nineteenth century. They were both unusual high-profile commissions, and did not typify the bulk of Roman Catholic patronage.

Perhaps there is no better evidence that Pugin had 'a good eye' than the late fifteenth century latten lectern which he acquired for St Chad's Cathedral. It is supposed to have been one of a pair from Leuven, disposed of in 1789.[73] The date is probably a misprint because the edict confiscating the property of the religious houses in Belgium was not issued until 6 November 1796.[74] It is more likely that the lecterns came from the auction of the fittings of St Peter's, Leuven, which is known to have possessed a pair in 1798. Pugin's lectern must have been in hiding for over thirty years, whilst its companion suffered an ignominious fate. It was being transported to the Louvre by the French invaders of the Low Countries, when, having almost completed its journey, whilst crossing one of the Seine bridges, it fell off the wagon into the river.[75] The St Chad's specimen was imported by Edward Hull, who obtained it, according to Samuel Meyrick, in Brussels. Meyrick included the drawing of it by Henry Shaw in his book *Specimens of Ancient Furniture etc.*, published in 1836.[76] Lord Shrewsbury seems to have purchased it and presented it to St Chad's cathedral. It was certainly one of the most idiosyncratic items of church furniture brought to England during the entire nineteenth century. It was purchased by the Metropolitan Museum, New York in 1967.[77]

As a private collector on an ambitious scale Pugin organised his own transport, as Benjamin Ferry, his biographer tells us:

First owner of a small boat which he kept for his own pleasure, he successfully commanded a smack, afterwards a schooner, in which amongst other merchandise he generally managed to bring over many interesting carvings, and other antiquities purchased in the old stores of Holland and Flanders. Thus he used these excursions as subservient to the object of forming a museum ... one of the chief attractions in his residence at Ramsgate.[78]

Ferry also quotes a letter from Pugin to his friend Osmond in Salisbury, written in about 1832-33, where Pugin says:

I fully hope and expect to join you for a few days in the spring on my way to Havre le Grace for a nine months journey in Normandy and the Low Countries to collect originals and sketches.

Some of his trips to the Continent may have been verging on the illegal. J.H. Powell tells us how Pugin's friend Talbot Bury used to rag him:

Having heard much of Pugin's early life he chaffed him about 'smuggling over antiquities for sale'...

But it is clear that Pugin was motivated far more by the idea of saving threatened works of art than any financial consideration.

J.H. Powell elaborated on Pugin's antiquarian activities abroad as follows:

Finding that abroad all care for preserving old medieval carvings was dead he bought up all he could and placed them in his churches, the stalls of St Chads, Museum at Oscott as instances, and his own cartoon room was filled, one oak newell with the figure of the B. Virgin, St Catherine and St Martin was snatched from under a plumber's pot, and the charred parts show what a narrow escape it had.[79]

To cover the market he needed to know the principal furniture dealers of his time, such as Edward Baldock of Rathbone Place and John Swaby of Wardour Street. His friendship with Edward Hull

and John Webb, upholsterer and cabinet maker of 8, Old Bond Street, was particularly useful in giving him access to the carved woodwork, sometimes in substantial quantities, that he required for his commissions. For instance, we find a note in his 1839 diary:

| Hull for crucifix | 25.0.0 |
| Ditto for canopies etc. | 30.2.6[80] |

It seems likely that these items were medieval objects which Pugin was collecting together for his projects of the time, namely Oscott College, St Chad's Cathedral and Scarisbrick Hall.[81] His contacts with dealers may have been of special importance to him at the beginning of his career. Ferry suggested that he may have been introduced to the Earl of Shrewsbury at Edward Hull's antique shop in Curzon Street.

Edward Hull was the most prominent dealer in woodcarvings. He had been running a broker's business since the late 1820s, but appeared as a 'curiosity dealer' in the 1830s.[82] He died in 1847, his son George taking over the business. *The London Post Office Directory* lists the firm as that of 'ancient furniture dealer, Gothic and Elizabethan oak furniture manufacturer'. Charles Scarisbrick was Hull's best customer, appearing as early as 1833 under the name C. Dickinson, before he took the name Scarisbrick.[83] The owner of Scarisbrick Hall, with his immense wealth, he indulged his love for wood carving.[84] He was a fanatical account keeper, although he did not always record the source of purchase. He dealt with Edward Hull throughout the decade 1836-46.[85] In sculpture, the St George and the dragon bought on 14 November 1838, the St Martin on horseback purchased in May 1840 and the gothic panel of a musical angel of June 1839 are all identifiable with works still at Scarisbrick Hall.[86] Many items of furniture still *in situ* are identifiable from the accounts, notably the two pairs of lavish double-sided double doors for the north and south libraries. Hull would occasionally resell pieces for Scarisbrick, as a scribbled note mentions: '34 lots of mine were put up at Hull's sale in May 1840 – at Deacons and 49-0-0 are marked sold'.[87]

Scarisbrick had found his interest in wood carving before his meeting with Pugin. The latter's association with Scarisbrick Hall dates from 1834.[88] From 1836 onwards Scarisbrick seems to have been including Pugin in his purchasing decisions. On 23 September of that year there is a letter from Edward Hull advising his client that he had sent a consignment of furniture 'safely packed in 28 Cases' to Lancashire.[89] On 25 October 1836 Hull acknowledged receipt of a cheque for the huge amount of £440 from Scarisbrick and notes:

My goods have just arrived at the customs house – I intend making a sale of them in Novr and will forward you a (list?) with a drawing of the panelling ... I have not yet seen Pugin but expect every day.[90]

On 1 June 1839, having acknowledged receipt of a further cheque for £400, Hull states:

My goods are now on examination at the customs home and I expect they will be here on Wednesday or Thursday next – I will take care you have the best of them – I suppose Pugin is with you by this time, if so you must talk to him about it.[91]

As Woods points out:

Edward Hull had close business relations with Pugin in his own right. Pugin's diaries contain payments made to Hull in 1835 and 1839-42.[92] In Pugin's sketchbook of 1840-41 he recorded the huge debt of £413 18s owed to Hull.[93] The drawing by Pugin of Scarisbrick Great Hall includes some corbels annotated in Pugin's own hand 'carvings at Hull's'.[94] In 1840 it seems to have been Hull who was forwarding letters from Lord Shrewsbury ....to Pugin....[95] Hull seems to have been the principal dealer with whom Pugin worked, but he was not the only one. On 16 March 1837 Pugin purchased stalls from John Webb,[96] ... in a letter to the Earl of Shrewsbury dated 3 November 1840 Pugin referred to the 'exquisite cross from Pratt's'.[97]

The debt of 1840-41 must have been associated with the Oscott and St Chad's commissions. Indeed in Pugin's diary at the start of September 1837 there is the entry 'Webb stalls 92', and on 20 December the payment by Pugin to Webb of £93.12.0 is recorded. The huge payment of £600 to Hull on the same date was considered by O'Donnell to have concerned the altar and reredos, although the Baroque altar rails could have been included here.[98] It is rather hard to understand why Hull should have been forwarding letters from Lord Shrewsbury to Pugin as late as 1840, given that he is thought to have introduced them to each other in 1837.

Plate 25. *Sketch of furnishings at St Mary in Capitol, Cologne by A.W.N. Pugin, B.L., MS 7820, h.24, Pl.69.*
By permission of The British Library

As a dedicated student of late Continental and English Gothic art and a professional architect, Pugin enjoyed a peculiar position, neither strictly speaking a patron nor a dealer. As an antiquary, we have his own record of some of the monuments he studied abroad, such as:

Oberwesel
21. Sketches of panels of Screen doors and details of same.
24. Stalls of choir and details.
25. Elevation, section & ground plan of screen.

Mayance
16. Details from pulpit in Mayance Cathedral.

Munich
30. Sketch of altar at Munich Cathedral

Ulm
53. Sketch of altar
54. Coloured sketches of stalls in the choir.

There are drawings by him of the choir-stalls at Amiens, Basel, and Cologne cathedrals and Ulm Minster, and one of the pulpit at Évreux, supposedly details of the stalls at St Mary in Capitol (Plate 25), Cologne and the choir-screen at St James, Antwerp.[99]

He must have used these records as a starting point for the designs of his modern church furniture. In *St Marie's College, designed and drawn by A.W.N. Pugin,* published in 1834, there are designs for a high altar, a small and a great candlestick, a monstrance (metal), a tabernacle for the Holy Sacrament, a cope chest, a lavabo (stone), a chest for altar cloths, a lectern (probably metal), an almery for vestments and a brazier (metal). In the following year he published *Gothic Furniture of the 15th century, designed and etched by A.W.N. Pugin,* which includes designs for a prie-dieu and a reading desk. At Oscott and St Chad's Pugin was also a supplier of functional secular furniture.[100]

Pugin's stone pulpit at Oscott, already mentioned above, seems to have been much admired. In 1905 it was described as follows:

A little incongruous perhaps as to position and utility, yet a wonderful piece of art, and another touch that relieves the dull monotony that would have otherwise palled upon us at the present day.[101]

Most of the other furniture at St Chad's, particularly the rood screen there, were newly made to Pugin's designs.

As we have seen, the Birmingham commissions were particularly well funded and it was possible to include a high proportion of antique furniture. It is unrealistic, on the other hand, to have expected Pugin to have interpolated ancient furniture into his bread-and-butter commissions. Even at the church of St Augustine, Ramsgate, where he was both architect and patron, the furniture was to his own design rather than brought in. But as Woods appositely puts it:

This demonstrates the fallacy of supposing Pugin to have been an antiquarian in the true sense of the word.

His interest in late Gothic woodcarvings appears to have been subservient to his main aim, which was to promote the production of modern British sculpture.[102]

Woods had based these remarks upon a careful examination of several of Pugin's modern altarpieces which in design terms clearly show an independence of spirit.

What is surprising about Pugin's furnishings at Oscott is that, in spite of his dedication to Gothic, the most important of them are from the Baroque period. In truth there was only a limited supply of medieval woodwork on the market and a glut of seventeenth and eighteenth century material. Indeed Pugin's perceived inconsistencies were quickly put right at Oscott soon after the commissioning of the chapel, when, according to Bishop Amherst, 'Dr Moore turned out of the chapel everything which was not Gothic', and replaced the railings with a screen designed by Pugin.[103] Luckily James Wheble was able to buy them back in 1872. It is not known if the choir-stalls were also removed.

To return to the art trade, we have seen how a few entrepreneurs took advantage of the Peace of Amiens to return to France. However, within a couple of years the war with Napoleon was renewed, forcing a prudent withdrawal to safer territory. None the less, a few dealers seem to have circulated around Europe during these troubled times. In any case we know that, some eight weeks before Waterloo, the London dealer John Coleman Isaac was making purchases in Germany.[104]

In London the market was being supplied by the furniture dealers and the auction rooms. On 10 November 1825 Christie's held a sale of '… a large collection of ancient and very curious carvings in wood many of which may be found suitable for the fitting up of private chapels, and, many of them applicable for the furniture in Gothic mansions … the whole of which have lately been imported from the continent'. Wainwright commented that, judging from an annotated copy of the catalogue, the carvings came from various sources, some being consigned by Edward Baldock.[105] Most of the buyers were dealers, including John Swaby and John Webb.[106] Swaby was a dealer in antiquities and ancient furniture from 1819 to 1834. He had a shop at 109 Wardour Street from 1822 to 1834. Webb was

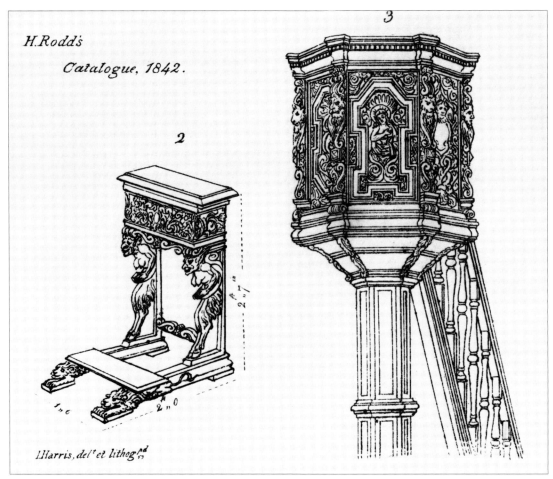

Plate 26. *Pulpit and prie-dieu. Illustrated in H. Rodd,* Catalogue of portraits, pictures, drawings, carvings in oak etc., *London, 1842.*

a well-known dealer in ancient furniture in Bond Street from 1826 to the mid-1850s. The made-up pulpit at St Martin's, Dorking, which incorporates high quality late fifteenth century figure carving, was purchased from Webb's shop.[107]

At the auctioneers, Deacons, on 15 June 1836, there was a 'splendid sale of Gothic and other oak XVIth carvings, just landed, comprising fine specimens of the XVth and XVIth centuries, a magnificent Gothic screen, containing numerous figures, … several fine Gothic doors, and upwards of six hundred Gothic panels, … a Gothic frieze, curiously carved in compartments etc. in all about 10,000 pieces; the whole well worthy the attention of the Nobility, Gentry, Architects and Collectors of Ancient Property'. Items of special interest were:

Lot 156. An oak screen or communion rail, in 5 compartments, with panels beautifully carved in fruit, flowers, and subjects, in high relief.

Lot 157. A set of four very fine spiral columns, richly carved in arabesque, with fine Corinthian capitals, 10 ft 6 high.

Lot 272. A prie-dieu, of solid oak, with panelled front, carved in relief.

Lot 281. A pair of Gothic stall ends, finely carved in oak, with mouldings, capitals and bold figures.

Lot 557. A very fine communion rail, containing fine panels beautifully carved in flowers and fruit, composed of fine oak.

Lot 568. A communion rail, consisting of 2 panels, exquisitely carved in bays, fruit etc. suitable for the lower part of a bookcase.

Lot 574. A magnificent Gothic screen or shrine, divided into 3 compartments, containing groups of figures, very spiritedly carved in oak, enriched with splendid tracery work, in canopies, friezes, pilasters, etc. a grand composition.

Lot 576. A set of three finely carved oak boy figures.

It is disappointing that none of the above descriptions is specific enough for any of the items to be recognisable.

In 1842 there appeared a sale catalogue with illustrations, a very rare occurrence for this date (Plate 26). The auctioneer, Horatio Rodd, published a 'Catalogue of portraits, pictures, drawings, carvings in oak, ivory and boxwood, antique furniture and plate, crosses, chalices, tabernacles, shrines, stained glass etc'. Two items of church furniture were illustrated, namely:

Prie-Dieu. A very excellent 'prie-dieu' of the time of Francois Premier 2ft 6in high. The desk supported by two grotesque Satyrs. The whole resting upon demi-lions. Clean oak; an original and choice piece of furniture.[108]

Another Pulpit, finely carved with the Symbols of the Four Evangelists. In clean oak, on a pedestal, with staircase, etc., etc. complete.[109]

Rodd was a prominent dealer in a wide range of second-hand goods during the second, third and fourth decades of the century. He described himself as 'dealer in curios etc.', and his premises were at 9 Great Newport Street, Long Acre. He had the good fortune to have G.W. Braikenridge, the Bristol antiquary and collector as a client.[110]

The existence of a line drawing in his 1842 catalogue is unsurprising, as he seems to have regularly provided pen and ink sketches in his letters to Braikenridge, one of them at least in colour.[111] The range of Braikenridge's interests, and, apparently, the depth of his purse, was enormous.[112] In 1834 Rodd tried to interest his client in a pair of apparently thirteenth century Limoges enamelled candlesticks (Plate 27). The letter which accompanied this sketch provides an unique insight into the pre-Victorian world of dealers and collectors.[113]

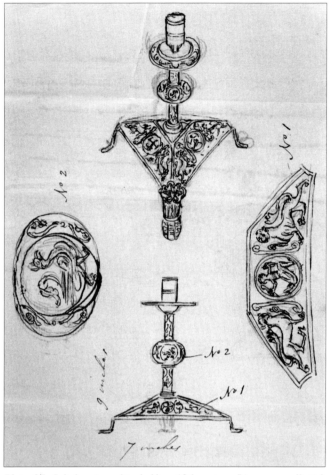

Plate 27. *Ink drawing of probably a 13th century Limoges candlestick by Horatio Rodd. 1834.*
COPYRIGHT BRISTOL RECORD OFFICE. MS.14182/HB/B/40

August 18 1834

Dear Sir,

On the other side I have made an attempt to sketch the representations of a pair of Candlesticks of the time and style of the two now-to-be-forgotten ones which unfortunately I let go through my hands a few years since and which eventually fell into the hands of Sir Samuel Meyrick – I do not remember the precise shape of these two or the figures that were enamelled upon them – but the general appearance I do not forget.

The ones I now have to offer you (in conjunction with Mr Swaby who has just reached this with me from the sale at Lee Priory near Canterbury where we were fortunate enough to meet with these) – are certainly as curious as the others – they are enamelled upon copper – and may be considered as very perfect and extraordinary specimens of antiquity – but it is a question if at the top they have not had a spike instead of the nozzle now upon them – i.e. it is a question with me who only pretend to any sort of knowledge in these matters – ... if you think you would like to possess them – the price fixed is the exact sum Dr Meyrick gave 12 Guineas.

At the Stowe sale of 1848 it transpires that there may have previously been some furniture of interest in the chapel. For £5.10s. John Swaby bought 'A music-desk, on a carved support'.[114] Also for £32.11s. the purchaser Walesby bought 'An altar-piece ... A very remarkable piece of early Flemish workmanship'.[115]

Pugin died in 1852 and there was an important sale of his effects on 12 February 1853. The catalogue was described by Sotheby's as 'of the valuable collection of mediaeval carvings in oak ...'. The range and richness of this assemblage is evident from the list. The very large number of single carved figures and a few groups demonstrates how when the fittings of the secularised churches were broken up such pieces were brutally removed from their artistic and liturgical contexts. Items in the catalogue of special relevance are:

1. A pair of oak doors with whole length figures of saints, painted and gilt, canopied with architectural fret work, and having four subjects from the life of the Redeemer carefully painted at the back of each, a fine specimen, in beautiful condition.
German work of the XVth century.
2. An altar-piece, comprising twenty figures, besides disjointed groups, representing the Passion of our Lord, gilt and richly painted; fine specimens.
German work of the 15th century.
3. A pair of panels, elaborately carved with heraldic work, shield, helmet, and crest, the mantling filling up the remaining spaces with great ingenuity, beautiful specimens, in fine state.
German work of the 15th century.

The purchaser of the altarpiece was Zimmerman who, according to Woods, may have been the person of that name 'whose collection of medieval carvings, ecclesiastical furnishings and artefacts was sold in Paris in 1875'.[116] Hull, probably George Hull, Edward Hull's son, was among the other buyers.

On 27 June 1856 the auctioneers Phillips offered:

the finely inlaid oak and sculptured marble fittings of the church of St John at Luneberg comprising the staircase of the pulpit, carved frames & monuments, doors, friezes, panelling, etc. About 1500 pieces, well adapted for the fitting of a Church or Gothic Houses.

Again it has not as yet been possible to identify any of the purchasers of this material, or the name of the enterprising dealer who shipped it over.

So far we have seen how, mainly through the agency of the trade, European ecclesiastical goods of all kinds were drawn into England during the first half of the nineteenth century. It remains now to investigate the behaviour and motivation of some of the collectors.

Sir Walter Scott was an early bargain hunter. In 1816 and, significantly, from Brussels, he wrote to Mathew Weld Hartsonge:

books and paintings are here wonderfully cheap, & with the latter I have nearly broke myself – I think it would be a good speculation for any person who was a competent judge to purchase paintings here & at Antwerp & freight a vessel with them & dispose of them in London the duty on importation into England is I understand an English pound for every square foot of canvas....[117]

Another visitor to Belgium, in this case to Antwerp, Lord Braybrooke of Audley End, wrote in 1829:

Steencering's collection of curiosities for sale were very odd and not uninteresting, but he was hardly civil & quite indifferent as to disposing of them ... I offered him 20 francs for 2 little articles which I bought since for fr12 thinking myself bound to purchase something but he refused it with disdain at another place I bought two armoires which will turn out well ... in no other town have I seen carved oak for sale the uniform answer to all enquiries being 'the Jews collect it all & send it to England'.[118]

In 1816 the twenty-three year old John Winn of Nostell Priory, Yorkshire, set off with his personal physician on the Grand Tour. A good deal of time was spent in Switzerland where the Swiss stained glass now at Wragby Church, adjacent to the family home, was probably purchased. It is said to be the largest collection anywhere of such material, apart from that at the Landes Museum, Zurich.[119] There is no evidence from the diaries that the Italian wood panels which were later worked up into the extant pulpit at Wragby were acquired on this journey. These diaries describe vividly the primitive conditions of the journey. A chance aside on some church furnishings notes:

Oratorio De santa Maria della Salisle [?sp.]. The altar of marble of Carrara verey fine. The bronze candlesticks … from Constantinople much resemble but less elegant than ours at Ratclif liberar fora [?sp.][120]

The peregrination ended tragically with the death of Winn, the story being taken up by Dr Harrison, who gives a full account of the mournful journey back to Nostell with the body.[121]

The astonishing assemblage of Flemish woodwork at the remote Bedfordshire church of St John the Baptist, Cockayne Hatley was introduced in 1826 by the Honourable and Reverend Henry Cockayne Cust, second son of Lord Brownlow of Belton, Lincolnshire. The memorial to him on the north wall of the chancel reads:

Lord of the manor
Fifty-five years rector of this parish.
Forty-eight years canon of St. George's Chapel, Windsor[122]
Second son of Brownlow Cust, Baron Brownlow
He died 19 May 1861 aged 80 years etc.

Cust was a man of his time. He was the scion of one of the greatest aristocratic landowning families in England,[123] and, as the second son, was fortunate enough to inherit the Hatley estate in Bedfordshire, which had come to the family through a distant connection with the defunct Cockayne family in 1745. The estate comprised 1,400 acres and produced a gross rental of about £1,500 a year.

On leaving Cambridge in 1805 he took up the position of Rector close to the family seat in Lincolnshire, at Scott Willoughby.[124] The following year he acquired another Rectorship at Sywell, Northamptonshire, and was appointed Vicar of Middle Rasen Drax, Lincolnshire, a position which he enjoyed until 1832.[125] For a man who was already a member of the aristocracy, the extra monetary income deriving from the holding of these pluralities would have represented a very real bonus, considering that in 1837 the average annual clerical income was £500.[126] In 1806, at the age of twenty-five, he came into the estate and settled at Cockayne Hatley as Rector and Squire. There had been no squire in residence since 1739. Not surprisingly he found that the church was in a 'most lamentable state of neglect'.

The stone of the east window had crumbled away, and

on Christmas Day 1806 snow fell through the roof on to the altar during the service. He undertook a major restoration, which was completed by 1830.[127]

The comprehensive refurnishing of the interior was the culmination of a thorough-going restoration and remodelling of the church. The roof of the nave was taken down and repaired or replaced, the east wall of the chancel was demolished and the chancel shortened and re-roofed. The whole of the south aisle had to be rebuilt and a large porch was removed.

Interestingly, these initial building activities at Cockayne Hatley were paralleled by those of Henry Cust's brother, John Cust (1st Earl Brownlow), at Belton Church, Lincolnshire, adjacent to the ancestral home.[128] There in 1816, amongst other work, he commissioned Jeffry Wyatville to design a chapel on the north side of the church, in memory of his first wife, Sophia Hume, who died in 1814. The centrepiece was to be Canova's large statue of Religion, which, like some of his younger brother's later imports at Cockayne Hatley, is awkwardly out of scale in a modest English parish church.

At last, in 1823, with the purchase from a dealer named Hill of a new altarpiece at a cost of £100, the furnishing campaign at Cockayne Hatley got under way.

Tradition has it that all the foreign material was acquired through a dealer in Charleroi, but Cust's journals, most of which have survived for this period, reveal a more complex picture (Appendix I). He was a wealthy man, and thought nothing of spending well in excess of £100 a year on books alone. With his appointment as a canon at St George's Chapel, Windsor, in 1813, his work-load must have increased considerably, over and above his preaching commitments, particularly after he had been appointed Canon Steward. His journals give the impression of a man almost constantly on the move, overseeing his other livings, visiting London regularly, where he had a house at 30 Hill Street, Berkeley Square, often attending the House of Lords, and conducting peregrinations around the country to visit friends and relatives. Yet somehow he managed to be back at Hatley to deliver the sermon on most Sundays. Apart from all this he had serious domestic responsibilities with a burgeoning young family. He seems to have travelled with his wife to the Continent regularly for three-week 'excursions'. He was an assiduous tourist. When he visited Cologne in July 1827 he saw all the main churches and combed the Rhineland for art and architecture of all periods.

He was sufficiently ambitious and wealthy to go to the source of the material he wanted for his church. However, he would not have had enough time to make the necessary contacts with foreign dealers himself. Until now the exact process of acquisition was quite unknown, but, thanks to his journals, and letters from his friend Robert Rushbrooke, his *modus operandum* has become clear. Colonel Rushbrooke, of Rushbrooke Hall, Suffolk, who in 1809 had been appointed Lieutenant-Colonel Commandant of the Suffolk Militia, acted as his agent. To judge even from a few of his letters, Rushbrooke was a natural connoisseur. It seems to have come naturally to him to append a sketch of an architectural feature to make a point. Indeed, we know that later, in a very modest way, he joined the ranks of the nineteenth century gentleman-architect, which were beginning to form at this time, for in 1838 he is recorded as being responsible for the design of a new main gatehouse at Melford Hall, Suffolk, for his neighbour, Sir Hyde Parker. He may have been largely responsible for converting Cust to his improbable devotion to Catholic furnishings. Rushbrooke may have served in Belgium during the Napoleonic War, but we cannot be sure of this.[129] He must have been a Belgo-phile for he lived in Brussels for about two years between 1826 and 1828. He was a mere two years his friend's senior. He quite probably went to Eton (he certainly sent his son there), where he would have cemented a bond of trust with Cust. Apart from negotiating with a single dealer or dealers, Rushbrooke was skilled at smoothing the path of his imports through the Customs House. His military background would have prepared him well for dealing with civil servants.

At Cockayne Hatley the Baroque monastic choir-stalls, originating from the Augustinian priory of Oignies in Belgium (M/9 and Plate 14), and the superb Mannerist pulpit, from St Andrew, Antwerp (K/4 and Plate 29), were shipped from Belgium and erected in the church in 1826 at the enormous cost of £345 (Appendix I). The rest of the woodwork was installed in 1827 and 1830 – no fewer than three sets of altar rails, two of which had to be mounted on the 'organ' screen, the material for the family pew, the pair of folding doors under the 'organ' etc. These items totalled over £311. All this was in addition to the restoration work that Cust had commissioned – the erection of a new west window, incorporating some English fifteenth century glass, but otherwise painted under the direction of Thomas Willement (£114.9.0.), the placing and painting of false organ pipes on the loft (£10), the painting of the roof by Thomas Fairs, and other painting, papering and plastering work (£224.10.5.). In 1827 Cust and Rushbrooke had discussed the possibility of obtaining some Continental stained glass for this window,[130] and Rushbrooke asked Cust to send him the measurements. Rushbrooke also mentioned that he might be able to obtain an organ case locally, but in the end Cust must have decided to buy some pipes and decorate them. It seems that Cust never intended to install a real organ and, interestingly, Rushbrooke installed a false organ in his own church in Suffolk in the 1840s. The musical deficit was made good at Cockayne Hatley in 1833 when a barrel organ was purchased for £36.17.0 (Appendix I). A view of the inside of the church from the east end was drawn by J.C. Buckler in December 1827 (Plate 28). It shows the stalls, with canopywork in the chancel, and canopyless seating in the nave. The lectern is in the centre at the west end of the chancel. The pulpit is at the west end, and the Dutch low screenwork can just be made out north of it. The doors now in front of the tower are not shown because they did not arrive until the following year. Nor is the false organ, installed in 1830.

The very unusual business relationship between patron and agent at Hatley is brought vividly to life in three surviving letters from Robert Rushbrooke (Appendix II). It is a pity that we do not have any of Cust's letters to confirm this, but the tone of familiarity and obscure humour in Rushbrooke's missives supposes a reciprocal level of fraternal trust.

A major problem for Cust was that Hatley church is essentially a long narrow space from end to end, with only meagre north and south aisles. As it turned out, the problem of fitting in a row of eleven choir-

Plate 28. *'Interior view of Cockayne Hatley Church, Bedfordshire. 26th-27th December 1827'. Pen and ink drawing by J.C. Buckler, B.L. MS 36356, f.30.* BY PERMISSION OF THE BRITISH LIBRARY

stalls on each side of the chancel was made impossible by the shortening of the chancel in the first instance. In consequence the canopy or the seating of the stalls occupy the chancel and most of the nave as well.

When the pulpit arrived, it must have been obvious that there was barely room for it anywhere. As Rushbrooke said in his letter of 13 June 1826 (Appendix II), soon after its arrival: 'Plague on the Primrose proportions what trouble they give you!' '… the *honest* pulpit is without the pale…', he states, as indeed it eventually was, finding a resting place only at the back of the nave! At this point Cust was clearly hoping that it would be possible to place it somewhere in the body of the church, since Rushbrooke mentions that there would be worshippers behind as well as in front. Rushbrooke was trying to be as encouraging as possible: ' – when it *is* set up, your choice of spot will be the most effective – it having no sounding board, of course no panel at your back will be required – so that those behind you will hear well'. In fact, according to his son, Robert, the pulpit came complete with its sounding board, although this was eventually discarded.[131] Clearly Henry Cust made an early decision to abandon it. The reason for this, acoustical or otherwise, is not clear. One can imagine his feelings at eventually having to accept that the only place for the pulpit was at the very back of the church. He would have realised that it was going to block the view of the soon to be installed 'gateway' at the base of the west screen. The addition of a sounding board would have hidden even more of it. Presumably, for the same reason, the back board with the figure of St Andrew was also found to be surplus to requirements, but it was retained, and made up into the lectern, which is still in the church today. Perhaps it was hoped that the organ screenwork behind the pulpit would project the preacher's voice forward.

Reviewing the entire project, Rushbrooke expresses relief: '…since I find my Commission has given *such complete satisfaction*'. And moreover: 'I am glad you are not alarmed at all the cost. By adding to that already incurred ….'

An item of particular interest to emanate from Rushbrooke's letters is the identity of one of the dealers used, who was probably based in Brussels. In his letter, dated 16 January 1827 (Appendix II), about the acquisition of stained glass, Rushbrooke says: 'I am on the scent both here and Gand & hope in a week or ten days to hear of my *Hammock* Joe. & in the meantime to have your illustrations (of the west window) for my Guide. … Joseph [Heminius] enquired how far from London was the *revived abbey*, & literally will *some* day pay you a visit of respect & curiosity….' Rushbrooke discusses the possibility of visiting Hatley, which he clearly had not done since the arrival of the pulpit and 'pewing'[132] eight months earlier: 'It was with great practice and forebearance that I eschewed the *Land of Cockayne* in my last flight to Britain. But I had to trespass on a day or two of the Boy's Vacation, and it was, for business sake & their desire of Reunion was too ardent to admit of it' (the boys were at boarding school in England). He then shows us how business was conducted between himself and Henry Cust, in a most gentlemanly way: 'As to the little Balance against me, let it rest. I pray, until it be *swollen* by the gateway' (the folding doors under the 'organ-loft'). 'You are so prudent a personage. No one will accuse you, or fear that you are

Keeping a more *swelling post*
Than what your means may grant continuance

For myself, on that head what with feelings of the present & fears for the future, I have resolved to extenuate my stay herein one twelvemonth more than at first intended. So that if you have more *Abbeys* to endow & to decorate, you may be assured of my Agency until September 1828. … Bye the Bye in the collection of *Candlesticks* from Gand, have you been so thoughtful as to reserve me a *pair*? I hope I sent as liberal a supply as to be able to xxxx a *Claim* for twain of these for *my* Altar piece, but do not spoil any of your plans if they be requisit for the – … Your delight with these well applied materials which my researches have procured so happily gives me an equal enthusiasm with yourself and fancy for my reward, I shall say, as the Poet to his mistress. "You are pleased & *your'e* my pleasure" – and it shall go hard but I will assist in its completion, by following the Skreening materials (probably for the family pew in the north aisle) to xxxxx distinction if times and dates allow.'

Finally, it is noticeable that the London dealers were mostly by-passed in the acquisition process. However, there is a journal entry for the week

PLATE 29. *Flemish pulpit at Cockayne Hatley Church, Bedfordshire. Drawing by H. Shaw. From R.N. Cust*, Some Account of Cockayne Hatley, Bedfordshire, *1851. B.L. Shelf Mark C 106 l.22, opp.10.*
BY PERMISSION OF THE BRITISH LIBRARY

commencing 14 July 1827 (Appendix I), which states: 'Swabey [*sic.*] for Wood Work for Cockayne Hatley Church £11.10.0.'. From Rushbrooke's letter dated 9 June 1829 (Appendix II), it is clear that he did make use of Swaby. If the item was a minor one, such as a short run of communion rails, it would

have been convenient to have been able to make a choice in London, and to have fully involved the patron in the decision. The letter implies that Swaby was used not only in 1827, but also again in 1829 over a considerably bigger purchase. Swaby's agency at this stage would have been inevitable since Rushbrooke probably moved back to England in September 1828. From the letter it is clear that the procedure was already well established: He says that he hopes Cust will come to London … 'And we must carry Swabey in our eye fit at Hatley vice [*sic.*] seeing what is wanted at Hatley to be supplied by S'. According to Cust's journal the only expenditure on 'Wood Work' that was made was one amounting to £64.5.0. It seems likely that this material, whatever it was, was furnished by Swaby.

Three years later in 1830 there is another journal entry referring to a London furniture dealer, this time John Webb of Bond Street. This says: 'Webb – woodwork for Hatley Church £5.3.10' (Appendix I). John Webb of Bond Street was to be used a great deal by Pugin at the end of the decade, at Oscott College and St Chad's Cathedral. In 1840 there is another entry in Cust's journal: 'window and altar rails at do £19.9.8'. From this we can conclude that one of the three altar rails purchased for the church came from a London dealer.

The pulpit must have become known to a limited circle of antiquaries. A drawing of it by Henry Shaw was featured in Robert Needham Cust's privately printed celebratory tribute to a father's extraordinary munificent piety (Plate 29).[133] Also in that volume, Henry Cust's daughter, Lucy, contributed a drawing of the east end of the church, showing the choir-stalls and communion rails (Plate 30).

Henry Cust's love of Baroque furniture is surprising considering the accelerating interest in Gothic in his day. His 'excursions' to Europe in 1825, 1827 and 1830 must have broken down any innate prejudice against such material. The first of these visits must have been defining because the most important purchases, that is the choir-stalls and the pulpit, happened the following year. A list of the places visited is convincing evidence of a rapid self-education:

Dunkirk church; Bruges; Ghent (Toured the churches

PLATE 30. *St John the Baptist, Cockayne Hatley, Bedfordshire. View of east end. From a drawing by Lucy C. Cust. From R.N. Cust,* Some Account of Cockayne Hatley, Bedfordshire, *1851. B.L. Shelf Mark C 106 l.22, Pl.12.* BY PERMISSION OF THE BRITISH LIBRARY

and the Béguinage); Cathedral of St Gudule, Brussels; Malines; Utrecht (Cathedral, public library and museum); Amsterdam; Haarlem, Delft and Rotterdam; Antwerp; Louvain; Liège; Rheims (Cathedral, palace and St Rémi); Paris (St Denis. monuments restored & repairs going on); Boulogne; Calais.

As a fitting postlude to the Cockayne Hatley episode,

we are lucky enough to have a contemporary description of this important early Gothic-Revival church refurbishment. The writer was John Mason Neale (1818-1866) who, as a young man of twenty-one years and still an undergraduate at Cambridge, visited the parish with a male companion. This description is an enthusiastic encomium of the project in the very year that he had co-founded the Cambridge Camden Society. Neale's High Church temperament was clearly excited and astonished by Cust's taste for Catholic furniture.

12 Dec. 1839 (ff.81-82d): It was getting dark, but we pushed on to Hatley Cockayne where we put up our horses at a farm, there being no inn. The church is magnificent beyond description. At the time the present Rector came it was almost ruinated, and had hardly a beautiful feature belonging to it. The outside is now in the most perfect repair. The drain that should never be omitted runs round the walls, and there is an iron fence, separating off a paved portion before the West End, where is the entrance. You enter by folding doors adorned in the most exquisite carving. They came from some Dutch church; all the additions were procured at or near Antwerp. The coup d'oil is very striking. The pulpit is a most elaborate piece of carving of the date of 1559. It has the 4 Evangelists exquisitely sculptured with the symbols. This stands at the West end of the North. The Clerk's desk is a little behind it, and also very beautiful. The reading stool is by the Altar & is supported by a figure of St.Andrew. The C [Chancel] is pannelled with the most gorgeous carving. Each side is divided into 8 niches, and in each side stands a Saint, about half the size of life with his name and legend. Between these are the figures of Cherubim etc. The Saint nearest the Altar on the South side is St.Thomas Archbishop and Martyr. There are also S.Prosper, S.Possidonius, S.Gregory, S.Antony, S.Nicholas, S.Bernard occupies the station on the North that S.Thomas does on the South side. There are also S.Ivo, S.Silvester and others. The East window is modern, both as to the stone work and the glass. The latter is however excellent, containing the history of the Saviour's life, The Crucifixion of course occupying the prominent station in the centre. Under this window is a series of pannelling, in which are inserted most beautifully illuminated in Lombardic characters, the Belief, Commandments, and Lord's Prayer. Behind these, and immediately above the Altar, the text is illuminated "The Law was given by Moses" on one side, then in the centre an illuminated Chalice, and on the other "but grace & truth came by Jesus Christ". The North Window in the Chancel is, as is every Window in the Church, filled with stained glass, the arms of the Cockaynes fill the side lights, the South window is similar, except that it has the Cust Arms. There is not a pew in the Nave. It is filled with Cathedral stalls having beautiful poppy-heads. The East Window of the North Aisle has nine Saxon Saints, the lowest are S.Edward the Confessor, S.Sebert, & S.Oswald. All this glass is ancient. The font was a plan 8L [octagonal]. It is now pannelled into most beautiful P [Perpendicular]. The basin is an ancient [one word illegible] ... piece of china, containing the History of Joseph and his brethren, though this is incorrect. In the Nave are 3 sets of brasses, containing 2,3 and 3 figures respectively. These all commemorate the Cockaynes, but very unfortunately enamelled, I could not take them. In the south aisle is an Elizabethan monument to Sir Patrick Hume. On the North West pier of the Nave is an exquisite modern EE [Early English] niche. We were forced to see this all by candle light and I could have cried with joy to see so much of the feeling of former times yet amongst us. Cust was gone to Bedford, or we should have called. As it was, we left our names. I was amused with the naivety of the clerk's reply to my question whether there were any Dissenters? Oh no, Sir, Mr. Cust doesn't like that there should be any. [There was a strong tradition of Non-Conformism in Bedfordshire.] I wish I could do something like justice to this glorious Church. We re-mounted our horses and rode through Hatley Cockayne wood. I never saw such a road. Oceans of mud up to the horses' knees, branches projecting across the road, twilight pitfalls and gates tended to make our passage neither pleasant nor safe. We were an hour getting to Hatley St. George which is little more than a mile and a half and our horses were dreadfully fagged. Indeed I think we should never have reached our destination at all, had not the moon fortunately, I might also say providentially, come out. We put up at the George....[134]

As we have seen, an interest in collecting Continental church woodwork seems to have percolated to the very top of English society. We even have a personal account of the intervention of a ducal grandee at a London auctioneer's, probably in the 1830s. The 6th Duke of Devonshire, describing the 'Oak Room' at Chatsworth in the 'Handbook of Chatsworth', published in 1844, tells us that:

One day, walking with a friend in Berners Street, we were tempted into the auction-room, and found carved oak being knocked down. I bought to the right and left, and became possessed of almost all that you see here, the fittings of some German monastery, and the woodwork of an old-fashioned pew. So inconsiderate a purchase was never made – however, look at the result. Is it not charming? What discussions might be raised upon it hereafter! – what names given to the busts unknown to the buyer as they were to the seller!

The 'Handbook' was published anonymously, but is generally agreed to be the work of the 6th Duke.[135] The oak panelling was installed at Chatsworth, and is still there today. It consists of wainscoting, divided by spiral columns with busts of ecclesiastics on

PLATE 31. *Chatsworth Hall, Derbyshire. Oak Room. Detail of German wall panelling.*

plinths (Plate 31). Although we do not know the date of the sale, Wainwright has suggested that it may have been an 'importation sale', held on 15 June 1836 at 2 Berners Street:[136]

> Sale of Gothic and other oak carvings just landed comprising fine specimens of the XV & XVI centuries about 10,000 pieces. The whole well worthy the attention of the Nobility, Gentry, Architects and collectors ... by Mr C. Deacon at his spacious rooms.

It is clear that the Duke was not particularly interested in or knowledgeable about woodcarving. At much the same time, another aristocrat, the 5th Lord Monson (1809-1841), was responsible for the much more self-conscious antiquarian enterprise at St Andrew, Gatton in Surrey (L/6, M/10 and M/11), mentioned above. During his short life he travelled

abroad a great deal. The marble hall which he built at nearby Gatton Park was supposed to have been a copy of the sixteenth century Corsini Chapel at St John, Lateran in Rome.

The Hibberts of Birtles Hall, Cheshire, were probably minor county gentry, although little seems to be known about the family that bought the estate in 1791.[137] Robert Hibbert built a new mansion in 1819 and it was probably he who filled it with paintings by Salvator Rosa, Bassano and Gainsborough.[138] The chapel was built for private use in 1840 by Robert's son Thomas and was presented in 1980 to the Diocese of Chester.[139]

With its fine collection of Flemish and Dutch sixteenth and seventeenth century stained glass, the chapel is another outstanding antiquarian interior, especially valuable because it is undisturbed (Plate

PLATE 32. *St Catherine, Birtles, Cheshire. West end of nave.*

32, I/1 and M/4). Most of the furnishings are made up, as usual. The pulpit comprises four different components, and has two different seventeenth century dates on it. An important feature is the remnants of a large suite of seventeenth century Flemish choir-stalls. Sadly there is only one complete stall left, but there are seventeen bays of stall back panels, arranged at the west end and in the north chapel, with the canons' names inscribed above each.[140] Three more have been incorporated at the base of the pulpit.

An antiquarian interior created by a member of the new class of wealthy businessmen and manufacturers is at Harwood Church, Lancashire.[141] It was paid for and created by Robert Lomax, a local velveteen and fustian manufacturer. He was a collector of church furniture in England and abroad. Apart from the items still in the church today, the Lomax Chapel in the south transept was fitted out some years later with Victorian seventeenth century style stalls and desks (Plate 33). The poppy-heads of the desk-ends were metal casts of 'Ripon School' originals. Attached to the desk-ends were eight Flemish wood panels, depicting the *Life of Christ,* one of which was dated 1635. These were saved and restored in 1974 when the chapel was cleared out.[142]

The Lancashire industrialist, Samuel Taylor, paid for the new church at Eccleston, which was completed in 1838 (Plate 34). An account of the opening ceremony was given in *The British Magazine* for November of that year:

On the 10th October, the Lord Bishop of the diocese, consecrated a new church at Eccleston, in the parish of

PLATE 33. *Christ's Church, Harwood, Lancashire. The Lomax Chapel before 1974.*
COPYRIGHT HARWOOD CHURCH

Prescot, built in great part and wholly endowed, at the expense of Samuel Taylor, Esq., of Eccleston Hall. The church is a neat Gothic edifice, adapted for the accommodation of 600 persons, and is fitted up in the interior in a manner much superior to the great majority of modern churches, and in a style which reminds us of the pious care bestowed by our forefathers on the decoration of God's house…. The front of the gallery, the enclosure of the altar, and the holy table itself, as well as the panels of the doors, are all of ancient carved oak, descriptive of sacred objects.[143]

The interior includes odd bits of foreign wood carving attached to the pews, and Flemish narrative panels to the north and south chancel doors. Of most interest are six panels with historiated scenes in

cartouches surrounded by Rococo foliage on the front of the west gallery and two more, which have been built into the modern framework of the narrow altar rails (B/6). These are early to mid-eighteenth century Flemish or French Rococo work of good quality. Eccleston church is a relatively unspoilt example of a pre-archaeological Gothic revival church.

Between 1837 and 1839 the cultured Anglican squire and friend of John Keble, William Crawley Yonge, supervised the building of a new church at Otterbourne, Hampshire, for the local landowner Sir William Heathcote. John Keble was Heathcote's tutor at Oxford, and he was persuaded by his former

PLATE 34. *Christchurch, Eccleston, Lancashire. View of high altar.*

student to accept the livings at Hursley and Otterbourne in 1836. Yonge had studied military engineering in the Army as a young man and undertook to build the church with the local professional architect Owen Carter (1806-1859).[144] The building incorporates the precepts of the Oxford Movement and is very definitely pre-Ecclesiological in character. It is still an auditorium with no chancel screen, originally. The choir was positioned in a gallery at the west end. The pulpit is on the north side, to the west of the chancel step, and the font was in the middle of the crossing.[145]

The pulpit is of some interest as a made-up piece.

It is based on the Prior Silkstede exemplar at nearby Winchester Cathedral. This monument was later to become very familiar to Carter, as he was commissioned to design new steps and a canopy for it in 1848.[146] The Otterbourne pulpit incorporates five fine late fifteenth century low-relief figural Flemish or German panels, illustrating the Virgin, St Jerome, St Augustine, a pope and a bishop. The other two panels of bishops are of wrought iron. They must have been copies from two other ancient panels from the same set which, for some reason were not available. Yonge's daughter Charlotte discusses the furnishings at Otterbourne, saying that:

Mr Yonge sought diligently for old patterns and for ancient carving in oak, and in Wardour Street he succeeded in obtaining five panels, representing the Blessed Virgin and the four Latin Fathers, which are worked into the pulpit.[147]

This reference to 'old patterns' is of interest in the study of the practices of the furniture trade at this time. We are reminded of the wrought iron body of the pulpit at Butterfield's Keble College chapel, built over twenty-five years later. Judging from the address, the dealer who supplied not only the pulpit, but the altar rails and altar at Otterbourne was most probably John Swaby (M/24 and B/9).

As already observed in the case of the Earl of Shrewsbury, Roman Catholic patronage of imported church furniture played a role perhaps more influential than substantive. However, as noted above, in terms of his dealings with Edward Hull and Pugin, the activities of Charles Scarisbrick, another Catholic, should not be underrated. During the 1830s he must have been the single most important purchaser of imported wood carvings in England. Five years after his father's death Charles inherited his entire estate, after a legal battle that went to the House of Lords.[148] He made his fortune from property in Southport and coal mining. His annual income is thought to have been around £60,000 in his later years.[149] Nathaniel Hawthorne, the American writer who lived at Southport in 1856-57, remembered him being described by fellow railway train passengers in the following terms:

He was an eccentric man they said, and there seems to be an obscurity about that early part of his life; according to some experts he kept a gambling house in Paris, before succeeding to the estate. Neither is it a settled point whether or no he has ever been married ... He is a very eccentric and nervous man, and spends all of his time at his secluded hall, which stands in the midst of mosses and marshes, and sees nobody, not even his own steward.[150]

The Scarisbricks were a Catholic family with traditionally strong Jacobite inclinations. It has been suggested that, being brought up before the enactment of the Catholic Emancipation Act of 1829, Charles would almost certainly have been sent abroad after his time at Stonyhurst School to finish his education.[151] No doubt this period laid the foundations for his love of Continental art.

The Scarisbrick Hall interiors do not contain any complete church furniture. Making-up was the order of the day and the Great Hall (Plate 35) and the other room schemes are epitomes of this taste. We cannot say whether the magnificent Dutch Baroque pulpit in the family chapel at Bescar was introduced by Charles Scarisbrick, although there is a note dated January 1833 from Edward Hull in the Scarisbrick papers, as follows:

One hundred Pounds shall be paid for Pulpit with all its accessories and then delivered restored and complete.[152]

Certainly, a pulpit costing £100 in the 1830s would have been of the best quality. This is a judgement that can certainly be made of the extant one (K/12). The chapel at Bescar has been rebuilt since Charles Scarisbrick's time and was in his day much smaller. There was no chapel at Scarisbrick Hall during Charles Scarisbrick's lifetime. The chapel built at the house for Scarisbrick's sister, by E.W. Pugin, after Charles Scarisbrick's death, is too small to contain a pulpit, so the intended use for this object is somewhat mysterious. Intriguingly, Scarisbrick also gives us an oblique reference to a 'Communion Rail'.[153]

The Scarisbrick Papers are the best evidence we have from the whole of the nineteenth century for the economics of the trade in foreign wood carvings. Laid out before us are the itemised bills from Hull's, with Scarisbrick's annotations upon them. In addition there are references to shipping arrangements to this country and internally. For convenience, consolidated excerpts are printed in Appendix III. Reading through them, it is possible to get an idea of the wide range of goods of all descriptions acquired. The destination of some, including a few of the most important ensembles in the house, is adverted in the annotations. For instance:

(Charles Scarisbrick's annotations in brackets)

£

5 Feb 1837
The Large Gothic Oak Doorway including the new Carvings and two Gothic figures on top (for library)
94.10

June 1839
Gothic Pillars for the (centre of)
Large Doors library
4.10

PLATE 35. *Scarisbrick Hall, Lancashire. View of west end of Great Hall.*

Dec 1840
Making pair of large Gothic Doors for Library   94.10
Making Gothic Chimney Piece for small room   58.00
The very fine Screen and Panelling Doors etc.
– for end of the Hall   1000.00

14 August 1841
Lot of fine canopy work and Group (now in
Scarisbrick anteroom)   100.00

October 1844
Lot of very fine Gothic Work to be used for the
Lanthorn over Staircase & window frame   150.00

Apart from the pulpit, the only complete piece of church furniture acquired seems to have been an Eagle lectern, as follows:

5 Feb 1837
Richly carved Oak Gothic Eagle Desk with figures under canopies   40.00

The first of several sales of Scarisbrick's effects took place after his death on 7 November 1860, at Christie's. A number of important items of portable church furniture was offered for sale:

51. Two Gothic carved oak crosses.
55. An old carved pulpit, on stand, with six panels and figures at the angles.
58. A fine old skreen consisting of three panels, boldly carved with busts of Christ, the Virgin, and a bishop, cherubs' heads and fruits in high relief, divided by three spirally twisted columns, with Corinthian capitals, infant angels & c.
85. A pair of gilt Gothic canopies; and sundry pieces of carving.
101. Twenty cathedral stall seats, the brackets formed of grotesque figures.
125. A fine carved oak eagle lectern, on openwork Gothic stand, with three figures of saints.

128. A set of eight very fine old Flemish oval panels, carved with subjects of the new Testament in high relief, supposed to be the work of Bergier: viz. the Annunciation, the Presentation in the Temple, the Baptism, the Last Supper, the Bearing of the Cross, the Crucifixion, the Resurrection, and the Ascension.

The two Gothic crosses were probably the ones noted in 1846 as 'not settled for', purchased for £24 (see Appendix III). The pulpit might be the one bought in 1833 for £100, although another does also seem to have been acquired, apart from the extant specimen at Bescar. The eagle lectern must have been the one purchased in 1837 for £40 (see Appendix III). As already mentioned, it is not clear where these items of church furniture can have been at Scarisbrick, or whether they were even in use at Charles Scarisbrick's death. Pugin's proposed chapel at the Hall was never built, and, as already mentioned, the chapel in the village at that time was only very small.

Another important Roman Catholic patron was Sir Henry Paston Bedingfeld (1800-1862) of Oxburgh Hall, Norfolk, although his building work is mainly undocumented. He started to refurbish the house in 1829 but the detached chapel in the grounds was not completed until 1837, and the furnishings installed in the following year.[154] Pugin was probably the architect, but there is no documentary proof. There are some fine late sixteenth century Flemish stalls (M/25), raised up at the back of the chapel. There are also altar rails at the west end (B/11), as well as others protecting the altar proper (B/10). The carved wooden altarpiece from Antwerp that is there now was not part of the original furnishings, but purchased in Bruges some time before Sir Henry's death in 1862. There seems to have been another altarpiece originally, which might have been the work of Pugin.[155]

Like Scarisbrick, Bedingfeld loved old wood carving. He was naturally drawn to the Low Countries as he had contacts there. Members of his family had entered convents in Ghent during the sixteenth and seventeenth centuries.[156] Augustina Bedingfeld, the great-granddaughter of Margaret Pole, who was beheaded for her faith in 1541, was Prior of the English monastery of Nazareth in Ghent during the mid-sixteenth century. She was later characterised in the *Register of the Acts of the Vicars*

General of Bruges as: 'Religiosa optima et prudentissima atque ad regendum capacissima'.[157] After the Napoleonic Wars the whole family settled in Ghent to live more economically. In the nineteenth century Sir Henry's own sister was a nun at a convent in Bruges. On a much smaller scale than the prodigious Charles Scarisbrick, Sir Henry also imported woodwork for use in the house.

The handful of patrons who have been discussed above represent only the tip of the iceberg when one considers the number of churches in England with fragments of Continental woodwork of one kind or another. It is clear that the motives for acquisition were legion, perhaps the principal one being the availability of the material. Unequivocally, however, the boom time for this activity ran from the second to the fourth decades of the nineteenth century. In the Anglican church many of the most idiosyncratic interiors, such as Gatton (1830s), Cockayne Hatley (1830), Brougham (late 1830s), Charborough (1837), Otterbourne (1839), Birtles (1840) and Old Warden (1841) were created well before the precepts of the Ecclesiologists had 'made it very difficult for …incumbents … to know what new types of furnishings could be inserted without offending either the bishops or the congregations'.[158] As Pevsner observed about Cockayne Hatley: 'Thirty years later no one would have dared to introduce such a display into an Anglican church'. By then the Ecclesiologists had turned their backs firmly on Rome.

For the English Catholics the espousal of European art where it was affordable is entirely understandable. The Anglicans who indulged in this activity were eccentric antiquaries smitten by the Romantic ideal. In any case, they were too socially and financially independent to concern themselves with the strictures of the church authorities. With family ancestral monuments crowding in on every side, and an ostentatious and comfortable provision of accommodation for the living, a rural parish congregation of grateful estate tenantry was probably prepared to tolerate an alien and perhaps mystifying display of theatricality in their village church, even if it meant that, as at Gatton, Cockayne Hatley and elsewhere, farmers were expected to sit every Sunday in the stalls of seventeenth century Belgian monks.

Chapter IV

CONSOLIDATION AND RESTITUTION
1860 TO THE PRESENT DAY

After 1860 there was a dramatic falling off in the amount of Continental church furniture being brought to England. This was due to a diminution in supply, but one should look also to the greater control of liturgical practice exercised within the Anglican church, engendered by the Ecclesiological movement.[1] Moreover the aristocracy and gentry suffered from a serious decline in rental and land values, particularly from the 1880s, and the clergy experienced by 1900 a halving in the value of their stipends.[2]

Interestingly the little material that was imported came mostly from beyond the traditional hunting grounds of The Netherlands, Germany, Switzerland and France. Italy, Spain and in one case Denmark were the source of supply in this quieter phase.

The Victoria and Albert Museum, which was founded in the 1850s, acquired the marble rood loft from St John, s'Hertogenbosch in 1871, probably its most significant acquisition since its inception. The cathedral removed the pulpitum in 1866, and sold it to a dealer.[3] The museum also acquired many Continental woodwork fragments. An important early collection of such was the one assembled by A.W.N. Pugin for the instruction of the craftsmen employed at the Palace of Westminster.[4] The only other English museum with any Continental church furniture is the Bowes Museum at Castle Barnard.[5] There can be seen a few items of interest, by far the most important being the choir-stalls from the Dominican convent of St Katharinenthal, Diessenhofen, Germany (M/2), and the carved Netherlandish altarpiece.[6] We do not know how the choir-stalls were acquired, no proper note having been made of John Bowes' acquisitions, as it seems that his wife's memory was considered a good enough substitute. The altarpiece was bought from Monbro *fils aîné*, Paris in 1859. It was kept at the ancestral home, Streatlan Castle until 1892, when the museum was opened.[7] William Burrell bought mainly secular furniture, both Continental and English. A catalogue of the collection, which is now in Glasgow, has never been published.

As has been pointed out already, the fierce arguments which raged for so much of the nineteenth century in the Anglican church about the liturgy post-dated the acquisition of the bulk of the continental church furniture. The introduction of carved altarpieces at St Peter's College, Radley, in the late 1840s,[8] and St John's, Tue Brook, Liverpool, in 1870[9] caused great offence. In the latter case the Bishop of Chester refused to consecrate the new church before the offending item was removed. On the whole, it seems that the ecclesiologists, who in the words of Alexander Beresford Hope, the president of the society in 1860, were 'strong in sacramental doctrine and aesthetic in worship', generally specified modern furnishings in their churches. Bodley, the architect of Tue Brook, favoured modern altarpieces, as did Gilbert Scott and other architects associated with the movement.[10]

By this time, of course, the high watermark of the Gothic Revival was well past. A new self-confident generation of architects, like Street, Butterfield and Burges, was sure enough of its own originality not to need to rely on imported Gothic, let alone second-hand Baroque furniture.

The relatively simple precepts of the early Ecclesiologists were soon overtaken by a more complex system of arranging a church interior:

> the simple solution of providing a large unified auditorium, from all points of which the congregation would see and hear the preacher, was soon outdated. Ecclesiology prescribed a new method of assembling characteristic elements borrowed from medieval English churches into a complex shell within which various sacramental rites would be 'rubrickally' performed.[11]

The manifestation of this philosophy clearly predicates the need to take control and remodel. The use of ancient furniture would have been inappropriate in this context, as fragments of any size tend to dictate their own space. It would have been much more convenient to copy the Gothic forms and decoration if appropriate, but to tailor-make the

PLATE 36. *St James, North Cray, Kent. View of chancel looking east.*

objects to the needs of the liturgical ensemble.

None the less, picturesque antiquarian chancels continued to be created, particularly as part of the re-orderings of medieval parish churches. One such, which will have to stand for many others, is that of 1871 at St James, North Cray, Kent (Plate 36). The reredos, altarpiece and wall panelling, which is mostly foreign, has been orchestrated into a convincing ensemble. The altarpiece consists of two fine German early sixteenth century panels in high relief, depicting the *Adoration of the Magi* and the *Flight to Egypt*. These have been either cut to fit or adapted for their present position. The bowed shelf below is modern. At ground level on either side of the altar are large Baroque panels, completely out of character with everything else. Both back and side walls are furnished with carved panelling and coved canopywork of various

periods, much of it modern. The canopywork could have been from a set of choir-stalls originally. Clearly the palm ornament uprights to each side of the altarpiece do not go with the canopywork above. All this woodwork is covered in a dark varnish to cover up the differences in provenance and colour of the various components.

A spectacular piece of made-up furniture from the later nineteenth century is the oak eagle lectern at Methley, West Yorkshire (Plate 37).[12] It consists of a massive proto-Disneyesque eagle made by Robert Ellis & Co. of New York and exhibited in Philadelphia in 1867. It sits on an elaborate hex-agonal stand packed with late-Gothic continental formal and decorative features. It was even validated by Pevsner, presumably on the basis that the three figures under the projecting canopies are themselves ancient. The base is indeed a very learned piece of work and the quality of the figures is very high. But the stand itself, as well as the eagle, is of nineteenth century workmanship.

Collecting continued during the second half of the century, as we have seen in the case of John Bowes. Alexander Beresford Hope, one of the leading figures of the Ecclesiologists, inherited a fortune in 1841 and proceeded to build up a huge collection of works of art, which he kept at his London home, 1 Connaught Place. He was visited by Dr Gustav Waagen who mentioned that the medieval objects were kept in a room resembling a chapel.[13] Three items of church furniture were noted:

A large altarpiece with wings, carved in wood, from a church at Ypres, in Belgium etc.

A crucifix of wood with some pretty angels around. This was executed between 1530-40.

The pedestal of a candelabrum in the Romanesque style, which, judging from the pure and small form, cannot be assigned to a period later than the year 1000.

Hope's collection was sold after his death, at Christie's on 12 to 15 May 1886. It included a painted triptych (Lot 302), and presumably the altarpiece noted by Waagen, namely: 'An old Flemish carved wood altar-piece, with the Crucifixion and four smaller subjects, from the Passion, in high relief under Gothic canopies'. This was purchased by the 15th Duke of Norfolk.[14]

Another collector, the 'eccentric and enthusiastic antiquarian', Vincent J. Robinson, F.S.A., of Parnham House near Beaminster, Dorset, had erected a set of seventeenth century Brescian choir-stalls around the walls of his dining-room (Plate 38).[15] In 1910, after his death, the house and contents were sold. The sale catalogue notes that: 'The walls are panelled in carved walnut, fitted with seats (the work having been brought from the Sacristy of a church outside Brescia...'. The stalls are no longer in the house. They must have been sold and, presumably, either returned to Italy or possibly sent to the United States. However, the Rococo double doors into the dining room, which are probably Flemish, have come to rest only a few miles away at Fordington, near Dorchester, Dorset (J/6).

The relative paucity of material available from

PLATE 37. *St Oswald, Methley, West Yorkshire. Lectern, 1860-70.*

Europe by the end of the century was underlined in the catalogue prepared by Julius Ichenhauser, a dealer of 68 New Bond Street, for a sale of ancient woodwork on 20 June 1888. *The Post Office Directory* of 1877 tells us that Julius Ichenhauser had a fine art gallery, warehouses in Bridle Lane, London, and Fürth, near Nüremberg.[16]

In 1888 he gave a second retail address in Little Goudge Street, claimed to have another warehouse in Brussels, and adverted a 'speciality for oak panellings'.[17] In the catalogue he boasts:

In offering the remarkable examples of antique wood carvings ... Mr J. Ichenhauser may safely say that such lots as the carved oak choir stalls from Buxheim, and the

PLATE 38. *Parnham House, Dorset. Dining Room, before 1910.*   COPYRIGHT COUNTRY LIFE

reredos from Maeseyck may never be put up again for public competition. It is a fact that a greater proportion of the finer antique wood carvings was executed in the monasteries and convents of Continental Europe; and, as the days of loot and wanton destruction are now happily over, and those religious orders which possess rarities of past ages not being likely to dispose of the same, the supply is stopped.

The stalls (Plate 39) came from the Carthusian monastery of Buxheim, south of Ulm. They are a bravura exhibition of both joinery and sculpture. The lots on offer consisted of thirty-one seats, with the remains of others, and the figures about a metre in height which surmounted them. The stalls were made by Ignaz Waibel between 1688 and 1700.[18] When the monastery was secularised in 1809 it was sold by the state to a local family. In 1880 Count

Hugo von Waldbott-Bassenheim sold some of the stalls, which ended up in London. At the sale they were bought by Edward Howly Palmer, Governor of the Bank of England, no less, who presented them to St Saviour's Hospital, Osnaburgh Street, London. In 1963 the hospital, the work of the architect Butterfield, was demolished for redevelopment. The refugee fragments were moved with the institution to Kent, but since then they have been returned to Buxheim to rejoin the portions of the furniture which had always remained in the church.

During the period of their refuge in this country the Buxheim stalls were not unappreciated. As Pevsner noted in 1952:

While the ornament with its lush foliage is already entirely Baroque in style, the figures have still the long,

PLATE 39. *St Saviour's Hospital, Osnaburgh Street, London (demolished 1963). Detail of German Baroque choir-stalls in chapel.* CROWN COPYRIGHT. NMR

slender bodies, small heads and hands, and thin folds of Mannerism, a style which in German sculpture kept alive right through the 17th c. The Buxheim stalls are the best example of German wood-carving of that date in England.[19]

As a sign of the changing times it is appropriate to quote from a letter about the Buxheim furniture written to Judith G. Scott, Secretary of the Council for the Care of Churches, by S.W. Wolsey, probably the best known of the English wood carving and furniture dealers of the twentieth century.[20] He was discussing the imponderable conditions which would in 1963 surround the public auction of such a monument:

Such an almost complete church interior in such condition has not come into the market, home or abroad in my fifty years connection with the trade and so far as one can foresee is not likely too [*sic.*]. Europe as a whole is taking greater precautions to return intact the artistic objects of the earlier periods.

Since 1860 the Roman Catholic church has played practically no part in the acquisition of Continental church furniture. The one exception is the only Roman Catholic private chapel to have installed European woodwork. The small architecturally modest Chapel of Our Lady of the Rosary, at Bursledon, Hampshire, built in 1906 by a Mrs Shawe-Storey, contains an almost overpowering ensemble of Baroque furniture, quite out of scale with the building, the climax of which is the large Flemish altarpiece from which the place takes its name (Plate 40, B/2 and C/1).

Similarly Anglo-Catholicism has played but a small part in the use of Continental material. At Coveney, Cambridgeshire, Athelstan Riley, the prominent Anglo-Catholic layman, was patron of the living from the late nineteenth century until his death in 1945. The rood screen, which was designed by a former rector, contains Riley's initials AR as well as the gridiron of St Laurence, his patron saint. The Danish pulpit was bought by him in a Continental antique shop (K/6), and he also presented the T-shaped supposedly German reredos of about 1500. Unfortunately the latter has been so heavily restored that it is impossible to say whether it is authentic or not. Riley had a private chapel in his London house. A Flemish relief of the Crucifixion from there is now in Cavendish Church, Suffolk.[21] He was also patron of the living at Little Petherick, Cornwall, where his wife is buried. For her monument he acquired another Flemish seventeenth century relief, and 'also collected a considerable number of vestments, altar furniture, etc., for example a chasuble with Spanish late 16th c. embroidery, two late 16th c. Italian copes, an Italian 13th c. silver cross, two 16th c. chalices and patens, one Elizabethan the other foreign, a 16th c. Venetian processional cross, and a Spanish 17th c. painting of the Magdalen'.[22]

The earliest of the patrons in this period, whose church, having been rebuilt in the neo-Romanesque style, was reopened in 1862, was Edward Law, Baron Ellenborough. He bought the Southam Delabere, Gloucestershire, estate in 1839, but did not spend much time there until his return from distinguished but controversial service in India in 1844. He was the son of a Chief Justice and the grandson of a bishop, but, although able, he was considered to have lacked judgement. He had a highly eventful career, attaining cabinet rank under Wellington and becoming Viceroy of India in 1842. An incident in his Viceroyalty shows what kind of a man he was:

> At the close of the Afghan Campaign, he arranged to receive the returning armies ... with more than oriental pomp; they were to march beneath a triumphal arch and between double lines of gilded and salaaming elephants, but the arch was a gaudy and tottering structure, and the ill-tutored elephants forgot to salaam and ran away.[23]

'I go to restore peace to Asia', he is supposed to have said as he departed for India.[24] His lack of judgement is instanced by the fact that he took his mistress with him. As Thomas Needham Cust tells us in his diary:

> Sorry to hear that the report of a mistress from England was true, as we ourselves had ocular proof of the individual, unworthy of so high a character as the Governor General.[25]

He fought three wars very successfully but was recalled in haste by the East India Company's directors for whom he had broken every rule in the book. Gloucestershire must have seemed very tame after the grandeur and pomp of the east, although until the end of his life he spent a good deal of time in London. On his return from India he was created Viscount Southam and Earl of Ellenborough. He was appointed First Lord of the Admiralty in 1846 and was later a successful speaker in the House of Lords. Tipping observed that there was no possibility that Ellenborough would leave the building alone, a typical unpretentious sixteenth century manor house. He continues:

> He possessed to the full the new romantic feeling and mediaeval leanings, which, with more zeal than discretion, were producing Eglington tournaments, 'restoring' cathedrals and erecting 'Gothic' town halls and villas. ... The returned Viceroy, the hero of three wars, should assuredly have a Norman keep and Edwardian towers to his dwelling. And so there they are.[26]

The church, which was restored as a chapel in memory of his wife, Lady Octavia Stewart, is tiny. The plain oak panelling on the walls throughout the nave

PLATE 40. *Chapel of Our Lady of the Rosary, Bursledon, Hampshire. 17th century. Flemish altarpiece. Detail (C/1).*

and chancel contrast with the stone 'Romanesque' pulpit, the original Norman stonework and the whitewashed walls. There is a fine, probably Flemish, corbel of an angel holding a chalice on the south side of the altar. The item of furniture of particular interest is the run of three stall seats on the north side of the chancel, quite out of proportion to the space available (M/30). They are exceptionally good quality Continental Mannerist work.

Another country squire of a very different stamp was Sabine Baring-Gould, of Lew Trenchard, Devon (1834-1924). To celebrate his birth his father cleared out the late medieval oak benches and rood screen of the unprepossessing but ancient family church, replacing them with pine pews and a pulpit, all painted 'a bright mustard yellow'.[27] Sabine inherited the patrimonial estates in 1872 and presented himself to the Rectory on the death of his uncle in 1881.[28]

Apart from restoring the parish church and re-building the manor house, he was the father of fifteen children. He is remembered today chiefly as a hymn writer, although he wrote prolifically, including many novels, and several hundred articles. He published fifteen volumes of the *Lives of the Saints* and he was a well-known local archaeologist and antiquary.[29]

From a tender age, we are told, he became interested in European history:

> His father's restless nature had caused him to be trailed round the Continent from childhood. At the age of fifteen, when most boys of his class would have been more concerned with the hope of winning cricket or football colours, he could not only speak several languages but had developed a cosmopolitan taste. Even at that age he was something of a scholar and we hear of him spending a happy winter in the public library of Pau translating Michaud's 'History of the Crusades'.[30]

The impression that the interior at Lew Trenchard gives today is of an over-restored Devon church. Gould managed to salvage some of the benches ejected by his father, had them refurbished, and commissioned a new pulpit and rood screen, both made by two Devon women wood carvers.[31] Overlaid is a veneer of Europeanism. The fifteenth century chandelier from St James, Mechelen, was bought in 1880 when the Belgian church was putting in new gas lighting.[32] The fifteenth century Flemish triptych was presented in 1881.[33]

The painting over the altarpiece is the work of the Swiss nineteenth century artist Paul Deschwanden. The eagle lectern is said to have been discarded by a church in Brittany. It was acquired in 1905.

A history of English artistic acquisition would not be complete without the agency of a plutocrat. In this case William Waldorf Astor, the most prodigious of them all, can be cited. In 1903 he bought Hever Castle in Kent, restoring and enlarging it at huge expense to provide the standards of comfort of a five-star hotel. In middle age he had become a Europhile, and enjoyed a spell as American Minister in Rome between 1882 and 1885. The large number of specimens of Italian furniture at Hever, including the interesting choir-stalls, must be the fruits of this ambassadorship.

By the early twentieth century the English landed classes had suffered a crisis of confidence. It is not surprising that the creation of antiquarian church interiors was virtually a thing of the past. However, it is pleasing that the phenomenon went out at All Saints, Tooting Graveney, London with a blaze of glory (A/3, C/3, C/4, D/1, E/6, I/7 and M/17). For this church is one of the most important repositories of Continental church furniture in England (Colour Plates 1, 3, 4, 5, 8, 9, 11, 17; Plates 41, 55, 96, 97, 103, 112, 148, 158, 307, 308). It was built in memory of Lord Charles Brudenell-Bruce (*ob.* 1856) with the large sum of £140,000 provided in his widow's will. Canon Otter Stephens, a life-long friend of Brudenell-Bruce, was appointed a trustee, and it was he who carried out the ambitious project. He conducted it from the beginning almost single-handed, bringing to the task some previous experience of church building. He had founded hospitals in Wiltshire and Norfolk, and built a church at Beaulieu-sur-Mer on the French Riviera with the architect Temple Moore, whom he appointed for the Tooting church. The foundation stone was laid in 1904, but the two men fell out over Stephens' plans for the furnishings. The latter had been buying from abroad material which Temple Moore considered 'unsuitable'. The architect, Sir Walter Tapper, was appointed to install Stephens' furniture, and the church was consecrated on 7 July 1906.

The disagreement was based on the long-running Victorian liturgical debate. Temple Moore, the rationalist and pupil of George Gilbert Scott, Jnr, wanted 'to give a sense of stately length characteristic of a medieval church, with the maximum of accommodation for a large congregation'.[34] Stephens, on the other hand, an Oxford man, favoured mystification. He got his way with the huge Baroque altarpiece that was, in the event, put in place. Temple Moore's reservations are wholly understandable, given that Stephens, the dilettante, proposed to use his neo-Gothic church as a repository for the latter's collection of Italian Baroque furniture.

The Edwardian 'Baroque' revival promoted by the Society of St Peter and St Paul did not prove to be a direct stimulus to the traffic in Continental church furniture. We are told that Geoffrey Heald, for instance, a curate at All Saints, Margaret Street from 1916-28, ransacked the back streets of Soho to find furniture of the Baroque and Rococo styles.[35] No doubt the opulent early eighteenth century Italian gilt chairs from Culford Hall, Suffolk, now in the chancel of the rural Wisbech St Mary Church,

PLATE 41. *All Saints, Tooting Graveney, London. View to east from chancel step.*

Cambridgeshire, were the kind of furniture Heald would have been looking for. They must have been placed in the church at about this time.

In practice most of the Anglo-Catholic re-furnishings of this period, such as Martin Travers' (1886-1948) work at Compton Beauchamp, near Shrivenham, Berkshire, were made up from modern materials. Travers' refurbishment of St Magnus the Martyr, Lower Thames Street, London, uses Wren's

original furnishings in the main. The transformation to the appearance of a seventeenth century Catholic church is achieved to a great extent through the use of white paint and gilding. The seventeenth century Flemish aumbry in the church was one of the last Continental ecclesiastical pieces to be imported into England (G/3). It was introduced by the incumbent of St Magnus, the Rev. H.J. Fynes-Clinton, who was a friend of the architect.

Chapter V

THE DEMISE OF NOSTALGIA

There can be few more bizarre sights in England than the great hall at Weare Giffard in Devon, with its fine fifteenth century hammer-beam roof, and a run of Flemish seventeenth century choir-stalls placed on a floral 1950s-style carpet. Unfortunately this scene is not simply picturesque, but evokes a general air of neglect. Non-ecclesiastical settings do not always provide an ideal environment for the storage of wooden furniture. But churches are public buildings and part of an institution that is committed to preserving its historic contents. At the start of a new millennium, however, this reassuring assumption cannot necessarily be taken as read. There is the continuing problem of having to adapt these buildings to the perceived needs of an evangelical liturgy. In the case of our rare Continental fragments, due no doubt to a mixture of their Catholic associations and alien style, a distinctly prejudicial attitude from church-wardens and clergy is often encountered.

Gone are the days when foreigners might mistakenly think that we were still endowing, reviving and decorating abbeys over here. On the contrary, clergy are often ashamed of these tokens of the nostalgia that epitomised a rejection of Georgian rationalism and the guilty backward glance to the vandalism of Protestantism. A pioneer of this nostalgia was Horace Walpole, who stoutly objected to the wholesale removal of the thirteenth century choir-stalls from Westminster Abbey in the late eighteenth century. At the time that Henry Cust was buying his furniture for Cockayne Hatley church, the movement was still in its first unfocused flush, and had not yet been strait-jacketed by Pugin, Ruskin and the Ecclesiologists into a specifically Gothic programme. In Cust's day Catholic Baroque artwork could comfortably evoke a golden past when the Church played as central a part in everyday life as the state. Surprisingly, this Catholic material, it seems, was equally effective in touching this chord as anything from the Gothic tradition. A similar tendency was the large amount of post-medieval Continental stained glass which flooded into England from the turn of the nineteenth century. Sadly today, in spite of the efforts of the Ecumenicists, this fellow feeling for Continental Catholicism has largely evaporated.

The story of a West Country church exemplifies the process well. An interesting collection of two seventeenth century Flemish carved panels, four miniature Solomonic columns and a high quality altar frontal, possibly from Bruges, were presented to the church in the 1950s. They are reputed to have reached England *via* Spain or Portugal. They were arranged in the south chapel of the church altar-wise with the frontal perched on the back of an English oak altar table, and the carved screen panels used as wings, interspersed with the columns. This interesting material has now been moved to make way for a carpeted communal area and rearranged meaninglessly under the tower. There is only one direction in which this particular part of our eccentric heritage can now go. My suggestion that the rare and beautiful frontal could be used on the main altar was met with disbelief. There might be practical problems in doing so, but, more significantly, such is the chasm between the increasingly dominant progressive elements of our Anglican clergy and these seemingly quirky historical traditions.

But affirmative action like this is better than indifference. Woodworm or wood rot can be neglected for so long that conservation almost comes too late. This is the case with the fine eighteenth century panels at Grittleton, and some of the furniture at Bishopstone, both in Wiltshire. In the latter place the interesting fifteenth century, probably northern French, choir-stall fragments had become infested with death-watch beetle. Only very rarely indeed is our native ecclesiastical furniture affected in this way, doubtless because it tends to be housed in well maintained churches. Undoubtedly the problem with this alien material is that it is so often found in quiet country parishes with low populations. Woodwork is vulnerable to damp, but it should be possible to isolate a threat at a reasonably

PLATE 41A. *Chelmsford Cathedral. Detail of Dutch altar rails. Removed in 1983.* R. AND H.J. PARSONS

early stage. Any deterioration is either not being noticed, or is being ignored. In any case more needs to be done to alert the long-suffering guardians of our heritage to the artistic importance of this alien material, to the inexorable appetite of the wood-boring beetle, and the acute vulnerability of wood to damp conditions.

As we have seen, in a few untypical instances the Roman Catholics introduced this material into their churches. This does not seem to have been as a result of any official encouragement but rather of the personal initiative of certain churchmen and patrons. The Catholic Church's finances being increasingly tight, along with the other treasures which have been acquired over time, woodwork is always at risk of being sold off. It was a matter of personal taste that caused, in the early 1850s, the communion rails at Oscott to be disposed of by the new rector Dr Moore, when he 'turned out of the chapel everything which was not Gothic'.[1] Although the rails were later bought back, the choir-stalls at Oscott have been neglected to the extent that they have needlessly lost some of their misericords. In the twentieth century, with the Catholic Church's

finances being perennially stretched, many of the most important items given to Oscott College in the nineteenth century have been sold, including the Flemish latten lectern. Important paintings and other valuables have also been disposed of by Stonyhurst College. The stalls from St Peter's Church, Stonyhurst, consecrated in 1835, were ousted many years ago. Some of them have been placed around the school, others until very recently were stored in an abandoned squash court, and still more in an old corn mill. A few of these stalls have been affected by storage in damp conditions and, again, misericords are missing. Is it too much to hope that this material could be reunited again in a place of worship? At parish level, in the little chapel at Bursledon, Hampshire, the future of the interesting assemblage of Continental fragments (B/2 and C/1) must be very uncertain.

In this catalogue of pitfalls, high on the list is destruction by fire. The redundant church of St Thomas, Tenison Court, Westminster, which has since been burnt down, had an early eighteenth century walnut Franciscan Italian confessional.[2] On redundancy the object was sent to St Matthew's,

Great St Peter Street, where it was destroyed in the devastating conflagration of 1977. An interesting eighteenth century Flemish pulpit was caught up in a redundancy at St Luke's, Cheetham Hill, Manchester. It is now in the Manchester City Art Gallery but in an undignified state of disassembly (K/9). One far-sighted donor, at Mark, Somerset (M/21), stipulated in his will that if his early sixteenth century choir-stall ends, allegedly from Bruges Cathedral, were ever removed from the church, for whatever reason, they would become the property of the South Kensington Museum, London.[3]

There are the largely, but not completely, apocryphal stories of vicars setting fire to unwanted furniture in the churchyard. One set of five early seventeenth century Netherlandish panels from a Berkshire church have certainly been destroyed. Another increasingly acute problem has become the theft of easily portable objects, such as the Italian sixteenth century chair from Cheveley Church, Cambridgeshire, and the Flemish chandelier from Lew Trenchard Church, Devon. The most serious loss of the last few years is thirteen of the figurative panels at Old Warden, together with three of the Evangelist pilasters on the pulpit. The stolen panels represent about eighty percent of the original total and were important components of this extraordinary assemblage. As for the pulpit there, the loss of the pilasters has ruined a good quality Flemish eighteenth century monument.

Another vicissitude is the unrecorded removal of items from a church and their disposal by sale or gift to unknown persons. Up until 1978, at least, there was an early eighteenth century Flemish or French vestment cupboard at St Mary's, Watford. This has disappeared and there is no explanation as to its whereabouts. The late seventeenth century Dutch altar rails at Chelmsford Cathedral, apparently of outstanding quality, were 'removed at a general scheme of reordering and refurnishing in the early 1980s' (Plate 41a).[4] They appear to have been subsequently disposed of in spite of the then Cathedral Advisory Commission recommending that they be retained against possible future re-instatement.[5] The Flemish early sixteenth century stalls from Knowsley Hall, which were probably brought from the Continent by the Earl of Derby between 1850-60 and

placed in Knowsley Church, were mentioned by Pevsner in 1969,[6] but have since disappeared without trace. They were presumably sold in the early 1980s to raise funds for the restoration of the church.

Finally at St Ninian, Brougham, in Cumbria, this remote rural church, according to a photograph taken in 1931, had a run of high quality Flemish choir-stalls (Plate 42). They have since vanished. No one locally seems to know their fate.

A perhaps unexpected hazard for one of these nineteenth century ecclesiastical ensembles was the proposal by the diocese of Southwark in 1952 to empty and dismantle Gatton Church, Surrey. The stalls and the stained glass were offered to Glasgow Cathedral and some of the other furnishings were considered for Bury St Edmunds Cathedral. Happily these plans did not materialise and the church with its furnishings intact is still there. The only successful cherry picker has been Carlisle Cathedral, which bought in 1963 for £500 the pulpit from St Andrew's Church, Antwerp, which had been part of the furnishings at Cockayne Hatley, Bedfordshire since 1826. At the time funds were needed at this isolated rural church for fabric repairs, in order to prevent closure of the church.[7] In 1930, in an earlier similar crisis, the disposal by sale of the pulpit was averted through the generous intervention of Mr. S.H. Whitbread.[8] The Flemish altarpiece at St Wilfrid's, Brougham, Cumbria, another highly important early nineteenth century import, was sent in the late 1970s to the Victoria and Albert Museum for conservation, upon the chapel becoming redundant. However, it was soon realised that, when properly assembled, the side wings would have effectively blocked the windows to each side of the altar at Brougham. In this case, inevitably, it was decided that the monument should be sent on loan to Carlisle Cathedral, to which it was despatched in 1979, on practical, conservation and security grounds.

One final hazard which needs to be mentioned is the danger of insensitive restoration, where a local amateur has been called in, rather than a reputable craftsman. The pair of late Gothic, c.1500, German candlestands, about six feet tall, at Stapledon Church, Shropshire,[9] have been recently painted in the worst possible taste. All traces of the original

PLATE 42. *St Ninian, Brougham, Cumbria. View of Flemish choir-stalls, taken in 1931.* CROWN COPYRIGHT. NMR

polychrome have gone. Another example is a probably Italian early seventeenth century lectern on triangular base and baluster shaft at Wolferton Church, Norfolk,[10] which has been severely compromised by a recent black and gold overpaint.

Given all these vicissitudes it is, perhaps, surprising that so much of this material still survives in our churches, country houses and other institutions. For those who may want to follow up the subject a county gazetteer is appended at the back. This will never be complete as items are sold,

moved or destroyed, and new ones discovered.

In this book I have tried to put the acquisition of this material into a historical context. But the search for a provenance and a stylistic context for the most interesting items really demands the specialist knowledge of a local furniture historian. The following section highlights the cream of the national collection, and perhaps the publication of this book will alert such people to the existence of the woodwork, and lead to fruitful locally-based research in the future.

PART II

THE NATIONAL COLLECTION

Introduction

One hundred and thirty more or less complete items of Continental church furniture in wood in England have been selected for close scrutiny in this section. The date of manufacture is from the fifteenth century to *c*.1800. The only major categories of wooden furniture to be omitted are wall panelling, of which there are only fragments in any case, and organ cases. To some extent a breakdown by type will give a picture of the collectors' priorities.

Altar frontals: 4
Altar rails: 14
Altar reredoses and canopies: 6
Candle stands: 3
Chairs and benches: 6
Chests: 12
Cupboards: 3
Faldstools: 2
Lecterns: 12
Miscellaneous (Water stoups, corbels, doors, a
    cross, font covers, reliquaries): 16
Pulpits: 17
Screens: 7
Portions of stalls: 32

Some of the items, such as altar frontals, altar rail panels and stalls, have been built into another piece of furniture, or, as in the case of communion rail panels, made up into full reproductions of the original. The pulpits have often been altered to fit into the new host church. The vast majority of the objects were manufactured abroad. On the other hand, some of the screens, such as the north Devon group (L/1, L/4, L/5), were clearly made in England but by aliens or at least denized foreigners. The proportions of the different types of furniture in this section are not typical of the complete collection of fragments to be found in England, which is dominated by loose refugee panels (see Gazetteer).

To give a rough idea of the provenance of this material, a table of percentages is shown below:

	%
Low Countries (mostly Flanders)	55
France (mostly northern and north-west)	22
Italy	13
Germany	6
Spain	2
Denmark	1
Portugal	1

Clearly, for various reasons, the Flemish material was most easily accessible to English buyers. What is perhaps *prima facie* more surprising is that most of it is post-medieval in date. But it must be remembered that before the trauma of the French Revolution and the confiscation by the state of all religious property in 1796, Belgium had suffered terribly from the devastating iconoclastic *beelderstorm* of 1566-67 during the Reformation, and then, more or less intermittently from 1572 to 1648, during the military struggle between the French and the Spanish for political supremacy over their territory.

The furniture that was put on the market following the Revolution was mainly the product of the systematic refurbishment of old churches, and the institution of many new ones, which necessarily followed the destructive fury of the iconoclasm and religious wars of the sixteenth and seventeenth centuries.

From the late sixteenth century and early seventeenth century Belgium experienced a state-led Renaissance of Catholic religious life, under the leadership of Archduke Albert and his wife Isabelle, who was Philip II's daughter (van Kalken 1954). The edicts of the Council of Trent (1545-63) were instigated in full. The Jesuits were given a free hand and between 1595 and 1626 the number of their priests increased from 420 to 1,574 (Pirenne 1950). But, in addition, many other Orders were established, thanks to a glut of donations. The

Récollets (Jesuits of the Poor), Carmelites *(Déchaussés)*, the Order of St Francis of Paola, preaching, teaching, contemplative and charitable Orders, all queued up for favours from the sovereign and the public. The percentage of family members who had joined an Order increased vastly. Clergywomen were hardly less numerous than clergymen. There were the Carmelite convents, the Order of St Teresa, the Brigittines, Ursulines, Franciscans and Poor Clares, amongst others.

The unprecedented rise in the number of clerics even alarmed the Archduke, who remarked that the number of clergy was growing like trees in a garden of which there are already too many. Such was the culture of piety at that time that even the Archduke would get out of his carriage to kneel before a passing sacramental procession. The Archduke and Duchess visited the pilgrimage sites at Laeken, Hal and Montaigu. Albert took part in the processions of the Sacrament, standing in as one of the bearers. Albert and Isabelle always humbly washed the feet of the beggars on the Thursday of Holy Week and after Albert's death, in 1621, his widow allotted six hours a day to her devotions. Also at this period the Italian Capuchin friar, de Casali, gave fanatical sermons at court, beating himself and donning a crown of thorns. This kind of behaviour was also adopted at public processions (van Kalken 1954 and Pirenne 1950).

A large number of new religious houses were built at this time, not to mention the wholesale refurbishment of parish churches, particularly in the big cities. Of interest to us, in connection with the altar rails at Otterbourne, Hampshire (B/9), is the Premonstratensian Order. Their abbeys, such as Floreffe, Ninove, Grimbergen and Averbode, were particularly numerous in Belgium. The Order's founder, St Norbert, was a bishop in the twelfth century, yet he was canonised only in 1582, and the Order was relaunched as a spearhead of the Counter-Reformation. He is usually represented as a bishop with mitre and cross, or in the costume of his Order. For attributes he has a chalice, a monstrance with the Sacred Host in his right hand, an olive branch, and the scapula, or short monastic cloak, which he is supposed to have given to the Virgin Mary (Husenbeth 1882) (Plates 73 and 93). Most of this iconography stems from the sixteenth century. He is frequently featured on pulpits, often about to be thrown off his horse at the moment of his conversion, as at St Rombouts Cathedral, Mechelen and St Peter's, Leuven.

The extraordinary story of Norbert's promotion in Rome by means of the erection of a statue of him at St Peter's is a symbol of Belgian national pride. In 1738 Nicolas Meyers, a Premonstratensian from Tongerloo, took on this difficult task. He insisted that Norbert should have a prominent niche in the church, and proposed the removal of an ancient image of St Andrew, which was in the position he had selected. It took two years of negotiation with the Pope for this to be agreed. He was then ready to commission the sculpture from the Fleming, François Jansens, only to find that the Trinitarians, taking advantage of the Pope's temporary absence from the Holy City, had moved the St Andrew statue themselves and started to prepare the space for their saint, Pierre Nolesque. Luckily, when the Pope returned, Meyers was able to get the Trinitarians removed. There was then a very considerable delay and at last it became clear that Jansens would never make the statue. So, in consultation with the Vatican, the Italian sculptor, Pietro Bracci, was chosen, and the monument was finally put into place twenty-nine years after the proposal was first initiated (Lamey 1941).

The renaissance in the fortunes of the Catholic church in the early seventeenth century in Belgium was also mirrored in France, in spite of the temporary expulsion of the Jesuits there. Later the church building boom in Belgium was brought to a complete halt by the invasion of Louis XIV's army in 1672. This culminated in the capture of Ghent in 1678. Thereafter peace was restored with the Treaty of Nijmwegen, but only gradually was there enough confidence to bring about the revival of the new building and refurnishing schemes of the eighteenth century under Austrian rule.

It was the second invasion of Belgium by the French after the Revolution, particularly in 1794, which once again destroyed or dislocated the furniture from Belgium's religious institutions. The treasuries of churches and monasteries were raided, all the precious objects taken away and melted down into ingots and coin (van Kalken 1954). The agents of the occupying power were known as 'les éponges françaises' and were seen to set off for Paris loaded up with the best paintings and art objects. Belgium was treated like occupied territory and the French were also dubbed *vampires delapidateurs*. Hardly a single religious house escaped this treatment. One of the very few exceptions was the church of the reformed Carmelites (the *déchaussés*) at Bruges, whose early eighteenth century interior is still intact. By contrast the *chaussés* Carmelites, who had been established in Bruges since the Middle Ages, fled to Holland, the order being already unpopular since, unusually for mendicants, it was identified with the aristocracy and other vested interests. On the other hand it was well known that the *chaussés* friars in Bruges had tended the plague victims of that city during the seventeenth century and lost several of their numbers in so doing.

Having briefly considered the organisational revival of the Catholic church in Belgium in the sixteenth and seventeenth centuries, and aspects of the presentation of dogma, against a summary political backdrop, we can move on to judge the ways in which the Counter-Reformation translated itself into the furnishings of churches in the Southern Low Countries. The three main forms we will consider are pulpits, confessionals, and choir-stalls.

The pulpit, or *chaire de verité*, was the second most important object in the church after the altar. It was the crucial vehicle of the Counter-Reformation. From it the true doctrines of the church could be illustrated in sculpture and propagated through the sermon. Each one presents a particular theme, such as *The Triumph of Truth over Error* at St Bavo's Cathedral, Ghent. The pulpit at the cathedral of St Michael and St Gudule in Brussels shows at the bottom the *Earthly Paradise* with plants, flowers, fruits and animals around the *Tree of Knowledge of Good and Evil* (Plate 43). Adam, wracked with shame on account of his disobedience, attempts to protect himself from the avenging angel who tries to banish him and Eve from *Paradise*. The terrified Eve still holds the apple in her left hand, the forbidden fruit and object of temptation. Overhead is a horrible skeleton, the bringer of death, which is the only reward for her sin. The cursed temptor, the serpent, slithers on the ground between the outcasts, and its

PLATE 43. *St Michael and St Gudule, Brussels. Pulpit. 1699. Lithograph by unknown 19th century. artist. The maker was Henrik-Frans Verbruggen.*

body stretches all the way up to the top of the sounding board. At the summit of this visual drama is a Virgin with stars around her head and the moon at her feet, and the Christ Child below. This is the Virgin described by St John the Divine in the Apocalypse (*Apoc.* 11,19 – 12,1):

> And the temple of God was opened in heaven, and there was seen in his temple the ark of his testament: and there were lightenings and voices, and thunderings, and an earthquake, and great hail.

> And there appeared a great wonder in heaven, a woman clothed with the sun, and the moon under her feet, and upon her head a crown of twelve stars.

The body of the pulpit is covered with a valanced curtain and decorated with a medallion with the Marian monogram and underneath a verse of the hymn *Ave Maria Stella*. On the underside of the sounding board is a dove, symbolising the *Holy Spirit,* which inspires the preacher announcing the *Good News.*

A nineteenth century Belgian lithograph gives an idea of the scale and impact of the St Gudule pulpit. In general an enormous amount of architectural and sculptural talent was expended on this furniture component and it is a characteristic and highly original invention of Baroque art. Examples tend to be of two types. The more traditional follow the medieval prototype, of wineglass shape, resting on a spreading base. The pulpit at St Kwinten, Leuven, of the second half of the seventeenth century is typical (Plate 221). However from the late seventeenth century a new architectural form emerges, with the structure hoisted up into the air, from where it could dominate the nave. This elevation above the con-gregation allowed a series of dramatic scenes with interacting figures to rise up above the worshippers, in the way that the players in the Baroque theatre are able to dominate their audience in the pit. One is reminded of the recommendations of Nicola Sabbatini (1574-1654) in his *Manual for Constructing Theatrical Scenes and Machines,* where he recom-mends that at the opera the 'Quality' should sit in the stalls so as to get the best view of the stage machines, which do not look so impressive from the wings. Sabbatini stressed that from the floor of the hall, preferably in the middle:

> They will have the greatest pleasure there, since in such a position all the parts of the scenery and the machines are displayed in their perfection, and they will not be able to see the defects which are sometimes discerned by those on the steps or at the sides. (Martin 1992.)

Generally speaking, in a church the worshippers remain on ground level, so there is, compared with the theatre, only a limited choice as to from where to view the pulpit. This gave the designer the scope to manipulate perspective on a human scale and in three dimensions.

At the lower level it was possible for the faithful to get right up close to the protagonists, such as St Norbert clinging to his horse, about to crash to the ground, a typically Baroque contrivance, at St Rombouts Cathedral, Mechelen, and St Peter, Leuven, or the exotic figures of the *Four Continents* at Antwerp Cathedral, inviting admiration and curiosity (Plate 44). In the same way they could commune with the images of *Faith, Hope* and *Charity,* or even the protagonists in a Christological scene, such as the group of the Christ Child, sitting on a globe, and the homely Virgin and St Joseph sheltering in some Classical ruins under a thatched roof, at the Lesser Béguinage in Mechelen. This is the intimate, even tactile zone, almost a 'themed experience' in contemporary terms, although it was invariably fenced off. The screens could be in metal, or stone, but are usually in wood, and resemble fictive paling. There is something disconcerting about wood masquerading as wood. It is effectively styleless, and could have been made yesterday.

The main body of the pulpit above is covered in decoration and usually includes the Four Evangelists, the first sermonisers, in a manner befitting the vessel of the preacher.

The crowning feature creates the ethereal region above the preacher's head and the sounding board, to launch a climax of rocks, trees, angels blowing trumpets, and perhaps fictive rays of sun shining down upon it all from the very top.

These massive structures gave ample scope for artistic creativity, piling on elements one on top of another, and exemplifying in three dimensions the gravity-defying diagonals of Baroque art. To look at them is to experience a sense of impending instability. They must have competed for popular attention with the secular carnival wagons of the period. They have a certain vulgarity worthy of twentieth century Hollywood, the experience of which is largely lost on us without an intimate familiarity with the religious processions and public art of the age. One of the most imaginative features is the design of the stairway. It can be a single sequence running directly behind the pulpit, with the figures of angels standing guard at the bottom. But if the budget would run to it there would be a stairway on either side (Plate 44), at the same time exhibiting figure work and often quite bizarre decoration. On the Antwerp pulpit of 1713, by Michiel van de Voort, the Elder, there are prominent birds perched on the newel posts, with trees and spreading foliage everywhere *(The Garden of Eden).* The serpent on the pulpit at St Rombout's Cathedral, Mechelen, as it slithers its way down to

PLATE 44. *Antwerp Cathedral. Pulpit with 'Four Continents' at base. By Michiel van de Voort, the Elder.*

PLATE 45. *St Rombout's Cathedral, Mechelen. Rear view of pulpit. By Michiel van de Voort, the Elder.*

floor level, uses a single spreading stairway, which is doing its best to look as if it is made of natural stone (Plate 45). Did the long wooden serpents at Old Warden, Bedfordshire escape from such a Belgian *Garden of Eden*, one wonders?

The importance of these pulpits as art objects has not to date been generally recognised. Most of them in cathedral churches were lost at the Revolution, but were often replaced by examples from the monastic and friary churches which had been closed down. The church of Our Lady of Sablon in Brussels now shelters a 'Pulpit of Truth' from the demolished Augustinian Abbey church at the Place de Brouckère in Brussels. At Antwerp Cathedral is the pulpit from the former Cistercian abbey at Hemiksem (Sint-Bernards-aan-Schelde). St Peter, Leuven's former pulpit was sold during the Revolution, and was

replaced in the early nineteenth century by that from the dissolved Premonstratensian abbey at Ninove.

The makers must have had a very high social status, since the cost of the pulpit, let alone all the other items of wooden furniture required, must have bulked substantially in the overall cost of erecting the new churches. Many of the techniques used are prodigious. The really spectacular examples date from the end of the seventeenth century through into the nineteenth century. A relatively early but attractive example is the pulpit by M. Devos at the Church of Our Lady of Sablon in Brussels of 1697. There is an early eighteenth century pulpit at the Carmelite church, Bruges, by Jacob de Coster, with the figure of Elijah, the founder of the Order, at its base. Another fine example from the first half of the eighteenth century, by the Mechelen artist Theodoor

PLATE 46. *St Michael and St Gudule, Brussels. Confessional. Lithograph by unknown 19th century artist. Maker Henrik-Frans Verbruggen.* COPYRIGHT CONWAY LIBRARY, COURTAULD INSTITUTE OF ART

Verhaegen (1700-1759), is at Our Lady's Church van Hanswijk, in that town. The pulpit at St Rombout's, Mechelen, was made in 1723 by Michiel van de Voort, the Elder, and the stylistic similarities with the pulpit at Antwerp (Plate 44) are all too evident. The Brussels Cathedral pulpit was originally the work of the Antwerp carver Henrik-Frans Verbruggen (1654-1724) in 1699, for the Jesuit church in Leuven. Of this artist's sculpture for churches, it has been said:

> They are conceived as richly articulated theatrical settings, not only designed as the main feature of the church interior to catch the eye, but also to create an extraordinary dynamic spatial effect with their accentuated three-dimensional character and the curving shapes of their architecture ... [H-F Verbruggen's] remarkable use of circular and elliptical elements, reveals that he must have been familiar with Bernini's ideas, and with Borromini's as well. (Vlieghe 1998.)

Of mid-eighteenth century date is the superb pulpit combining Danish oak and Carrara marble at St Bavo's, Ghent, by L. Delvaux. These talented artists were often asked to supply all or most of the furniture in a single church. Mechelen was the home town of the renowned architect and sculptor Lucas Faydherbe (1617-1697). He was responsible for fitting out much of the Grand-Béguinage Church there (dedicated to St Catherine and St Alexis). At the Carmelite Church at Bruges in the early eighteenth century the Carmelite friar Jacob de Coster, from Brussels, was commissioned to fit out the chapel completely.

Surprisingly little research has been done on Belgian Baroque church furniture, although art historians are just starting to take an interest in this rich subject. Doubtless in due course some current attributions will be changed as the subject begins to

THE NATIONAL COLLECTION – INTRODUCTION

PLATE 47. *St Paul's, Antwerp. Confessional. 1657-59 by Peter Verbruggen I.*

come into focus in terms of patronage, iconography and technique.

The confessional played a major part in the practices of the reformed Catholic church. The sacrament of penance, rejected by the Protestants, was central to post-Tridentine doctrine. Confession was assiduously propagated, particularly by the Jesuits. The earliest surviving confessionals in Belgium are from the early seventeenth century, but these are rare. The same nineteenth century artist who drew the 'pulpit of truth' in Brussels Cathedral also illustrated the practice of Confession in the same church (Plate 46). The confessionals at the cathedral are the work of Henrik-Frans Verbruggen. Earlier examples of the form are the ones at St

Paul's, Antwerp, made by Peter Verbruggen I, Henrik-Frans' father, between 1657 and 1659 (Plate 47). The exquisite confessionals at the Church of Our Lady of Hanswijk, Mechelen, of *c.*1690, were made by Jan Frans Boeckstuyns (*c.*1650-1734), who, twenty years later, created the altar-rails at the Grand Béguinage (Plate 64). Lucas Faydherbe, who was jointly responsible for the stone statuary at Brussels Cathedral with Jérôme Duquesnoy, also made the remarkable early eighteenth century confessionals at the Grand-Béguinage, Mechelen. Jacob de Coster excelled himself in the confessionals in the chapel of the Carmelite Church in Bruges of the early eighteenth century. And at the former Cistercian monastery of St Bernard at Hemiksem, and now at

PLATE 48. *Grand-Béguinage, Mechelen. Confessional by Lucas Faydherbe.*

Antwerp Cathedral, the confessionals were made by Guilliemus Ignatius Kerrickx (1680-1745) and Michiel van de Voort the Elder (1667-1737). The angels which stand guard in front of these structures illustrate sentiments of contrition and penitence.

Some confessionals usually offer a modicum of privacy, such as those at the Grand-Béguinage, Mechelen (Plate 48). But there is a type, used from the middle of the seventeenth century, which affords very little indeed, such as those at the Dominican St Paul's, Antwerp (Plate 47), or the ones now in Antwerp Cathedral from Hemiksem Abbey. In the latter cases the wainscoting behind looks almost as if it might have been prepared to house choir-stalls. Instead standards, or partitions,

with a saint or angel at the front are placed in groups of four. The spaces at the sides are recessed back from the two in the front, the centre pair with or without a low door between them for the use of the priest. Behind the door is a seat on which the priest sits to hear Confession. He speaks through a grille on either side at which the penitent kneels. This type of arrangement and design was common at the time, and it begs the question as to how the sacrament was organised. In the larger religious houses, as for instance at Hemiksem (the furniture now at Antwerp Cathedral), there were at least two banks of confessionals, each providing accommodation for two priests. Presumably when they were used the members of the establishment attended *en masse*, and four priests were able to process a large number of monks and lay brothers in a relatively short time.

In England, if we discount Pugin's confessional at Oscott College (Colour Plate 19), which is largely made up, there was only ever one genuine specimen imported into England. This was the now destroyed eighteenth century Italian example in walnut formerly at St Thomas, Tenison Court, Westminster, London (page 89).

Choir-stalls proliferated in the late sixteenth century and seventeenth century in Belgium, thanks to the development of the new monastic orders, and went on being made through the eighteenth century and beyond. The remarkable post-medieval Classicising set of choir-stalls of 1596 at St Walburga, Veurne, in West Flanders has seat standards with hoofed feet and a coved backing screen divided by columns with geometric panelling in between. The stalls at St Martin's Cathedral, Ypres, of 1598, in the same part of Belgium, are of similar style and architecture. In the seventeenth century panelled backs remained popular, but the use of human busts in medallions or cartouches started in the second half of the century, as at Oignies Abbey in 1689 (M/9). By the end of the seventeenth century a variety of decoration and architecture proliferated throughout the region, including the use of full-size human figures incorporated into the superstructure, as on the stalls at Wouw, now in the south Netherlands (Plate 290). These were made originally for Hemiksem abbey church by Artus Quellinus the Younger (1625-1700), Henrik-Frans Verbruggen and Ludovicus Willemsens (1630-1702).

In prestige commissions altarpieces received the most lavish embellishment. They were generally made of expensive marble, although the framework could be of wood disguised as stone. It was normally in less wealthy churches that altarpieces were made exclusively of wood, like the one in England at Bursledon, Hampshire (B/2).

Other important categories of furniture are altar frontals and altar rails. Wooden Baroque frontals are rather rare, although there are good examples at St Anne's church, Bruges, Notre-Dame de la Rose at Lessines (Plate 53), and Our Lady's Church, Aarschott.

Altar rails were a post-medieval Catholic innovation. They gave ample scope, often on account of their inordinate length, for illustrating the Old Testament liturgy, as well as some New Testament patristic references. Unfortunately, they were the principal victim of the re-orderings resulting from the second Vatican Council between 1962 and 1965. Most were moved back from before the high altar, truncated and re-located in front of the choir-screen. Sometimes, as at St Bavo's, Ghent, parts were transported to a side chapel. In all cases, even if they have been moved to the east end of the nave, they rarely cross the church as they were supposed to. It is therefore a comparatively rare pleasure to find communion rails *in situ* and unmutilated, as at the Grand-Béguinage, Mechelen. Here they are no less than 25m (82ft.) in length and comprise thirteen different panels.

Most of the scenes that are illustrated come from the Book of Exodus, such as *Aaron and the Brazen Serpent* and *Aaron's Rod*, the *Tabernacle*, the *Ark of the Covenant*, the *Table*, the *Lampstand* and the *Altar of Incense, Collecting The Manna, Moses and the Tablets of Stone*, and *Moses Striking the Rock*. The images of the *Shewbread* and the *Tabernacle* denote the twelve loaves for the twelve tribes, arranged in two piles on the table of shittim wood, set beside the altar each week. The *Table* itself, which was also to be used for holding the *Vessels* 'for the pouring out of offerings', follows very closely the prescription laid down in *Exodus 25, 26-30*:

> Make four gold rings for the table and fasten them to the four corners, where the four legs are. The rings are to be close to the rim to hold the poles used for carrying the table. … Make its plates and ladles of pure gold, as well as its pitchers and bowls for the pouring out of offerings. Put the bread of the Presence on this table to be before me at all times.

The Ark of the Covenant is also clearly denoted, with its carrying poles. We can recognise the *Atonement Cover*, which was made of pure gold, with the two cherubim. Also we can see that 'The cherubim had their wings spread upwards, overshadowing the cover with them', and that 'The Cherubim faced each other, looking towards the cover'.

There are images of the priestly vestments, in particular the *Breastplate*, mounted with four rows of precious stones, one for each of the names of the sons of Israel (Plate 71). From the *Book of Kings* the scene of *Elijah in the Wilderness*, comforted by the angel, is common, as is *The Gift of Bread and Wine from*

Melchizedek to Abraham (Genesis 18), which was a powerful pre-figuration of the Eucharist. Images of *The Lamb of God and the Cross,* and animal sacrifice, as at the Grand-Béguinage, Mechelen, are, of course, also antetypes of the Christian story. *The Pelican in her Piety* comes from St Jerome.

There is plenty of New Testament symbolism also. Some altar rails at Antwerp Cathedral, formerly in the chapel of *Our Lady of Praise,* and made by Ludovicus Willemsens in 1680, display putti holding symbols of the Virgin – star, sun, rosary, censer and lily and dove. Evangelist symbols are common. Occasionally there are scenes from the New Testament, such as *Peter washing Christ's Feet ,* the *Last Supper* and the *Emmaus.*

At the Grand-Béguinage at Mechelen the Old Testament scenes in the altar rails, made *c.*1710 by Jan Frans Boeckstuyns, are, disconcertingly, mainly acted by putti. The scene of Melchizedek offering Abraham bread and wine is an example (Plate 49). The two patron saints of the church, St Catherine with her wheel and St Alexis with a ladder, adore the Chalice and Host on each side of the entrance gates. Donors feature on the Premonstratensian altar rails at Otterbourne, Hampshire (B/9 and Plates 76 and 77).

Stoups for Holy Water were no longer used in the Protestant church but were *de rigueur* for Catholics. Also, after the Reformation, reliquary coffers and shrines stood on the high altar, or above it, exclusively in the Roman church.

In considering the design sources for these objects, it is as well to be aware, in the earlier period, of the influential Flemish artists who published prints, such as Cornelis Floris, Peter Coeck van Aelst and Hans Vredeman de Vries, all from Antwerp. None of these, however, seems to have produced any printed furniture designs for ecclesiastical use. Only a handful did. There is a drawing of a pulpit by Crispin de Passe I, published in Utrecht in 1621; the work of Hendrick Hondius I (1573-after 1649), born in Duffel in Brabant, who lived in Mechelen, Antwerp and Brussels; and that of Jean Du Breuil (1602-1670), who was born in Paris and became a Jesuit at Dijon. The latter provides very elaborate designs for pulpits, panelling, fonts etc. (Jervis 1974).

PLATE 49. *Grand-Béguinage, Mechelen. Altar rails. Panel with Melchizedek greeting Abraham by Frans Boeckstuyns. 1710.*   COPYRIGHT IRPA-KIK, BRUSSELS

From Italy, the late fifteenth century or early sixteenth century North Italian cedarwood chests, referred to as 'Cypress' chests in the records, are an important group of Continental objects rather well represented in England. They seem to have almost entirely escaped the attention of scholars to this day (see F/2, F/3, F/8, F/10, F/11 and F/12). The penwork decoration applied to them is often very faded and it seems miraculous that any of it has survived at all. This technique is much more fugitive than the better known 'poker work', or *pirograffiata,* also applied to northern Italian cedarwood chests, where the design is burned directly into the wood (Yorke 1989). Under the chest lids the backgrounds to the drawings are slightly recessed and cross-hatched with a metal punch. On the chest fronts a similar woodcut-type technique is used, with the images, again, drawn in penwork, although in our cases the latter has long-since disappeared.

Of even greater interest, perhaps, is the function of these objects. In five out of six cases, the underside of the lid is decorated with the scene of the *Crucifixion,* surrounded by sketches of other Gospel events, particularly the *Annunciation,* and the symbols of the Evangelists in fictive panels. The Redenhall, Norfolk, chest is the odd man out in not featuring the *Crucifixion* under the lid (F/11). It is possible, but by no means certain, that these chests had a secular function. The subject on the cut-out fronts, which must originally also have been decorated with penwork drawing, is now hard to make out, but most of it seems to have been of a contemporary Italian Petrarchian type (see the illustrations of the *Trionfi* in Hind 1938, Part I, Volume II, Pl. 24, and Part I, Volume III, Pls. 191-96).

Two possible functions spring to mind. Firstly their manufacture from cedarwood, said to have had moth-proofing properties, and, in most cases, their unusual length, would qualify them as vestment chests. But also the possibility of there having been an inner lid, and the placement of the *Crucifixion* scene under the lid proper, must mean that they were used as portable altars. The integral strong boxes, or safes, under the lid could have been used for storing money or plate. At Carlisle there is circumstantial evidence for a monastic provenance, supporting the case for an ecclesiastical rather than a purely domestic devotional function. Three of the six chests, or fragments thereof, are now in modest parish churches, two in cathedrals, and another component is at the Victoria and Albert Museum.

Examples in Italy of the *Crucifixion* scene used as an altar reredos, or the centrepiece of a triptych, are now much less common than they probably used to be. A well-known early altar with the *Crucifixion* as centrepiece is that in the left transept of the upper church at Assisi by Cimabue (1280-1283). The complex scenes, with three crosses and many protagonists, as also found on these chests, are a development of the late thirteenth century, from the earlier type with the *Crucifix* in the centre and Mary and John on either side, which typically would have been seen above every parish church rood screen. The number of figures was increased, each personally involved in the event. They had ceased to be merely types and had become active human protagonists. Duccio's former high altar at Siena Cathedral, of 1308-11, had a *Crucifixion* as its centrepiece. A later example of this scene, used as a reredos centrepiece, and this time on a polyptych painted in 1348 by Bernado Daddi, is owned by the Courtauld Institute Galleries in London. Depictions of the *Crucifixion* in frescos are much more numerous, such as that by Giotto, *c.*1305 at Padua, Barna da Siena, of 1350-53, at San Gimigniano, and Andrea da Firenze, of 1366-68, at Santa Maria Novella in Florence.

Schiller has suggested that this novel way of showing the *Crucifixion* stemmed from a new-found interest in historical events, in the first place from the experience of the Crusades. Also the rise of the Passion play in the second half of the thirteenth century, possibly inspired by the Italian mendicant orders, reached a climax in Jacopone's *Stabat Mater Dolorosa* (Schiller 1972). What these images have in common with the chests are the angels, and devils, on either side of the crucified figures, waiting to catch the souls; the crowd with men on horseback, one of them usually pointing up to the figure of Christ; the figure of the Virgin being consoled by attendants on the left; the Mary Magdalene on her knees, holding the foot of the Cross; the men on Christ's left holding the seamless robe; the centurion Longinus on the left with his spear;

PLATE 49a. *Rouen Cathedral. North portal. Detail of archivolt decoration. Early 12th century.*
COPYRIGHT CONWAY LIBRARY, COURTAULD INSTITUTE OF ART

Stephaton holding the staff and carrying the hyssop-steeped sponge; and the Jews standing about disconsolately or frightened by the unnatural events at the *Giving up of the Ghost.*

The style of the drawing on the fragment in the Victoria and Albert Museum is distinctively different from the others, and must have been the product of a different workshop. The chests at Carlisle Cathedral, Chilcombe, Dorset, Norwich Cathedral and Swaffham Bulbeck, Cambridgeshire, are similar and close in style. The recycling of the *Crucifixion* scenes on these chests, probably in the early sixteenth

century, was a decidedly *retardataire* activity. One would like to know since when these joinery workshops had been in business and from whence they obtained the prototypes to copy from. Most probably they relied on engravings like the ones produced in Florence in the period 1470-90 (Hind 1938, Part I, Vol.II).

The dating is conservative since there are decorative motifs on these chests, such as the tied acanthus branches repeated in the borders, which are reminiscent of early sixteenth century work. On the other hand some of the pen drawing, such as the

103

Annunciate Virgin on the Chilcombe chest, looks decidedly fifteenth century.

The woodcut-type technique, with the punched decoration in the negative spaces, is reminiscent of so-called 'chip-carving' on chests, a technique which has a tradition probably going back to classical times. Interestingly, something very similar to the method used on the cedarwood chests was utilised in stone on the north and south portals at Rouen Cathedral in the early twelfth century (Plate 49a).

There is certainly more work that could be done on the stylistic sources for these images, and on finding out how exactly the chests were used.

———————

It is very rarely difficult to distinguish foreign workmanship in English churches. Only in a few instances where the furniture was manufactured in England, such as the choir-stalls at St George's, Windsor (1478-83), at the Henry VII Chapel, Westminster Abbey, *c.*1512 (both Tracy 1990), or those at King's College, Cambridge (M/7 and Woodman 1986), the Devon group of late fifteenth century French-influenced screenwork (L/1, L/4 and L/5), or the Salkeld Screen at Carlisle Cathedral (L/3), is there genuine ambiguity.

The foreign-influenced woodwork in Devon (L/1, L/4 and L/5) is part of a wider corpus of screens in the county which has been previously cited, such as those at Holbeton (Spanish), and Swymbridge, Lapford, Atherington, Morchard Bishop, Poltimore, Lustleigh, Marwood, South Pool, and Bridport in Devon (Italian) (Bond 1902).

But how easy is it to recognise foreign influence, or even manufacture, in England in the Baroque period? Throughout his astonishing career Grinling Gibbons (1648-1721) developed a unique technique of undercut and additive decorative carving, using foliage, flowers, game animals and birds. The style is not unreasonably described as English, since it flourished here and was by no means simply transplanted from abroad. Yet if we examine the sculptural and decorative *milieu* from which Gibbons came, that is the Low Countries, we can immediately recognise the essential character of his early work. In

particular it is instructive to look at the decorative carving of his contemporary, Jan Frans Boeckstuyns, of *c.*1690. His confessionals at Our Lady's Church, van Hanswijk, share Gibbons' interest in the reproduction of fine texture on clothing and the miraculous reproduction of lace, traits inherited from an earlier generation of sculptors, such as Peter Verbruggen I and Lucas Faydherbe. This kind of attention to detail goes back ultimately to Rubens, in whose studio Faydherbe is known to have made ivory carvings (Vlieghe 1998). Faydherbe's lively, decorative and highly naturalistic treatment of foliage and fruit can be seen on his confessionals at the Grand-Béguinage, Mechelen, as well as his handling of birds. It shares the same Classicising well-spring as Gibbons' work.

Finally, in this connection, we shall look at two apparently 'borderline' objects, which must be, on

PLATE 50. *St Mary, Stoke D'Abernon, Surrey. Late 17th century aumbry.*

PLATE 51. *St Mary, Wisbech St Mary, Cambridgeshire. Late 17th century bracket.*

reflection, English: the aumbry at Stoke D'Abernon Church, Surrey and the bracket at Wisbech St Mary, Cambridgeshire (Plates 50 and 51). To quote the informative NADFAS inventory description of the aumbry: it consists…

> of a shield shaped panel carved in high relief with a central round headed door covering the locked aumbry safe. The panel is surmounted by a stylised pelican with outstretched wings below which on each side is a cherub above a phoenix, all surrounded by acanthus leaves. The frame of the door is carved with a leaf and feather like decoration (surely, a laurel wreath?) and a central scroll. The door has two brass hinges and the socket for a lock on the back but no keyhole at the front, and is lined with cream damask. It is decorated with a central incised Latin Cross enclosed within two curved flower stems terminating at the top and bottom in reversed flower heads. Leaves spring from each junction and the Cross stands on a mound which has a chiselled finish.

At the time that it was acquired, the Victoria and Albert Museum suggested that the aumbry was of the Wren period and English, although they mentioned a detectable influence of Grinling Gibbons. Nikolaus Pevsner had remarked on the 'violent Baroque design' (BOE, *Surrey* 1971) and suggested that it might be German. Also at the time the then vicar, the Reverend John H.L. Waterson, remarked in a letter to *Country Life,* dated 26 July 1956, that the simple cross

seemed somewhat austere for a product of the early Restoration period. He rightly commented that if it had been of Continental origin it would have been provided if not with a 'refulgent Host, then an elaborated Crucifix'.

He pointed out that at this date aumbries, that is a closed recess built into a wall, had been out of fashion on the Continent for a long time. So who would have wanted such an object? Had it been made for a recusant country house, as had been suggested by the museum?

The absence of any overt post-Tridentine symbolism on this aumbry puts it apart from Continental Catholic work. Similarly on the Wisbech St Mary bracket, of early eighteenth century date, the religious propaganda element is, again, virtually missing. Moreover, in that case the use of the cherub's head in the centre bears an unmistakable Wrenian hallmark.

———————

Finally, a word on the nomenclature used to describe the ethnic and geographical areas comprised by modern Belgium and the Netherlands. Although in the Middle Ages Flanders stretched from the Netherlands province of Zeeland, through the modern Belgian provinces of East and West Flanders, to the modern French department of the Nord, the term Flemish is usually loosely applied to cover the whole of modern Belgium. But sometimes, of course, it can specifically be used to denote the medieval county of Flanders, based on Ghent. Also, some of the other medieval principalities, such as Hainault and Brabant, are referred to. The Netherlands describes the area covered by modern Holland, as we sometimes call it, although 'Holland' was historically merely the southernmost province of the Protestant 'Netherlands'. The term 'Dutch' is used occasionally to describe anything pertaining to the modern Netherlands. This appellation has been used in England for a very long time, as in the reference to 'Ducheman Smyth' in the royal accounts pertaining to the furnishing of the Henry VII Chapel, Westminster Abbey, in 1505-06. The term 'Low Countries', or even 'Southern Low Countries' is occasionally convenient to use.

A: *Altar Frontals*

A/1. St Mary, Harefield, Middlesex (Plate 52)
Oak. Flemish. Late 17th century
Main panel 3.05m x 88cm (10ft. x 34½in.)
(For Harefield, see also B/7)
The frontal is placed behind the altar, and forms part of a late 18th century ensemble of altar furnishings, incongruously, but delightfully, interspersed with two family tombs (Plate 52). The design consists of two broad horizontal ribbands, bound together with flowers and fruit. It is secured in a later frame. The latter is probably associated with the present arrangement, incorporating the sculpted angels, also of Continental origin, and the Commandment boards above. The date of this installation can be inferred from the late 18th century style of these Commandment boards. The wing brackets of the present 'reredos' can be associated stylistically with the altar rails (B/7).

The style is reminiscent of the early 18th century altar frontal on the high altar at the Musée de l'Hôpital Notre Dame de la Rose Church at Lessines in Hainault (Plate 53).

From 1675 the rights over the chancel of the church belonged to the Newdigate family of Arbury, Worcestershire, who owned Harefield Place. In 1841 Charles Newdigate put in hand a major restoration of the whole church (MRO History Notes, 12 December 1956; VCH, *Middlesex*, 3, 240-58). It is very likely that the Continental material was introduced then, rather than in the late 17th century or early 18th century, when extensive restoration work was also undertaken, as has been suggested elsewhere, following a complaint about the lack of 'seats and desks' in the chancel (WRCO, CR. 136/B; MRO, CR. 136/MX./PEC. 2-9; VCH, *Middlesex*, 3, 254-55).

PLATE 52. *St Mary, Harefield, Middlesex. View of high altar (Altar frontal A/1; Altar rails, B/7)*

A/2. Hever Castle, Kent (Plate 54)
Gilded and polychromed, probably walnut. Northern French or Netherlandish. Early 16th century
62cm x 167cm (24½in. x 5ft.5¾in.) (front of panel) x 48cm (19in.) (depth of chest)
(For Hever Castle see also E/4, H/2 and M/13)

The frontal has seven niches; the *Virgin and Child,* in the centre, is flanked by the Mary Magdalene and St Catherine, with St John the Divine and St Paul on one side, St James the Great and St Peter on the other. The figures stand under tent-like canopies, the curtains of which are raised by angels standing on the flanking pilasters. The sides are carved with linenfold decoration and Gothic foliage. The three ancient panels, comprising the altar, have been framed in modern times into a chest, possibly part of a travelling altar/chest.

The same conceit of angels holding up the tent curtains can be seen on a 16th century French chest, formerly in the Gorisse Collection, Orléans, with pairs of saints under the canopies and God the Father in the centre. Another chest of similar date at the Château de Sully, Upper Loire, shows saints in niches. The Renaissance chest in the Victoria and Albert Museum (F/6 and Plate 128) has similar tent tops above standing figures, in this case the curtains being held up in the beaks of birds.

Hever Castle was acquired by William Waldorf Astor in 1903. In middle age he had become a Europhile, especially after a spell as American Minister in Rome between 1882 and 1885. In 1893 he bought Clivedon in Buckinghamshire and settled in England for good. The large number of specimens of Italian secular furniture at Hever are the fruits of Astor's ambassadorship (page 86).

PLATE 53. *Lessines, Musée de l'Hôpital, Notre Dame de la Rose. High altar. Early 18th century.* COPYRIGHT IRPA-KIK, BRUSSELS

PLATE 54. *Hever Castle, Kent. Altar in chapel. Early 16th century altar frontal. French or Netherlandish (A/2)*

PLATE 55. *All Saints, Tooting Graveney, London. Late 17th Italian altar frontal (A/3. reredos C/3)*

PLATE 56. *Nativity of the Virgin, Madley, Herefordshire. Flemish altar frontal under west tower.*
Late 17th century. (A/4)

108

PLATE 57. *Grand-Béguinage, Mechelen. Altar frontal. Late 17th century.*

A/3. All Saints, Tooting Graveney, London (Colour Plate 1, Plate 55)
Painted wood. Italian. Late 17th. century
83cm x 299cm (32½in.x 9ft.9¾in.)
(For Tooting, see also C/3, C/4, D/1, E/6, , H/3, I/7 and M/17)

The design of this altar frontal consists of three candelabrum motifs, framed by voluted scrolling foliage. It is carved in openwork technique and the continuous panels are framed and applied to a backing-board. Unfortunately, the frontal was repainted in yellow and green, to match the reredos, when placed in the church. It would probably have been gessoed, gilded and painted originally. There seem to be traces of gilding below the yellow-painted parts.

All Saints, Tooting Graveney, is one of the most important repositories of Continental church furniture in England. Interestingly, it is one of the most recently formed collections, dating back only to before 1906 (page 86).

A/4. The Nativity of the Virgin, Madley, Herefordshire (Plate 56)
Oak. Flemish. Late 17th century

83.5cm x 194cm 33in. x 6ft.4¼in. (excluding frame)
Presented by Major H. Ll. F. Bucknall in 1953. Said to have been bought in Portugal or Spain

The frontal, two unrelated but coeval decorative panels and two miniature Solomonic columns were given to the church in the 1950s. Initially they were arranged in the south aisle chapel quite incoherently, with the frontal, as at Harefield (A/1), acting as a reredos. The piece attached to the top of the frontal was not originally associated with it. Recently the arrangement has been disassembled and the components have been given a temporary home under the west tower.

The frontal, or antependium, consists of bold inhabited scrollwork, with cherubs holding up and adoring a monstrance in the centre. The central element is framed on the sides and the base with a plain moulding, but above a gadrooned fillet stretches from end to end. Around the outside is a frieze using the same decorative carving on a smaller scale. The thin frame is a modern addition.

Similar Flemish altar frontals, of a rather later date, are at the Church of Our Lady, Aarschott, and the Grand-Béguinage, Mechelen (Plate 57). These show a chalice in the centre, with the Host suspended above.

B: *Altar and other Rails*

B/1 St Paul's, Brighton (Plates 58 and 59)
Oak. Northern French. *c.*1700
52cm x 5.33m (20½in. x 17ft.6in.

These altar rails are not straight but bowed forward in a tripartite arrangement (Plate 58). In the centre is the widest panel on a segmental plan, incorporating scrolling foliage with an image of the *Sacrifice of the Lamb* in the centre (Plate 59). The gates are placed on either side. They display grapes, sheaves of wheat and oak leaves. On the outer flanks is another pair of identical panels. They are in-curving and feature the monogram JMB in the centre. There are doubled pilasters at the points of intersection and at the ends.

The communion rails were introduced to the church *c.*1970 by the incumbent, the Reverend John Milburn. Following the Second Vatican Council, and even before, he had been buying up unwanted vestments in France.

B/2 Chapel of Our Lady of the Rosary, Bursledon (Plate 60)
Oak. Flemish. Late 17th century/early 18th century
Five complete panels and two half panels all 52cm (20½in.) high
(For Bursledon, see also C/1)

The chapel contains the remains of a set of altar rails. They are distributed in various places, including on either side of the main altar (Plate 40). There are two complete panels (52 x 38.5cm, 20½in. x 15in.), decorated with scrolling foliage, with zones either side displaying swags of grapes. Most of the panels were probably of this kind. There is also a pair, one of them cut down, which were probably both 90cm (35½in.) wide. They are on a slightly curving plan and display the *Lamb of God and the Cross* and *The Pelican in her Piety* (Plate 60). These were probably the gates of the altar rails.

This small and architecturally modest chapel was built in 1906 by a Mrs Shawe-Storey. It seems to be the only Roman Catholic private chapel in England with mainly European furnishings (page 84).

B/3 St John the Baptist, Cockayne Hatley, Bedfordshire. West end (Plate 61)
Oak. Flemish. Second quarter 18th century
The panels 48cm x 69cm (19in. x 27in.). Height to top of rail 71cm (28in.)
(For Cockayne Hatley, see also B/4, B/5, J/5, K/4 and M/9)

A length of altar railing has been hoisted up into the air and now serves, somewhat inappropriately, as an organ loft, although the instrument behind is purely for show. Conventionally, these refugee panels depict the Sacramental themes of the *Grapes*, the *Manna*, *The Ark of the Covenant*, and *The Vessels for the Wine*.

Robert Cust (Cust 1851) implied that this woodwork was originally part of the Mechelen altar rails in the chancel (B/4). However, stylistically there is no connection.

PLATE 58. *St Paul's, Brighton, East Sussex. General view of altar rails from south. French c.1700 (B/1).*

110

PLATE 59. *St Paul's, Brighton, East Sussex. Altar rails. French, c.1700. Central panel with* Sacrifice of the Lamb. *(B/1)*

PLATE 60. *Chapel of Our Lady of the Rosary, Bursledon, Hampshire. Altar rails. Flemish, late 17th/early 18th century. Detail of panel with* Pelican in her Piety. *(B/2)*

B/4 St John the Baptist, Cockayne Hatley, Bedfordshire. East end (Plates 62 and 63)
Oak. Flemish. Early 18th century
The panels 49cm x 70cm (19¼in. x 27½in.). Height to top of rail 67.5cm (26½in.)
Supposed to have come from a church in Mechelen
(For Cockayne Hatley, see also B/3, B/5, J/5, K/4 and M/9)

The rails are in good condition apart from a few minor restorations. However, the capping has been cut where it curves back on the left. The original rails were probably considerably wider than they are now. The subject matter of the remaining four panels certainly suggests a more leisurely approach adopted in this case to the Sacrament iconography. They illustrate *The Israelites finding Water from the Rock, Harvesting the Corn, Making the Wine* and *Picking the Grapes* (Plates 62 and 63).

PLATE 61. *St John the Baptist, Cockayne Hatley, Bedfordshire. General views of altar rails at west end. Flemish, second quarter 18th century. (B/3)*

PLATE 62. *St John the Baptist, Cockayne Hatley, Bedfordshire. Altar rails at east end. General view. Flemish, early 18th century. (B/4)*

PLATE 63. *St John the Baptist, Cockayne Hatley, Bedfordshire.* Collecting the Grapes *panel from altar rails at east end. Flemish, early 18th century. (B/4)*

PLATE 64. *Grand-Béguinage, Mechelen. Altar rails by J.F. Boeckstuyns.* Collecting the Grapes
panel. c.1710.   COPYRIGHT IRPA-KIK, BRUSSELS

The high quality of the carving suggests that these altar rails came from a large and important church. There are parallels with the communion rails at the Grand-Béguinage (St Alexis and St Catherine) church at Mechelen, of 1710, by J.F. Boeckstuyns (Plate 64), although those at Cockayne Hatley are unlikely to have been made by the same artist. The *putti* at Cockayne Hatley have the scenes to themselves, as they do mostly at the Béguinage, but they do not stand in for the protagonists, as at Mechelen. The Cockayne Hatley railings share an attempt to make

something decorative of the reverse side of the panels, like the railings at the Grand-Béguinage. It would not be unreasonable to take this feature as the trade-mark of a workshop, but in any case we can assume that the Cust family provenance is correct.

The miniature ivory panels in the Victoria and Albert Museum, after François Duquesnoy (1594-1643), of putti playing with a wine vat are prototypes for this kind of style and composition (Plate 65). Duquesnoy lived in Rome for most of his life and associated with Poussin.

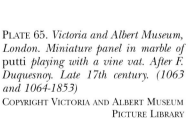

PLATE 65. *Victoria and Albert Museum, London. Miniature panel in marble of* putti *playing with a vine vat. After F. Duquesnoy. Late 17th century. (1063 and 1064-1853)*
COPYRIGHT VICTORIA AND ALBERT MUSEUM PICTURE LIBRARY

PLATE 66. *St John the Baptist, Cockayne Hatley, Bedfordshire. Organ gallery in tower. Flemish, c.1700. Detail (B/5)*

B/5 St John the Baptist, Cockayne Hatley, Bedfordshire. West end (Plate 66)
Gilded oak. Flemish. *c.***1700**
3.884m. x 59.8cm x 15-52mm (12ft.6in. x 23½in. x ½-2in.)
(For Cockayne Hatley, see also B/3, B/4, J/5, K/4 and M/9)
This length of organ gallery railing has been truncated from the original. The composition consists of cartouches alternating with framed arrangements of musical instruments, including a viola, recorders, oboe and hunting horns. Rowland-Jones advises that the type of recorder shown was made in about 1680.

Organ galleries were presumably not uncommon at this time in the Low Countries. An example with railings showing musical instruments can be seen at St Gertrude, Leuven.

B/6. Christchurch, Eccleston, Lancashire (Plates 34 and 67)
Oak, Flemish or French. Mid-18th century
Two larger panels in the extant altar rails, 120cm x 59cm (47¼in. x 23¼in.), from a set of nine
The two larger panels have been built into the early Victorian narrow altar rails, which were provided with a new framework, with authentic foliage panels either side of the entrance. Seven additional smaller panels have been attached to the front of the west gallery and to a pew on the south side of the chancel arch. All nine panels are stylistically similar. The Old Testament subjects depicted

PLATE 67. *Christchurch, Eccleston, Lancashire. Altar rails.* Israelites gathering the Manna *panel. Flemish or French, mid-18th century. (B/6)*

114

are *The Israelites gathering the Manna*, while Moses points to where it is (Plate 67), and *The Ark of the Covenant* (both of these on the altar rail), *Noah and the Ark* and a further six New Testament subjects – *The Life of Christ, The Birth of Christ, The Presentation in the Temple, The Moneychangers, The Baptism of Christ* and *The Procession to Calvary*.

The carving is of excellent quality and, notably, the larger panels, at least, have been carved completely from the solid. The style is Rococo and could be French or Flemish.

Some of the panels were acquired for the new church, which was completed in 1838. Others are said to have come to Eccleston much later, as they were acquired after 1922 when St Peter's Cathedral, Liverpool, was closed prior to demolition. The panels on the west gallery are referred to in the newspaper report of the church opening, so perhaps it is only the larger ones within the altar rails which came from St Peter's (pages 73-74).

B/7 St Mary, Harefield, Middlesex (Plates 52, 68 and Frontispiece)
Oak. Flemish. Late 17th century
Height 70cm (27½in.) to rail
(For Harefield, see also A/1)

These now polygonal railings are *en suite* with the 'reredos' behind. However, the latter is a made-up piece and only the buttresses can be associated with the altar rails (A/1 and Plate 52). There is a double bay at the front for the entrance gates, on either side of which are panels with carved busts of a man (north) and a woman (south) in clerical dress. The south-east bay has been omitted to make room for the Countess of Derby tomb (1637). The fine voluted buttresses, placed at right-angles to the made-up reredos behind, have been mutilated to fit into their present positions (Plate 68). They display some stylistic affinities with the carving on the altar rails, such as the treatment of human hair, faces and particularly eyelids. Also the foliage in both cases is comparable.

PLATE 68. *St Mary, Harefield, Middlesex. Buttress on south side of 'reredos'. Flemish, late 17th century.* (B/7)

PLATE 69. *St Mary Magdalene, Littleton, Surrey. Altar rails Pelican in her Piety. Flemish, mid-18th century.* (B/8)

PLATE 70. *St Mary, Magdalene, Littleton, Surrey, Altar rails. Gates. Flemish, mid-18th century. (B/8)*

PLATE 71. *St Mary Magdalene, Littleton, Surrey. Altar rails. Panel showing the* Breastplate *from the priestly vestments. Flemish, mid-18th century. (B/8)*

B/8 St Mary Magdalene, Littleton, Surrey (Plates 69-71)
Oak. Flemish. Mid-18th century
Height 43cm (17in.) to rail; side panels of variable widths, but probably all originally 70cm (27½in.); present length 5.02m (16ft.6in.)
(For Littleton, see also M/16)

No doubt these altar rails were originally much wider. The plinth may be original, but the uprights and all the top framing and rail are new. The plinth has been cut in places, probably when the rails were shortened to fit into the available space. Most of the decorative panels, including the gates, have been truncated as well, particularly *The Pelican in her Piety* (Plate 69) and the *Shewbread*.

The panels on the gates have two angels adoring the Chalice and Host (Plate 70), and the *Bread and Wine* are represented on adjacent panels on either side. At each end are Old and New Testament references, the former showing the *Tables of the Law, Aaron's Rod*, a censer and the *Breastplate* from the priestly vestments (Plate 71), the latter a chalice with wafer above, a Cross and a Bible. The style is Rococo.

Although they were made about thirty years earlier than those at Littleton, the panels of *Angels adoring the Host* on the altar rails at the Carmelite Church in Bruges have a good deal in common with these (Plate 72).

PLATE 72. *Carmelite Church, Bruges. Altar rails. Centre panel. Early 18th century.*
COPYRIGHT IRPA-KIK, BRUSSELS

B/9. St Matthew, Otterbourne, Hampshire (Plates 73-77)
Oak. Flemish. Late 17th century
86.5cm x 2.58m. (34in. x 8ft.5in.)
Bought in Wardour Street by W.C. Yonge
(For Otterbourne, see also pages 74-76 and M/24)

These altar rails are in far from authentic condition. They have lost their gates, and all of the framework, including the plinth, capping and naturalistic frieze are 19th century. However, what remains, particularly the large carved panels on either side of the entrance, is very grand indeed, and is said to come from a Premonstratensian abbey in Flanders. It is an example of 'Wardour Street' adaptation.

There is another pierced panel, 150cm (4ft.11in.) wide, from the original rails, converted into the altar frontal. The sides of the altar must have been made up at the same time as the rails because their decoration is similar.

St Norbert, who lived in the twelfth century, was the founder of the Order named after him. In the 16th century he was used by Rome as a standard bearer of the Counter-Reformation. He was re-launched in the mid-17th century as the Apostle of the Blessed Sacrament, hence his attribute is the monstrance, a transparent vessel in which to display the Host (Plate 93). The choice of a monstrance probably also reflected Norbert's itinerant pastoral activities, which were centred on his preaching and the miracles he performed. He is often shown with the figure of the mythical Antwerp heretic Tankeln at his feet, whom he is supposed to have subjugated. At Otterbourne he appears to the right of the former communion rail entrance. He is wearing a pallium, over a scapula and rochet. He is carrying a reliquary in his right hand, with the long archiepiscopal cross and an olive branch in the left. His mitre is placed on the ground behind him (Plate 73). In 1126 Norbert was appointed archbishop of Magdeburg. On the altarpiece at Bursledon, he carries the more usual monstrance in the left hand (C/1). As well as the two examples featured here other Norbertine material can be seen at the London Oratory, including some stained glass and two 16th century painted Annunciation panels.

PLATE 73. *St Matthew, Otterbourne, Hampshire. Altar rails. Flemish, late 17th century. Figure of St Norbert on right of former entrance. (B/9)*

PLATE 74. *St Matthew, Otterbourne, Hampshire. Made up 'altar' with figures of St Eloi on left and St Thomas Aquinas on right. Flemish, late 17th century. (B/9)*

PLATE 75. *St Matthew, Otterbourne, Hampshire. Altar rails. Flemish, late 17th century. Figure of priest in monk's habit with kneeling (?) ass. (B/9)*

The two figures on the 'altar' at Otterbourne, which has been made up from the altar rails, are possibly St Eloi on the left, holding a reliquary and St Thomas Aquinas on the right (Plate 74). St Eloi (*c*.588-660) was born at Chaptelet, in the Haute-Vienne. He became a renowned goldsmith, hence his attribute of the hammer, which he holds in his right hand. He was a successful preacher and founded monasteries in France. He was particularly active in the Tournai area and was a pioneer apostle in much of Flanders. St Thomas Aquinas, the Dominican friar and theologian, is recognisable by the star with sun on his breast and the book in his left hand. Other figures on the rails include a canon, a nun, and a priest in monk's habit with what appears to be a kneeling ass beside him. In his left hand is a large disc-like object (Plate 75).

On either side of where the entrance gates would have been appears to be the patron, kneeling on a cushion with his Ducal crown on the ground in front of him, wearing the Order of the Golden Fleece and accompanied by his *entourage* (Plate 76). This includes his assistant, who carries a sword. On the left are a group of young women and girls, presumably the latter's family (Plate 77). One carries a pot of flowers and at the back is probably the patron's spouse and mother of the children. Perhaps the scarves worn by the three young women at the front denote that they are the married ones. This group seems to be kneeling in front of an altar with a reliquary placed on it. Flanking them to the right is the figure of a nun, the twin to the St Norbert figure on the other side.

On stylistic grounds, this woodwork is likely to have come from the Liège/Maastricht area. Also, if the identification of St Eloi is correct, it would be another reason for placing the monument in southern Belgium.

PLATE 76. *St Matthew, Otterbourne, Hampshire. Altar rails. Flemish, late 17th century. Male donor figure and entourage on right of former entrance. (B/9)*

PLATE 77. *St Matthew, Otterbourne, Hampshire. Altar rails. Flemish, late 17th century. Panel on left of previous entrance, with female donor and daughters. (B/9)*

119

PLATE 78. *The Chapel, Oxburgh Hall, Norfolk. Altar rails at east end. Flemish, early 18th century. Entrance gates. (B/10).*

PLATE 79. *The Chapel, Oxburgh Hall, Norfolk. Altar rails at east end. Flemish, early 18th century. Panel with* Abraham Sacrificing Isaac. *(B/10)*

B/10 Chapel, Oxburgh Hall, Norfolk. East end (Plates 78 and 79)
Oak. Flemish. Early 18th century
Length 5.54m (18ft.2in.). Height to rail 71cm (28in.)
(For Oxburgh, see also B/11, C/5 and M/25)
The central entrance panel of these altar rails, which gives the appearance of a continuous piece of carving (see also Plates 57, 70, 72 and 82), is flanked by a wider section each side. Four putti heads adore the *Chalice and Host* in the central panel (Plate 78). The space between plinth and rail is carved with a network of bold C scrolls, interspersed with cartouches containing bishops' busts and *Moses presenting the Manna and Wine* and *Abraham sacrificing Isaac* (Plate 79).

The chapel at Oxburgh was commissioned by Sir Henry Bedingfeld in 1837 and has been attributed to A.W.N. Pugin (Wainwright 1976). The carved Flemish altarpiece, from Antwerp, was bought in Bruges by Sir Henry some time before his death in 1862, as a replacement for Pugin's original. Sir Henry's sister Charlotte was a nun at Bruges for fifty years (page 78).

PLATE 80. *The Chapel, Oxburgh Hall, Norfolk. Altar rails at west end. Flemish, late 17th century. Entrance gate with* Pelican in her Piety. *(B/11)*

PLATE 81. *The Chapel, Oxburgh Hall, Norfolk. Altar rails at west end. Flemish, late 17th century. Detail of the* Shewbread on the Table. *(B/11)*

B/11 Chapel, Oxburgh Hall, Norfolk. West end (Plates 80 and 81)
Oak. Flemish. Late 17th century
Length 5.54m (18ft.2in.). Height to rail 86.5cm (34in.)
(For Oxburgh Hall, see also B/10, C/5 and M/25)
The entrance panel of these altar rails, with the *Pelican in her Piety*, is hinged on one side only, and flanked by a wider adjoining section (Plate 80). Cherubs with crosses stand on either side of the entrance. The carving consists of a network of scrolling foliage interspersed with plain and historiated cartouches. The two figurative cartouches display the *Shewbread on the Table* (Plate 81) and the *Ark of the Covenant*. The only foliage decoration, apart from acanthus, are thistles.

Probably the thistle refers to *Silybum marianum*, or 'Our Lady's Thistle', which, tradition has it, owes the white markings on its leaves to milk from the Virgin's breast. Equally the spikiness of the plant could simply be a metaphor for the *Passion*. References to the Virgin are common in communion rail iconography.

These rails act as the desking for the family pew behind.

PLATE 82. *St Peter, Reymerston, Norfolk. Altar rails. Probably Flemish, c.1700. General view. (B/12)*

B/12 St Peter, Reymerston, Norfolk (Plates 82 and 83)
Oak. Probably Flemish. *c.*1700
2.02m (6ft.6in.) long. Panels 72cm (28¼in.) high
Said to have been bought in Belgium
The central double-hinged entrance panel of these communion rails has angels flanking a chalice with the Host above. The panels either side are filled with thick leafy acanthus scrolling foliage, with two small historiated medallions containing the *Baptism of Christ* and *The Sermon on the Mount* (Plate 83). All the framing is modern, including the end and central buttresses. Parts have been

painted over in a grey-green to obscure the joins of the new work.

The *Sermon on the Mount*, according to the account in Matthew (Matthew v-vii) was thought by St Augustine to correspond to *Moses receiving the Ten Commandments on Mount Sinai*, a popular subject for depiction on communion rails. In this interpretation Jesus is seen as the New Moses.

The prodigious foliage on these panels is similar in spirit, if not in style, to the treatment of the altar rails at the Church of Our Lady, Aarschott (Plate 84).

PLATE 83. *St Peter, Reymerston, Norfolk. Altar rails. Probably Flemish, c.1700. Detail of the*
Sermon on the Mount *panel on north side. (B/12)*

PLATE 84. *Church of Our Lady, Aarschot. Altar rail in south nave aisle. Detail. Flemish, 18th century.*

B/13 St Mary's College, New Oscott, Sutton Coldfield, Warwickshire
Oak. Flemish. Inscribed 1680 on south gate of entrance (Colour Plate 2; Plates 85-88)
9.144m (30ft.) long, 76cm (30in.) high
Obtained by Lord Shrewsbury and A.W.N. Pugin at Leuven and put in place in 1839. Shortly afterwards the rails were sold to St Mary's, Chelsea, London but bought back in 1872 by James Wheble.
(For Oscott College, see also J/12, J/13, J/14 and M/31)

Some restoration work has been done to the altar rails, and the capping is new. The decoration is very classical with scrolling foliage running along the frieze at the top, and upright acanthus leaves below (Plate 85). The main panels consist of cherubs harvesting in the interstices of large-scale scrolling foliage. The only specific liturgical or dogmatic reference is the reliquary on the front of the gates (Plate 86). The monogram MR *(Maria Regina)*, with crown above and the *Sacred Heart* below, is located on the north side. The rails were painted a dark brown in the 19th century.

PLATE 85. *St Mary's College, New Oscott, Sutton Coldfield, Warwickshire. View of altar rails from N.W. Flemish. Inscribed 1680. (B/13)*

PLATE 86. *St Mary's College, New Oscott, Sutton Coldfield, Warwickshire. Flemish altar rails. Detail showing reliquary at centre of entrance gates and date inscription (1680). (B/13)*

PLATE 87. *St Mary's College, New Oscott, Sutton Coldfield, Warwickshire. Flemish altar rails. Detail showing IHS symbol (the first three letters of the name Jesus in Greek) on south side. Inscribed 1680. (B/13).*

The treatment and subject matter of the railings, with the cherubs playing in the scrolling foliage, owes something in a general sense to Francis Duquesnoy (Plate 65). The Marian monogram at the north end and the IHS symbol on the south side are worked in a kind of 'bobbin' technique (Plate 87). This can also be seen on Peter Verbruggen I's wall panelling at St Paul's, Antwerp, of 1657-59, but also much later on Jacob de Coster's grand double doors at the west end of the Carmelite Church in Bruges. If we look at the frieze on the Antwerp panelling we can recognise a strong stylistic affinity with the Oscott altar rails, even though the latter were carved some twenty years later (Plate 88).

The fitting out and the furnishings of the Oscott College chapel were the responsibility of A.W.N. Pugin, who was introduced to the college by the Earl of Shrewsbury in 1837. Joseph Potter of Lichfield and Dr Kirk, the missioner at Lichfield, had designed and erected the college between 1835 and 1838. The chapel building was nearly complete when Pugin came on the scene. But there was plenty of scope for his imaginative talents, which he lavished on the walls, ceilings and windows, and on the furnishings. Pugin's etching of 1837 and a late 19th century photograph of the chapel interior (Plate 24) both show that the altar rails were originally much further east than they are now. No doubt it was only due to their considerable span that they were placed west of the choir. They have since been pushed back even further away from the altar by the introduction, probably in the 1920s, of another bank of ten choir-stalls west of the line of the north vestry door. The photograph also depicts Pugin's original canopied stone pulpit high up in the north-east corner of the chancel, and behind the altar his reredos. Today the altar rails are positioned incongruously just to the east of the north and south main entrance doors.

B/14 St Nicholas, Worth, West Sussex (Plates 89-92)
Oak. The pierced panels Flemish, mid-18th century. The low relief panels Netherlandish, early 17th century
Flemish panels 75cm x 6.56m (29½in. x 21ft.5in.). Dutch panels 46.5cm x 33.5cm (19¼in. x 13in.)
Said to have come via an Oxford College
(For Worth, see also K/17)

PLATE 88. *St Paul's, Antwerp. Wall panelling. Detail. 1657-59.*
COPYRIGHT. K. FREMANTLE

This not a completely authentic set of altar rails. The six pierced panels and the shield, and probably much of the framing and the plinth, are of the mid-18th century. The attractive Evangelist panels on either side of the gates are intrusions, and the rail itself is probably modern. The

PLATE 89. *St Nicholas, Worth, West Sussex. Altar rails. General view. Netherlandish early 17th century and Flemish mid-18th century. (B/14)*

PLATE 90. *St Nicholas, Worth, West Sussex. Netherlandish panel depicting St Luke. Early 17th century. (B/14)*

PLATE 91. *St Nicholas, Worth, West Sussex. Altar rails. Circumcision panel. Flemish, mid-18th century. (B/14)*

gates, with their original hinges, are authentic (Plate 89).

The 16th century panels depict the Evangelists Luke (Plate 90) and John. The six pierced panels illustrate the usual motifs found on altar rails. Reading from left to right they are: *The Table* with dish on it; an *Altar of Burnt Offering with the Lamb of God;* a loaf of bread and a flagon on an 18th century style *Table;* the *Manna* piled up in two mounds on another 18th century type *Table;* the *Altar of Incense* with a pot and an oil lamp on it; and the *Circumcision* (Plate 91).

The arms in the centre (Plate 92) depict a shield with a plain cross, surmounted by a coronet, and an abbot's staff with the velum or *sudarium.* According to Goodall the type of coronet in this case is normal for the Court in Belgium in the 18th century. The velum was used by bishops and abbots who had not had the honour of being granted the *pontificalia* by the Pope, which meant that they could not wear gloves. In this case the velum, which was a cloth hanging down the crozier, was provided so that the latter could be carried without direct contact with the hand. Commonly at that time the religious houses were denizened by members of the aristocracy. Whether or not an abbot was aristocratic himself, he would often have been one by virtue of his office and the estates of the institution. All the canons of Lyons Cathedral, for instance, were Counts as of right, and were entitled to wear a French comital crown. Goodall suggests that, in the case of Worth, the head of this particular institution could have been an abbess, since the arms are on a lozenge and there is no mitre.

PLATE 92. *St Nicholas, Worth, West Sussex. Altar rails. Flemish, mid-18th century. Coat of arms in centre. (B/14)*

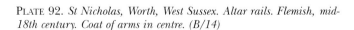

127

C: *Altarpieces, Reredoses and Canopies*

PLATE 93. *Chapel-of Our Lady of the Rosary, Bursledon, Hampshire. Altarpiece. Flemish, 17th century. Detail of image of St Norbert. (C/1)*

PLATE 94. *Chapel of Our Lady of the Rosary, Bursledon, Hampshire. Altarpiece. Flemish, 17th century. Detail of Virgin and Child. (C/1)*

**C/1. Chapel of Our Lady of the Rosary, Bursledon
(Plates 40, 93 and 94)**
**Painted and gilded wood. Provincial Netherlandish. 17th
century**
240cm x 246cm (7ft.10½in. x 8ft.)
(For Bursledon, see also B/2)

The centre of this reredos (Plate 40) consists of three
niches for sculpture, with probably the figures of St
Dominic, with a star on his forehead, and holding a rosary
in his right hand, and St Norbert, wearing the robes of his
Order, with the pallium and scapula, over a rochet, and
holding a monstrance in his right hand (Plate 93), on
either side. The *Virgin and Child* are placed in the centre
in a rounded recessed *aediculum* which breaks through
the entablature above (Plate 94). The Virgin is crowned
and stands on the serpent, holding the other end of the
rosary with her right hand. The panels are divided by
Solomonic columns. These are repeated above in the attic
storey, which contains the figure of *God the Father*. The
broken entablature supports winged cherubs on either
side. Most of the background colouring is original,
including marbling effects in red and green. The figures

have been touched up recently.

This is a delightful provincial altarpiece.

**C/2 St Nectan, Hartland (or Stoke), North Devon (Plate
95)**
**Wood, gessoed and gilded. Probably French. Mid 14th
century**
**Height of canopywork, 63cm (24¾in.). Width 129cm
(4ft.2¾in.)**

This is the top of a reredos consisting of three canopied
niches with a central spire above. It is a very impressive
object with the gilding still in good condition and traces
of blue polychrome in the hollows. There is much
restoration work, however, including most of the central
spire and two of the main finials. None the less, what we
see probably reflects the original form of the object.

The design has a metropolitan feel about it, which stems
ultimately from the late 13th century French Rayonnant
style. The carver was even careful to distinguish between
one canopy and another by choosing different leaf forms
(ivy, vine and trefoil) for his crockets, a tradition that goes
back at least as far as the early 14th century.

PLATE 95. *St Nectan,
Hartland, Devon. Reredos
canopy. Probably French,
mid-14th century. (C/2)*

C/3 All Saints, Tooting Graveney, London (Colour Plate 3; Plates 41 and 96)
Painted wood. Bolognese or Modenese. 18th century
3m x 3m (9ft.10in. x 9ft.10in.) approx.
From the same unknown church as the choir-stalls at Tooting Graveney (M/17)
(For Tooting Graveney, see also A/3, C/4, D/1, E/6, I/7 & M/17)

The high altar reredos, in late Renaissance style, serves as a very large picture frame, enclosing a copy by Raoul Maria of a *Crucifixion* by Velasquez now in the Prado, Madrid. Its harmonious disposition of fluted columns and pilasters is surmounted by a broken semi-circular pediment, with attic, vases and a statue above. Between the broken pediment at the top is the figure of St John the Baptist, holding the *Lamb*. The altarpiece is enhanced by the original muted colour-scheme of pale green and gold.

On the plinths below the columns at each end are heraldic cartouches. The identification by Goodall of these identical arms suggests a provenance of Modena, in spite of the received opinion that the altarpiece came from Bologna. But of course these cities are not far from each other, in the region of Emilia Romagna. The coat, which is *azure, a fess lozengy and three molets six points gold,* belongs to the Forni of Modena (Crollalanza 1886) (Plate 96). It is curious that the arms are the same on both sides and perhaps suggests that the altarpiece was the centrepiece of a Forni chapel.

PLATE 96. *All Saints, Tooting Graveney, London. High altar reredos. Bolognese or Modenese, 18th century. Detail of heraldic cartouche. (C/3)*

PLATE 97. *All Saints, Tooting Graveney, London. Canopied reredos on south side of choir. Probably Italian, early 18th century. (C/4)*

C/4. All Saints, Tooting Graveney, London (Colour Plate 4; Plate 97)
Probably of stained pine. Probably Italian. Early 18th century
233cm (from top of modern base) x 137cm (7ft.7¾in. x 4ft.6in.)
(For Tooting, see also A/3, C/3, D/1, E/6, I/7 and M/17)
On the south side of the choir. Backboard with gilded mouldings and attached decorative carving. Canopy with pelmet and the ceiling with moulded double-S centrepiece.

C/5 Library, Oxburgh Hall, Norfolk (Plates 98-100)
Oak. Mosan. Late 15th century
143cm x 180cm (4ft.8¼in. x 5ft.11in.).
(For Oxburgh Hall, see also B/10, B/11 and M/25)
The canopied reredos is used as a mantelpiece (Plate 98). At the top are three net-like vaults, the central being higher than the others. The arches have a basket profile, but are elaborated at the sides with canopy heads made up from ogee and intersecting tracery (Plate 99). The foliage is spikily convoluted. There is a plain depressed ogee pediment at the top in the centre. The canopy is supported on standards either side, incorporating figures intertwined in the branches of a tree (Plate 100). Inevitably with a piece including so much delicate carving, transported from its original location, quite a lot of restoration has been necessary. There is much new wood in the framework, the canopywork and the double columns either side, but the cresting is mostly original and the vaults and the figure carving down the sides are intact.

The late 15th century style of the Flamboyant tracery on the reredos is similar, but much more complex, to that on the lower panels of the St George altarpiece at St Nicholas, Kalkar of about 1480. The uprights on either side of the reredos at Oxburgh and their setting are similar to those flanking the 'reredos' in the Dining Room at Scarisbrick Hall. In particular the canopywork at the sides is in both cases populated with figures.

The ancient carved woodwork, which has been incorporated into the house, could have been installed by J.C. Buckler, the main restoration architect, A.W.N. Pugin, to whom the chapel has been attributed, or Sir Henry Bedingfeld himself (Wainwright 1976).

PLATE 98. *Library, Oxburgh Hall, Norfolk. Reredos canopy. Mosan, late 15th century. Detail of upper part. (C/5)*

Plate 99. Library, Oxburgh Hall, Norfolk. Reredos canopy. Mosan, late 15th century. Detail of upper right-hand side. (C/5)

PLATE 100. *Library, Oxburgh Hall, Norfolk. Reredos canopy. Mosan, late 15th century. Detail of figures on right side. (C/5)*

Plate 102. St Michael and Our Lady, Wragby, West Riding, Yorkshire. Reredos. Probably Mosan, early 16th century. Pietà *panel (C/6)*

C/6 Wragby, West Riding, Yorkshire (Plates 101 and 102)
Oak. Probably Mosan. Early 16th century
Twelve small panels (96cm x 36.5cm, 37½in. x 14⅖in.)
each side and one large panel (96cm x 55cm, 37½in. x
21⅘in.) in the centre

The reredos consists of a central *Pietà*, flanked by figures of the twelve apostles (Plate 101). Prominent at the base of the central panel is a heraldic shield, with two stars, a chevron, crescent and scallop (Plate 102). The saints stand under shell hoods. All the framing is modern, and the buttresses at each end are 17th century.

This may have been acquired by John Winn, owner of the adjoining Nostell Priory, who introduced the Swiss stained glass at the beginning of the 19th century (see page 64 and Brockwell 1915), or possibly later by his brother Charles.

This is a difficult work to pin down stylistically. Didier has suggested that it was probably made in the Mosan region, but was attempting to emulate Brussels work.

Plate 101. St Michael and Our Lady, Wragby, West Riding, Yorkshire. Reredos. Probably Mosan, early 16th century. (C/6)

D: *Candle Stands*

D/1. All Saints, Tooting Graveney, London (Colour Plate 5; Plate 103)
Painted and gilded wood. Florentine. 18th century
162cm (5ft.3¾in.) high. Sides of tripod bases 55cm (21⅛in.) high
(For Tooting Graveney, see also A/3, C/3, C/4, E/6, I/7 and M/17)
Conventional design with terminal figures standing on the scrolls of the tripod, surmounted by a vase. The stone base is modern.

The polychrome and gilding on the woodwork were applied in the early part of the 20th century and the cartouches bear the arms of the superseded diocese of Rochester.

PLATE 103. *All Saints, Tooting Graveney, London. Candle stand Florentine, 18th century. (D/1)*

134

D/2. St Michael, Milverton, Somerset (Plate 104)
Mahogany. Netherlandish. Late 17th century
209cm (6ft.10¼in.) high
With scrolled tripod, the shells and terminal figures riding dolphins.

The base of a Paschal candle stand at Brussels Cathedral is of about the same date (Plate105).

PLATE 105. *Brussels Cathedral. Base of Paschal late 17th century candle stand.*

135

PLATE 106. *St John the Baptist, Stapledon, Shropshire. Candle stands. Netherlandish, c.1500. (D/3)*

D/3. St John the Baptist, Stapleton, Shropshire (Plate 106)
Polychromed wood, probably oak. Netherlandish. *c.*1500
Height to top of abacus 177.5cm (5ft.10in.)
A pair of candle stands, on modern hexagonal bases. The

body and capital is carved with a mixture of low relief and deeply undercut typical Northern Continental late Gothic foliage. Unfortunately the importance of these pieces is mitigated by a recent redecoration using modern paints.

E: *Chairs and Benches*

E/1. St Mary and All Saints, Beaconsfield, Buckinghamshire (Colour Plates 6 and 6a; Plate 107)
Unknown wood, Italian. Mid-18th century
Height including canopy 222cm (7ft.3⅛in.); height of seat 53cm (21in.); width of back 67.5cm (26½in.); width of seat 73cm (28¾in.); depth of seat 53cm (21in.)
Presented to the church by Benjamin Disraeli on his becoming Earl of Beaconsfield in 1876. Said to have come from Lombardy.

Gilt wood armchair with ogee ribbed canopy in the form of a crown, surmounted by a cherub. The chair back has in-curved side posts, straight bottom rail and the arched top is decorated with carved scrolling acanthus and three cherub heads in the centre amidst rays, with a cherub head at each side. The scrolled and curving arms have cherub heads at each end. The underside of the arms are painted red, and the top surfaces are treated with a punched decoration of flowers. The cabriole front legs have pad feet, whilst the back legs splay in a curve. The seat and back are covered with embossed and stained leather. There are some old paint losses on the side posts and the right-hand arm. There is also some new paint loss and some areas are lifting. It is not clear whether the beetle infestation is old. Otherwise the paint surfaces are in excellent condition. The seat is rather worn.

On the back the embossed cartouche contains a painting of a nimbed figure in clerical habit, kneeling beside a table in a cave (Colour Plate 6a). He appears to be holding a stone to his chest. On the table are a crucifix, a book, a skull, an unidentified object and a flail. There is a bucket in the background and on the floor possibly a snake. Inscribed on the table cloth are the words:

S. CORRADO EREMITA

This must be the 12th century St Corrado of Chiaravalle, who was the son of Henry the Black, Duke of Bavaria. He became a Benedictine monk and later went to Palestine to experience the eremitical life. He then returned to Italy and lived in a cave dedicated to the Virgin, near Modugno, not far from Bari in Apulia, where he died in 1154. His body was carried to the cathedral of Molfetta, which is dedicated to him. It is recorded that his bones were moved on 10 July 1785 to another position within the church. His head has always been kept separately and is displayed in procession on special occasions. His cult was confirmed by Pope Gregory XVI on 6 April 1832 (Damiani 1669).

Although this is pure speculation, given the style of the chair it is possible that it was made to commemorate the translation of the bones of St Corrado in 1785.

PLATE 107. *St Mary and All Saints, Beaconsfield, Buckinghamshire. Armchair. Italian, mid-18th century. (E/1)*

PLATE 108. *Exeter Cathedral, Devon. Arm chair. Portuguese, late 17th century.* (E/2)

E/2. Exeter Cathedral, Devon (Plate 108)
Oak. Portuguese. Late 17th century
126cm (4ft.1⅛in.) high to top of back; width 57cm (22½in.); height of arms 74cm (29in.); depth of arms 61cm (24in.); height of cresting 24cm (13½in.) (without finial)
(For Exeter Deanery, see E/3)
High-backed chair with legs and uprights with spiral turning. The seat and back of tooled leather, secured by

rows of prominent brass-headed studs. The substantial cresting at the top contains a framed cross, and brass baluster finial above. There are mortises for two more, now lost, on either side.

The lively decoration of the tooled leather is based on the Bérain style prints available at this time.

E/3. The Deanery, Exeter Cathedral, Devon (Colour Plates 7 and 7a; Plate 109)
Gessoed, painted and gilded chestnut (or possibly cherry); carcase of beech or poplar. Probably Italian. Second quarter 16th century
Height 212.5cm (6ft.11⅛in.); width of seat 72.5cm (28½in.); depth of seat 51cm (20in.); height of seat 49cm (19¼in.); height of back to springing of vault 146cm (4ft.9½in.)
Given by the Reverend Sir Patrick Ferguson Davie, Bt., *c.*1960. Bought in London
(For Exeter Cathedral, see E/2)
A pair of thrones with box-type seats, short arms, and high canopied backs based on half a dodecagon (Plate 109). The backs are treated with a thick layer of gesso and were certainly not meant to be seen. Moreover, the sides of the thrones are angled off and there is no sign of any fixing, so that it would appear that they were originally built into a wall and plastered up to the edges.

The seat-backs are painted delicately and in muted unrestored pale pink, blue and brown with scrolling foliage, inhabited by birds and female figures, against a gold flecked background (Colour Plate 7a). The five-sided canopies have a late Gothic appearance, with corbels, finials and cusped arches. Inside the canopy is a star-shaped vault. In the vaults and down the sides of the thrones is a running foliage motif in gold against a red background. Underneath the seat capping on both sides is a coat of arms. On the fronts of the seat stiles are Renaissance-type human masks and foliage. In between the stiles and on the seat sides are fields of Moresque decoration on a blue background.

The use of female figures emerging from flowers can be compared to the work of the engraver Marco Dente from Ravenna (d. 1527), or another Italian artist, Thomas Vincidore, who was active 1520-36. But perhaps the best comparison would be with the work of the Vicenzan Battista Pittoni (1520-1584). Silhouette, or Moresque, work was common throughout Europe in the early 16th century, for example, in the hands of the Frenchmen Jean de Gourmont (active 1520-51) and J.A. Duçerceau (*c.*1520-*c.*1584), the Italian Francesco Pellegrini (active 1528-41), and the German Virgilius Solis (1514-1562) from Nüremberg. The latter's engravings were widely influential in the applied arts in general and in furniture. Finally, the use of masks like these is seen in the work of the Bolognese Antonio Fantuzzi, who was born *c.*1510 and was working at Fontainebleau after 1537 and before 1540.

Goodall has suggested that the coat of arms on these chairs is undoubtedly Italian, but its organisation is

PLATE 109. *Chapel, Bishop's Palace, Exeter, Devon. Canopied throne, one of a pair. Italian or Spanish, second quarter 16th century. (E/3)*

E/4. Hever Castle, Kent (Plate 110)
Oak. French. Late 15th century
153cm x 70cm x 53cm (5ft.½in. x 27½in. x 21in.)
(For Hever Castle, see also A/2, H/2 and M/13)
A high-backed chair, with open sides but closed base. Hinged seat for locker with original straps. The centre panel at the back features a crown, whilst the panel at the front underneath the seat displays shields. The side panels at the base have linenfold decoration. There are inscribed crosses at the top and bottom on three sides of the seat rail struts. A genuine piece in authentic condition.

A similar French chair of this period, described as 'Chaire à coffre de la fin du xvième siècle', is illustrated in Boussel 1979, p.21, fig.2.

PLATE 110. *Hever Castle, Kent. Armchair. French, late 15th century. (E/4)*

somewhat uncertain. He suggests that it probably was *Bendy gules and gold with a chief supported by a fillet gold a demi-lion sable holding a ?lily vert with the chief of Anjou.* He also points out that the scroll should have a motto on it.

There is an ambiguity as to the function of the thrones. Were there just two of them? As a pair they might have been set up in the throne room of a royal or aristocratic establishment. On the other hand, if there were more, they might have been the seats in a cathedral chapter house.

E/5 St John the Baptist, Thaxted, Essex (Plate 111)
Oak. Probably French. Mid-17th century
Bench-ends, 146cm x 37cm (4ft.9½in.); seats 34cm
(13½in.) high x 201.5cm (6ft.7¼in.) long
The ends of the six benches are of panelled construction.
Most of the seats have a double roll moulding each side
and new supporting brackets underneath. Others are
plain. It is possible that the seats are all modern.

The bench-ends, whilst all similar in overall design,
contain a variety of unusual motifs, such as crossed fire-
brands, books, crossed-sticks with knobs on the ends, glass
phials, bells, and a crossed pick-axe and spade. These
motifs presumably stand for various trades. At the top
there are *memento mori*, including a child with a spade,
bells, skull and crossed bones, and an hour glass.

E/6. All Saints, Tooting Graveney, London (Colour Plate
8; Plate 112)
Wood not identified, possibly chestnut. Netherlandish.
Mid-18th century
98cm x 153cm x 58cm (3ft.2⅛in. x 5ft.¼in. x 22¾in.)
(For Tooting, see A/3, C/3, C/4, D/1, I/7 and M/17)
A bench with panelled base in the form of an apron.
Sturdy voluted arms each end. Cartouche in the centre of
the seat back, decorated with a Jerusalem cross. The feet
seem to have been altered or restored.

Use of the Jerusalem cross identifies the bench with the
Order of the Holy Sepulchre. This institution still exists as
one of the Papal Orders, which can confer upon cardinals
the rights to create their own Knights.

PLATE 111. *St John the Baptist,
Thaxted, Essex. Bench end. One of
twelve. Probably French, mid-17th
century.* (E/5)

PLATE 112. *All Saints, Tooting
Graveney, London. Bench.
Netherlandish, mid-18th century.*
(E/6)

F: *Chests*

PLATE 113. *The Bowes Museum, Barnard Castle, County Durham. Oak chest. French, early 16th century. (F/1)*

F/1. The Bowes Museum, Bishop Auckland, County Durham (Plate 113)
Oak. French. Early 16th century
80cm x 160cm x 69cm (31½in. x 5ft.3in. x 27in.)
(For Bowes Museum, see also J/1 and M/2)
Panelled chest with three compartments in the lower zone, two each on the sides, and a decorative band above, on the front, incorporating the lock. The central panel displays a representation of the *Annunciation*, with two pairs of saints either side, including St Christopher and St Peter at the extremities. On the sides are two pairs of Renaissance-style profile busts. The lid is original except for the modern surround. The hinges are modern, but the scars of the original ones are visible on the underside. The original metal lock plate is missing. The wood was probably cleaned in the 19th century. The front feet seem to be original, but the back ones have been renewed. There is a security compartment inside.

The style of the figure carving is typical of French work of the beginning of the 16th century as we find on the choir screen and stalls at King's College Chapel, Cambridge (Plate 278) and the refugee panels at Harwood, Lancashire (Plate 296).

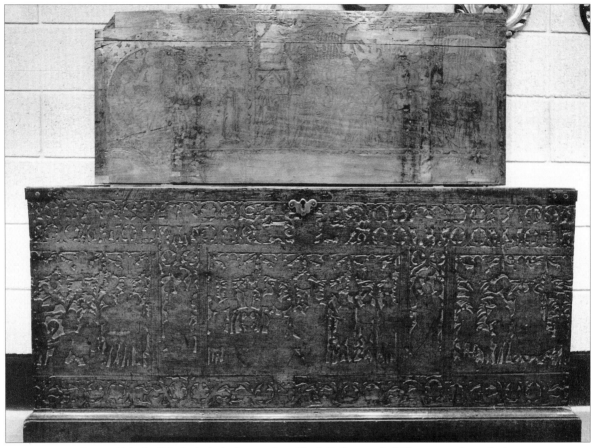

PLATE 114. *Carlisle Cathedral. Cypress chest. North Italian, early 16th century. General view (F/2).*

F/2. Carlisle Cathedral, Cumbria (Plates 114-116)
Cypress, cembra-pine or cedarwood, North Italian. Early 16th century
55cm x 140cm x 57cm (21½in. x 4ft.7in. x 22½in.)
The chest was presented to the Dean and Chapter of Carlisle in 1939 by the Sewell family of Brandlingill, near Cockermouth.
This is one of a group of six North Italian cypress vestment and/or altar-chests, or fragments thereof, in England (See F/3, F/8, F/10, F/11 and F/12)
(For Carlisle Cathedral, see also K/4, L/2 and L/3)
This flat-bottomed 'cypress' altar-chest has been truncated to about two-thirds of its original length. Originally it would have been about 206cm (6ft.9in.) long. The front panel, and the lid, have been cut down at both ends *pro rata* to the overall reduction in length. The sides are plain and 17th century carrying handles have been applied. The lid is split in two places towards the front and a modern metal retaining bracket has been screwed into it on the top side. The top left-hand corner of the lid has been damaged on the inside only. Under the lid on both sides there are lidded security boxes, which

are probably a modern feature. The chest is made out of five solid planks, which would have originally been joined together with dovetails.

The front panel is handled in the usual woodcut-type technique, and would have been drawn over in penwork. The original subject matter is hard to distinguish. There seem to have been three main scenes of Petrarchian type. There are two single panels with figures on either side of the central scene. The latter possibly depicts the *Annunciation.*

We can estimate the original width of the chest by extrapolating the amount of missing figurative content on the inside of the lid to the right of the *Crucifixion* scene, this portion having been removed. The basic layout of the picture would have been exactly the same as at Chilcombe, Swaffham Bulbeck and Norwich, with large roundels either side. In the 'spandrels' of the left-hand roundel, top right, there are the hindquarters of a griffin (Plate 115). There was probably another drawing on the other side. At Carlisle, Chilcombe and Norwich the scene on the left hand side is the *Scourging of Christ*. At Carlisle the companion roundel scene on the right is missing.

Immediately to the right of the roundel on the left-hand side, at Carlisle, is a nimbed friar with book, very similar in appearance to those at Chilcombe and Norwich, but carrying a double, as opposed to a single, cross and standing on a small plinth as at the other places (Plates 115 and 116). Is this the founder of one of the preaching orders? From him we move from the left into the *Crucifixion* scene, with a full complement of protagonists, starting, as in the four other cases, with an urban tower. The scene spreads across, but is truncated abruptly after the crucified robber on Christ's left. As at Norwich, Swaffham Bulbeck and Chilcombe fictive predella panels with the symbols of the Evangelists were inserted at each corner of the *Crucifixion* scene, although only one of these, St John, survives at Carlisle. Below the *Crucifixion* scene, the outline of the compartments of a decorated frieze can just be made out.

If such a chest was able to be used as a temporary altar it would have been necessary to have a platform, or inner lid, underneath the main one when open, to place things on. At Norwich the inner lid, which is modern, is plain, but the original one would probably have been decorated. At Carlisle there are two fragments of wood which have been sawn from a large decorated panel, presumably parts of the original inner lid. On the right-hand side the piece, about 18cm (7in.) wide, fits the space perfectly. On it are drawn in penwork secular male and female figures.

PLATE 115. *Carlisle Cathedral. Cypress chest. North Italian, early 16th century. Lid underside.* Scourging of Christ *scene on left side. (F/2)*

PLATE 116. *Carlisle Cathedral. Cypress chest. North Italian, early 16th century. Detail of right end of lid underside, with figure of friar at extreme left. (F/2)*

On the left-hand end the decoration is mostly foliate, but there are the heads only of a man and a woman. This fragment has been cut down to fit the wrong way up and clearly was intended to run along the top of the false lid.

According to a report made when the chest was acquired by the cathedral, it was found in the dairy of a farm in the Holme Cultram district of West Cumbria. As is mentioned in connection with the Gondibour screen at Carlisle (L/2), there was an important Cistercian abbey there, which had links with the cathedral in the late 15th century. It is tempting to speculate that the chest is a refugee from there. Its date is certainly early enough to have reached Holme Cultram before the Reformation.

F/3. Chilcombe Church, Dorset (Plates 117-121)
Cypress, cembra-pine or cedarwood, North Italian. Early 16th century
62cm x 190cm (24⅛in. x 6ft.2⅜in.)
This is a fragment of one of a group of six North Italian cypress vestment and/or altar-chests, or fragments thereof, in England (See F/2, F/8, F/10, F/11 and F/12)

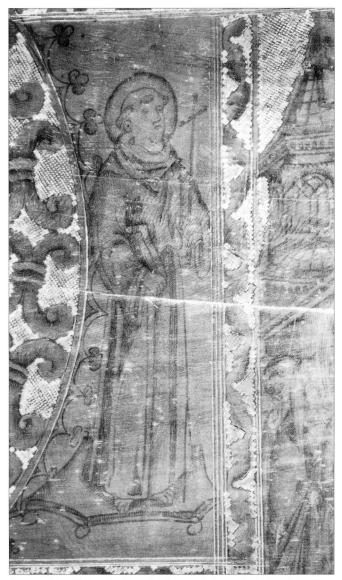

PLATE 118. *Chilcombe Church, Dorset. Cypress chest. North Italian, early 16th century. Detail of friar. (F/3)*

PLATE 117. *Chilcombe Church, Dorset. Cypress chest. North Italian, early 16th century. Detail of* Crucifixion. *(F/3)*

The surviving lid, or reredos, from a 'Cypress' vestment and/or altar-chest has been reset into a later framing of oak, and hangs on the north wall of the church. It uses the penwork drawing technique typical of these chests, combined with a recessing of the negative spaces between the main scenes, which are treated with stamped decoration. The *Crucifixion* is represented in the centre (Plate 117). On the corners outside the picture are the four Evangelist symbols, between them a friar with halo, book and cross, standing on a small plinth, as at Carlisle (Plate 118), and an anchorite with halo and scroll. At either end are scenes in roundels, the *Scourging of Christ* on the left (Plate 119) and the *Resurrection* on the right

PLATE 119. *Chilcombe Church, Dorset. Cypress chest. North Italian, early 16th century. Detail of* Scourging of Christ *under lid. (F/3)*

PLATE 121. *Chilcombe Church, Dorset. Cypress chest. North Italian, early 16h century. Detail of* Annunciation *under lid. Figure of Virgin Mary. (F/3)*

(Plate 120). On either side of the IHS monogram above the *Crucifixion* scene, in penwork, are placed the two protagonists of the *Annunciation*. The Virgin's lectern has a kink in the upper portion of the stand (Plate 121), similar to the one on the Victoria and Albert Museum panel (F/8) and at Redenhall (F/11). This is probably a poorly-drawn reference to the standard type of adjustable medieval lectern, often portrayed in manuscripts and sculpture, which uses a swivelling bracket attached to the stem.

In most cases, where the woodcut-type technique is used, there are traces of gesso in the background of the silhouetted drawings and scenes. This may well have been deliberate, as we know that coloured chalk was used in the comparable North Italian poker-work or *pirograffiata* decorated cypress chests (Yorke 1989). The white or coloured backgrounds would have thrown up the figural scenes in sharp relief. They are also carefully stamped to provide an overall texture.

The chest lid, a solid piece of timber, has been truncated at each end on the top and bottom. There are several bad splits in the wood and circular wear grooves in the bottom right- and left-hand corners. Also there are some small repairs.

PLATE 120. *Chilcombe Church, Dorset. Cypress chest. North Italian, early 16th century. Detail of* Resurrection of Christ *under lid. (F/3)*

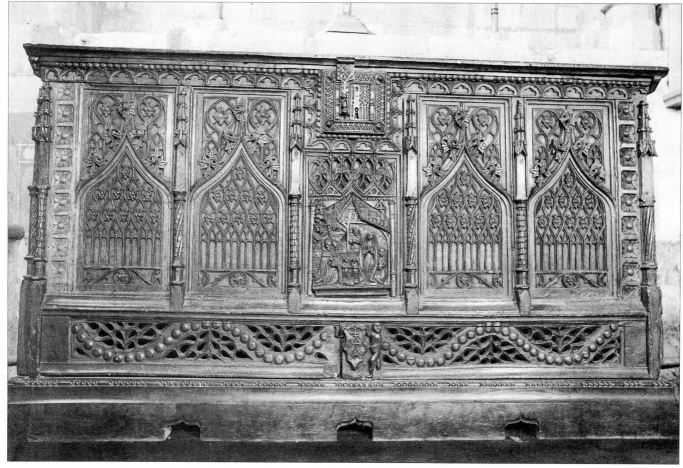

PLATE 122. *Church of the Holy Cross, Crediton, Devon. Oak chest French (Normandy), after 1500. (F/4)*

F/4. Church of the Holy Cross, Crediton, Devon (Plate 122)
Oak, French (Normandy). After 1500
95cm x 170.5cm x 64cm (3ft.1½in. x 5ft.7in. x 2ft.1in.)
Said to come from the old manor house of Trowbridge, Wiltshire, home of the Yarde family.

A boarded plinth chest, with a *Nativity* scene in the central panel with lock plate above, two pairs of traceried panels separated by buttresses either side, and a panel running the length of the chest at the bottom with serpentine moulding and pierced work. There is a supporter and emblazoned shield in the centre of this frieze, the dexter figure now missing. The shield carries a merchant's mark and initials. The traceried panels and the frieze below continue around the ends of the chest. There are four aediculae on the front buttresses for small statues, now missing. The chest's plinth is modern. The original lock plate has flat openwork. Inside not seen.

The placing of the *Nativity* scene in the centre of the front panel can be paralleled in the late 16th century Normandy chest at East Dereham, Norfolk (Plate 125).

This particular style of chest is not uncommon in England, for example at North Frodingham, East Riding, Yorkshire, the 'Corporation Chest' in the Christchurch Mansion Museum, Ipswich (Plate 123) and the chest front at Middlewich, Cheshire (F/9). The same kind of blind tracery can also be seen on the pulpit at the Musée Nationale du Moyen Âge, Paris (Plate 124).

PLATE 123. *Christchurch Mansion, Ipswich. 'Corporation' chest. French (Normandy), after 1500.*

PLATE 124. *Musée Nationale du Moyen Âge, Paris. 15th century pulpit.*

PLATE 125. *St Nicholas, East Dereham, Norfolk. Oak chest. Northern French (Normandy), late 16th century. (F/5).* COPYRIGHT BATSFORD

PLATE 126. *St Nicholas, East Dereham, Norfolk. Oak chest. Northern French (Normandy), late 16th century. Left end. (F/5)*

F/5. St Nicholas, East Dereham, Norfolk (Plates 125-127a)
Oak. Northern French (Normandy). First half 16th century
89cm x 182.5cm x 77cm (2ft.3in. x 6ft. x 2ft.6¼in.)
According to an inscription fixed to the chest, it was presented to the church in 1786. It is said to have formerly belonged to the Dukes of Norfolk and to have been rescued from the ruins of Buckenham Castle.

A plinth chest of boarded construction, with much restoration inside and out. The carved panels, lock plate and uprights are all original. The bases of the uprights at the corners, the base rail, the entire plinth and the chest lid are modern. The original highly decorated wrought-iron lock plate displays Renaissance inhabited scrolls and decorative nail heads. The hasp is in the form of a canopy with profile heads each side.

The front board is decorated with six standing female figures in aediculae between 'candelabra' columns, with the *Nativity* in the centre underneath the lock. The boards at each end incorporate another three female figures (Plates 126 and 127). It had been suggested that the standing figures represent the twelve Sibyls. Reading from left to right, their attributes are as follows:

1. Coronet.
2. Reed or spear.
3. Mirror.
4. Sword in the right hand, scales in the left.
5. Pincers in the right hand.

6. A church.
7. Cross in the right hand.
8. Heart in the left hand.
9. A tower in the left hand, with a dragon emergingfrom it.
10. A spear-head in the right hand, and a scourge in the left.
11. Long cross.
12. Bottle-shaped object sheathed in reed.

In fact, the carved images seem to be a series of *Cardinal and Theological Virtues*. There are five more than the usual seven, and the identity of many of them is ambiguous. The presence of the *Nativity* scene in the centre of the front panel is paralleled on the earlier French Crediton chest (F/4). However, there is a very close parallel to this chest at the Musée des Antiquités, Rouen (Plate 127a). Here the original plinth, with typical Renaissance decoration, is intact and there are differences in the treatment of the arch hoods and plinths for the figures. At Rouen the central panel under the lock piece depicts the Virgin and Child (Thirion 1998). There are five panels depicting *Virtues* built into a late 19th century chest, albeit of inferior artistic quality, at Berwick-upon-Tweed, Northumberland (Gazetteer).

PLATE 127. *St Nicholas, East Dereham, Norfolk. Oak chest. Northern French (Normandy), late 16th century. Right end. (F/5)*

PLATE 127a. *Musée des Antiquités de la Seine Maritime, Rouen. Oak chest with Virtues.First half 16th century.*

F/6. Victoria and Albert Museum, London (Plate 128)
Oak. Northern French. Mid-16th century
78cm x 135cm x 61cm (2ft.6¾in. x 4ft.5in. x 2ft.)
(Acq. No. W.38-1938)
(For V & A Museum, see also F/7, F/8, J/8, J/9, J/10, L/7, M/18, M/19 and M/20)

Of panelled hutch-type construction, the chest incorporates two figural panels, carved in high relief on the front, on either side of a representation below the oblong lock plate of the *Virgin and Child* and goldfinch (the figure of the Child is damaged). Pairs of panels, carved in low relief, are at each end. Four Gothic-style saints are depicted under Renaissance-type canopies, namely St Barbara on the left, two unknown in the centre, and St Margaret at the other end. The figures on the front are combined with areas of Renaissance grotesque decoration. The end panels display medallions under birds.

It is noticeable that the decorative carving on the margins of the main panels is incomplete, petering out about one-third the way along the front towards the right-hand side. Also on the end panels one medallion has not been executed, having been only lightly inscribed.

The conceit of tent tops above the saints being held up in the beaks of birds is reminiscent of the angels holding up the tent curtains on the early 16th century French altar frontal at Hever Castle (A/2).

F/7. Victoria and Albert Museum, London (Plate 129)
Oak. Netherlands/Northern France. c.1500
49cm x 71.5cm x 61cm (19¼in. x 2ft.4in. x 2ft.)
(Acq. No. W.12-1945)
(For V & A Museum, see also F/6, F/8, J/8, J/9, J/10, L/7, M/18, M/19 and M/20)

This chest is of boarded construction, with the sides dovetailed into the front and back panels. There is a deeply excavated space for a lock plate and mechanism, but this is now missing. There are security batons at each end of the lid. The front board displays a high-relief carving of the *Annunciation* with the lily pot in the centre. The sides are pseudo-panelled in diaper-work.

F/8. Victoria and Albert Museum, London (Plate 130)
Cypress, cembra-pine or cedarwood, North Italian. c.1500
52.7cm x 74.3cm x 3.2cm (20¾in. x 2ft.5¼in.x 1¼in.)
(Acq. No. 470-1882)
(For V & A Museum, see also F/6, F/7, J/8, J/9, J/10, L/7, M/18, M/19 and M/20)
This is a component of one of a group of six North Italian cypress vestment and/or altar-chests, or fragments thereof, in England (see F/2, F/3, F/10, F/11 and F/12).
Like the fragment at Chilcombe (F/3), this is a detached lid, or 'reredos', from a 'Cypress' vestment and/or altar-chest. The four recesses underneath the front of the lid

PLATE 128. *Victoria and Albert Museum, London. Oak chest with Virgin and Child. Northern French, mid-16th century. (F/6)*

PLATE 129. *Victoria and Albert Museum, London. Oak chest with the* Annunciation. *Netherlandish/Northern French, c.1500. (F/7)*
COPYRIGHT VICTORIA AND ALBERT MUSEUM, PICTURE LIBRARY

PLATE 130. *Victoria and Albert Museum, London. Cypress chest panel. North Italian, early 16th century. (F/8)*
COPYRIGHT VICTORIA AND ALBERT MUSEUM, PICTURE LIBRARY

PLATE 131. *St Michael and All Angels, Middlewich, Cheshire. Oak chest. French, after 1500. (F/9)*

must have been for the original hinges. The underside surface is decorated with penwork drawing, typical for this class of object, combined with a recessing of the negative spaces between the main scenes, which are cross-hatched. This lid is up to two-thirds shorter than the others in the group, but the present size is authentic.

On the main panel, as usual, the *Crucifixion* is represented in the centre and in the corners are the four Evangelist symbols, as at Chilcombe, Swaffham Bulbeck, Norwich and Carlisle. In spite of the fact that this lid is so much narrower than the others in the group, it has many more ancillary scenes, in this case in a strip around the outside, predella-wise. There is the *Annunciation,* which also occurs at Norwich Cathedral, Chilcombe and Redenhall, as well as Chilcombe and Redenhall's kinked lectern stand (Plate 121). However, it is the only one to show the *Entombment* scene. This is followed by the *Resurrection,* which is also to be found at Norwich, Chilcombe and Swaffham Bulbeck. The London panel has other scenes not otherwise evident in this group, such as the *Pietà,* the *Procession to Calvary* and the *Visitation,* as well as the figures of St Katherine, two monks and a secular male. The *Scourging of Christ* scene in London parallels those at Carlisle, Norwich and Chilcombe. The ordering of the scenes does not seem to have any logic to it.

The five additional chest fragments, associated with it, do not conform to the shape of the lid. They display probably an Angel, a Friar, and musician Angels standing around a fountain. There is another small fragment decorated with scrolling foliage inhabited by dragons. It is generally difficult to compare the style here with that on the main panel, because of the secular/religious divergence in subject matter. But they may be fragments of an inner lid from another chest of about the same date.

F/9. St Michael, Middlewich, Cheshire (Plate 131)
Oak. French. After 1500
63.5cm x 151cm x 62cm (25in. x 4ft.11⅛in.x 24½in.)
(For Middlewich, see also M/22 and M/23)
A simple chest with four traceried panels across the front, and space for the lock piece, which is missing. It has been transformed into a cupboard by being placed on a stand. The front panel has been sawn down the middle, the hinges fitted each end. Inside there are mortises for a money box. An ecclesiastical purpose is indicated by the IHS monogram on the front left-hand panel.

The tracery is very similar to that particularly on the sides of the Crediton chest (F/4), the Ipswich chest (Plate 123) and the pulpit at the Musée Nationale du Moyen Âge, Paris (Plate 124).

PLATE 132. *Norwich Cathedral. Cypress chest. North Italian, early 16th century. Detail of* Crucifixion. *(F/10)*

F/10. Norwich Cathedral (Plates 132-135)
Cypress, cembra-pine, or cedarwood. North Italian. c.1500
70cm x 197cm x 62.5cm (2ft.3½in. x 6ft.5½in. x 24½in.)
This is one of a group of six North Italian cypress vestment and/or altar-chests, or fragments thereof, in England (see F/2, F/3, F/8, F/11 and F/12)
A flat-bottomed 'Cypress' altar-chest of boarded construction (Plate 135), with double lid (the inner undecorated one is modern). The planked sides are dovetailed together. A small key-hole has been placed at the top of the centre of the front panel, but there is no lock plate. The two key-holes on either side may be modern additions. There are three original hinge straps on the underside of the outer lid, with two later ones, screwed in insensitively, over the drawing. The ends of the chest are plain and accommodate probably later carrying handles. The outer lid is lipped at both ends for security, as at Swaffham Bulbeck and Redenhall. This chest, and the one at Swaffham Bulbeck, are the only two of the group to survive in an authentic state.

PLATE 133. *Norwich Cathedral, Norfolk. Cypress chest. North Italian, early 16th century. Detail of* Scourging of Christ. *(F/10)*

PLATE 134. *Norwich Cathedral, Norfolk. Cypress chest. North Italian, early 16th century. Detail of* Resurrection of Christ. *(F/10)*

PLATE 135. *Norwich Cathedral, Norfolk. Cypress chest. North Italian, early 16th century. View of front panel. (F/10)*

The decoration of the lid, or reredos, uses the penwork drawing technique typical of these chests, with recessed areas in the background. It depicts the *Crucifixion* in the centre (Plate 132), with the *Scourging of Christ* to the left (Plate 133), and the *Resurrection* to the right (Plate 134). At the four corners of the *Crucifixion* are the four Evangelist symbols, as they also appear at Chilcombe, Swaffham Bulbeck and, as they would originally have been positioned, at Carlisle. Above is a band containing the IHS symbol in the centre, with sketches of birds and angels each side, as well as the *Annunciation*, again as at Chilcombe. As at Carlisle and Chilcombe, to the left of the *Crucifixion* scene there is a standing friar, although this one is on *terra firma* and without a book (Plate 133).

The front panel (Plate 135) is elaborately carved in the manner of a woodcut block, like the fronts on the other cypress chests. The design is of overall scrolling foliage top and bottom, with strips of Renaissance 'candelabra' design at each end. In the centre of the panel are three medallions, the middle one with two figures in a landscape. Between the medallions are two more areas containing 'candelabra' designs with flanking figures. The 'positive' areas, which would have carried the imagery, are as usual now blank but were originally drawn over in penwork.

F/11. Assumption of the Blessed Virgin Mary, Redenhall, Norfolk (Plate 136)
Cypress, cembra-pine, or cedarwood, North Italian.
Early 16th century
62cm x 146cm x 52cm (24⅜in. x 4ft.9½in. x 20½in.)
Said to have been used to store vestments in the chapel of nearby Gawdy Hall (now demolished). Placed in the Gawdy Chapel in the north aisle at Redenhall church in 1922
This is one of a group of six North Italian cypress

PLATE 136. *St Mary, Redenhall, Norfolk. Cypress chest. North Italian, late 16th century. (F/11)*

vestment and/or altar chests, or fragments thereof, in England, although in this case the original function is ambiguous (See F/2, F/3, F/8, F/10 and F/12)

A flat-bottomed 'Cypress' chest of nailed box construction with lid, lipped at each end for security, with 17th century carrying handles. There must have been an internal lock in the first place. A small lock plate can be seen at the centre of the front panel at the top, which could be original. The hinge straps placed under the lid appear to be modern. The elaborate woodcut-style front panel consists of three large enthroned figures, and below them possibly the *Annunciation* on the left and two angels conversing on the right. From the top there are four tiers of putti amongst scrolling foliage.

Like the Carlisle example this chest appears to have been cut down at some time. Its width is some 52.5cm (20⅝in.) less than the full-size chests at Norwich Cathedral and Swaffham Bulbeck, and approximately the same as the Carlisle Cathedral chest. The front has suffered the same treatment. As at Carlisle the front and the side panels have had to be nailed together. Originally they would have been dovetailed, as on the completely authentic specimens at Norwich Cathedral and Swaffham Bulbeck.

Unusually, on the underside of the lid there is a mixture of painted and penwork images. At the top is a fleet of three-masted ships on the high seas and below is the *Annunciation* with the Sacred Monogram in the centre. The Virgin's lectern is kinked, as at Norwich and Chilcombe. Inside the chest itself, on the back panel, there are penwork drawings of dragons. Pevsner found this painting 'rustic', and suggested that it is probably later than the chest itself (BOE, *North-West and South Norfolk* 1999). Due to the later alterations, already mentioned, the paintings on both panels have been abbreviated. This fact is not so apparent on the lid as it is on the lower back panel. Possibly this is why Pevsner thought that the latter was later than the work on the underside of the lid. In fact the painting style is unmistakably the same in both cases as on the other chests in the group.

This chest may always have had a predominantly secular function. The cypress example at Berkeley Castle, Gloucestershire, which belonged to Sir Francis Drake, is also painted on the inside of the lid with ships. It is supposed to have furnished Drake's cabin. There, penwork drawing on the front panel is clearly discernible. Any sign of such treatment on the chest fronts in our group has been entirely effaced.

PLATE 137. *St Mary, Swaffham Bulbeck, Cambridgeshire. Cypress chest. North Italian, early 16th century. (F/12)*

F/12. St Mary, Swaffham Bulbeck, Cambridgeshire (Plates 137-141)
Cypress, cembra-pine or cedarwood, North Italian. Early 16th century
67cm x 197.5cm x 71cm (2ft.2½in. x 6ft.5¾in. x 2ft.4in.)
This is one of a group of six North Italian cypress vestment and/or altar-chests, or fragments thereof, in England (See F/2, F/3, F/8, F/10 and F/11)
A flat-bottomed 'Cypress' altar-chest of dovetailed boarded construction with carved front (Plate 137). The lid is original and has a security overlap at each end, as at Norwich and Redenhall. The two strap hinges at the sides are probably not original, but the central T-shaped one may be. The chest has been fitted with three locks, although the central one has been changed at some time. The two on the outside may be later additions. The lock plates are 17th century. This, and the chest at Norwich Cathedral (F/10) are the only two of the group to survive in an authentic state.

The altar frontal plank has a decorative border of inhabited scrolling foliage, in the woodcut-type technique invariably used in this position, with winged putti around the edges. On the left is what appears to be a king, sitting on a dais under a canopy with various attendants to the right. In the centre is a procession moving from the right. On the right there is a cart drawn by two horses moving to the left, with a standing figure in front and two more to the right (Plate 138). Between each of the main pictures is a seated figure, similar to those on the Carlisle chest. As

has been suggested in the latter case, this could be a depiction of the *Annunciation*.

On the inside of the lid, or reredos, in the centre is the *Crucifixion* (Plate 139), with the Evangelist symbols outside the corners, drawn in penwork. On the sides are roundels, one on the left with the *Assumption of the Virgin* (Pl. 140), and that on the right with the *Resurrection* (Plate

PLATE 138. *St Mary, Swaffham Bulbeck, Cambridgeshire. Cypress chest. North Italian, early 16th century. Detail of 'woodcut-type' decoration on chest front. Right end. (F/12)*

PLATE 139. *St Mary, Swaffham Bulbeck, Cambridgeshire. Cypress chest. North Italian, early 16th century. Detail of* Crucifixion. *(F/12)*

PLATE 140. *St Mary, Swaffham Bulbeck, Cambridgeshire. Cypress chest. North Italian, early 16th century. Detail of* Assumption of the Virgin. *(F/12)*

PLATE 141. *St Mary, Swaffham Bulbeck, Cambridgeshire. Cypress chest. North Italian, early 16th century. Detail of* Resurrection of Christ. *(F/12)*

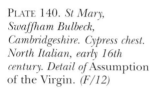

141). The rectangular space above the *Crucifixion* may originally have had decoration on it but is now blank. The image of the *Assumption of the Virgin* is unique in this group of English altar-chests.

The use of a metal punch is evident as usual on the crosshatched backgrounds to the scenes. On the underside of the chest lid there are the traces of original gesso, which must have been worked into these negative spaces. When newly finished, with the white or colour of the gesso setting off the raised and articulated shapes of the forms, the altarpiece images in particular must have appeared much more impressive than they are today.

G: *Cupboards*

G/1. Private Collection (Plate 142)
Oak carcase. Chestnut doors, Southern French. Mid-17th century
189cm x 126cm x 163cm (6ft.2½in. x 4ft.1in. x 5ft.4in.)
This cupboard has a panelled carcase in oak with moulded and decorated stiles and architrave (Plate 142). The double doors, which are made from chestnut wood, hang from the original metal hinges and incorporate their metal lock plates. The doors are subdivided into four panels. Those at the top display a cross, centrally, with a rayed paten superimposed, and candlesticks on either side. On the next level, beneath the top of a fleur-de-lis, is another cross in an oval with the sacred heart superimposed on to what may be also intended for a paten. The doors are decorated with birds and rosettes.

Although this may have been a vestry cupboard, it must be borne in mind that religious symbols were routinely applied to secular furniture in France at this time, including also the chalice and IHS symbol. They merely expressed the faith and devotion of their owners. In Brittany there is a suite of such furniture still *in situ* at the *Ferme Kervazégen*, Pont L'Abbaye, Finistère.

PLATE 142. *Private Collection. Vestry cupboard. Southern French, mid-17th century. (G/1)*

PLATE 143. *St John the Baptist, Oxenton, Gloucestershire. Fitted aumbry. Probably Flemish, early 16th century. (G/2)*

PLATE 144. *St Magnus, Upper Thames Street, City of London. Aumbry. Flemish, 17th century. (G/3)*

G/2. St John the Baptist, Oxenton, Gloucestershire (Plate 143)
Oak, Probably Flemish. Early 16th century
52cm x 42.5cm (20½in. x 16¾in.)
An aumbry, in the north-east corner of the chancel, is in the form of a vaulted receptacle, encased within a three-sided box and built into the north chancel wall. The tracery is missing in the left-hand spandrel. The outside framing is modern.

The hole in the wall appears to be a rare 13th century aumbry for altar books. The box which has been placed in it, however, is not likely to have carried out the same function. It seems to be part of the framing of a Flemish altarpiece, such as that which houses the central *Pietà* group in the Flemish retable from Omstreeks at St Walbürgeskerk, Netterden in the Netherlands (de Werd 1978). From the relatively small size of our 'aumbry' it is perhaps more probable that the box formed part of the structure of a larger multi-image altarpiece.

G/3. St Magnus, Upper Thames Street, City of London (Plate 144)
Oak. Flemish. 17th century
64.5cm x 44.5cm x 9.5cm (25⅛in. x 17½in. x 3¾in.)
The gift of the Rev. H.J. Fynes-Clinton (WWW, 1951-60)
Said to house a relic of the True Cross
A small aumbry with door in the centre, with lock, and drawer underneath. Architectural design, including a gabled roof with flat moulded top and segmental pediment of scrolled foliage. Figure of Christ displaying his wounds carved on the door, with female figures either side, attached to pilasters. The drawer front with more scrolling foliage. There is the sparing use of punched and incised decoration. The brackets underneath are modern.

H: *Prie-dieu*

PLATE 145. *St Mary, Elham, Kent. Prie-dieu. French, inscribed 1767. (H/1)*

H/1. St Mary, Elham, Kent (Plate 145)
Oak. French. Inscribed 1767
89cm x 118cm x 70cm (depth including integral kneeler)
(2ft.11in. x 3ft.10½in. x 2ft.3½in.)
(For Elham, see also I/3)
With wooden kneeler and sloped desk, on cabriole legs. The arms of Bourbon and Medici in the centre of the desk apron. The front legs of the desk are slightly sloped, whilst the back ones are upright.

The mid-18th century *prie-dieu* at St Rombouts Cathedral, Mechelen in Belgium makes a good comparison (Plate 146)

PLATE 146. *St Rombouts Cathedral, Mechelen. 18th century prie-dieu.*

PRIE-DIEU

PLATE 147. *Hever Castle, Kent. Prie-dieu. Italian, early 17th century.* *(H/2)*

H/2. Hever Castle, Kent (Plate 147)
Pine, Italian. Early 17th century
89cm x 60.5cm x 43cm (2ft.11in. x 2ft. x 17in.)
(For Hever Castle, see also A/2, E/4 and M/13)
A prie-dieu with lidded box at the top and cupboard with single shelf in the centre. The cupboard door has brass wire staples for hinges and the brass inverted heart-shaped handle is fixed in a similar way. At the base is a locker (inside not inspected). There are crude moulded legs, clearly fitted later, at the back and incongruous claw-feet at the front, to lift the piece off the ground. The same type of nail has been used to fix the front feet as the back. The former can also be recognised on the mouldings and on the close-boarded back. The front surfaces are decorated in relief with Mannerist-type low relief scrolling foliage and other Classical decoration.

H/3. All Saints, Tooting Graveney, London (Colour Plate 9; Plate 148)
Walnut, Italian. Early 17th century
87.5cm x 66.5cm x 63cm (2ft.10½in. x 2ft.2in. x 2ft.1in.)
(For Tooting, see also A/3, C/3, C/4, D/1, E/6, I/7 and M/17)
Front with panelled inlaid scrolling foliage pattern. Classical foliage swags each side with angel heads, and masks above. The plinth is modern.

PLATE 148. *All Saints, Tooting Graveney, London. Prie-dieu. Italian, early 16th century. (H/3)*

161

I: *Lecterns*

PLATE 149. *St Catherine, Birtles, Cheshire. Lectern. The eagle from the Namur region, 15th or 16th century. (I/1)*

I/1. St Catherine, Birtles, Cheshire (Plate 149)
Oak, and mahogany (stand). Namur region. The eagle 15th or 16th century
Height of stand 85cm (2ft.9½in.); height of eagle, including ball, 79cm (2ft.7in.); wing span 65cm (2ft.1⅛in.)
(For Birtles, see also M/4, and pages 72-73)

The eagle with its claws on a ball is much earlier than the stand, which is decorated with classical scrolling foliage around the base. The book-rest is modern.

The eagle seems to be imitating those in latten from Dinant. There must have been a flourishing export trade in these, as plenty survive in English parish churches. There is another very similar wooden example at St Cross, Winchester (I/11).

The chapel was built for family use by Thomas Hibbert in 1840. It is full of Continental woodwork, including a western screen made up from panels which were Netherlandish stall backs.

I/2. St Mary the Virgin, Buscot, Oxfordshire (Colour Plate 10; Plates 150 and 151)
Wood unknown. Spanish. 17th century
Height 162cm (5ft.3¾in.); width of reading desk 59cm (23¼in.); depth of reading desk 63cm (24¾in.)
(For Buscot, see also M/6)

A double reading desk is supported on a tripod, consisting of three scrolled feet and a baluster column above. Carved foliage to match that on the feet fill up the sides of the lectern (Plate 151). Apart from a certain amount of damage to the base, including much paint loss, the piece is in authentic condition. The lectern has a background covering of green, with gilding and silvering superficially on a red ground.

PLATE 150. *St Mary the Virgin, Buscot, Oxfordshire. Lectern. Spanish, 17th century.*

PLATE 151. *St Mary the Virgin, Buscot, Oxfordshire. Side view of lectern. Spanish 17th century.* (*I/2*)

Double reading desks were for the use of the choir in a great church. This desk must have come from an institution founded by Charles V (1500-1558), as it displays the arms of Castile and Laon quarterly against a double-headed eagle and imperial crown.

I/3. St Mary, Elham, Kent (Plate 152)
Gilt wood and brass. French. Late 17th century
130cm (4ft.3in.) high
(For Elham, see also H/1)
The traditional eagle motif on top is supported by a baluster column mounted on tripod legs (Plate 152). The base of the cut-out sheet-metal book-rest is probably original.

The bird is not stamping on a serpent, as it is at St Sulpice, Fougères, Brittany (Plate 153), and its pose is more conventional by comparison. The Elham monument is a more provincial work.

The lectern is said to have been bought in Calais for the church in 1914 (Williams 1959), during the incumbency of a vicar of French extraction, Alard Charles de Bourbel.

I/4. Great Dixter, Kent (Plate 154)
Oak. book-rest French. Stem French. Stand possibly Italian. 14th to 16th century
153cm (5ft.) high. book-rest 23cm x 51cm x 36cm (9in. x 20in. x 14in.)
The lectern has a double book-rest, the front face of which is decorated with a pierced cusped wheel, with triangular punched indentations around the circumference (Plate 154). At each end is an acute-arched opening. There are burn marks on top of the reading desk on both sides. The stem, which pierces to the top of the reading box, has a scale motif decoration at the top, below which are three graduated zones of moulding. There is evidence of a gesso preparation on the surface of the stem. The triangular base has carved lions on the extensions, which lift the rest of it off the ground. Behind

the lions' manes are shallow mortises about 2.5cm (1in.) wide, which cut right across the feet of the lectern base.

This is a piece of considerable antiquity, but it is not authentic. The three components probably came from as many different objects. The book-rest must be of the early 14th century and is probably French. The stem is of the early 16th century and again may well be French. The base is clearly reused and may be early 14th century Italian.

PLATE 152. *St Mary, Elham, Kent. Lectern. French, late 17th century.* (*I/3*)

163

PLATE 153. *St Sulpice, Fougères, Ile et Vilaine. Lectern.*

PLATE 154. *Great Dixter, Kent. Lectern. 14th to 16th century. (1/4)*

PLATE 155. *Christ's Church, Harwood, Lancashire. Lectern. Detail of eagle. Eagle probably Flemish,* c.*1700. (I/5)*

I/5. Christ's Church, Harwood, Lancashire (Plate 155)
Oak. Probably Flemish. *c.*1700
77cm (2ft.6in.) high; wing span 51cm (1ft.8in.)
(For Harwood, see also M/12)
The eagle stands on a large ball, which includes a blank cartouche displaying a bishop's mitre between two croziers (Plate 155). The fine stand (not shown) with inscription is Victorian.

The presence of the mitre above the blank coat of arms suggests that the lectern was made for a cathedral or abbey church. The piece is supposed to have been conveyed from the Pyrenees area of southern France.

The eagle is much more naturalistically depicted here than in the early Baroque period, when the conventional medieval treatment still more or less prevailed. Baroque asymmetry is much more uninhibitedly exploited here than at the perhaps slightly earlier lectern at St Sulpice, Fougères, Brittany (Plate 153). The eagle is not stamping on a serpent, which is common in Northern France.

Robert Lomax, a velveteen and fustian manufacturer from a local family of some standing, was instrumental in building the new church at Harwood in 1848 (See page 73 and Plate 33).

I/6. St Peter, Lew Trenchard, Devon (Plate 156)
Oak, French, from Brittany. 16th century
Height 178cm (5ft.10in.)
The eagle with wings unfurled stands on a ball, supported by a baluster column on a later tripod stand. The eagle has been repainted gold quite recently.

Stylistically this sculpture represents a modest development towards naturalism, by contrast to the well-established Flemish medieval tradition, as seen at Birtles (I/1). Instead of the fierce hieratic pose the eagle presents a tendency even to domestication. It seems that it might almost fly. By contrast the French example from the late 17th century, at St Jean, Lamballe, also in Brittany, displays an eagle in repose, and not so very different from that at Birtles (Plate 157).

PLATE 156. *St Peter, Lew Trenchard, Devon. Lectern. French (Brittany), 16th century. (I/6)*

PLATE 157. *St Jean, Lamballe, Côtes d'Armor. 17th century. Lectern.*
CLICHÉ ARCH.PHOT./CENTRE DES MONUMENTS NATIONAUX, PARIS

The lectern was acquired during the incumbency of the patron of the living, the Reverend Sabine Baring-Gould (1834-1924). He inherited the family estates at Lew Trenchard in 1872, on the death of his father, and presented himself to the Rectory of Lew Trenchard on the death of his uncle in 1881 (WWW 1916-28). Between 1880 and 1914 he collected items of furniture for his church from Belgium, Germany, Switzerland and France (See pages 85-86).

I/7. All Saints, Tooting Graveney, London (Colour Plate 11; Plate 158)
Oak. Italian. Late 17th century
168cm (5ft.6in.) high

(For Tooting, see also A/3, C/3, C/4, D/1, E/6 and M/17)
The double book-rest, which is decorated with cresting, sits on a baluster column, supported by a tripod stand on ball feet (Plate 158). A modern deeper book-rest has been placed on top of one of the original ones. A cartouche on the base, with crown above, carries a heraldic design including three stars. These arms are those of the Carmelites, the blazon being *chapé-ployé the point ending in a cross formy silver and azure with three stars countercoloured.*

Being double-sided this lectern must have been designed for use in a choir.

PLATE 158. *All Saints, Tooting Graveney, London. Lectern. Italian, late 17th century. (I/7)*

PLATE 159. *All Saints, Nuneham Courtenay, Oxfordshire. Lectern. Italian, early 18th century. (I/8)*

PLATE 160. *All Saints, Nuneham Courtenay, Oxfordshire. Lectern. Italian, early 18th century. Figure of St Peter as Pope on base. (I/8)*

I/8. All Saints, Nuneham Courtenay, Oxfordshire
(Colour Plate 12; Plates 159 and 160)
Walnut or chestnut. Italian. Early 18th century
Height to top of reading desk 200cm (6ft.6¾in.); width
of each side 64cm (2ft.1in.)
(For Nuneham Courtenay, see also J/11)

The lectern is rectangular in plan, with a double reading desk perched on a baluster. It is difficult to tell the kind of wood employed, partly because the whole has been rather crudely overpainted. However, where the paint has fallen off, the red colour of the natural wood can be seen. The base can be used as a cupboard and one of the sides is fitted with a door. Inside, at the top, the dowel for the superstructure protrudes. This has recently been strengthened. There is a key hole but no lock any more. The original brass handle and lock piece survives.

At each end of the book-rest there is conventionalised symmetrical foliage. There is a pair of leather straps for holding the books open, complete with baluster-shaped brass weights. Only one of the weights is still attached to a strap; the other is stored in the cupboard below.

On the corners of the base are swags of grapes, acorns and vegetables. On the three sides of the base are standing figures in low relief within decorative frames. On the cupboard door there is the figure of St Peter as Pope (Plate 160), a mitred bishop or abbot with staff, wearing a cope, and a monk with staff. It seems unlikely that the lectern was originally painted.

Such double-sided lecterns were designed for use in the choir of a great church. The cupboard was where the antiphonary would have been kept. This contained the verses of the Psalms, which were to be intoned or sung in turn by alternating choirs during Divine Office.

The neo-classical church, a successor to the former parish church, was designed, built, and no doubt furnished, in 1764 by Simon, 1st Earl Harcourt.

PLATE 161. *St John the Evangelist, Sidcup, Kent. Lectern. Netherlandish, dated 1776. (I/9)*

I/9. St John the Evangelist, Sidcup, Greater London (Plates 161 and 162)
Oak and brass. Netherlandish. Reading desk dated 1776. Column possibly early 18th century and tripod feet probably 19th century
Height to base of book-rest 124cm (4ft.1in.)
(For Sidcup, see also K/13)
This is a made-up piece. The sheet-metal brass double-sided reading desk incorporates inscriptions, although much of them has been worn away by over-enthusiastic brass polishers (Plate 162). Happily, however, the full text was recorded in the early 19th century (Anon, 1844), as follows:

On one side

> *Cura zeloque reverendi patris Antonii Prioris erectum, concentibus exultandum ferventius,*

> *Decorantes excelsum vocibus excolendum.*

On the other side

> *Exacto fervore Pulpitum decorate. Cuncti, exultemus Deo. Exaltamus pectore et laudibus excellamus.*

Richard Palmer has kindly translated this as follows:

> Erected by the care and zeal of the reverend father Prior Anthony, for more fervent rejoicing in harmony, praising and honouring the Most High with voices.

> Adorn the lectern with the required fervour. Let us all rejoice in God, exalting Him in our hearts and extolling him with praise.

Around a star in the centre, the only inscription which is legible reads:

> *Orietur stella ex Jacob N.N.M. 34.*

Palmer has pointed out that 'N.N.M. 34' seems to be a mis-transcription for 'NUM 24', and refers to Numbers chapter 24, verse 17, 'There shall come forth a star out of Jacob'. This is taken to be a prophesy of the Messiah.

The dating inscription reads – *Pid. Largille, me construxit, Anno. Dom. 1776.* The transcriber noted that the style of the main inscriptions 'have an appearance so grotesque, that one is surprised at the comparatively recent date of the dating inscription'.

The lectern was described as having been surmounted by an 'Imperial eagle', presumably in brass. It was suggested that (Anon 1844) it 'probably belonged to one of the suppressed convents in the Austrian Netherlands', and that it had probably been a gift from the prior to the choir. Flanders was under the rule of the Austrian Empire from 1713.

The continental furniture at Sidcup was assembled for the first church on the site, consecrated in 1844. Since then the building has been completely reconstructed in two phases, 1882 and 1899.

PLATE 162. *St John the Evangelist, Sidcup, Kent. Lectern. Netherlandish, dated 1776. Brass book stand. (I/9)*

PLATE 164. *St Andrew, Wickhambreaux, Kent. Lectern. Italian (Lombardic), late 18th century. Detail of swinging putto. (I/10)*

PLATE 163. *St Andrew, Wickhambreaux, Kent. Lectern. Italian (Lombardic), late 18th century. (I/10)*

PLATE 165. *St Gertrude, Leuven. X-frame lectern. 1490-1510.*
COPYRIGHT IRPA-KIK, BRUSSELS

PLATE 166. *Wooden bracket of putto playing on a swing, in the style of Andrea Fantoni. Italian (Lombardic), 18th century. (Private Collection)*
COPYRIGHT SOTHEBY'S, LONDON

I/10. St Andrew, Wickhambreaux, Kent (Plates 163 and 164) Gilt and gessoed wood. Italian, Lombardic. Mid-18th century

169cm (5ft.6½in.) high

X-framed construction, with a cupid as if swinging through the foliage of the lower section. The top of the reading desk luxuriates with foliage. In the centre is another cupid holding a shield.

This object is evidently rare. There is a much earlier example in gilded wood of late 16th century date at the Villa La Pietra, Florence (*Gonzalez-Palacius*, 1969, pl.18). A late medieval folding-type lectern exists in Belgium, dating from 1490-1510, at St Gertrude, Louvain (Plate 165).

The Wickhambreaux lectern is quite close to the work of Andrea Fantoni from Lombardy, and particularly his sons Graziosa the Younger and Francesco Donato, who continued his style of decorative wood carving during the 18th century (Bossaglia 1978, pls. 32-34, 182 and 214-15; Mallé 1965, pls. 284-85). A carving of a boy on a swing in the form of a bracket in a private collection is particularly close to the putto at the base of the lectern (Plate 166).

PLATE 167. *St Cross, Winchester. Lectern. Namur region, 15th or 16th century. Detail of eagle. (I/11)*

I/11. St Cross, Winchester (Plate 167)
Oak. Namur region. The eagle 15th or 16th century
Height of ancient part (eagle), 46cm (18in.); wing span 69cm (2ft.3in.)
The eagle with its claws on a ball is much earlier than the neo-Gothic stand (not shown), which must have been designed for J.L. Pearson, who worked at the church at the end of the 19th century.

This appears to be a type of lectern eagle which imitates the latten ones from Dinant. There must have been a flourishing export trade in these, as they are quite common in English parish churches. There is another wooden eagle of the same date and provenance at Birtles, Cheshire (I/1 and Plate 149).

I/12. St Peter, Wolferton, Norfolk (Plate 168)
Painted wood. Italian. Third quarter 17th century
185cm (6ft.1in.) high
With double reading desk, classical vase, column and tripod feet. There are female terms above the scrolls of the feet. The ends of the book-rest are decorated with masks. Unfortunately the piece has recently been re-decorated with modern paints in black and gold.

PLATE 168. *St Peter, Wolferton, Norfolk. Lectern. Italian, third quarter 17th century. (I/12)*

J: *Miscellaneous*

J/1. The Bowes Museum, Barnard Castle, County Durham (Plate 169)
Kingwood. French. 18th century
30cm x 14cm (12in. x 5⅓in.)
(For Bowes Museum, see also F/1 and M/2)
A small water stoup, framed by a bulrush cartouche. It is cup shaped with bay leaves around the bowl. Above is the Cross, hanging from which is the Crown of Thorns.

This seems to be a domestic stoup. It is unusual in being in wood, as most of them were in ceramic or metal (Chaperon, 1985).

PLATE 170. *Capesthorne Hall, Cheshire. Chapel. Seraphim with symmetrically folded wings. Flemish, late 17th century. (J/2)*

J/2. Chapel, Capesthorne Hall, Cheshire (Plate 170)
Oak. Flemish. Late 17th century
193cm (6ft.4in.) high, including base
(For Capesthorne Hall, see also J/3 and K/3)
Four figures of angels with wings folded, hanging at the west end of the family pew (Plate 170). They are composed as term figures on pedestals, decorated with foliage and fruit swags.

From the late 19th century photograph of the interior of the chapel at Capesthorne, it seems that these figures were originally placed in the eastern apse (Plate 2).

They are typically found on wall panelling, confessionals and pulpits in late 17th century and 18th century Flemish churches. Other sets of figures were imported into Britain, as there are pairs of angels, used as the uprights of a mantelpiece, at Welburn Hall, North Riding, Yorkshire, at Dyffryn House, Glamorgan, Wales (Plate 171) and another pair used in the same way at Oteley Park, Shropshire.

PLATE 169. *The Bowes Museum, Barnard Castle, County Durham. Water stoup. French, 18th century. (J/1)*

172

PLATE 171. *Dyffryn House, Glamorgan. Fireplace with Flemish Seraphim.*

J/3. Chapel, Capesthorne Hall, Cheshire (Plate 172)
Oak. Flemish. Late 17th century
Both 132cm (4ft.4in.) high, including base
(For Capesthorne Hall, see also J/2 and K/3)

Two figures of angels in the corners of the family pew. They have thick stylised hair with 'torn' garments clinging to their legs (Plate 172).

The sculptural quality is very high and in general one is reminded of the work of Artus Quellinus, the Older (1640-1660), and the wooden fittings at St Paul and St James, Antwerp. In particular at St James (Plate 173) the seraphim at the corners of the confessionals share the same heavy viscous treatment of the lower garment found at Capesthorne. The door of the 'Wedding Chapel' at St James, Antwerp, of 1667, by Quellin the Younger, provides other close parallels.

J/4. St Mary, Charborough, Dorset (Plates 18, 174 and pages 51-52)
Oak. Netherlandish. 17th century
43cm x 22cm (maximum)

A pair of corbels of two cherub heads. The plinths are later.

PLATE 172. *Chapel, Capesthorne Hall, Cheshire. Angel with single wing. Flemish, late 17th century.* (*J/3*)

PLATE 173. *St James, Antwerp. Late 17th century. confessional.*

PLATE 174. *St Mary, Charborough, Dorset. Corbel with two cherub heads, the lower one singing. Netherlandish, 17th century. (J/4)*

PLATE 175. *St John the Baptist, Cockayne Hatley, Bedfordshire. Pair of folding doors at west end. Flemish, early 18th century. (J/5)*

J/5. St John the Baptist, Cockayne Hatley, Bedfordshire (Plates 175 and 176)

Oak, Flemish. Early 18th century
264cm (floor to cornice) x 241cm (both doors) (8ft.8in. x 7ft.11in.)
Said to have come from Leuven (Cust 1851)
(For Cockayne Hatley, see also B/3, B/4, B/5, K/4 and M/9)

A pair of folding doors (Plate 175). The upper portion, with scrolling foliage, was originally pierced, but has been covered over from behind with a pine board (Plate 176). The space left by the inverted profile of the top of the doors is filled with integral Baroque screenwork. The beam above and the pelmet must be modern. The screenwork on either side of the doors has been curtailed to fit into the existing space. On the inside it is very plain, there being only one small piece of carving each side. On the inside of the doors in the lower zone there are two scars where roundels, complementary to those on the front, must have been positioned. The door handle is missing on both sides, and possibly a lock also.

The doors were probably acquired by Henry Cockayne Cust in 1828, and may refer to the item in his accounts for the week commencing 3 March – *Bill for Wood & Work etc. Hatley Church £74-0-0.* This entry is associated with a reference to the 'gateway' at about this time. Henry's son Robert tells us, in his account of his father's restoration of the church, that the doors came from Louvain (Cust 1851), but, although they are clearly Netherlandish, the provenance adduced may be unreliable.

PLATE 176. *St John the Baptist, Cockayne Hatley, Bedfordshire. Folding doors at west end. Flemish, early 18th century. Formerly pierced panel. Detail. (J/5)*

J/6 St George, Fordington, Dorchester, Dorset (Plate 177)
Oak. Flemish. Mid-18th century
Doors 273cm x 94cm (8ft.11½in. x 3ft.1in.). Height to top of cornice 340cm (11ft.2in.)

The door panels have exuberant curvilinear mouldings at top and bottom, with Rococo scrollwork in the centre (Plate 177). On either side are fluted pilasters with acanthus bracket-type capitals. The door handles are probably original, but a modern lock has been inserted. The doors, which are positioned underneath the tower on the east side, are said to have been reset there in 1935.

These doors used to be at Parnham House, Dorset before the contents were scattered in 1910 (Plate 38 and page 81).

A general stylistic comparison would be with the double doors at the west end of the south nave aisle at Our Lady's Church, Aarschott (Plate 178).

PLATE 177. *St George, Fordington, Dorset. Folding double doors at west end. Flemish, mid-18th century. (J/6).*

PLATE 178. *Our Lady's Church, Aarschott. 18th century folding doors.*

PLATE 179. *The London Oratory. Figure of an angel on confessional. Flemish, late 17th century.* (J/7)

J/7. The London Oratory (Plate 179)
Oak. Flemish. Late 17th century
Both figures 131cm (4ft.3½in.) high, including base
Two figures of angels on the westernmost of the two confessionals in the south nave aisle. The confessional itself has been made up from ancient and modern material.

The figures were carved originally from one piece of wood, but cracks have since developed. The wings were originally attached from the back with wooden pegs. The right-hand figure holds a large key ring with two large keys attached, whilst the other grasps a slate-board and sponge.

177

J/8. The Victoria and Albert Museum, London (Plate 180)
Oak, Northern French. *c.*1500
165cm x 152cm (5ft.3in. x 5ft.)
Museum Acq. No. 600-1895 (Ex Peyre Collection).
(For V & A Museum, see also F/6, F/7, F/8, J/9, J/10, L/7, M/18, M/19 and M/20)

A cross from a rood screen, with Evangelist symbols in quatrefoils at each of the four corners (Plate 180). There is an iron hook for the Crucifix at the base of the central boss. The Cross was originally decorated along the edges of the shafts with leaf crockets. These are now much damaged, and there are many missing. There are traces of gesso to indicate that the cross was originally polychromed.

A roughly contemporary wooden rood cross survives in France, at Marpent, Brittany. Of interest in this connection is the Crucifix at the Victoria and Albert Museum, London from the Brabant/Hainault region of the Low Countries, dated to *c.*1480 (Plate 181 and Williamson 2002).

PLATE 180. *The Victoria and Albert Museum, London. French rood cross. Northern French, c.1480 (J/8)*
COPYRIGHT VICTORIA AND ALBERT MUSEUM, PICTURE LIBRARY

PLATE 181. *The Victoria and Albert Museum, London. Flemish wooden cross with Crucifix and figure of St Mary and St John (714-1895). c.1480.*
COPYRIGHT VICTORIA AND ALBERT MUSEUM, PICTURE LIBRARY

PLATE 182. *The Victoria and Albert Museum, London. Font cover. French, first half 16th century. (J/9)*

J/9. The Victoria and Albert Museum, London (Plates 182-184)
Oak. French. First half 16th century
47.4cm x 103.5cm (18½in. x 3ft.6¾in.)
Museum Acq. No. 723-1895.
(For V & A Museum, see also F/6, F/7, F/8, J/8, J/10, L/7, M/18, M/19 and M/20)

This dome-shaped font cover is divided into eight compartments by heavy ribs which radiate from the top to the octagonal base (Plate 182). The triangular compartments contain the following scenes:

1. St Katherine of Siena. She holds a heart in her left hand and prays to a Crucifix in an image that is reminiscent of those of St Francis of Assisi. Like him St Katherine received the pain of the *stigmata* although not the physical injury (Plate 183).
2. *The angel troubling the water of the Pool of Bethesda* (John v.4) (Plate 183a).
3. *Christ and the woman of Samaria* (John iv.7) (Plate 184).

PLATE 183. *The Victoria and Albert Museum, London. Font cover. French, first half 16th century. St Katherine of Siena panel. (J/9)*

179

4. *Christ and Nicodemus* (John iii.2).
5. *St Philip Baptising the Eunuch* (Acts viii.27).
6. Man in 'kilt' and cloak.
7. *Christ asking the Chief Priests and Scribes concerning the Baptism of John* (Matthew xxi.25).
8. Man holding a scroll.

The knop is in two tiers, the lower of which is quatrefoil in plan, and carved with two lions' masks and two cherubs' heads. The upper tier is much smaller and octagonal in shape.

The decorative carving is still typical of the northern Renaissance of around 1530.

J/10. The Victoria and Albert Museum, London (Plates 185 and 185a)
Limewood, gilded. German. Late 15th century
Measurements 61cm x 89cm x 44.5cm (2ft. x 2ft.11in. x 17½in.)
Museum Acq. No. 357-1854.
Said to have come from the Franciscan church in Constance, the monastery attached to which was dissolved in 1808. Entered two private collections and was sold in London in 1854
(For V & A Museum, see also F/6, F/7, F/8, J/8, J/9, L/7, M/18, M/19 and M/20)

This is a substantial chest-reliquary in the shape of a house shrine, with removable triangular lid set on a chest, which sits on diagonally placed square feet with buttresses above set at the corners. The buttresses contain niches for the figures of saints on plinths, the finials of which are missing. The moulding at the apex of the lid has five holes in it for the pegs to hold the original cresting. Only the pupils, lips and eyelids of the sculpted figures are painted black. There are some traces of red colouring under the gilding. The body of the chest has been carved in the solid on all four sides, the eight different scenes being divided into discrete panels by the application of moulded frames. The moulding divisions are of a simpler profile on the lid, but three of these are missing. On the triangular 'roof' are eight more scenes arranged in the same way. The head of St Stephen, the hands of the figure of an angel, both placed at the corners, are missing. The crockets of the triangular gables at each end are damaged.

The Passion story is related in two circuits of the shrine, starting at the lower level, as follows (Plate 185a):

PLATE 183A. *The Victoria and Albert Museum, London. Font cover. French, first half 16th century.* Angel troubling the water of the Pool of Bethesda *panel. (J/9)*

PLATE 184. *The Victoria and Albert Museum, London. Font cover. French, first half 16th century.* Christ and the Woman of Samaria *panel. (J/9)*

PLATE 185. *The Victoria and Albert Museum, London. South German chest-reliquary. Late 15th century. (Side B.) (J/10)*

PLATE 185A. *Victoria and Albert Museum, London. South German chest reliquary. Late 15th century. Subject sequence. Sides A and B. (J/10)*

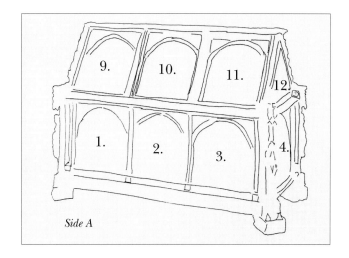

Side A

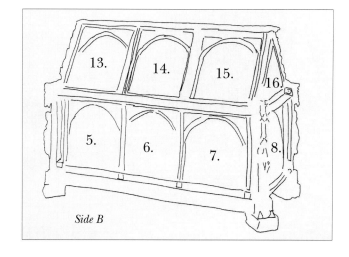

Side B

1. Long side A. Lower left. *Christ's Entry into Jerusalem.*
2. Long side A. Lower centre. *The Last Supper.*
3. Long side A. Lower right. *The Agony in the Garden.*
4. Short side A. Lower part. *Arrest of Christ.*
5. Long side B. Lower left. *Christ before Annas.*
6. Long side B. Lower centre. *The Flagellation.*
7. Long side B. Lower right. *The Crowning with Thorns.*
8. Short side B. Lower part. *Christ carrying the Cross and the encounter with St Veronica.*
9. Long side A. Upper left. *Christ in Distress.*
10. Long side A. Upper centre. *Crucifixion.*
11. Long side A. Upper right. *The Entombment.*
12. Short side A. Upper part. *Harrowing of Hell.*
13. Long side B. Upper left. *Resurrection.*
14. Long side B. Upper centre. *Incredulity of St Thomas.*
15. Long side B. Upper right. *Ascension.*
16. Short side B. Upper part. *The Trinity.*

In the spandrels above the scenes are beasts, mostly crouching dogs, but there is also a monkey, an ibex and a lion. The spandrels of scenes 9, 10 and 11 are decorated with foliate scrolls, while those of scenes 13, 14 and 15 show the *Two Marys,* two prophets and two angels respectively. The figures under the canopies at the corners are an angel, a prophet, St Stephen and St Catherine.

The shrine's late 15th century origins have long been recognised. The passion scenes are close in composition to the engravings of Martin Schongauer (*c.*1430-91). (For scenes 9-13, see Bartsch 1980, 8, p.222-226, nos 9-13; for scenes 10-13, see *ibid.*, pp. 229-233, nos 16-20). As Jopek has pointed out: 'The stylistic features ...reflect carvings in Constance, for instance the *Scenes of the Life of Christ* on the door-wings of the main portal, dated 1470, and the figurative reliefs of the choir-stalls of the Minster in Constance of about 1466-71, probably executed by the workshop of Heinrich Iselin, who was active in Constance from about 1466-1513' (Jopek 2002). Most of Schongauer's engravings were produced between 1470-90, so this gives us a reasonable dating bracket for the shrine.

This house-shaped shrine in gilded wood imitates the more valuable mainly German silver-gilt reliquaries in this format, most of which were melted down at the Reformation. Jopek points to examples of these now rare objects, such as the one in Überlingen, and two in the treasury in Reichenau-Mittelzell, all three of which were made in Constance about 1470-80. However, he stresses that there is no reason why some of the wooden versions should not have graced the treasury of a cathedral. Moreover, if positioned on a 'high shrine', a founder's relics were displayed behind the high altar (Crook 2000). In this context this late medieval reliquary would have been intended to be seen as the pilgrims circulated around it, when the Passion scenes could have been read in sequence.

PLATE 186. *All Saints, Nuneham Courtenay, Oxfordshire. Font cover. Italian, 17th century. (J/11)*

J/11. All Saints, Nuneham Courtenay, Oxfordshire
(Colour Plate 13; Plate 186)
Unknown wood. Italian. 17th century
Bottom section 62cm (24½in.) high; top section 155cm (5ft.1in.) high
(For Nuneham Courtenay, see also I/8)
The font cover is hexagonal in plan, and in two stages. The lower part is a series of panels decorated with cartouches, separated from each other by prominent scrolled brackets. The centre panel is a door, which has been repainted on the inside with blue and gold stars. On the outside is painted the IHS symbol on a sun motif. The top section has matching brackets of strapwork scrolls at the joins of the panels. The decoration of the panels alternates between scrolling foliage and fruit swags below a human mask. The field for this decoration is inscribed imbrication. The monument is painted and gilded. Some green paint has been added later. At the top is the figure of St John the Baptist.

The Neo-Classical chapel, a successor to the former parish church, was designed, built, and no doubt furnished, in 1764 by Simon, 1st Earl Harcourt.

J/12. St Mary College, New Oscott, Sutton Coldfield, Warwickshire (Colour Plate 14; Plates 187 and 189) Gilded wood. Probably French. Late 15th century Height 180cm (5ft.11in.) (For Oscott, see also B/13, J/13, J/14 and M/31)

This was described as a 'reliquary coffer' in the catalogue of works of art from the college, dated 1880 (Plate 187). It is certainly a very elaborate container, or open tabernacle, which could have been placed on the high altar to protect the reserved Host and the vessels used in the sacrament of Holy Communion. There is a large circular opening at the centre of the top of the main compartment, and a small one in the same place in the section above. It is therefore possible that there may have been a hook below the apex of the spire, from which was suspended a cord to which the Host was ultimately attached.

In the Netherlands and the German-speaking world these objects are known as sacrament houses. It could also have been a reliquary to contain the bones and other relics of a saint. It is six-sided and consists of three graduated sections, filled with Flamboyant tracery. The top part is a spire surmounted by the figure of St Peter. Relatively recently it has been decorated with gold paint.

In 1899 this very unusual object was described as follows: 'The Reliquary Coffer in the form of an hexagonal tower and spire, carved in wood and gilded, with flamboyant tracery, cusps and finials in French of the XVI c. There is a fellow to it in the Musée Cluni, in Paris. It is identical in size and shape and gilding with ours; but instead of St Peter it has on the summit, an image of the Blessed Virgin' (Greaney 1899).

The important medieval wooden tabernacle in Paris (Plate 188) is somewhat earlier in date than the one at Oscott. However, it is not clear whether this is the object to which Greaney referred, as it is not gilded. It is not identical in shape, being in three tiers rather than two. It also is about half as high again as the Oscott piece. It does not have a figure of the Virgin on the top but a foliate pinnacle. Perhaps Greaney was referring to another tabernacle at the museum.

At Oscott there is access to the lower section through a hinged door in the main compartment (Plate 189). Also at the Musée Nationale du Moyen Âge two of the tracery panels of the bottom section are left open for ready access. The rather absurd feet at Oscott hardly look Gothic and seem to have been applied, rather than carved in the solid, which is what one would expect.

There is a French tabernacle which is coeval with the one at Oscott at Crouy en Thelle, Oise, with a cross on top. Later, very elaborate specimens can be seen in the Aube region, at Bouilly, near Troyes, of the early 16th

PLATE 187. *St Mary's College, New Oscott, Sutton Coldfield, Warwickshire. Reliquary coffer. Probably French, late 15th century. (J/12)*

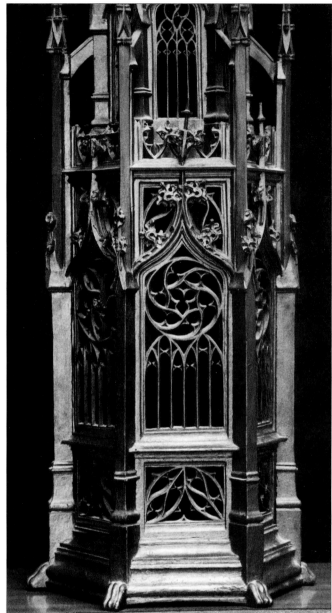

Plate 189. *St Mary's College, New Oscott, Sutton Coldfield, Warwickshire. Reliquary coffer. Probably French, late 15th century. Detail of lower section. (J/12)*

Plate 188. *Musée national du Moyen Âge, Paris. Reliquary coffer. First half 15th century.*

PLATE 190. *St Gertrude, Leuven. Fragment of a late-medieval tabernacle. Early 16th century.*

J/13. St Mary's College, New Oscott, Sutton Coldfield, Warwickshire (Colour Plate 15; Plates 191 and 192)
Painted and gilded oak. Probably French. Early 18th century
80cm x 87cm x 46cm (2ft.7½in. x 2ft.10¼in. x 18in.)
(For Oscott, see B/13, J/12, J/14 and M/31)

The presence of the chalice and censing angels on the sides of this imposing box (Plate 191) suggests that it was probably a closed tabernacle, for the containment of the Host, and the vessels used in the sacrament of Holy Communion, rather than a reliquary. It is probable that originally there would have been some sort of crowning feature above. The tabernacle would have been placed on the high altar at the base of the reredos.

The structure is half-hexagonal in plan. The door in the front displays a chalice with grapes and ears of corn above, and the Cross in the centre with light rays radiating from it (Plate 192). There are traces of red paint behind

PLATE 191. *St Mary's College, New Oscott, Sutton Coldfield, Warwickshire. Closed tabernacle. Probably French, early 18th century. View from side. (J/13)*

century, and the abbey of Menthier-la-Celle, St André-les-Troyes. Other late Gothic examples can be seen at St Maure, Auch, and St. Lô, Foucarville in Normandy (*L'Art du Moyen Âge* 1998).

Part of an early 16th century Flemish tabernacle can be seen at St Gertrude, Leuven (Plate 190). This has no door mechanism, but could perhaps have been raised on a pulley.

PLATE 192. *St Mary's College, New Oscott, Sutton Coldfield, Warwickshire. Closed tabernacle. Probably French, 18th century. View from front. (J/13)*

the figures and chalice. The columns at the corners are gilded against a background of brown paint.

Tabernacles of this period are common throughout France and in other Catholic regions.

J/14. St Mary's College, New Oscott, Sutton Coldfield, Warwickshire (Plate 193)
Probably mahogany. Probably French. 17th century
46cm x 33cm (18in. x 13in.)
Stolen 2000
(For Oscott, see also B/13, J/12, J/13 and M/31)
A water stoup with the figure of *God the Father* in the centre, his right hand raised in blessing, and in his left hand an orb (Plate 193). Above his head is a garland of flowers and acanthus ornament. He is surrounded by angels, and one at the bottom holds up the stoup with his hands raised. This subject is not included in Chaperon's typology (Chaperon 1985).

J/15. St Mary, Wisbech St Mary, Cambridgeshire (Plate 194)
Mahogany. Origin unknown. Late 18th century
30cm x 23cm x 14cm (12in. x 9in. x 5½in.)
A water stoup of simple Neo-Classical design, with fluted

PLATE 193. *St Mary's College, New Oscott, Sutton Coldfield, Warwickshire. Water stoup. Probably French, 17th century. (J/14)*

PLATE 194. *St Mary, Wisbech St Mary, Cambridgeshire. Water stoup. Late 18th century. (J/15)*

and gadrooned body. Until recently it has been used as a money box, the hinged lid being later.

186

PLATE 195. *Wroxton Abbey, Oxfordshire. Chapel door. Probably Flemish, third quarter 17th century. (J/16)*

PLATE 196. *Carmelite Church, Bruges. One of a pair of doors flanking the high altar. 1691-1700.* COPYRIGHT IRPA- KIK, BRUSSELS

J/16. Wroxton Abbey, Oxfordshire (Plate 195)
Oak. Probably Flemish. The main door, third quarter
17th century
204cm x 922cm (6ft.81/4in. x 30ft.3in.)
The outer face of the chapel door, an elaborately carved and panelled composition, has been attached to a much older one (Plate 195). Judging from the wrought-iron door handle this is of the mid-14th century. It has been re-built to fit this space, and there are portions of new wood around the outside. In the centre of the upper part is a cartouche containing a representation of the *Flight into Egypt*. The pediment seems to be from a different door, and has probably been modified to fit. On the lower part is a date of 1618.

A possible use for this door might have been as one of a pair on either side of an altar, like the doors which flank the altar of St Ignatius at St Walburga, Bruges. Another example, which gives us a general comparison of this type of door is the pair flanking the high altar at the Carmelite Church, also at Bruges (Plate 196). These are later than the Wroxton door, and date from 1691-1700.

The Continental furnishings in the chapel at Wroxton Abbey (see Gazetteer) were introduced by Col. John and Lady North in the middle of the 19th century. It has been suggested that the date may have been put on the door on their orders, along with several other such inscriptions around the house (Cornforth 1981).

K: *Pulpits*

K/1. St Chad's Cathedral, Birmingham (Plate 197)
Oak. Probably from the abbey of St Gertrude, Leuven,
whose furnishings were sold in 1798. Before *c*.1520
114cm (3ft.9in.) high, from top to base; panels 82cm
(2ft.8¼in.) high, 43cm (17in.) wide
No back board or sounding board.
Originally intended for New Oscott, a gift of the 16th
Earl of Shrewsbury
(For St Chad's, Birmingham, see also M/3)

With a hexagonal body comprising elaborately-carved
concave panels flanked by columns (Plate 197). It sits on
a plain moulded and panelled pendent vault. The
existing entrance stairs and door were supplied by Pugin.
They probably do not penetrate on the side of the
original entrance, which may have been on the side now
attached to the stone nave arcade pier. The modern
entrance was probably originally another decorated

panel, judging from the portion of plinth decoration still
in situ. If the pendent vault is original, it is not clear how
the pulpit can have been supported, unless it fitted into a
stand, as at Abcoude (Plate 208).

The four remaining figurative panels are supposed to
represent the four Latin doctors of the church – Jerome,
Gregory, Ambrose and Augustine. They sit on
recognisable thrones or chairs under elaborate three-
dimensional canopies.

The style is clearly transitional between Gothic and
Renaissance. The Renaissance did not come to Leuven
until about 1520, as the epitaphs in the cathedral and at
St Peter's Church evince (*Ars Sacra* 1962). Whilst con-

PLATE 197. *St Chad's Cathedral, Birmingham. Pulpit. Probably from St Gertrude, Leuven, before* c.*1520. Detail. (K/1)*

PLATE 198. *Our Lady's Church, Nieuwpoort, Flanders. Pulpit. Early 16th century.*

forming to the new style, however, the Brabantine workshop which made the St Chad's pulpit was looking back to late Gothic tradition exemplified at the church of Our Lady at Nieuwpoort (Plate 198), and the church of St Géry, at Roucourt, Peruwelz, near Tournai (Plate 199). The columns at the intersections of the sides are reminiscent of the prints of Heinrich Vogthern I (1490-1556), the German painter, sculptor and engraver (Jervis 1974, pls. 42 and 43), although it seems improbable that our carver could have seen any Vogthern engravings before c.1520. There is no stylistic connection with the choir-stalls at St Gertrude, which were made a whole generation later (1540-54).

The frontispiece of *The History of St Chad's, 1841-1904,* published in 1904, shows the pulpit standing on the south side of the rood screen, against the south-west pier of the crossing. It also is provided with a Puginian sounding board. It has clearly been moved since to its present position on the north side, and the 19th century sounding board has gone.

PLATE 200. *St Michael and All Angels, Brownsover, Warwickshire. Pulpit. Flemish, 18th century. (K/2)*

K/2. St Michael and All Angels, Brownsover,
Warwickshire (Plate 200)
Oak. Flemish. 18th century
168cm (5ft.6in.) high; Panels 48cm (19in.) wide
Given by the local landowner, Allesley Boughton-Leigh,
at the end of the 19th century

There are four panels on the body. Two are decorated with motifs, one with a chalice, seal and book, the other with chalice, censer, bell and quill. A third is plain, but the fourth, in the centre, has a male head and shoulders within a cartouche. The carving on the string-course of the base seems to match that on the body of the pulpit, yet the proportions seem very modest in comparison with the base.

Unusually the sounding-board has survived (out of picture). It is 18th century in character. A pelmet with swags, and boards arranged underneath in rays.

The medieval church was rebuilt for Allesley Boughton-Leigh by George Gilbert Scott in 1877. The former was a skilled amateur wood carver. He apparently re-assembled the pulpit and was also responsible for installing the large amount of decorative woodwork in the church, including the choir screen.

PLATE 199. *St Géry, Roucourt, Peruwelz, Tournai. Pulpit. Early 16th century.* COPYRIGHT IRPA-KIK, BRUSSELS

PLATE 201. *Chapel, Capesthorne Hall, Cheshire. Body of pulpit. Flemish, early 16th century.and late 17th century. (K/3)*

PLATE 202. *Chapel, Capesthorne Hall, Cheshire. Body of pulpit. Flemish, early 16th century and late 17th century. Human supporter figure from pulpit. One of a pair now in the entrance hall supporting a mantelshelf. (K/3)*

K/3. Chapel, Capesthorne Hall, Cheshire (Plates 2, 201 and 202)
Oak. Flemish. Early 16th century and late 17th century
Term figures 169cm (5ft.6½in.) high; body of pulpit 74cm (2ft.5in.) high. No back board or sounding board
(For Capesthorne Hall, see also J/2 and J/3)
In its original form at Capesthorne the pulpit was a double-decker without tester. The pair of human supporter figures, now incorporated into the hall mantelpiece in the house itself, supported a clerk's desk in front. The body of the pulpit, which was originally hexagonal, rose up above to a height of approximately 3m (10ft.), if we allow for the seat-back panels for the clerk, now missing. It is quite likely that the supporter figures were taken from a secular context, as they appear to be wood spirits (Plate 202). Both have oak leaves at the base of the pilaster. The man is wearing a vine wreath and the woman an oak wreath. The arms of these figures have

been damaged, and there is further damage elsewhere. The third finger of the right hand is missing from the man.

A double tier only of panels survives on the pulpit itself. Two of the six sides were sacrificed when it was pushed against the north wall of the chapel. There are three historiated panels, depicting *Mary and Joseph in the Stable*, *Christ rising from the Tomb*, and the *Adoration of the three Kings* (Plate 201). At the corners there are 'lozenge' posts with, above, finials and figures under archlets. The fourth panel is decorated with a Renaissance-type candelabra design with flat foliage suggesting an early form of strapwork

The chapel, for which the pulpit, seraphim (J/2) and angels (J/3) were intended, was built by John Ward of Capesthorne. The architect was, almost certainly, William Smith of Wergs, the elder brother of the better-known Francis Smith of Warwick. The chapel was consecrated in 1722 (Bromley-Davenport 1974).

K/4. Carlisle Cathedral, Cumbria (Plates 203-206)
Oak. Netherlandish. From St Andrew, Antwerp.
Inscribed 1559
Height 274cm (9ft.). No sounding board extant. Back
board at Cockayne Hatley, Bedfordshire
Formerly at St John the Baptist, Cockayne Hatley,
Bedfordshire
(For Carlisle, see also F/2, L/2 and L/3)

The pulpit is hexagonal in plan (Plate 203). The main carved panels on the sides of the body present the four Evangelists in classical *aediculae* (Plate 204). The remaining two sides also have the same feature, but with

PLATE 204. *Carlisle Cathedral, Cumbria. Pulpit from Cockayne Hatley, Bedfordshire. Netherlandish, from St Andrew, Antwerp, inscribed 1559. Detail of St John panel (K/4).* CROWN COPYRIGHT. NMR

PLATE 203. *St John the Baptist, Cockayne Hatley, Bedfordshire. Pulpit in 1937. Netherlandish, from St Andrew, Antwerp, inscribed 1559. (K/4)* CROWN COPYRIGHT. NMR

a cartouche implanted in the middle and distinctly out of proportion with their surroundings, although they do not appear to be later additions. There are Corinthian columns at the corners with decorated bases, and a Classical frieze to complete the higher zone. The body is supported by a deep plinth, modern but probably reliably renewed, on which stand claw-footed brackets echoed by term-brackets above. The strings of the access stairs, which go with the pulpit, are decorated with an arcade of rounded arches, formerly pierced, with pilasters (Plate 205). The form and decoration is Renaissance with Mannerist overtones. Unusually the existing, but not original, sounding board was purchased with the pulpit (Cust 1851) but never used. The backing board behind

Plate 205. *Carlisle Cathedral, Cumbria. Pulpit from Cockayne Hatley, Bedfordshire. Netherlandish, from St Andrew, Antwerp. inscribed 1559. Detail of access stairs. (K/4)*

there are two putti between a vase of flowers, but this seems to be no more than a routine Renaissance decorative conceit.

The pulpit has been attributed to Jan Terwen Aertsz (Jeannin de Téruenne) (1511-1589), who was probably from Thérouanne in Artois (van Balen 1677 and Kavaler 1994). Van Balen also attributed the choir stalls at the Church of Our Lady, Dordrecht in the Netherlands to Terwen. The latter is dated 1538-40 and is somewhat earlier in style than the pulpit (Plate 207). Recent research done by van Duinen on Jan Terwen has produced no evidence for his existence as a leading artistic figure either at Dordrecht or elsewhere (van Duinen 1997). Van Balen, a historian, was writing some one hundred and forty years after the event, and would

Plate 206. *St John the Baptist, Cockayne Hatley, Bedfordshire. St Andrew panel from former pulpit. Netherlandish, from St Andrew, Antwerp, inscribed 1559.*

the preacher, which was also acquired, still exists at Cockayne Hatley, where it was later made up into a reading desk. It has a carving of St Andrew on it in the same style as the rest of the upper part (Plate 206). The 1827 drawing of the interior of the church looking west by J.C. Buckler shows the pulpit in its original position (Plate 28). A photograph taken in 1937 shows it still there at that time (Plate 203).

According to Goovaerts one of the panels displayed the arms of the city of Antwerp, with the emblem of the Fuggers, a lily between two putti, but this is not there now (Goovaerts 1978). On the upper frieze above St Mark

it was given a new sounding board, which had above it the figure of Christ (Goovaerts 1978). It seems to have survived the Revolution, but was sold to the Netherlands, probably around 1820, because a new one by J-F. van Geel and J-B. van Hool is recorded as having been installed in 1821 (Goovaerts 1978).

PLATE 207. *Church of Our Lady, Dordrecht. View of choir-stall seating. 1538-40.* COPYRIGHT RIJKSDIENST VOOR DE MONUMENTENZORG, ZEIST

probably have been relying on hearsay. Van Duinen believes that the Dordrecht stalls, and related monuments were most probably made by the Flemish court artist Jehan Mone (*c.*1485-1550), who came from Metz in Lorraine and, as a young man, studied in Italy. In 1521 he was in Antwerp, where he met Dürer, and in 1524 moved to Mechelen where he was appointed 'Maître Artistes de l'Empereur' by Charles V (van Duinen 1997). Mone died before the St Andrew's pulpit was made in 1559 and so all we can say about its manufacture is that it may be the product of the Mone successor workshop.

It needs to be studied as part of the group of Netherlandish Renaissance pulpits made in the middle of the 16th century, for example, St Janskerk, 's-Hertogenbosch (1547-61); St Cosmas and St Damian, Abcoude (Plate 208); St Jacob, 's-Gravenhage; and St Gomarus, Enkhuizen (1567-68) (Bangs 1997).

Of the later history of the pulpit we know that in 1608

PLATE 208. *Abcoude Church. Renaissance pulpit. Mid-16th century.* COPYRIGHT RIJKSDIENST VOOR DE MONUMENTENZORG, ZEIST

K/5. St James, Congleton, Cheshire (Plate 209)
Oak. Flemish. Third quarter 17th century
Height 179cm (5ft.10½in.). No back board or sounding board
Hexagonal in plan, with plain panelled two-tier base, probably not original. The upper section is again chaste, with deep plain frieze and dentilated cornice. The decorative carving consists of framed cartouches with four of the corner pilasters representing the Evangelists. Also there is one figurative panel showing the Mary Magdalene holding a chalice.

The body of the pulpit is probably the only part which is original. The base and top section do not fit the middle section very well, and the staircase is clearly modern. This poor cobbling together must have been done, perhaps by a local joiner, when the church was fitted out.

St James, Congleton was a 'Commissioners' church, and was erected in 1847-48.

K/6. St Peter-ad-Vincula, Coveney, Cambridgeshire (Plate 210)
Oak. Danish. Inscribed 1706
Height 179cm (5ft.10½in.). No back board or sounding board
The body is a segment of an octagon, each panel 36cm (14in.) wide, with an hour-glass base and pendent corbel below. It is painted all over. The main panels display the full length figures of Christ and the four Evangelists, with an inscription above and their symbols below. St Peter appears on the outside of the door, and Moses on the inside, with the Ten Commandments at his feet, and, above, the inscription 'Mosis: Anno 1706'. The stiles of the framing show figures of the three Theological Virtues (Faith, Hope and Charity), and the four Cardinal Virtues (Prudence, Temperance, Fortitude and Justice). The paintwork has been much distressed with age and needs conserving. The original brass door furniture has been preserved.

The pulpit and reredos (see Gazetteer) were given by Athelstan Riley, the prominent Anglo-Catholic layman, who was patron of the living from the late 19th century until his death in 1945.

The Danish inscription around the base has been translated as follows: 'To the glory of the Holy Name and for the hearing of God's work is this pulpit presented to this house of God by the widow of that blessed man Capt. Fedde Pieffer, the virtuous and God-loving matron Margareta Bendsdatter. Blessed are they that

PLATE 210. *St Peter-ad-Vincula, Coveney, Cambridgeshire. Pulpit. Danish, inscribed 1706. (K/6)*

K/7. St Peter and St Paul, Kettlethorpe, Lincolnshire (Plate 211)
Oak. From Brittany. *c.*1700
Height 196cm (6ft.5in.). No back board or sounding board

A waisted top section leads down to the sharply tapering centre of this hexagonal pulpit (Plate 211). At the base is a faceted baluster. The original plinth is missing. The steps are probably unrelated. The piece is heavily stained. The top section is decorated with low relief panels exhibiting *Christ before Pilate* and the *Stations of the Cross*. The latter carries on in the panels of the tapering section below. Almost the entire object is covered with decorative carving, displaying a definite *horror vacui*.

PLATE 211. *St Peter and St Paul, Kettlethorpe, Lincolnshire. Pulpit. French (Brittany), c.1700. (K/7)*

hear the word of God and keep it. Luke xi.28. 1706' (Hodder 1984).

Ebbe Nyborg, from the National Museum, Copenhagen has contributed some interesting comments on this pulpit. To paraphrase:

There would not be much chance to identify the individuals, since Pieffer is such a common name. However it is certainly Frisian, making it most probable that it is from the south-west of the country. Also the style of the painting fits in quite well with the traditions of this area. As the language of the inscription is Danish, the pulpit could hardly come from a church south of the present Danish-German border, as the language there was German. So the pulpit probably comes from one of the south-western counties of present-day Denmark: Haderslev, Tonder, Abenra, Sonderborg and Ribe.

All five counties have been published in the Danish survey of churches (*Danmarks Kirker*).

PLATE 212. *All Saints, Landbeach, Cambridgeshire. Supporting angel from base of pulpit. Probably Netherlandish, mid-17th century. (K/8)*

K/8. All Saints, Landbeach, Cambridgeshire (Plate 212)
Oak. Probably Netherlandish. Mid-17th century
Height of figure 122cm (4ft.); wingspan 138cm (4ft.6in.)
Said to have been purchased in 1822 from an antique dealer in York.
The figure is supposed to have been the base of a Dutch pulpit (Plate 212). It must have been fashioned into a lectern in the 19th century, judging from the existing base and book rest. There is peripheral damage to the sculpture, for example. the loss of three fingers and the thumb of the left hand, and one finger on the right hand. Also damage to the big toe of the left foot. This is an additive work and the joins in the wood can be easily discerned.

K/9. Manchester City Art Gallery (formerly at St Luke's, Cheetham Hill Road) (Plate 213)
Wood and composition. Belgian. 18th century
Base 197cm (6ft.5½in.) high, including the panelled

plinth below (not shown) and the balustrade with winged cherubs' heads above (not shown)
The monument, as it was in its English Victorian guise and before disassembly in the 1970s, consisted of the sculptured foot section on a panelled plinth, surmounted by the Flemish base section. Above this was an oblong pulpit body decorated on the outside with Gothic Revival 14th century type canopywork. In the same vein were the stairs with cast-iron railings and a returned entrance. The concave Flemish sculptured section exhibits two half life-size female weepers and the figure of Christ sitting on rocks (Plate 213). Behind and above them are the 14th century type foliage bosses and trails, and a pollarded tree trunk. The original patina of this section has been entirely obscured by five layers of paint, the latest colour scheme being cream for the figures and the rocks, and mauve for the background.

Although this is only a fragment of the original pulpit, it deserves a place here on account of its rarity and high sculptural quality.

PLATE 213. *Manchester City Art Gallery. Base of pulpit from St Luke, Cheetham Hill Road. Belgian, 18th century. (K/9)*

Plate 214. *St Thomas, Newport, Isle of Wight. Body of pulpit. Made by Thomas Caper of Salisbury, dated 1637. (K/10)*

away. At the Restoration of the monarchy only one could be found, but the other was reinstated.

K/11. St Leonard, Old Warden, Bedfordshire (Plate 215)
Oak. Belgian. 18th century
162cm (5ft.3¾in.) high from top to pendent corbel; two main decorative panels 72cm x 64cm (2ft.4¼in. x 2ft.1in.). No back board or sounding board
Introduced by Colonel Shuttleworth in the late 19th century and bought in Scotland

The hexagonal pulpit is complete with stairs, but with no canopy. The body consists of three large high-relief sculptured scenes punctuated by three Evangelist symbols on projecting Roman-type brackets (stolen in 1997). The sculptured panels depict Christ and the *Samaritan Woman at the Well* and *Christ blessing the Children*. On the door there is the figure of St John the Baptist with the Lamb on his shoulders. The pulpit may originally have been free-standing and not leant up against a wall as now. In this case there would have been room for another sculptured panel and Evangelist symbol.

K/10. St Thomas, Newport, Isle of Wight (Plates 1 and 214)
Oak. Made by the Fleming, Thomas Caper of Salisbury.
Dated 1637
Height to top of desk 280cm (9ft.2¼in.); approximate height of canopy from ground 421cm (14ft.)

Octagonal sounding board with elaborate cresting above, and pendent corbels underneath (Plate 1). Around the canopy in gilded letters is the text: 'Cry aloud and spare not; lift up thy voice like a trumpet'. In the front panel of the cornice, between the two seraphim blowing trumpets, are reclining figures representing Justice and Mercy. The underside of the canopy has stars, cherub heads and, formerly, two pendent gilded doves (one now missing), representing the Holy Spirit. The back panel bears the coat of arms and the crest of the donor, and the date of erection, 1631. The book board is supported with brackets. Beneath it are cherub heads and the *Pelican in her Piety*.

On the body of the pulpit are two rows of seven panels incorporating low-relief carvings of the seven *Virtues*, above, and the seven *Liberal Arts* below (Plate 214). The latter are all labelled underneath.

The architecture of the pulpit is rather ambitious, but the artistic level of the figure style is only provincial. It is difficult to point to a Flemish prototype, yet the carving is certainly not English.

The pulpit was the gift of the Mayor of Newport, Stephen Marsh.

In 1643 the churchwardens 'received a warrant to remove and destroy in their Church all things of a superstitious nature'. At this time the doves were taken

PLATE 215. *St Leonard, Old Warden, Bedfordshire. Pulpit. Belgian, 18th century. (K/11)*

K/12. St Elizabeth's, Scarisbrick (Bescar), Lancashire (Plates 216-218)
Oak. Dutch, mid-17th century. Stairs, Dutch or Flemish, late 17th century/early 18th century.
229cm (7ft.6in.) high; large panels 80cm x 76cm (2ft.7½in. x 2ft.6in.); small panels 80cm x 40cm (2ft.7½in. x 15¾in.); height of stairs at highest point 216cm (7ft.1in.). No back board or sounding board

The octagonal pulpit stands on a waisted base (Plate 216), spreading down to the floor. The sides of the octagon alternate between wide and narrow. The main panels are decorated with a cartouche in the centre, inside a frame, and ending in scrolls at the base. These panels are devoid of figurative carving except for putti heads at the top. The smaller panels display the symbols of the four Evangelists. Very lavish base with large dolphins acting as buttresses. The pierced scrolling acanthus-type foliage of the later stair balustrade incorporates putti, cornucopias and fruit (Plate 217). The balustrade itself is of superb quality, and looks back, via the Antwerp-type carving on the

PLATE 216. *St Elizabeth, Scarisbrick (Bescar), Lancashire. Pulpit. Dutch (stairs Dutch or Flemish), mid-17th century. (K/12)*

PLATE 217. *St Elizabeth, Scarisbrick (Bescar), Lancashire. Pulpit. Dutch (stairs Dutch or Flemish), mid-17th century. Entrance staircase. (K/12)*

communion rails at Oscott College (B/13), to Peter Verbruggen I's wall-panelling frieze at St Paul's, Antwerp (Plate 88).

As a general comparison from another pulpit of this date, a detail from the example at St Elizabeth's Gasthuis, Antwerp is given (Plate 219). The latter is somewhat later, and of better quality, than the Bescar example.

The present chapel was built by the Marquis de Castéja, and consecrated in 1889. The pulpit may have been introduced by him, or was possibly bought by Charles Scarisbrick for the earlier but smaller chapel there.

PLATE 218. *St Elizabeth, Scarisbrick (Bescar), Lancashire. Pulpit. Dutch (stairs Dutch or Flemish), mid-17th century. Evangelist panel. (K/12)*

PLATE 219. *St Elizabeth's Gasthuis, Antwerp. Pulpit body. Late 17th century. Detail.*

PLATE 220. *St John the Evangelist, Sidcup, Kent. Pulpit. Inscribed Antwerp 1651. (K/13)*

PLATE 221. *St Kwinten, Leuven. Pulpit. 1651-1700.*
COPYRIGHT IRPA-KIK, BRUSSELS

K/13. St John the Evangelist, Sidcup, Kent (Plate 220)
Oak. Inscribed Antwerp 1651
Height of body 117cm (3ft.10in.). Side panels 72cm x 42cm (2ft.4¼in. x 16½in.). No back board or sounding board
(For Sidcup, see also I/9)

Only the body of the pulpit is original. The rather under-sized modern base accounts for the apparent top-heaviness of the body. The pulpit is hexagonal in plan, the side panels incorporating robust carvings of the Four Evangelists between twisted columns. The fifth figure, depicting Hope, was introduced in the 1840s, this panel having previously been blank, presumably where the pulpit was attached to a pier. The staircase is also modern.

This is an interesting example of part of a mid-17th century Flemish pulpit. The decorative carving is still quasi-Renaissance in style and the Corinthian capitals and twisted columns at the angles are very carefully made. To get an idea of what this pulpit might originally have looked like, a comparison with the probably slightly later example at St Kwinten, Leuven is useful (Plate 221). If it was free-standing the Sidcup pulpit may have had a Classicising bracket base like this, which reminds us of those on the fully-blown Renaissance pulpits at Abcoude (Plate 208) and Carlisle (Plate 203). Whereas the medallion carvings at Sidcup are still in relatively low relief, as we find again at Abcoude and Carlisle, the Leuven figures are in rather higher relief. A distinct tendency to naturalism at Leuven is of course apparent in the vegetal swags on the intermediate stiles of the pulpit body. The stairs at Leuven, guarded at the bottom by Seraphim, are of the type which may have existed on the

PLATE 222. *St Mary, Slaugham, West Sussex. Pulpit. Netherlandish, early 17th century. (K/14)*

Sidcup example. Interestingly, there are more Seraphim underneath the sounding board, which is another application for these multi-purpose figures (J/2).

K/14. St Mary, Slaugham, West Sussex (Plate 222)
Oak, Netherlandish. Early 17th century
Height 166cm (5ft.5¼in.); width across the back 114cm (3ft.9in.). No back board or sounding board
Presented in 1890
The monstrance-shaped body of this pulpit is complete with its original base, with projecting plinths, the stage above being decorated with cabochons. The body, with detached Corinthian columns, is decorated with a mixture of Renaissance and Mannerist motifs. There is a fine strapwork panel in the centre. Unfortunately the original scheme has been curtailed at the back and the

pulpit has lost its door.

The form and decorative details of this pulpit are typical of the furniture designs of Paul Vredeman de Vries (de Vries 1630).

K/15. Holy Trinity, Stowupland, Suffolk (Plate 223)
Oak. Flemish. Early 17th century
Height approx. 200cm (6ft.6in.); main panels 36cm x 26cm (14in. x 10¼in.). No back board or sounding board
Presumably part of the original fittings of the church, erected in 1843
The pulpit was originally six-sided with the entrance at the back, although only five sides survive. Its tapering foot rests on a rectangular stem base. Each of the main sides have figurative scenes in cartouches as follows: S.E. *Presentation of the Virgin;* S.W. Two Kings; W. Female saint with cross; N.W. *Circumcision;* N.E. Christ child in centre naked, two women on either side, and angel blessing above.

The removal of the back has resulted in the loss of probably the door panel. The other panels have been straightened up so that the plan has been transformed into half a decagon. Also two of the panels have been reduced in size.

PLATE 223. *Holy Trinity, Stowupland, Suffolk. Pulpit. Flemish, early 17th century. (K/15)*

PLATE 224. *St Andrew, Trent, Dorset. Pulpit. Flemish, c.1600 (K/16).*

PLATE 225. *St Andrew, Trent, Dorset. Pulpit. Flemish, c.1600.* Christ with Simeon *panel. (K/16)*

K/16. St Andrew, Trent, Dorset (Plates 224-226)
Oak. Flemish. *c.*1600
Height 90cm (2ft.11⅛in.) excluding the top cornice and base. No back board or sounding board

The body of the pulpit is ancient, but it is now mounted on a modern base and capped with a later cornice (Plate 224). The corbel-like form of the original base can be seen in the drawing of the crossing of the church, done before the pulpit was grounded. It was probably originally mounted on a pier about 1.5m (5ft.) above floor level, as it was at Trent when first introduced at the end of the 19th century. It is octagonal in plan with projecting triangular terminal brackets interspersed with historiated low relief carved panels. The latter measure 87cm (2ft.10¼in.) in height, but vary in width from 31cm (12¼in.) to 36.5cm (14¼in.). The original entrance door and staircase are gone.

There are no terminal buttresses on either side of the *Annunciation* panel, now at the back of the pulpit. This is the first in a Christological series, including the *Annunciation, Nativity, Adoration of the Kings, Christ with Simeon* (Plate 225), *Circumcision,* and *Christ in the Temple* (Plate 226), which starts and finishes on either side of the entrance door. It seems unlikely that the *Annunciation* panel would not have been flanked with brackets, particularly as it would have been well in view, unlike today where it is out of sight between the pulpit and the rood screen. It would not be surprising if the pulpit had been tampered with in this area. Perhaps the lone figure of David to the left of the door has been interposed, possibly from another now lost part of the monument.

Although this is almost certainly a Flemish work, it is hard to locate it exactly. Nor is it any easier finding parallels through the medium of prints. The style is thoroughly Mannerist and Italianate, yet the decorative carving appears provincial.

The pulpit was given by a former incumbent, the Reverend W.H. Turner (Rector 1835-75) and his wife. They both made frequent visits to the Continent to buy furniture and window glass. The latter was placed in the east window of the church and in the rectory. It is Swiss and German in origin of the 16th and 17th centuries.

PLATE 227. *St Nicholas, Worth, West Sussex. Pulpit. German, dated 1577 (K/17).* CROWN COPYRIGHT. NMR

K/17. St Nicholas, Worth, West Sussex (Plates 227-231)
Oak. German. Dated 1577
Height 193cm (6ft.4in.). No back board or sounding board
Bought from a London furniture dealer by the
incumbent, the Reverend G.C. Bethune (1841-58). It was
said to have once belonged to a pastor of Wittenberg
Church, Schleswig-Holstein
(For Worth, see also B/14)

The structure is ten-sided in plan, but the scheme has been truncated on the side nearest the wall (Plate 227). The entrance door, which still exists, was probably originally further back, and the pulpit free-standing. Some of the panelling on the inside is original. The base consists of fluted pilasters with human heads in the capitals and recessed panels, decorated with strapwork, in between. The main part is composed of fluted angle columns on decorated plinths, with reliefs of the Four Evangelists (Plate 228) and God the Father (Plate 229) in shell-topped *aediculae* in between.

Under the figures are Renaissance naturalistically carved panels. Included amongst these is one with an

PLATE 226. *St Andrew, Trent, Dorset. Pulpit. Flemish, c.1600.* Circumcision *panel. (K/16)*

203

PLATE 228. *St Nicholas, Worth, West Sussex. Pulpit. German, dated 1577. St Mark panel. (K/17)*

PLATE 229. *St Nicholas, Worth, West Sussex. Pulpit. German, dated 1577. God the Father panel. (K/17)*

angel in the centre holding two shields, with a shield of arms on the dexter side, and the figure of Justice on the sinister side (Plate 230). Goodall points out that the arrangement must record a marriage. There are inscriptions in low German above and below the figures. The protagonists are identified in a legend below, that under the figure of God the Father, standing on the serpent, reading ICK. BIN. ALLENE. DI. HERE. UNDE. GODT. (I am alone thy Lord and God). The text of the inscription on the top rail is from *John* xiv, 23, as follows:

WOL. MI. LEVET / DE. WERTH. MIN / WORDT. HOLDEN / UND. MIN. VADER / WERTH. EN. LEVE / UND. WI. WERDE / THO. EM. KAME / UND. EIN. WANNIGE / BI. EM. MAKE.

(If a man love, he will keep my word: and my Fatherwill love him, and we will come unto him, and make our home above with him). 10A:14 / ANNO. DNI. 1577

The watercolour drawing of about 1850 by R.H. Nibbs

shows the pulpit hoisted up in the air as part of a Georgian triple-decker scheme (Plate 231). The body was raised clear of the box pews and above was a panelled backing board and canopy. The backing seems to have been placed where the old entrance would have been, the existing entrance having been made where it is now. The pulpit was moved to the other side of the chancel arch in the subsequent restoration. The photograph used here shows it before the fire in 1986. At that time the structure was raised on a deep plinth, which was much too low to have been the Georgian one, and the entrance given an L-shaped staircase. On the north side the Georgian railings visible in the Nibbs drawing had been reused. Today the plinth has gone and new steps, set at a right-angle, fitted. The Georgian railings have also disappeared, and the pulpit has been moved eastwards about three feet.

It has not been possible to locate the pulpit precisely, in spite of the fact that we seem to know the name of the place from which it came. Even though Martin Wentz

PLATE 230. *St Nicholas, Worth, West Sussex. Pulpit. German, dated 1577. Coat of arms. (K/17)*

from Hanover has pointed out that it cannot come from Lower Saxony, it must have emanated from the area north of the River Elbe, since the text is in Low German. Wentz has also suggested that the lower part of the structure may not be original, as it is more likely to have had a single column underneath it. The constituents of the present base seem to be old, but they could have been assembled to make a replacement. There seems to be no doubt that the pulpit came from a Lutheran church.

Unfortunately there are also doubts as to whether the monument came from Schleswig-Holstein. Dirk Jonkanski from Kiel has written:

> …A parish by the name of Wittenberg is not known. We only know of an estate by that name which is near Preetz. This estate belonged to the Rantzau or perhaps the Reventlow family at this time. However, neither of their coats of arms appears on the pulpit.

Herr Dr Teuchert, who is an expert in church art in Schleswig-Holstein, has examined the photograph of the pulpit. He thinks that other former locations could be possible, i.e.: Wittenberg – Luther's town; Wittenberg near Königsberg; Gross Wittenberg, west of Schneidemühl; Wittenberg on the Elbe in Sachsen-Anhalt and Wittenberg, west of Oldenberg and north of Friesoythe.

The double coat of arms as shown is not known to Dr Teuchert as a coat of arms of the aristocracy in Schleswig-

Holstein. There is a certain similarity in the way the pulpit has been built which compares with others from the same area in Schleswig-Holstein. However, the decagonal shape is also unusual for that time.

Jonkanski stresses that similar pulpits in Schleswig-Holstein, like the one from Klanxbüll, for instance, are in fact stylistically very different from the Worth example.

PLATE 231. *St Nicholas, Worth, West Sussex. Interior of church in 1850, looking east. Etching by R.H. Nibbs. (K/17)*

PLATE 232. *St Mary, Brushford, Devon. West side of choir screen. Franco-English, c.1480. (L/1)*

PLATE 233. *St Mary, Brushford, Devon. East side of choir screen. Franco-English, c.1480. (L/1)*

L: *Screens*

L/1. St Mary, Brushford, Devon (Plates 232 and 233)
Oak. Franco English. *c.*1480
Height from floor to top of dado rail 100cm (3ft.3¼in.);
rail to top of architrave 157cm (5ft.2in.); panel bays
53cm (21in.); width of screen 4.33m (14ft.2½in.).
This screenwork is one of a set of three found in Devon
in close proximity and of similar alien design. The
comments below should be read in conjunction with those
on the woodwork at Coldridge (L/4) and Colebrooke
(L/5)

Although the chancel was rebuilt in the 19th century,
the screen, which is perfectly symmetrical, shows no
evidence of mutilation (Plate 232). Moreover, on the east

side at each end the architrave mouldings stop, as if the
screen was never intended to be any longer. It would,
therefore, be safe to assume that it has not been
transferred from another building. It consists of three
bays either side of a double-bay entrance. This has a
flattened ogee door head above, foliage and the
mutilated remains of statue plinths. Harrison has pointed
out the use of 'gun-stock' shoulders for the door heads
(Plate 238) is extremely rare in England. It can also be

PLATE 234. *Lambader Church, Plouvorn, Finistère. Choir screen. 1481.*
East side. COPYRIGHT CONWAY LIBRARY, COURTAULD INSTITUTE OF ART

PLATE 235. *St Fiacre du Faouët, Morbihan. Choir screen. 1480. Detail of centre part, West side.*

PLATE 236. *Chapelle de Kerfons, Ploubezre, Côtes d'Armor. Choir screen. Early 16th century. West side.*
CLICHÉ ARCH.PHOT./CENTRE DES MONUMENTS NATIONAUX, PARIS

seen at Colebrooke (L/5 and Plate 245). This is a method whereby a wider entrance is obtained by narrowing the door stiles below the level of the door head. The fact that the door posts have moulded faces might seem to preclude the use of an entrance door. Moreover, on the reverse faces of the posts there are prolific mouldings which would rule out the use of the rather crude wing hinges in this position which occur at Colebrooke (Plate 244). The interposition of the haunching feature between the door post and door head mouldings is a solecism rather than a change of plan, since the very same thing occurs in the entranceway at Colebrooke. The flattened ogee carved door head with plinths at Brushford was probably also found originally at Coldridge, where it has been removed.

The tracery is presented directly underneath the architrave with no intervening archlets, which one usually gets in England. The same formula is also adopted at Coldridge, but not on the north-south screen at Colebrooke, where delicate ogee archlets with finials are superimposed (Plate 246). The Flamboyant handling of the tracery is complemented by the extreme thinness of

the sub-tracery members. The bars have a flat fret-cut profile and are only about 8mm (⅜in.) thick. Unfortunately, most of this sub-tracery has been knocked out, including the sub-cusping of the archlets. The spiral decoration of the columns in the tracery panels is unidirectional at both levels. There is linenfold panelling on the south-west side of the dado screen, but it continues on the north side only in the first bay. Presumably there was a pew in front of the plain panels originally, or possibly even a nave altar, which made any special decoration unnecessary. This confirms that the screen was purpose-built for the church. The screen still has its coat of brown Georgian paint.

On the east side of the screen there is a series of filled rectangular housings, cut into the top of the architrave, making five equal spaces for something rising above. Interestingly, these housings do not follow the architecture of the screen. The mortises must have originally been for pinnacles, as seen at Coldridge and Colebrooke. The verticals above the transom conform to the dado arrangement below, which is not always the case at Coldridge and Colebrooke. The carving style here seems

PLATE 237. *Carlisle Cathedral, Cumbria. St Catherine's Chapel parclose screen. Anglo-Flemish, c.1490-1500. West side of west section. (L/2)*

to be closest to that at Colebrooke. Also the mouldings on the door edges in the two places are identical.

The use of the fret-type tracery is not found anywhere else in England apart from this group of three Devon churches. On the other hand, direct parallels can be found in Brittany, such as the choir screen at Lambader, Plouvorn, Finistère (Plate 234), which is dated to 1481, and St Fiacre, du Faouët, Morbihan, dated to 1480 (Plate 235). A similar flattened ogee door head is found at Lambader, and it seems unlikely that there was ever a

door there either. It is common in England for the spiral twists on divided columns to go in both directions. The uni-directional spirals in these three churches may perhaps reflect the tall uninterrupted spiral columns found in Brittany, such as at the Chapelle de Kerfons, Côtes d'Armor (Plate 236). The use of linenfold panelling at Brushford, Colebrooke and Coldridge, must be an early occurrence of this feature in England, since it was not generally introduced until the opening of the 16th century.

The evidence at Brushford that allowance had been made for the placing of a pew, or other structure, in front of the north side confirms that this screen is most unlikely to have been manufactured in France. At the same time, in many respects, it is typically English in form. The most strikingly different feature is the tracery. The sensible conclusion would seem to be that it was made on site by English craftsmen with the active participation of a Breton.

L/2. Carlisle Cathedral, Cumbria (Plate 237)
Oak. Anglo-Flemish. *c.*1490-1500
North screen 3.62m (11ft.10½in.) long, west screen 2.69m (8ft.10in.) long; Height 3.14m (10ft.3⅛in.)
(For Carlisle Cathedral, see also F/2, K/4 and L/3)

The screens, which have been reconstructed from original and 19th century material, enclose the north and west sides of the former St Catherine's Chapel, to the east of the south transept (Plate 237). They comprise a deep cornice with curvilinear tracery and cresting at the top, a soffit with carved bosses, and a zone of open panelling sub-divided by buttresses with disciplined proto Flamboyant-type tracery in the heads. Above the dado rail there is curvilinear brattishing, only originally on the north screen. Below it there is a zone of openwork tracery panels, using a variety of designs. The dado panels proper are decorated with a simple chamfered linenfold-type ornament, with one wide leaf and a single arris each side, and a spreading and curving profile at top and bottom. A mutilated heraldic shield is positioned on the cornice on each side. There is a door in the centre of the western screen which has been cut in later. It bears the initials of Prior Thomas Gondibour (1484-1507), although these are a 19th century replacement.

According to Billings, writing in 1840, until the 1760s similar screenwork enclosed the chancel at Carlisle. Unfortunately, these screens were removed when Bishop Lyttleton 'beautified' the cathedral, leaving only the woodwork surrounding St Catherine's Chapel, some panels in the choir-stalls, and three more at nearby Featherstone Castle. Billings stated that:

some of the most beautiful of these panels were broken up and altered to enrich the door of the quire near the Bishop's throne. The great mass, however, was removed from the cathedral either into the fratry or the crypt beneath it, and much of it, it is said, was actually used for firewood. Some of it came into the hands of Lord Wallace, in whose castle at Featherston [*sic*.], Northumberland, are three beautiful specimens of these panels. (Billings 1840).

Other fragments ended up in a public house in Carlisle, which was demolished in 1916. *Pace* Billings, however, it is unlikely that the screenwork surrounding the St Catherine's Chapel was ever intended for this location. Each length of screen has been cut down and made up to

fit as well as possible, assorted tracery panels being inserted where necessary. Indeed there is clear evidence where disparate elements have been cobbled together. Although some new wood was used in a mid-19th century restoration, most of these screens, including the 'linen-fold' panelling, seem to be genuine.

Parallels with Carlisle's overlapping arcs in the tracery have been drawn in the past with the pulpitum at Hexham Abbey, another Augustinian foundation, and the parclose screen around Prior Leschman's chantry there (Billings 1842). Indeed it was suggested that the Carlisle and Hexham woodwork could have been the product of the same workshop (Bulman 1955). Hexham's rood screen probably dates from the time of Prior Thomas Smithson (1491-1524), and the date of the Leschman chantry is 1491. In view of the political situation at the time, and in 1491 Henry VII's war with France, it seems likely that the craftsmen in both places would have come from the north of England or the Lowlands of Scotland, rather than metropolitan England. The style of the surviving tracery panels at Carlisle is certainly not metropolitan or lowland English and seems ultimately to come from Flanders. The possibility that some of the craftsmen, here and at Hexham, were immigrants or first generation foreigners cannot be dismissed. But these monuments were probably not the product of the same workshop.

In Brittany there are fully-fledged linenfold panels at St Fiacre du Faouët dated to 1480 (Plate 235), and at Colebrooke, Coldridge and Brushford in Devon, all *c.*1480 (L/1, L/4, L/5) at approximately this time, although the tracery in the Devon churches, which are related to each other, is quite different from that at Carlisle. The style of the Gondibour screen tracery is earlier than the northern French panelling on the

PLATE 237a. *St. Salvator, Bruges. Choir-stalls. Detail of seat-back tracery head. Second quarter 15th century.*

cathedral Prior's stall door, on so many chests, here and in France (for instance, see F/4 and F/9), and on loose panels in many other contexts. Linenfold panels similar to the primitive type at Carlisle do occur elsewhere in England at this time, although it is not possible to be precise about their dating. The screen from Brightleigh, Devon, in the Victoria and Albert Museum, which can be dated on style between 1490-1510, has them (Tracy 1988, Cat.266). Another example is the extant settle in the abbot's parlour at Muchelney Abbey, Somerset (Tracy 1988, fig. 57), which is probably from the last quarter of the 15th century. The tracery style at Carlisle has distinct Flamboyant tendencies, but, with the exception of the heart-shaped design on the door of St Catherine's Chapel and that used for all the tracery heads in the long panels, it is too dense and convoluted to rival the flickering incandescence of its Continental models in France. On the other hand, the two-tier undulating and cusped running ornament on the dado rail of the north screen can be paralleled on the mid-century choir-stalls at 's-Hertogenbosch, in the Netherlands. It also has some affinity with the small-scale ornament on late 15th century Flemish altarpieces, such as that in the Wallfahrtskirche, Clausen, Germany, or the triptych in the St Annen Museum, Lübeck. But both of these parallels are still only very general and running ornament is a

common decorative architectural feature at this time in Flanders as it as in England.

Perhaps the best Flemish comparison is with the choir-stalls at St Salvator, Bruges (Plate 237a), probably of the second quarter of the 15th century (Debergh 1982). Here there is a similarly adventurous tracery, which is always restrained and firmly rooted in the Gothic tradition. Also the tracery elements in both places are flat-fronted, rather than arrised.

Ecclesiastical and trading links between Carlisle and Scotland certainly existed at the end of the 15th century. Bulman posited the connection between Melrose and Holmcultram, both Cistercian houses, both with direct connections with France, and cites the visit of the abbot of the latter house to Rose Castle to receive the episcopal benediction from Bishop Bell of Carlisle around 1480. The choir-stalls at King's College, Aberdeen, 1506-09, have also been invoked (Bulman 1955 and Simpson, in Geddes 2000), but their style is distinctly *retardataire,* and poorly executed by comparison, although the tracery at Aberdeen is, in its way, quite Netherlandish in appearance. One clear difference between each place is the absence in Carlisle of any small-scale sub-tracery. This is typically found in Flanders at the end of the 15th century, and in Brittany. There were plenty of links in Scottish ecclesiastical circles with Flanders (see pages 12-13),

PLATE 238. *Carlisle Cathedral, Cumbria. 'Salkeld' screen. Franco-Flemish, 1542-47. Entranceway. North side. (L/3)*

PLATE 239. *Carlisle Cathedral, Cumbria. 'Salkeld' screen. Franco-Flemish, 1542-47. South side. (L/3)*

exemplified as early as the 1440s at Melrose Abbey with the commissioning of a complete set of choir-stalls from Bruges. Indeed that monument must have radiated stylistic influence in all directions. In many ways Carlisle at that time could have been as much exposed to Continental cultural influence, both French and Flemish, direct and indirect, as to that from metropolitan England. The swathe of alien-looking tracery appearing at about the same time on the same latitude, at Carlisle, Hexham and Brancepeth (Billings 1845), is surely testament to this.

L/3. Carlisle Cathedral, Cumbria (Plates 238 and 239)
Oak. Franco Flemish. 1542-47
3m (9ft.10in.) (3.64m (11ft.11¼in.) with cresting) x 3.96m (13ft.)
(For Carlisle Cathedral, see also K/4 and L/2)
The 'Salkeld' screen stands on the north side of the choir in the fourth bay from the crossing. It is in three tiers with

elaborate cresting, and of three sub-divided bays with a door in the centre. The north, or 'public', side displays classical portrait heads in medallions beneath the dado, and the royal arms, the Prince of Wales' feathers with the lettering GSPE (God Save Prince Edward) and a Tudor rose (Plate 238). On the inside face are more medallioned portraits, the initials of Prior Salkeld, the last Prior and the first Dean of Carlisle, and Henry VIII (Plate 239). On the cresting of the south side, at each end, are the symbols of the Passion (the shield at the west end is probably 18th century).

The screen is said to have been erected to celebrate the birth of Edward to Jane Seymour. The widest dating bracket would be 1537, Edward's birth date, to 1548, the date of Prior Salkeld's resignation (Bulman 1955).

From the way that the screen has been fitted into its present position, it is clear that it has been reused and was not originally intended for this location. There have also

PLATE 240. *Fécamp Cathedral. Choir aisle stone parclose screen. 1505-19. Detail.*
COPYRIGHT CONWAY LIBRARY, COURTAULD INSTITUTE OF ART

been a number of later additions.

This monument has been linked with a group of Renaissance carvings in England, probably made by the workshop of foreign denizened craftsmen (Brears 1972; Gilbert 1978, and Strange 1927). In particular the panelling, thought to have come from the house of Sir Thomas Wingfield in Ipswich, and the bed and cupboard made for Sir Thomas Wentworth of West Bretton in the West Riding of Yorkshire, are comparable.

Similar wooden screenwork of this period in Belgium at St Gertrude, Nivelles, and examples in stone in Northern France at Evreux Cathedral, early 16th century, and Fécamp Cathedral, 1505-19 (Plate 240), both in Normandy could be cited.

L/4. St Matthew, Coldridge, Devon (Plates 241 and 242)
Oak. Franco English. *c.*1480
Height from floor to top of dado rail 121cm
(3ft.11⅛in.); from dado rail to top of cornice 141cm
(4ft.7½in; bays 62cm (24⅛in.) wide; door 179cm x 62.5cm
(5ft.10⅛in. x 24⅝in.); total length 2.64m (8ft.8in.).
Said to have been the gift of Sir John Evans, a Park
Keeper of the Marquess of Dorset's deer park at
Coldridge, and to be a component of his chantry chapel

This screenwork is one of a set of three found in Devon in close proximity, and of similar alien design. The comments below should be read in conjunction with those on the woodwork at Brushford (L/1) and Colebrooke (L/5).

In its present form this is a three-bay parclose screen, in the second bay of the north choir aisle to the east of the rood screen, with two half bays each end and a door in the centre (Plate 241). There is also a discontinuity between the dado zone and the superstructure, which do not match up. This irregularity confirms that the screenwork cannot originally have been made for this position.

There is a linenfold dado on a chamfered plinth, with buttresses, on the south, or outside face only, running up the full height of the screen along the divisions of the bays (Plate 241). Above are open lights, sub-divided by columns with tracery in the heads. As at Brushford, the cutting of this tracery is exceptionally delicate and has the appearance of fretwork. The colonnettes of the lights are of various spiral designs. On the north, or inside face, there is an undecorated architrave (Plate 242), while on the south side the same feature carries a vine-scroll frieze. Above the architrave there seems to have been a cresting punctuated by finials, of which only some of the latter survive. The intention that there should be a more or less important side is confirmed by the use of the linenfold panels on the south, or inside face only. This is the case at Brushford also. At Coldridge, however, it is curious that the public side of the screen is now located on the inside, or north side. It seems most unlikely that the patron would have originally intended to present his monument inside out, as it were. The logical conclusion is that these fragments of screenwork have been placed back to front, and cut back on both sides to fit the space. They seem to be the remnants, as at Colebrooke, of a formerly more ambitious scheme, or might even have come from another church. The vine-scroll frieze may have been fitted *de novo,* but is certainly English.

The Coldridge screenwork has less in common with the other two churches than they do with each other. Admittedly at Brushford the screen also has a decorated and plain side. But the mouldings on the door frame at Coldridge, and its construction, are different from the identical treatment of this feature at Brushford and Colebrooke, and the south side at Coldridge completely lacks the English emphasis on verticality.

Did the woodwork once form part of a much bigger ensemble in the church, including a rood screen? The door of the present 'chantry' is modern but, as Harrison has pointed out, the shafts, being shorter than the others, must have come from a different and lower screen. The present rood screen of rather later date has been forced into the church in a most inelegant manner. Part of a linenfold panel from our screen can be seen jammed up in the existing rood screen vaulting, on the east side of the first bay from the east on the south side of the choir aisle. Admittedly, the bay widths of our screen (62cm: 24⅜in.) are

PLATE 241. *St Matthew, Coldridge, Devon. North choir aisle. Parclose screen. Franco-English, c.1480. View from south side. (L/4)*

PLATE 242. *St Matthew, Coldridge, Devon. North choir aisle. Parclose screen. Franco-English, c.1480. View from north side. (L/4)*

PLATE 243. *St Andrew, Colebrooke, Devon. Choir, north side. Parclose screen. Franco-English, c.1480. East-west section from north. (L/5)*

much narrower than those in the rood screen (87cm: 34⅛in.), which completely overwhelms the scale of the church. It is possible that, in the twentieth century, another segment of screenwork was removed when the organ was installed in the third bay of the north choir aisle.

Direct parallels can be found in Brittany, such as the choir screen at Lambader, Plouvorn, Finistère, which is dated to 1481, and St Fiacre, Le Faouët, Morbihan, dated to 1480 (Plates 234 and 235). Most of the Breton examples highlight an important difference in the national aesthetic, whereby the dado zone is allowed to express its classical function as basement, and can run in a horizontal direction with the minimum interruption. By contrast, of course, English late-medieval screenwork exploits the unique national Perpendicular style, which can often emphasise the vertical almost to the exclusion of the horizontal.

The chantry chapel in the north-eastern corner of the chancel, which is bound on the north-south axis by our screen, is said to have been given by Sir John Evans, for use in his memory. The latter died in the early 1480s. Evans was a member of the circle of Henry Tudor, and spent time in Brittany, where he presumably caught his enthusiasm for Breton furniture. His monument is placed beneath a four-centred arch on the north wall. In the east window of the chapel is a small figure in ancient glass, believed to be Prince Edward, eldest son of Edward IV, and one of the two princes

who were murdered in the Tower of London in 1483. The window has usually been dated *c.*1480, which can probably be taken as the date of the setting-up of the chantry chapel.

L/5. St Andrew, Colebrooke, Devon (Plates 243-246)
Oak. Franco English. c.1480
East-west section: Height from floor to top of dado rail 107cm (3ft.6in.), height from dado rail to top of cornice 154cm (5ft.½in.), bays 65cm (25½in.) wide, door 166cm x 63cm (5ft.5¼in. x 24¾in.), length 4.33m (14ft.2½in.)
North-south section: height from floor to top of dado rail 103cm (3ft.4¼in.), height from dado rail to top of cornice 161cm (5ft.3½in.), bays 69cm (2ft.3in.) wide, door 174.5cm x 42.5cm (5ft.8¾in. x 16¾in.), length 3.83m (12ft.6¾in.).
This screenwork is one of a set of three found in Devon in close proximity, and of similar alien design. The comments below should be read in conjunction with those on the woodwork at Brushford (L/1) and Coldridge (L/4)

The screen surrounds the Copplestone Chantry Chapel in the north choir aisle, measuring 6.8m by 3.77m (22ft.3¾in. by 12ft.4½in.). The east-west section fills the first bay of the choir (Plate 243). According to Harding, the north-south section, which closes off the chapel to the west, and incorporates what is now the main entrance (Plates 244 and 245), formerly stretched across the entire width of the church (Harding 1853). The southern exten-

PLATE 244. *St Andrew, Colebrooke, Devon. Parclose screen. Franco-English, c.1480. North-south section from east, facing the nave. (L/5)*

PLATE 245. *St Andrew, Colebrooke, Devon. Parclose screen. North-south section from west, facing into the Copplestone Chapel. (L/5)*

Plate 246. St Andrew, Colebrooke, Devon. Parclose screen. Franco-English, c.1480. North-south section. Detail of tracery from W. (L/5)

repertory of motifs than at Coldridge. The spirals here, in the two stages of the posts, are not always consistently uni-directional, as they are at Brushford and Coldridge. Also the variety of reticulated tracery patterns is wider and more ambitious than at Coldridge. This includes the ogee reticulated shapes of the major tracery, but also some more complex asymmetrical Flamboyant forms, in both the main tracery mouldings and the sub-tracery net-like mouchette arrangements (Plate 246), which can be compared to that found in the upper stages of the choir-screens at Lambader, Plouvorn and St Fiacre du Faouët in Brittany (Plates 234 and 235).

The door posts on the north-south axis are haunched in exactly the same way as they are at Brushford with the characteristic 'gun-stock' shoulders appearing on the door head (Plates 244 and 245). On both sides of the western entrance of the screen there was profuse and elaborate extra embellishment, including ogee archlets with foliage and finials, some of them still in place, and buttress elements, all of which have gone (Plate 246). Additional decoration must have been provided by means of paint above the linenfold of the dado panels on the west face to either side of the door, where the carved decoration starts only some two-thirds of the way up from the bottom. Here there are traces of a red wash and the shadow of superimposed human heads. Since there is no masonry rood stair, it is possible that access to the central rood loft was by means of a wooden staircase as at Plouvorn. The screens carried a similar, but not identical, type of cresting to that at Coldridge. They seem to have been designed to be housed in their present positions in this church from the beginning.

As has already been stated in connection with the Brushford and Coldridge screens, the stylistic connec-tions with Brittany are clear. On the other hand, the trea-tment of the foliage on the ogee archlets at Colebrooke (Plate 246) is not particularly close to any of the Breton examples, and the the semi-circular mouldings inside the voussoirs and other idiosyncrasies seem to be unique. Curiously, the Devon foliage is typical of that found on Norman chests (Plates 122 and 123) and Flamboyant woodwork in Northern France and Flanders, both of which are usually considered to have been made about a generation later. It should be said that the stylistic connec-tions with the Breton rood screens in these Devon monuments can have been only a pale reflection of their archetypes, with their much more lavishly decorated entrance doors, profusion of figure sculpture and greater scale.

Tradition has it that it was in the second half of the 15th century that the north aisle of the chancel was rebuilt and a chapel installed where it is now. John Coplestone died in 1447. But Philip Coplestone, of Copplestone and Warley, who was High Sheriff of Devon in 1471, appears to be the founder of the Chantry Chapel. There is a fireplace and chimney in the north wall, as well as a priest's door, forming the original entrance to the chapel.

sion was removed by faculty in 1805, although some portions of it were still visible on the south side as late as 1850. All traces of this choir screen were finally expunged in the extensive restoration and rebuilding of the chancel around 1875.

On these last two remaining portions of this formerly extensive screenwork there is a linenfold dado on a moulded plinth. Above are open lights, sub-divided by colonnettes with tracery in the heads. As at Brushford and Coldridge, the cutting of this tracery is exceptionally deli-cate, and has the appearance of fretwork. The colonnettes are of various spiral designs, with a slightly bigger

PLATE 247. *St Andrew, Gatton, Surrey. Fragment of screenwork, made up into altar rail. Flemish, early 16th century. (L/6)*

L/6. St Andrew, Gatton, Surrey (Plate 247)
Oak. Flemish. Early 16th century
81cm x 3.35m (2ft.8in. x 11ft.
Said to come from Tongres, Belgium
(For Gatton, see also M/10 and M/11)
This fragment of screenwork has been made up into an altar rail, with the plinth, rail and decorative panels at each end having no stylistic or functional connection (Plate 247). It consists of a series of cusped oculi, resting on cusped ogee archlets, supported on quatrefoil columns.

Pevsner thought that this was probably late 16th century 'Gothic Survival' work (BOE, *Surrey* 1971), but the joinery and the decorative carving mitigates against this. The

tracery head is carved in substantial lengths in the solid. This typically medieval technique went out of use in the early 16th century. Moreover, the foliage, and the treatment of the jesters, is perfectly consonant with the late 15th century. There is a useful comparison in Belgium of a similar miniature screen, from St Nièrge, Pipaix, Leuze-en-Hainault (Plate 248). Here, although the arches are intersecting, the figurative and decorative carving is broadly comparable.

Given that altar rails did not exist before the Reformation, these fragments must have been salvaged from some other structure. One possibility is that they were the front of the loft of a rood-screen. Another is that they were intended to fence in a tomb.

PLATE 248. *St Nièrge, Pipaix, Leuze-en-Hainault. Miniature screen. Late 15th century.*
COPYRIGHT IRPA-KIK, BRUSSELS

L/7. Victoria and Albert Museum, London (Plates 249 and 250)
Oak. Dutch. *c.*1700
1.45m. x 4.55m. x 16.5cm (4ft.9in. x 14ft.11in. x 6½in.
Museum Acq. No. 429 to H-1901
Formerly in the Lutheran church, Alkmaar
(For V & A Museum, see also F/6, F/7, F/8, J/8, J/9, J/10, M/18, M/19 and M/20)
The pulpit screen, originally painted and gilded, bears the arms of Dol Lange, the Minister, and P. Haerboe and J.D. Roode, the two churchwardens (Plate 249). Along the top there are brass fittings, typical of the period, which were not originally in these positions. The brass candlesticks at each end are interlopers, and must have

come from a synagogue.

There are three panelling sections and two doors at right-angles to the ends. Each compartment is divided by a horizontal moulding, the upper portion being carved in pierced scrolling foliage, and the following heraldic devices in the centre, each with helmet and mantling:

1). *A shield quarterly,* 1 and 4, a hare, 2 and 3, a fountain, with a hare for crest; below, two scrolls inscribed P.HAERBOE and OUDERLINGH (Plate 250)

2). A shield bearing an arm holding three roses, with three roses for crest; below, two scrolls inscribed I.D. ROODE and OUDERLINGH

PLATE 251. *Interior of the Lutheran Church, Alkmaar, after 1692. Watercolour drawing by C. Pronk, dated 1736.* COPYRIGHT GEMEENTEARCHIEF, AMSTERDAM

3). A shield bearing a heart pierced by two darts with points upwards surrounded by a laurel wreath, with a similar heart for crest; below, two scrolls inscribed DOL LANGE and PREDIKANT (the Minister).

The panels are separated by pilasters with pendants of leaves and flowers, those at the ends having each two decorated sides. In the lower zone the panelling has plain raised centres. The side doors are treated similarly to the front panels, except that a rosette replaces the arms.

Above the middle panel is a brass book rest, decorated in openwork with floral scrollwork inscribed MARGARETA HOBBE HOYSVROV VAN D. HENRICUS VAN BORN, and over this is a twisted ogee arch surmounted by a knob. Above each of the side panels is a larger arch, composed of scrolling bands resting on twisted columns and surmounted by a Lutheran swan. These arches originally stood above the small doors on the screen wings. According to Pont the central arch stood on the pulpit, but was removed in 1875 (Pont 1915). Above each end pilaster is a moulded candlestick with a Jewish mark, signifying 'The Hague Congregation'.

The church can be identified because a small portion of the screen has remained there. The Lutheran church in Alkmaar was built in 1692 and consecrated on 14 September of that year by the Reverend Laurentius Lange (Pont 1915). Inside the screen stood the pulpit, and a table. On both sides were the pews for the church-wardens, the elders and the deacons. In the centre was the place for the reader, or parish clerk. The latter stood in front of the brass book-rest, a present of Mrs van Born (Margareta Hobbe). Her husband Henricus van Born was a clergyman in Alkmaar from 1658-1662 and it would seem that she was a native of the town. Laurentius Lange was a German, born in Ratzeburg, in Schleswig-Holstein. The screen was in the church until 1875 and in 1879 it was sold for fl.285 (£24), it is said, to a synagogue in The Hague, which would provide a reason for the candlesticks.

A watercolour drawing of the east end of the Lutheran church in Alkmaar, made in 1736, shows the pulpit complete with its screen still *in situ* (Plate 251).

There used to be a similar screen at the church of Ooltgensplaat, on the island in the mouth of the confluence of the River Maas and River Rhine, which may still be there.

M: *Stalls, Misericords and other fixed Seating*

PLATE 252. *St Margaret, Barming, Kent. Stall end. Flemish, c.1300. (M/1)*

PLATE 253. *St Margaret, Barming, Kent. Stall end with* Samson and the Lion. *Flemish, c.1300. (M/1)*

PLATE 254. *St Margaret, Barming, Kent. Stall end with* Harrowing of Hell. *Flemish, c.1300.*

M/1. St Margaret, Barming, Kent (Plates 252-254)
Oak. Flemish. *c.*1300
Centre to centre width of seating about 64cm (2ft.1in.);
height of seat capping 120cm (3ft.11¼in.); height of seat
42cm (16½in.); depth of seat 40cm (15¾in.) Small desk
end 76cm (2ft.6in.) high, three tall stall ends are about
2m (6ft.6in.) high.
The local tradition is that the carvings were brought
back from Flanders by two brothers in 1871.
This is the rump of a large set of choir-stalls, consisting of, on the south side, four seats, a stall end carved with *Samson and the Lion*, and one odd desk end with a lion on top (Plate 252), now made up into a priest's desk. On the north side there is only one seat standard, and two stall ends (Plate 253). The latter displays *St Michael slaying the Devil* and the *Harrowing of Hell* (Plate 254). There are no misericords.

The treatment of the seat standards is generally reminiscent of the Cologne choir-stalls of this date, such as those at St Maria in Capitol, St Severin, and formerly at St Aposteln (now in the Schnütgen Museum), with prominent figurated and foliage elbows, and columns at the base of the standards and underneath the seat

PLATE 255. *Bowes Museum, Castle Barnard, County Durham. Run of stalls from the Dominican church of St Katharinenthal, Diessenhofen. First decade 17th century. One of two. (M/2)*

capping. The treatment of the desk ends is also similar. However, the carving of the stall end figures is not in the same league, being frankly poor. It is tempting, perhaps, to see these as crude modern reproductions, but their authenticity is guaranteed by the fact that they are carved in the solid with the lower part of the stall ends, a procedure which was normal for the period.

Placing this material geographically is not easy because there is virtually nothing comparable extant from the Low Countries. Even allowing for the provincial quality of the carving, they are not likely to be German. Since they were acquired in Flanders, it would be safer to attribute them to that region. A reasonable comparison in terms of contemporaneity would be with the probably also Flemish stall standards at Otterbourne, Hampshire (M/24 and Plate 329).

M/2. Bowes Museum, Barnard Castle, County Durham (Plates 255 and 256)
Oak. Germany. First decade 16th century
Centre to centre width of seats 60cm (23½in.); height of capping 110cm (3ft.7¼in.)
From the Dominican convent of St Katharinenthal, Diessenhofen. Obtained by John Bowes through a dealer in Bâle, Switzerland in 1876
(For Bowes Museum, see also F/1 and J/1)
Two runs of seven stalls, with plain turned misericords (Plate 255). They have been identified as the central section of the original nuns' choir-stalls. The most striking feature is the fine carved busts on the stall ends. Below these are inset panels of curvilinear tracery. There are also traceried oculi carved in the solid on the seat rails. Busts of the Evangelists were grouped on the north side of the church. The segment in the Bowes Museum from this

PLATE 256. *Bowes Museum, Castle Barnard, County Durham. Stall end displaying unidentified king, from the Dominican convent of St Katharinenthal, Diessenhofen. First decade 17th century. (M/2)*
COPYRIGHT THE BOWES MUSEUM

side has the busts of St Luke and St John, and that from the south side those of St Bartholomew and an unidentified king (Plate 256). The balance of the stalls, two sets of three seats, originally on the east side, and two sets of four seats, originally on the west side, have been preserved in the museum at Frauenfeld.

The main carver has been identified as Augustin Henckel, whose securely attributed works include the high altar at Einsedeln (Deutsch 1964). A second carver seems, like Henckel, to have come from Constance. A third unknown apprentice sculptor has also been recognised.

M/3. St Chad's Cathedral, Birmingham (Plates 7, 257-261)

Oak. Netherlandish. *c.1520*

Centre to centre width of seating 71cm (2ft.4in.); height of seat capping 110cm (3ft.7¼in.); depth of seat 41cm

Erected by A.W.N. Pugin after 1838. Said to have come from St Mary in Capitol, Cologne

(For St Chad's Cathedral, see also K/1)

There are five seats on the south side (Plate 257) and six on the north, with another isolated stall, now the

PLATE 258. *St Chad's Cathedral, Birmingham. Choir-stalls. Netherlandish, c.1520. Stall end. Detail of Virgin and Child with Magus. (M/3)*

provost's chair (Plate 258), further east on the north side. There is a good deal of restoration, with some replacement misericord carving and new seat backs. There is the unusual use of linenfold for the seat backs, originally placed vertically above and horizontally below. There was never any canopywork. Although the desks are 19th century there are some fine original desk ends. They are traceried at the sides and have figure sculpture above, for example. one of the *Magi presenting a chalice to the infant Christ,* who sits on his mother's lap (Plate 259), a *Pietà* (Plate 260), two monks preparing food (Plate 261), and two secular figures, one with clawed feet holding a shield with the imperial eagle (Plate 257).

At the back of the provost's chair is a carving of the Virgin holding the infant Christ, being crowned by two angels (Plate 258). At her feet are two monks praying. On either side, under the arches, are two male saints, probably St Peter on the right, and St Paul, on the left. Under them are panels of finely carved late Gothic vine foliage and grapes, with punched and incised flowers on the background, suggesting the original use of polychrome here. The wings and the back seem to go together and the former are probably stall ends. Their width is the same as the desk ends in the main stalls. If it were possible to be certain about the dependent saints, one might be able to identify the monastery from which this panelling, and the choir-stalls came.

It is not easy to locate these stalls stylistically. However, they seem on balance most likely to have come from the Mosan area. The way that the lid of the misericord is sub-

PLATE 257. *St Chad's Cathedral, Birmingham. Choir-stalls. Netherlandish, c.1520. South side. (M/3)*

PLATE 259. *St Chad's Cathedral, Birmingham. Choir-stalls. Netherlandish, c.1520. Stall end. Detail of* Pietà. *(M/3)*

divided is echoed at St Nicholas, Kalkar (the stalls 1505-08), and the Minorite Franciscan friary at Klever (the stalls 1474). The mythical beasts, at St Chad's one clawed but wingless, the other winged and hoofed, are similar to those at Klever (Meurer 1970, pl. 25) (Plate 262). Their treatment is closely based on a drawing by the Master of St Sebastian, who was active 1460-80 (Lehrs 1921, L.iv, 124, 349). The figures cooking at St Chad's are broadly similar in treatment to others at Klever (Meurer 1970, pls. 2 and 24).

The heavy ungainly folds of the sculptural drapery, as well as a similar facial expression, are found on the Virgin and Child of *c*.1510 at St Lambert's Church, at

Opglabbeek in Limburg (Plate 263) (Laat-gotische 1990, Cat. ii, 30). The quality at St Chad's is provincial by comparison. Even so, a provenance in the western part of Belgium looks the most likely.

It seems doubtful that Pugin's stalls came from St Mary in Capitol, Cologne, as was traditionally thought. They bear no resemblance to the ones there now, probably datable to *c*.1300. Pugin's drawing, which is supposedly of part of these German stalls (Plate 25), may not relate to this church at all.

A.W.N. Pugin was commissioned to design a cathedral for Birmingham following the completion of Oscott College in

PLATE 260. *St Chad's Cathedral, Birmingham. Choir-stalls. Netherlandish, c.1520. Stall end. Detail of monks preparing food. (M/3)*

PLATE 261. *St Chad's Cathedral, Birmingham. Choir-stalls. Netherlandish. c.1520. Stall end on north side with dragons. (M/3)*

PLATE 262. *St Lambert, Opglabbeek, Limburg. Virgin and Child. c.1520.*
COPYRIGHT IRPA-KIK, BRUSSELS

PLATE 263. *St Catherine, Birtles, Cheshire. Single choir-stall. Flemish, late 16th century. (M/4)*

1838. Unusually for this date and in the Catholic church, a sumptuous assemblage of furnishings was provided by the architect and the Earl of Shrewsbury. Besides the stalls, this included the Flemish pulpit (K/1), as well as much fine modern furniture designed by Pugin himself. Also there was the 15th century brass lectern from Leuven (pages 58-59, a ciborium, a ewer and basin, and a pair of brass candlesticks, and six plates which had belonged to Cardinal Odescalchi in the 17th century. The cathedral, which cost £20,000 to build, was dedicated in 1841 (Hodgetts 1987).

M/4. St Catherine, Birtles, Cheshire (Plates 263-265)
Oak. Flemish. Late 16th century
Width of seat 79cm (2ft.7in.); height of seat capping 108cm (3ft.6½in.)
(For Birtles, see also I/1)

The evidence of the recessed quadrant for the tip-up seat on either side tells us that this single choir-stall seat has been extracted from a run of stalls (Plate 263). The seat standards are decorated with strapwork and acanthus, and their bases form shaggy cloven hooves. The misericord is in an Italianate Mannerist anthropomorphic manner (Plate 264). The elbows are carved heads, one a cleric and the

PLATE 264. *St Catherine, Birtles, Cheshire. Misericord. Flemish, late 16th century. (M/4)*

PLATE 265. *St Catherine, Birtles, Cheshire. Choir-stall. Flemish, late 16th century. Elbow with boy's head. (M/4)*

other probably a chorister (Plate 265). Both seem to be singing. There is no evidence that this seat has anything to do with the choir-stall backing at the west end and elsewhere in the church (pages 72-73, Plate 32 and Gazetteer).

The church at Birtles was built by the Hibbert family as a private chapel for the Birtles Hall tenantry (Richards 1973). It became a parish church in 1890. There is plenty of Continental stained glass, as well as a mass of heterogeneous Flemish and Dutch woodwork.

M/5. St John the Baptist, Bishopstone, Wiltshire (Plates 266-271)
Oak. Probably German, for example Westphalian. Early 16th century
The six stall ends must have all originally been 114cm (3ft.9in.) (max.) x 44cm (17¼in.)

A set of six stall ends. Two of them have been made up into a reading desk (Plates 267 and 268). Four, with a Spanish 19th century painted gesso panel and sundry pieces of woodwork of different dates, were composed into a pulpit (Plate 266). The two panels in the reading desk have been cut off at the top and sides, thereby losing their sloping mouldings at the top, surmounted by fantastic beasts, and

PLATE 266. *St John the Baptist, Bishopstone, Wiltshire. General view of 'pulpit'. (M/5)*

PLATE 267. *St John the Baptist, Bishopstone, Wiltshire. Reading desk. Choir-stall end with figure of bishop or abbot. Probably German, early 16th century. (M/5)*

PLATE 268. *St John the Baptist, Bishopstone, Wiltshire. Reading desk. Choir-stall end with figure of St Catherine Probably German, early 16th century. (M/5)*

PLATE 269. *St John the Baptist, Bishopstone, Wiltshire. 'Pulpit.' Stall end with abbot between Spanish gesso panel and figure of a bishop. Probably German, early 16th century. Notice complete stall end. (M/5)*

PLATE 270. *St John the Baptist, Bishopstone, Wiltshire. Stall end with St Mary Magdalene. Probably German, early 16th century. (M/5)*

PLATE 271. *St John the Baptist, Bishopstone, Wiltshire. Stall end with St Barbara adjacent to 'pulpit' entrance. Probably German, early 16th century. (M/5)*

PLATE 272. *St Mary's College, New Oscott, Sutton Coldfield, Warwickshire. Museum. Figure of bishop, probably Westphalian, early 16th century.*

PLATE 273. *St Mary the Virgin, Buscot, Berkshire. Single choir-stall. Netherlandish, early 17th century. (M/6)*

the generous buttresses each side (Plate 269). The standing figures on the stall ends represent St Catherine (Plate 268) and a mitred bishop on the reading desk (Plate 267), and the Virgin and Child (not shown), Mary Magdalene (Plate 270), St Barbara (Plate 271), and a mitre-less abbot with crozier and book on the pulpit (Plate 269). At his feet are the remnants of gesso and red paint. The composition of the panels is varied as to the placing and scale of the figures and the treatment of the canopies. In spite of this there is a consistency in the mouldings, and the treatment of foliage, drapery folds and physiognomy.

There seem to be two sculptors at work here. A rather conservative one has carved three of the four bishops, or abbots, in a heavy, static style. Of his carvings there are two semi free-standing figures, on early 16th century type plinths, one of which can hardly be seen as it faces the north wall (Plate 266, centre) (There are four more of these plinths on the pulpit stairs.) Both the figures by this first carver are stylistically different from the other stall end sculpture, except for the bishop on the desk (Plate 267), squatter in build, and in a much more conservative figure style, but still probably of a similar date. The five other figures, carved by the second sculptor, are all female, except for the mitre-less

abbot (Plates 268, 269, 270 and 271). The Virgin and Child, also by him, is not shown. They display heavy drapery folds and, in some cases, exhibit a serpentine profile.

The figure of a bishop in the museum at Oscott College (Plate 272), also thought to be German, is quite similar to the bishops at Bishopstone, carved by Hand A (Plates 266 centre, 267 and 269 right).

M/6. St Mary the Virgin, Buscot, Berkshire (Colour Plate 16; Plate 273)
Oak. Netherlandish. Early 17th century
Height of elbow 72cm (2ft.4¼in.), depth of elbow to back 37cm (14½in.); height of capping 94cm (3ft.1in.); depth of capping extension 30cm (11¾in.); depth of seat 39cm (15¼in.); width of seat 48cm (19in.)
(For Buscot, see also I/2)
The exuberant seat standards of this stall are in the form of a griffin, with head under the seat capping and clawed feet on the ground. They are made from two pieces of wood, an 11cm (4¼in.) strip having been added at the back. The seat back is original and features a coat of arms. The misericord is probably English and late 17th century, and has been cut to fit the stall.

PLATE 274. *King's College Chapel, Cambridge. Choir-stalls. South side of return seats. Early 1530s to after 1540. (M/7)*

M/7. King's College Chapel, Cambridge (Plates 274-278)
Oak. Probably made in Cambridge by Continental and English craftsmen. Early 1530s to after 1540
Centre to centre width of seats 76.5cm (2ft.6in.); height of seat capping 107cm (3ft.6in.); depth of seat capping 44cm (17¼in.); height of seats 45cm (17¾in.)
The furniture consists of a massive wooden pulpitum, 13 metres (42ft.7in.) wide, at the west end with single entranceway, eight return stalls and thirty lateral back stalls each side (Plates 274 and 275). There are also

twenty-five substalls each side with their original desks intact (Plate 276).

In about 1515 Henry VIII had been given a rough estimate of outstanding work in the chapel, including an item for £100 'for the workmanship in karving and joynyng … with Imagery, Tabernacles, doores, stayers and every other of' (here is a blank) 'concernyng the same workes to be made accordyng to the plat thereof devysed'. The total sum did not include the price of materials, 'the timber having been already purchased and laid by to season' (Willis and Clark 1886). Other items listed as not having yet been carried out were the carving and joining of ten return 'stalls against' the east side of 'the screen, with their tabernacles, five on each side, and a pulpytt over the doore at the comying in to the quire'. In practice there was a lapse of a further twenty years before work on the pulpitum and choir-stalls was resumed. Since the pulpitum carries the arms, badge and initials of Anne Boleyn, work on it is unlikely to have recommenced much before the year of her accession in 1532. Eight, not ten, return stalls were finally built.

The central doors of the pulpitum bear the arms of Charles I and the date 1636. They are the work of 'Woodruffe, le Joyner', who received £32 for his work (Willis and Clark 1886). 17th century also are the canopies of the lateral stalls. The panelling dates from 1633 and was made by William Fells (Willis and Clark 1886). The canopies were erected in 1675-78 to designs by Cornelius Austin at a cost of £305 (Willis and Clark 1886).

Consistent with English medieval precedent, the return stalls carry extra embellishment, notably the sculptured panel above the seat of honour on the south side, carved with a depiction of St George and the Dragon, and God the Father above (Plate 277). The dignitaries' seats on either side of the entranceway are much wider than the others, and the elbows of all the return stalls are carved with rosettes (Plate 278). The canopies of the return stalls are unquestionably original, with the heads of the dignitaries' seats projecting forward and the arms of King's College and Eton College above. In the corners of the return stalls there is a pair of canopy uprights, the mouldings of the easternmost of which conform to the 17th century canopywork of the lateral stalls. Surprisingly these were canopyless originally.

The pulpitum and the stalls, which are impossible to separate, are evidently the work of several craftsmen, some of whom must have been foreigners. Indeed we know that on 1 January 1535, 'Philip and another stranger' dined at the college with three local carpenters (*King's College Muniments Kitchen Accounts*, and Oswald, 1949). On 6 January 'Philippus Sculptor' and 'five other strangers' were given hospitality. Although the business of these craftsmen may have had nothing to do with the chapel furniture, the employment of several tradesmen at this time, most probably all carpenters, may indicate the period when much of the decorative carving was carried

PLATE 275. *King's College, Cambridge. Choir-stalls. North lateral stalls. Early 1530s to after 1540. (M/7).*   BY KIND PERMISSION OF THE PROVOST AND FELLOWS OF KING'S COLLEGE, CAMBRIDGE

out. These references in the college accounts could refer to the start of work on the pulpitum in the early 1530s. Woodman has shown on archaeological grounds that, in fact, the choir-stalls cannot have been completed until as late as shortly after 1540. However, since the coving of the pulpitum above the return stalls bears the quartered arms of Henry and Boleyn, and the 'AR' monogram, and the floor on which the pulpitum and the stalls stands was only laid in 1535, the entire monument must have had to be placed in storage for around four years before it was finally erected (Woodman 1981).

It is possible that the lateral stalls were made a little after the return stalls. By comparison they are quite plain with the snail-type decoration on the seat standard elbows, reminiscent of a design commonly found throughout Northern Europe (Plate 276). The elbows on the return stalls are much more typically English in form, but the fronting of the lower part of the standards with Renaissance baluster columns is novel (Plate 278). By comparison the side stall seat standards are simply

moulded without balusters. There are two types of misericords employed, those with foliage and some figurative carving with supporters, and the much more numerous Continental-looking simple triangular type without supporters on most of the lateral stalls.

Woodman has made a case for the workmanship of the pulpitum being English, and he cites certain design features which are quotations from the national architectural style. It would be absurd to suggest that the stalls were made abroad and shipped over to England, since we know that they were in any case an integral part of the unique wooden pulpitum, which must have been made on site. However, as in the late 15th century choir-stalls at St George's Chapel, Windsor, and the early 16th century choir-stalls at the Henry VII Chapel, Westminster Abbey, whether or not the craftsmen could be shown to be English, denizened foreigners or foreign visitors, there was in England at the time an openness to certain alien styles, the motifs from which could be reproduced if stipulated by a patron (Tracy 1990). By the 1530s the

231

was undertaken mainly by English craftsmen, but that some of the leading protagonists were either foreign visitors or at least of denizened status. Although Woodman has suggested that the man in overall control of both pulpitum and stalls was probably an English master-mason, under him would have been two carvers responsible for the very un-English looking medallion behind the seat of honour on the south side of the return stalls (Plate 277) and the fine lunette carvings on the west side of the pulpitum. Another might have had overall responsibility for the design and execution of the seating.

The architectural syntax is thoroughly Italianate, and closely related to other early Renaissance work in England, from the tomb of Henry VII at Westminster Abbey, of 1512-18, the Layer Marney, Essex tombs of the mid-1520s, the Jannys tomb at St George, Colegate, Norwich, after 1524, and the Oxburgh, Norfolk tombs of *c.*1525. By the early 1530s, this kind of work was well established. It is different from the coeval Italianate style on the stalls at Dordrecht, Holland (Plate 207) made

PLATE 276. *King's College, Cambridge. Choir-stalls. Detail of substalls seating in north side. Early 1530s to after 1540. (M/7)*

wider availability of prints would have made this process even easier. Throughout the period of the making of the stalls at Cambridge, King's College was a major employer of glass makers from Germany and Flanders. There would have been no shortage of advice on offer. As at Westminster and Windsor, much of the joinery work at King's College is English through and through, such as the constructional design of the seats and the way that the lateral ones are joined on to the return stalls. Interestingly at Cambridge the way that the desks of the back stalls are used to form decorated canopies for the substalls in front is exactly what happens at Westminster Abbey some twenty years before. On balance, therefore, would it not be more prudent to assume that, as a quarter of a century earlier at the Henry VII Chapel, Westminster, the joinery

PLATE 277. *King's College, Cambridge. Choir-stalls. St George panel in south return stalls. Early 1530s to after 1540. (M/7)*

PLATE 279. *King's College, Cambridge. Choir-stalls. View of south return seats. Early 1530s to after 1540. (M/7)*

BY KIND PERMISSION OF THE PROVOST AND FELLOWS OF KING'S COLLEGE, CAMBRIDGE

between 1538-41, which seems to have been filtered via Germany (van Duinen 1997). Other Dutch comparisons have been put forward by Bangs, notably the choir screens at the Westerkerk, Enkhuizen and St Bartholomeus, Schoonhoven (Bangs 1997). These deserve close attention, but are unlikely to be conclusive.

Judging from the limited amount of figure carving at Cambridge, notably the St George panel, the provenance of this element of the monument is more likely to have been via France, and the work of Italian artists, such as Battista Rosso and Primaticcio at Fontainebleau in the early 1530s, albeit that the Cambridge work is but a pale reflection. Other second-hand examples of this debased Fontainebleau-style figure carving in wood are occasionally met with in England, such as the figures at Ewyas Harold and Kinnersley, Herefordshire (Gazetteer), and those in the collection of loose panels at Harwood, Lancashire (M/12 and Plate 296). Pevsner attributed the Herefordshire material to the Netherlands and Flanders.

M/8. St George and St Mary, Church Gresley, Derbyshire (Plate 279)
Oak. Flemish. Third quarter 17th century
Centre to centre width of seats 73.5cm (2ft.6in.); height of seat capping 109cm (3ft/7in.); depth of seat capping 42cm (16⅛in.); height of seat 45.5cm (18in.)
From Drakelowe Hall, Derbyshire

The stall seating is arranged in two blocks of two, and two of three. The twos are made from pairs of end stalls. The threes are lifted from a run of stalls with the successive quadrants for the neighbouring seats exposed at each end. Typically for their time the misericords are not carved in the solid with the seats, the forward projections of the seat capping are separate, and the seats are metal-hinged. The carving is elaborate, with acanthus decoration along the front of the seat capping, angels' heads positioned under the seat capping, and elaborate seat elbows with human and animal busts, and claw and hoofed feet below. The range of classical ornament

PLATE 279. *St George and St Mary, Church Gresley, Derbyshire. Choir-stalls. Flemish, third quarter 17th century. Detail of seating. (M/8)*

employed is wide, including bead and reel, bay leaves, acanthus and laurel. Behind the seats are cut-out shaped and plain panels. The misericords are on the same generous scale as the rest of the carving, using various shell and cartouche motifs. The woodwork is largely un-restored, although it has suffered some recent damage.

M/9. St John the Baptist, Cockayne Hatley, Bedfordshire (Plates 15, 28, 30 and 280-284)
Oak. Flemish. Dated 1689-92
Centre to centre width of seats 72-74cm (2ft.4in.-2ft.5in.); height of seat capping 108cm (3ft/6⅛in.); depth of seat capping 30.5cm (12in.); height of elbow 81cm (3ft.3in.); height of seat 42cm (16½in.); depth of seat 33.5cm (13in.); width of seat 76cm (2ft.6in.); height of superstructure 1.585m (5ft.2½in.)
Introduced by the Honourable and Reverend Henry Cockayne Cust in 1826. Said to have come from 'Aune [Aulne] near Charleroi' (Cust 1851)
(For Cockayne Hatley, see also B/3, B/4, B/5, J/5, K/4 and pages 65-71)
The seating consists of eleven lateral stalls each side (Plates 280 and 281), with one return seat at the west end and the other one moved to the north chapel. The seats are placed in the church in two blocks, four seats in the chancel and seven in the nave (Plate 28). Original terminal seats, with their panelled and veneered closures, survive at the east end of the chancel blocks (Plate 282) and on the return stalls at the west end. As the chancel arch protrudes into the central space, the line of the stalls

had to be broken. It was, therefore, necessary to terminate the canopywork at that point. The rest of it was ingeniously extended into the presbytery, a rather curious expedient that is largely camouflaged by the altar rails which hide much of the lower zone at the east end (Plate 30). As a result only the first four seats from the east have any canopywork above them. Where the stalls return at the west end there are fine seat junctions with juxtaposed cherub heads, an uncommonly fine treatment of this perennially challenging passage (Plate 283). There is another of these seat junctions in the former family pew in the north nave aisle. Could there originally have been another single return stall on each side at the east end? This seems unlikely, since we know that a total of sixteen 'medallions' and twenty-four seats were sold in 1826 to the dealer in Brussels (Pickford 1995). Had there been an additional two return seats, the stall count would have been twenty-six. It is more likely that this spare seat junction is the remnant of a set of sub-stalls. The year 1689, the date of the initial setting up of the furniture, is recorded in two places, for instance, on the seat back of the westernmost stall on the south side of the chancel (Plate 281). The prior's coat of arms appears below on the misericord as well as on two other panels (Plate 284).

The joinery, decorative carving and sculpture is bold, imaginative and of high quality. There is pleasing variety in the use of mouldings and misericord types. The use of black inlay figuring on the seats, on seat terminations and return stalls adds richness to the overall effect, the motifs on the stall backs being of several different patterns.

PLATE 280. *St John the Baptist, Cockayne Hatley, Bedfordshire. Choir-stalls. Flemish, dated 1689-92. Detail of superstructure on north side. (M/9)*

PLATE 281. *St John the Baptist, Cockayne Hatley, Bedfordshire. Choir-stalls. Flemish, dated 1689-92. Detail of stall seating on south side of chancel. On the seat back of the right-hand stall the date is inlaid in bog oak. Below on the misericord are carved the arms of the prior.(M/9)*

Another touch of opulence is added by the foliage carving at the base of the seat standards and on the seat capping. Panels of scrolling foliage appear on the west side of the single return stalls, together with inset shell and foliage swags. Finally, the elevation of the super-structure was, according to an early 18th century source, originally surmounted by carved urns filled with flowers above the heads of the saints, balanced on each side with cornucopias (Saumery 1738-44). There are also pilasters with cherubs and foliage between each 'medallion'.

There is much restoration work in the superstructure, particularly in the framing behind the saints and the cornice work above. The carving of the busts, and of the angels between them, holding the instruments and symbols of the Passion, is in remarkably good condition. The date, 1826, of the setting up of this very Catholic furniture in a remote church in Bedfordshire, a county more usually connected with Non-Conformism, is recorded on a modern inlaid panel at the junction of the nave and chancel seats on the south side. The saints' names, from the Calendar of a Regular Augustinian house (Braconnier n.d.), are inscribed in a cartouche at the bottom of each panel. Reading from east to west, they are as follows:

North side – Bernardus, Anthonius, Ivo, Guarinus, Gilbertus, Aquilinus, Gaudentius, Nikolaus.

South side – Thomas, Anianus, Prosper, Dominicinus, Gregorius, Guilelmus, Ubaldus, Possidonius.

The names are followed by initial letters, indicating their status, i.e., E for Evangelist, C for Confessor, M for Martyr and P for Pope.

In his 'treatise' on the church, written in 1851, Robert Needham Cust, son of Henry Cust, stated that the choir-stalls came from Aulne Abbey, near Charleroi (Cust 1851). However, as Pickford has pointed out, Robert would have been but a boy when work on the church was in progress, making this claimed provenance: '...seem(s) rather credulous', given that he also notes the destruction by fire of the abbey in 1794, which most probably would have destroyed the stalls (Pickford 1995). The adduced provenance is certainly incorrect.

In the late 19th century a paper was written in Belgium about the stalls at Ragnies, south-west of Charleroi (Braconnier n.d.), in which it was claimed that they had come from the Regular Augustinian priory of Oignies, due east of that town (Plate 285). The furniture at Ragnies, it was claimed, consisted of the six easternmost stalls from Oignies. The others, according to the writer's informant, 'ont été vendues à un Anglais qui les ait fait transporter en son pays'. The Englishman was Colonel Robert Rushbrooke, of Rushbrooke Hall, Suffolk, who was living in Brussels at the time, and acting as agent for

PLATE 282. *St John the Baptist, Cockayne Hatley, Bedfordshire. Choir-stalls. Flemish, dated 1689-92. End standard, South-east end. (M/9)*

PLATE 283. *St John the Baptist, Cockayne Hatley, Bedfordshire. Choir-stalls. Flemish, dated 1689-92. Detail of seating junction. (M/9)*

his cousin and life-long friend Henry Cust.

The stalls at Ragnies are unquestionably from the same set of furniture as those at Cockayne Hatley. Adding the two collections together, and knowing how many stalls went to the Brussels dealer in 1826, we can say that the original number of stalls at Oignies was thirty-eight, on the basis of there having been four return stalls. The seats and medallions are distributed between Cockayne Hatley and Ragnies as follows:

	Number of lateral seats	*Number of medallions*
Cockayne Hatley	22	16
Ragnies	12	12
TOTAL	34	28
Return stalls	4 (1 missing)	
GRAND TOTAL	38	

Regrettably six of the canopy panels are still unaccounted

for. They are very likely to have been the so-called 'wainscotting' acquired by St Christophe, Charleroi, which is discussed below.

At this stage it may be helpful to record the list of saints above the twelve stalls at Ragnies, in case, by reference to an Augustinian Calendar, it helps to settle once and for all the question of the original number of seats provided. They are as follows:

> John (? John of Bridlington), Truden, Malachy, Lawrence, Bergisus, Fulcrus, Alype of Tagoste, Marcelin, Augustine of Hippo, Ablinus, Patrick, Herculanus.

After the abbey of Oignies had become the property of the state in 1796, it was offered to the mayor of Aiseau for the sum of four thousand florins for use as a parish church. Unfortunately, the curé of Aiseau was an ardent Revolutionary and the offer was refused (Fichefet 1977). In any case, the church would have been far too large for the needs of a hamlet. It was bought two years later by

PLATE 284. *St John the Baptist, Cockayne Hatley, Bedfordshire. Choir-stalls. Flemish, dated 1689-92. Panel with prior's arms. (M/9)*

Philippe Joseph Néverlée. The contents of the abbey's treasury, which had already been hidden from the covetous inclinations of invaders in 1648, were immured in a farmhouse by the last prior in 1794, and kept safe until 1817. Consequently the collection of peerless metalwork from the abbey's treasury, the product of Hugo of Oignies' late 12th and early 13th century workshop, and the extraordinary bequest of the Parisian administrator, Jacques de Vitry, cleric, historian, administrator, antiquary and bishop of Acre between 1216-28, still survives to this day at a convent in Namur. Also the much venerated 13th century figure of the Virgin and Child from the abbey was saved and is now in the Metropolitan Museum, New York.

The arms on the choir-stalls have been identified as belonging to the family of Castaigne. Guillaume de Rouillon, a member of this family, was Prior of Oignies Abbey in 1692 (Fichefet 1977). Pickford has done some useful work on this heraldry. As he says:

A clue to their origins is to be found in the arms on the stalls at Cockayne Hatley, which are dated 1689. There is also a date, 1692, in a chronogram under the medallion of St Ivo. It is difficult to match the arms with certainty. The archives of the Abbey of Oignies were

destroyed in 1940, and it has not been possible to identify the arms of Guillaume de Rouillon dit Castaigne, 'prieur' of the Abbey from 1679 to 1694. The arms of the family Rouillon de Castaigne are to be found on the portal of a farm at Montignies sur Sambre belonging to the Abbey at Oignies and they have the same arrangement of stars and flowers as those of the stalls at Cockayne Hatley [Plate 284]. This certainly links the stalls with Oignies instead of Aulne.

Fichefet contended that the dealer who sold the stalls in 1826 came from Brussels, rather than Charleroi, as was claimed by Robert Cust (Fichefet 1977). This makes sense as we know that Rushbrooke, Henry Cust's agent, was based in Brussels.

The abbey's furnishings were not finally sold and dispersed until 1826. As mentioned above, wainscoting 'associated with the choir furniture' was set up at the parish church of St Christophe, Charleroi, along with altars, confessionals, an organ, paintings, a pulpit, and the marble paving. Twelve of the stalls were sold to the church of Ragnies, a few miles south-west of Charleroi for 272 francs. But the greater part of them, consisting of twenty-four seats, sixteen medallions, two lecterns and two fronts of the *jubé* went to a dealer in Brussels, known to have

PLATE 285. *St Martin, Ragnies, near Charleroi. Choir-stalls.*   IRPA-KIK, BRUSSELS

been acting for an English collector, for 1,700 francs (Pickford 1995).

A passage from Saumery's mid-18th century *Les Délices du Pais de Liége* (Saumery 1738-44) on Oignies enthuses over the woodwork in the following terms:

Le choeur est décoré d'un magnifique Boisage orné de Medaillons d'un Relief délicat, ou sont représentés les Saints de l'Ordre, entre lesquels sont des Anges en forme de Pilastres, qui portent chacun un instrument de la Passion. Ils ont au-dessus de leurs têtes des Atiques surmontés de pots de fleurs, cantonnés de Cornes d'Abondance. Les quatre extrémités des stales [*sic*] sont ornées de quatre Colones torses assorties de leurs Bases et Chapiteaux d'Ordre Composite, qui servent de piedestaux à quatre Figures représentant quatre saints Personnages.

The Oignies stalls are stylistically on the cusp between the High and Late Baroque, with markedly less attention being paid to Classical detail and decoration than was later the case. Also the designer suffers much less from the *horror vacui* of his predecessors. Consequently a clearer and more intelligible overall design emerges with its contrasts in rhythm, and light and shade.

The use of busts emerging from medallions can be paralleled almost thirty years earlier in Flanders, in the stalls at St Jans Hospital, Bruges of 1661 (Debergh 1982, pls. 112-120). There are regional differences in the carving style, and the Bruges material inevitably looks old-fashioned by comparison. The Oignies work has a lightness and stylishness which animates the entire composition.

**M/10. St Andrew, Gatton, Surrey (Plates 12 and 286-288)
Oak. Said to have come from a Benedictine monastery in Ghent. *c.*1700
Centre to centre width of seats 67cm (26¼in.); height of seat capping 110cm (3ft.7¼in.); depth of seat capping 34cm (13½in.); height of elbow 74cm (29in.); height of seat 44cm (17¼in.); depth of seat 36.5cm (14¼in.); width of seat 62cm (24½in.)
(For Gatton, see also L/6 and M/11)**

As arranged here, there are sixteen back stalls on the north side and fifteen on the south, with fifteen substalls each side (Plates 12 and 286). However, only ten of the substalls are ancient. Originally all of the old seats were back stalls. In the modern entranceways between the substalls the seats have been arbitrarily terminated, leaving the quadrants exposed. The modern substalls are at the east end. Some of the stall ends with geometrical panelwork seem to be authentic. If the furniture did come from a monastery, there may not have been any substalls. From the number of seats at Gatton we can surmise that there were at least fifty-two stalls in the first place.

The design of the seat standards is conventional, with cherub heads under the seat capping and claw feet (Plate 287). The seats have plain panelled backs and the misericords, which are homogeneous, are in the form of human masks (Plate 288). The carved labels above the seat capping extensions must be modern as they decorate the timbers which make the transition from the 17th century seating to the 16th century superstructure.

The seating at Gatton resembles in some ways that on the Flemish choir-stalls from Hemiksem Abbey, in Flanders and now at St Lambert, Wouw in Holland (Plate 289). They were designed by the town architect of Antwerp, Jan Balthasar Bouvaert, and made between 1690-99. Three artists worked on them: Artus Quellinus the younger, Ludovicus Willemsens and Henrik-Frans Verbruggen.

M/11. St Andrew, Gatton, Surrey (Plates 12, 286, 290 and 291)
Oak, Netherlandish. Dated 1515
Height of superstructure from base of columns to top of cornice 164cm (5ft.4½in.)
Said to have been brought from Our Lady's Church, Aarschott, Brabant
(For Gatton, see also L/6 and M/10)

This Gothic stall backing consists of cusped ogee arches with perpendicular tracery in the spandrels (Plates 290 and 291). Typical Netherlandish late Gothic foliage crockets, and mini canopies with spirelets above and corbels for sculpture below. There are forty-four original small carved wooden figures of saints still *in situ*. Above is a coved canopy with pendent corbels, a carved inscription frieze, with its blue background paint intact, and a row of pinnacles. On the south side some of the backing has been sacrificed, where windows interpose. On the north,

PLATE 286. *St Andrew, Gatton, Surrey. Choir-stalls. Flemish, c.1700. View of seating. (M/10)*

PLATE 287. *St Andrew, Gatton, Surrey. Choir-stalls. Flemish, c.1700. Detail of seating. (M/10)*

PLATE 288. *St Andrew, Gatton, Surrey. Choir-stalls. Flemish, c.1700. Stall standard and misericord. (M/10)*

five of the segments of backing have had their panelling removed along the front of the family pew. There are other minor alterations associated with the problem of adapting the woodwork for use in this church.

The inscription reads as follows:

1. *Ghebenediit en gheloeft si die heiligen gloriosen soete namen ons liefs here ihu xpi en der gloriosen maget maria (?) sijne (?) lieuer moeder ewel*
2. *alre heilichste oro / iuve (sic.) maria moeder gods conighinne des hemels poerte des paradiis / missing*
3. *du onfincste ihm sonder en du diepste ghebaert den scepper en der verlosser der ganser werlt in welcke ick niet en twivel verlost mi va alle qwade amen an*
4. *In de jaer ons heren MCCCCCXV Is dit gh(ebeurt)*
5. *Volmaeckt bi ons keirkmeisters stansen (?) van diest jan / Kaemerlinc (?) in Jan Borchma(ns) hevet gema*
6. *Ke ame deo gracias*

The translation seems to be as follows:

1. *Blessed and praised be the holy, glorious, sweet names of our dear lord Jesus Christ and the Blessed Virgin Mary his dear mother ...*
2. *O Most holy Lady Mary, Mother of God, Queen of heaven, gate of Pa(radise)...*
3. *Thou didst conceive Jesus without ... thou hast brought forth the creator and redeemer of the whole world in whom I do not doubt. Redeem me from all evil. Amen ...*
4. *In the year of our lord MCCCCCXV (1515) is this ...*
5. *... completed by us Churchwardens Stasen van Diest, Jan Kaemerlinc (?) and Jan Borchma(ns) have made ...*
6. *Amen, thanks be to God*

The gaps in the text indicate that parts of the stall backing are missing.

Jan Borchmans (*c.*1450-*c.*1520), a wood carver and joiner from Eindhoven, is best known today for the set of choir-

PLATE 289. *St Lambert, Wouw. Choir-stalls. Detail of elevation. 1690-99.*
COPYRIGHT RIJKSDIENST VOOR DE MONUMENTENZORG, ZEIST

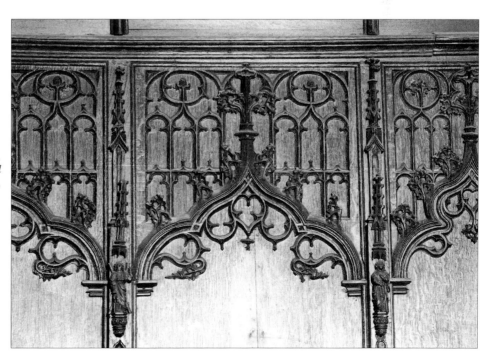

PLATE 290. *St Andrew, Gatton, Surrey. Stalls canopywork. Netherlandish, dated 1515. Probably from Our Lady's Church, Aarschott. Detail. (M/11)*

PLATE 291. *St Andrew, Gatton, Surrey. Drawing of Netherlandish stall backing, probably originally from Sint-Niklaasberg, Aarschott, but subsequently moved to Our Lady's Church, Aarschott. The seating is still at Aarschott (Plate 294). From F.A. Crallan,* Details of Gothic Woodwork, *London, 1897, Pl. xxxii.*

stalls he made for the cathedral church of St Peter, Oirschot in 1508. In the contract it was stipulated that the joinery should be finished within two years, and that the sculpture should be ready by the end of the following year. He was to base the design of the stalls on those at 's-Hertogenbosch Cathedral (Elias 1944). The whole job was to be finished four years before the date on the superstructure at Gatton. At Oirschot we are not able to make a direct comparison with the stall backs at Gatton, because the artist chose not to decorate the superstructure there, in virtual conformity with den Bosch in this respect. But, perversely, the vocabulary of the decorative sculpture on the stall backs at Gatton, although later in date, is less progressive than that at Oirschot. For the appearance of

the stalls at Oirschot we have to rely on old photographs, because the monument was destroyed in the Second World War (Witsen-Elias 1944, pls. 68-88). Indeed in many ways one would even be tempted to classify the Gatton stall backs, for instance, with those at St Martin, Bolsward of the late 15th century (Plate 292).

The stalls to which the superstructure at Gatton belonged are the ones today at Our Lady's Church, Aarschott, in Brabant (Plate 294). They were not made for this church, but for the convent of Sint-Niklaasberg in Aarschot, from where they were moved some time between 1586 and 1597 (Vanhoof 1987). A careful comparison of the stall ends at Aarschot (Plate 293) and the superstructure at Gatton throws up a number of stylistic similarities in the details

PLATE 292. *St Martin, Bolsward. Choir-stalls. Detail of stall elevation. Late 15th century.*

COPYRIGHT RIJKSDIENST VOOR DE MONUMENTENZORG, ZEIST

PLATE 293. *Our Lady's Church, Aarschott. Choir-stalls. Early 16th century. South side. Detail of stall end.*

COPYRIGHT CONWAY LIBRARY, COURTAULD INSTITUTE OF ART

PLATE 294. *Our Lady's Church, Aarschott. Choir-stalls. Early 16th century. Detail of stall end.*

COPYRIGHT CONWAY LIBRARY, COURTAULD INSTITUTE OF ART

between the two components, such as the triangular-shaped cusps, with indented triangles behind; the treatment of the foliage with regular holes pierced in it; and the form of the corbel mouldings below the arches of the superstructure and the misericords.

Between the Oirschot and Aarschot commissions Borchmans was employed making the choir-stalls at Averbode, a short distance away to the north-east.

M/12. Christ's Church, Harwood, Lancashire (Plates 295-297)
Oak. Flemish. Second quarter 17th century. Inserted panels *c.*1540
Centre to centre width 60cm (23½in.), height of capping 105cm (3ft.5¼in.)
(For Harwood, see also I/5)
This pair of stalls has been cut from a row, quadrants showing each side for the adjacent seats (Plate 295). The seat standards are decorated with strapwork and acanthus. At the top under the seat capping and on the

PLATE 296. *Christ's Church, Harwood, Lancashire. Pair of choir-stalls. Flemish, second quarter 17th century. View from front. (M/12)*

PLATE 295. *Christ's Church, Harwood, Lancashire. Pair of choir-stalls. Flemish, second quarter 17th century. (M/12)*

PLATE 297. *Christ's Church, Harwood, Lancashire. Misericords Flemish, second quarter 17th century. (M/12)*

elbows, angels' heads seem to have alternated with human heads. Claw and hoof feet were probably used throughout in equal proportions.

The stall backs contain an arch, embellished with a chain motif, with foliage in the spandrels (Plate 296). The figures of St Peter and St Paul, carved in low relief on the seat backs, have been put there recently. They demonstrate the typical figure style in the Low Countries and France *c.*1540. Two more of them have been built into the sides of a modern made-up desk. More yet are loose in the church. They must originally have belonged to a chest or reredos perhaps. The misericords of anthropomorphic foliage heads are original, but they have been remounted on to modern seats (Plate 297).

These stalls are not unlike those at St Peter, Lô, in West Flanders, of 1624 (Plate 298) (Debergh 1982).

TALLES
XVIᵉ Siècle.

ST·ALLES en bois de chêne sculpté décorant le chœur de l'église de Loo. Les frises, les miséricordes, la décoration des fûts sont autant de motifs différents. Ce remarquable objet d'art pourrait bien être l'œuvre du sculpteur yprois Taillebert. (Voir seconde série, Stalles, PL. 5 et 6).

Phototypie
STALLES

Jos. Maes, Anvers.

PLATE 298. *St Peter, Lô, West Flanders. View of choir-stalls. 1624.*   COPYRIGHT IRPA-KIK, BRUSSELS

PLATE 299. *Hever Castle, Kent. Settle with stalls attached. Italian, c.1500. (M/13)*

M/13. Hever Castle, Kent (Plates 299 and 300)
Walnut. Italian. *c.*1500
Width of left-hand seat 73cm (2ft.4¾in.), width of right-
hand seat 69cm (2ft.4in.), depth of seats 41cm (16in.);
height of capping, from original floor level 106cm
(3ft.5¾in.); height to top of stall back panelling from
original floor level 149cm (4ft.10¾in.)
(For Hever Castle, see also A/2, E/4 and H/2)
Two choir-stalls, and two misericords have been placed at
either end of a settle/chest (Plate 299). The four stall
standards have probably been cut from a continuous row of
seats, and some of the quadrants for the adjoining tip-up
seats, are exposed on each side (Plate 300). The standards at
the extremities of the present pew have been panelled over,
so that any evidence for these having been end seats, which
is possible, is hidden. They have been mounted on a short
plinth to bring them in line with the adjoining settle. At each
end the seat capping has been broken in two places.

The geometric ribband inlay on the seat backs and the
low-relief foliate carved panels above with the associated
cornice probably have nothing to do with the original

PLATE 300. *Hever Castle, Kent. Settle. Italian, c.1500. Detail of choir-stall on left side. (M/13)*

choir furniture. They may always have been associated
with the settle, but we cannot be sure. Prominent carved
discs decorate the stall standard elbows and the C-scroll
wings above the seat capping. Most are carved with lions,
but there are two with human heads. The surviving
misericords underneath the tip-up seats are probably
original, although they are not carved in the solid.

M/14. All Saints, Holdenby, Northamptonshire (Plates
301 and 302)
Oak. French. *c.*1720
Width of seat 76cm (2ft.6in.); height of seat capping,
excluding plinth, 107cm (3ft.6in.)
The surviving stall has been made up from two stall ends,
decorated with a long panel from which hangs a double-

curving bunch of leaves (Plates 301 and 302). The seat standards have scrolls under the rather thin seat capping, and simple acanthus carving on the fronts. On the insides, at the top, are small panels of foliage (not visible in the plates). The profile of the standards is very unusual with a double curve, and there is considerable undercutting at the bottom. They rest on claw and ball feet.

The chancel was rebuilt in 1843-45 by the then rector, the Reverend J.L. Crawley, at his own expense (Dalton 1985). It is probable that this French stall was introduced then.

M/15. St Nicholas, Leckford, Hampshire (Plates 303 and 304)
Chestnut or walnut. Central or North Italian. *c.*1650
Centre to centre width 68.5cm (2ft.3in.); height of seat 53cm (21in.); height of seat capping 110cm (3ft.7¼in.); depth of seat capping 46cm (18in.); height of superstructure 145cm (4ft.9in.)
Presented to the church in 1923
There are seven stalls each side, with their original seats without misericords (Plate 303). There are no substalls. The back of the seat capping has been removed on one

seat each side at the east end, where the altar rail passes through. The two easternmost seats have been raised up 30.5cm (12in.) The stall standards have scroll-shaped indentations (Plate 304). On the seat capping above rest foliage brackets. Between Corinthian pilasters there are indented mouldings on the superstructure. Across the top of the backing screen are winged putto heads.

At the top of the seat backs there are some old paper labels. On one is written *Vita mor* ... Others seem to be in Italian, but are indecipherable. Further down are more labels, such as:

On the north side	On the south side
SERVABIS	.. RIN(A)
... NON ...	DIRIGE
INVANUM	DOMINE
...IGVA ...	.. RA ..

These stalls are quite similar to the ones at Tooting Graveney, London (M/17), except that they are probably somewhat earlier in date. Like those at Tooting, they must originally have had some crowning decorative feature above the stall backing.

PLATE 301. *All Saints, Holdenby, Northamptonshire. Single choir-stall. French, c.1720. (M/14)*

PLATE 302. *All Saints, Holdenby, Northamptonshire. Choir-stall from side. French, c.1720. (M/14)*

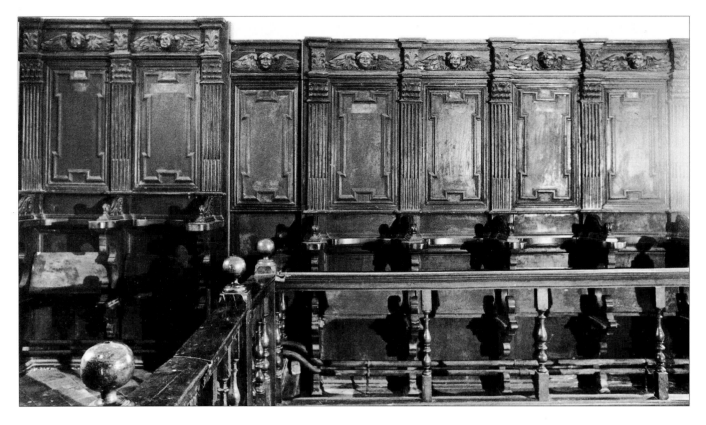

PLATE 303. *St Nicholas, Leckford, Hampshire. Choir-stalls. Central or North Italian, c.1650. South side. (M/15)*

PLATE 304. *St Nicholas, Leckford, Hampshire. Choir-stalls. Central or North Italian, c.1650. View of seating. (M/15)*

M/16. St Mary Magdalene, Littleton, Surrey (Plate 305)
Oak. French. Early 18th century
98.5cm x 32cm (max.) (3ft.2¾in. x 12½in.)
(For Littleton, see also B/8)
Fragment of a choir-stall seat standard from the elbow to the top, in the form of a scroll (Plate 305).

The delicate carving on this fragment is not dissimilar to a refugee standard in the Victoria and Albert Museum of about the same date (Museum Acq. No. 79-1898) (Plate 306).

PLATE 306. *Victoria and Albert Museum, London. Fragment of choir-stall end. Probably French, early 18th century.*

PLATE 305. *St Mary Magdalene, Littleton, Surrey. Fragment of stall standard. French, early 18th century. (M/16)*

PLATE 307. *All Saints, Tooting Graveney, London. View of choir-stalls. Bolognese or Modenese, third quarter 17th century. (M/17)*

PLATE 308. *All Saints, Tooting Graveney, London. Choir-stalls. Bolognese or Modenese, third quarter 17th century. View of seating. (M/17)*

M/17. All Saints, Tooting Graveney, London (Colour Plate 17; Plates 307 and 308)
Mahogany. Bolognese or Modenese. Third quarter 17th century
Centre to centre width of seats 72cm (2ft/4¼in.); seat height 44.5cm (17½in.); height of seat capping 112cm (3ft.8in.); overall height including superstructure 2.6m (8ft.6¼in.)
From the same church as the altarpiece at Tooting Graveney (C/3)
(For Tooting, see also A/3, C/3, C/4, D/1, E/6 and I/7)
There are two blocks of six stalls each side (Plate 307). The seats, which form a continuous fixed bench, are modern, as are the desks and substalls. Only the columns and seat arms are in solid wood. Otherwise, practically throughout, the surfaces are veneered. The design of the stall standards is strikingly different from the traditional form. The seat standard is now in two parts, a large volute for the base, and a combined buttress and arm rest above (Plate 308). The seats would have originally been discrete, and able to tip up, as at Leckford, Hampshire (M/15 and Plate 304). The superstructure is a conventional looking single-screen design, with large detached columns set at the back of the arm rest. The back rests at both levels are decorated with plain moulded panels cut out to two standard shapes. On the architrave are lively looking winged putto heads and a cresting of alternating acanthus sprays and urns.

PLATE 309. *Victoria and Albert Museum, London. Netherlandish bench end with* Life of Christ. *Early 16th century. (M/18)*
COPYRIGHT VICTORIA AND ALBERT MUSEUM, PICTURE LIBRARY

PLATE 310. *Victoria and Albert Museum, London. Netherlandish bench end with* Prodigal Son *story. Early 16th century. (M/18)*
COPYRIGHT VICTORIA AND ALBERT MUSEUM, PICTURE LIBRARY

M/18. Victoria and Albert Museum, London (Plates 309-311)
Oak. The Netherlands. Early 16th century
155cm x 49cm x 9.5cm (5ft.1in. x 19¼in. x 3¾in.)
Museum Acq. No. W.8 and W.9-1956.
(For V & A Museum, see also F/6, F/7, F/8, J/8, J/9,
J/10, L/7, M/19 and M/20)
A pair of bench ends, pierced and carved with subjects from the *Life of Christ* and the parable of the *Prodigal Son.* Each comprises the upper half only of a complete end, but lacks the cresting. The ends must have stood originally about 2.5m (8ft.) high.

There are four carved scenes on each, enclosed within circular and semi-circular panels, formed by a running scroll. The *Life of Christ* scenes on W.8 (Plate 309) comprise the *Annunciation,* at the bottom; the *Adoration of the infant Jesus by Mary and Joseph;* the *Baptism of Christ;* and *Christ's Vigil on the Mount of Olives.* On the front, supported on a

twisted column and surmounted by a late Gothic foliate canopy, is a figure of St Paul. The *Prodigal Son* scenes on W.9 (Plate 310) comprise *the Son receiving Money from his Father,* at the bottom; *the Son with a Harlot; the Son as a Swineherd;* and *the Son's Return.* Again, on the front, supported by a twisted column and surmounted by a canopy, there is another figure, this time of St Simon the Zealot (Plate 311). On the table cloth upon which the father counts out his money, in the first scene, is the following inscription:

+ VADER + GHEFT + MI +
+ MIN + DEEL + VAN + MIN + GOED + (Father gave me my share of my property).

A bench attached to the ends, but of a later date, was not retained by the museum.

One bench end must have been intended to stand against a wall, as the carving is only roughly finished off at

PLATE 311. *Victoria and Albert Museum, London. Figure of St Simon the Zealot on bench end. Netherlandish, early 16th century. (M/18)*
COPYRIGHT VICTORIA AND ALBERT MUSEUM, PICTURE LIBRARY

PLATE 312. *St Janskerk, 'sHertogenbosch. Stall end with inhabited scrolls. 1440-60.*
COPYRIGHT RIJKSDIENST VOOR DE MONUMENTENZORG, ZEIST

the back. There is some restoration at the base of W.9, and the base of the rear upright is worm-eaten. Each end is carved entirely in the solid. There is some damage to both carving and decoration. From the disposition of the surviving tenons, it seems that the ends were linked by comparatively light rails, engaging into the back of W.8 and the front of W.9. It seems unlikely that there was ever any more substantial back.

These bench ends are reminiscent of the highly elaborated Netherlandish late Medieval versions of the tall pierced back-stall end, exemplified at St Janskerk, 's-Hertogenbosch, dated 1440-60 (Plate 312). Similar stall ends with pierced scrolling branch-work in the upper zone, and containing Biblical scenes, could also be seen in the now destroyed choir-stalls at St Peter, Oirschot (Elias 1944, pls. 68 and 69). These were carved by Jan Borchmans (See M/11) in about 1510.

252

PLATE 313. *Victoria and Albert Museum, London. Misericord of girl with horned headdress and wimple (W.24). Netherlandish, c.1441-45 (M/19).* COPYRIGHT J.A.J.M. VERSPAANDONK

PLATE 314. *Victoria and Albert Museum, London. Misericord of man looking out of a window (W.30). Netherlandish, 1441-45. (M/19)* COPYRIGHT J.A.J.M. VERSPAANDONK

M/19. Victoria and Albert Museum, London (Plates 313-317)
Oak. South Netherlands. c.1441-45. Probably sculpted by Claes de Bruyn
29cm x 78cm (max.) (11½in. x 2ft.6¾in.)
Museum Acq. No. W.24 to W.41-1910
(For V & A Museum, see also F/6, F/7, F/8, J/8, J/9, J/10, L/7, M/18 and M/20)

This collection of eighteen misericords, probably all from the same set of choir-stalls, was given to the museum in 1910. They are vigorously carved with a wide variety of typically late medieval subject matter, as follows:

W.24-1910 Girl with prominent ears, horned head-dress and wimple (Plate313).
W.25-1910 Two animals issuing from a turret.
W.26-1910 Male head with bat's wings.
W.27-1910 Owl.
W.28-1910 Two men dancing.
W.29-1910 Two jesters or wrestlers.
W.30-1910 Man looking out of a window (Plate 314).
W.31-1910 Boy yawning.
W.32-1910 Woman with horned head-dress.
W.33-1910 Two (?) parrots.
W.34-1910 Grimacing male head.
W.35-1910 Two birds back to back (Plate 315).
W.36-1910 Winged dragon with head turned back (Plate 316).

PLATE 315. *Victoria and Albert Museum, London. Misericord with two birds back to back (W.35). Netherlandish, 1441-45. (M/19)*

W.37-1910 Wivern.
W.38-1910 (?) Pelican with young.
W.39-1910 Crouching two-legged beast (Plate 317).
W.40-1910 Two-winged animal.
W.41-1910 Affronted griffins.

It was thought at first that the misericords were English, since it was alleged that they had been removed from a Northamptonshire church. However, their European origin has long been recognised, although not until recently has it been specifically tied down. The Dutch misericord specialist, J.J. Verspaandonk, having examined them, has adduced some very convincing parallels from

PLATE 316. *Victoria and Albert Museum, London. Misericord of winged dragon with head turned back (W.36). Netherlandish, 1441-45. (M/19)* COPYRIGHT J.A.J.M. VERSPAANDONK

the South Netherlands (Verspaandonk 1986).

In the choir-stalls of about 1440, at the Grote Kerk, Breda, is a misericord of two birds (probably storks) pecking at two eels coming out of a basket. It was pointed out that these birds are similar to those found on contemporary playing cards, such as the 'five' and 'nine' by the Master of the Playing Cards (Plate 318). This engraver, from the Upper Rhine, was active between 1430 and 1450. The misericord at the Victoria and Albert Museum shows another pair of birds which seem to be modelled on the work of the same engraver (Plate 315). In this case the central bird on card five was probably used. As at Breda a single drawing has been selected and used again in reverse to make a pair of birds.

It is in the church of St Peter, Leuven, whose surviving choir-stalls were made between 1438 and 1441, that a series of really convincing parallels can be found for the museum's carvings. To start with, it will be seen from the illustrations that the seat shapes are almost identical. The rounded quality of the carving in both sets is well displayed in a comparison of two dragons (Plates 316 and

PLATE 317. *Victoria and Albert Museum, London. Misericord of crouching two-legged beast on protruding spike (W.39) Netherlandish, 1441-45. (M/19)* COPYRIGHT J.A.J.M. VERSPAANDONK

PLATE 318. *Card five. Master of the Playing Cards (Upper Rhine, 1430-50).* COPYRIGHT VICTORIA AND ALBERT MUSEUM, PICTURE LIBRARY

PLATE 319. *St Peter, Leuven. Misericord with dragon with head turned back. 1438-41.*   COPYRIGHT J.A.J.M. VERSPAANDONK

319). Both animals cling determinedly to the side of the seat in a similar way. The curious two-legged animal at the V & A displays the protuberances of his spine exactly like the dragon at St Peter's, Leuven (Plates 317 and 319).

In European misericords of the 14th century the whole carving often consists simply of an abstract faceted triangular shape, finished off at the bottom, as here, with a

PLATE 320. *St Peter, Leuven. Misericord with lion on protruding spike. 1438-41.*   COPYRIGHT J.A.J.M. VERSPAANDONK

PLATE 321. *St Peter, Leuven. Misericord with face framed by window. 1438-41.*   COPYRIGHT J.A.J.M. VERSPAANDONK

plain spike, and as also on the museum's curious two-legged beast. The motif of the spike appearing below the animal on the misericord can also be seen under the lion at St Peter's, Leuven (Plate 320). This compositional parallel provides important corroboration for the stylistic agreements. Finally, the two sets of misericords share another unmistakable compositional motif – that of a head peering out of a window (Plates 314 and 321). This conceit is also found at the Grote Kerk, Breda, where St Barbara is shown at the window of her tower.

The horned hair-style of the V & A Museum's girl in a wimple (Plate 313) can be dated to the second quarter of the 15th century. It is the fashion adopted by Giovanna Cenami in the *The Marriage of Arnolfini* by Jan van Eyck, at the National Gallery, London. This painting is inscribed with a date of 1434.

The shape of the ledge above the misericords at the Victoria and Albert Museum and St Peter's, Leuven is almost identical. The joinery at Leuven was undertaken by Gort Gorys and the carving by Claes de Bruyn, between 1438 and 1441. Both craftsmen came from Brussels. It seems most likely that the museum's collection is the work of Claes de Bruyn, and that they were made between 1441-45.

PLATE 322. *Victoria and Albert Museum, London. French stall backing. Early 16th century.(M/20)* COPYRIGHT VICTORIA AND ALBERT MUSEUM, PICTURE LIBRARY

M/20. Victoria and Albert Museum, London (Plate 322)
Oak. French. Early 16th century
2.447m. x 1.844m (8ft. x 6ft.)
Museum Acq. No. 410-1905
From the church of Toussy, between Auxerre and Montargis
(For V & A, see also F/6, F/7, F/8, J/8, J/9, J/10, L/7, M/18 and M/19)
This is a section of stall backing with the spaces for three

seats (Plate 322). The right-hand end seems to be where the stalls stopped, whilst the left-hand side has been crudely severed. In the centre there are portions of the original seat standards. For a general stylistic comparison of this French Renaissance wood carving, the room panels from the Château de Gaillon in Normandy (1500-10) are pertinent, although the vocabulary there is wider and the style more sophisticated.

256

PLATE 323. *St Mark, Mark, Somerset. Stall end figure of St Matthew. Flemish, c.1524. (M/21)*

PLATE 324. *St Mark, Mark, Somerset. Stall end figure of St John. Flemish, c.1524. (M/21)*

M/21. St Mark, Mark, Somerset (Plates 323 and 324)
Oak. Flemish. *c.*1524
91cm x 61cm, including bases (2ft.11¾in. x 2ft.)
From the choir-stalls of the former cathedral church of St Donation, Bruges. Inscribed 'André'
These four figures of the Evangelists must have formed the upper parts of the choir-stall ends. Two are illustrated here. All of them are designed to be seen fully in the round. The bases may not be original. The figures have been coated in a thick varnish, which is now badly discoloured.

The former cathedral was sacked in 1794. On 1 May 1799 a sale of the contents was held, including, according to the local official Joseph van Valleghem: 'Altars, choir-screen, pulpit, choir-stalls, metalwork, candelabras'. The

carvings now at Mark Church were purchased by a former vicar, the Reverend F. du Sautoy (his incumbency 1860-91), and given to the church. He paid £70 for them.

M/22. St Michael and All Angels, Middlewich, Cheshire (Plate 325)
Oak. Probably Flemish. *c.*1600
Centre to centre seat width 70cm (2ft.3⅛in.); height of seat capping 104cm (3ft.5in.)
(For Middlewich, see also F/9 and M/23)
A single stall. The misericord does not belong (M/23). There is strapwork on the sides of the standards, with a Roman mask and a Roman head under the seat capping. The left-hand divider is tantalisingly inscribed 'ANo'.

PLATE 325. *St Michael and All Angels, Middlewich, Cheshire. Single choir-stall. Probably Flemish, c.1600. (M/22)*

PLATE 326. *St Michael and All Angels, Middlewich, Cheshire. Lion misericord. Probably French, early 16th century. (M/23)*

PLATE 327. *Tréguier Cathedral, Côtes d'Armor. Lion misericord. 1508-09. (M/23)*

M/23. St Michael and All Angels, Middlewich, Cheshire (Plate 326)
Oak. Probably French. Early 16th century
36cm x 57cm (14in. x 22⅟₂in.)
(For Middlewich, see also F/9 and M/22)

This misericord depicts a lion sitting on a rock with, either side, two stalks bearing leaves for supporters (Plate 326). It was always peg-hinged into the seat standards on either side. Round pegs were fashioned at the back of the ledge in the solid and the seat was clamped in between the seat standards as they were assembled. Before the 14th century this was the preferred method of hinging seats. After that the use of metal hinges was practically ubiquitous. At Middlewich slivers of wood have been added either side of the seat to make it fit into its new housing.

A reasonable comparison is the lion misericord from Tréguier Cathedral, Brittany (Plate 327). The animal there has a forked tail and it perhaps makes one wonder if the Middlewich lion is supposed to share this feature. The stalls at Tréguier are dated to 1508-09.

M/24. St Matthew, Otterbourne, Hampshire (Plate 328)
Oak. Probably Flemish. Early 14th century
Height of elbow 84cm (2ft.9in.); depth from elbow to back 35cm (13¾in.)
(For Otterbourne, see also B/9)

The front portions of only two matching seat standards survive, up to the level of the capital above the elbow (Plate 328). The rest has been cut away. The lower part of the seat standard and the portion under the seat capping are fronted by columns. The elbows consist of boldly projecting birds and foliage.

The standards share the same vocabulary of form as the early 14th century stalls in Cologne, yet they are clearly not German. There are no comparable stalls surviving from this date in the Low Countries yet, given the provenance of the other imported material in this church, it would probably be safe to assume that they came originally from Flanders.

PLATE 328. *St Matthew, Otterbourne, Hampshire. Single choir-stall. Probably Flemish, early 14th century. (M/24)*

PLATE 329. *Oxburgh, Hall, Norfolk. Chapel. Section of choir-stalls at west end. Flemish, early 17th century. (M/25)*

M/25. Church of Our Lady and St Margaret, Oxburgh Hall, Norfolk (Plates 329 and 330)
Oak. Flemish. Early 17th century
Centre to centre seat width 66cm (2ft.2in.); height of seat capping 116cm (3ft.9½in.)
(For Oxburgh Hall, see also B/10, B/11 and C/5)
There are two blocks of four stalls. Both have been cut from a larger run of seats, there being no stall ends extant (Plate 329). All but one of the misericords have the same double-curve ledge moulding (Plate 330). The odd one out has a simple rounded profile. The decoration on the seating is elaborate, with human and animal supporters under the seat capping projections, volute foliage elbows with some figurative elements, flowers down the front of the seat standards, and fluting on the front and sides of the lower parts. An unusual feature is the flowers in the corners of the seat quadrants.

The stylistic mixture of late Mannerism and early Baroque in the hands of an outstanding decorative sculptor is highly successful.

PLATE 330. *Oxburgh Hall, Norfolk. Mask misericord. Flemish, early 17th century. (M/25)*

PLATE 331. *Scarisbrick Hall, Lancashire. Choir-stall standard on right side of made-up seat of honour in Great Hall. Flemish, 1440-45. (M/26)*

PLATE 332. *St Peter, Leuven. Choir-stall standards. 1438-41.*
COPYRIGHT IRPA-KIK, BRUSSELS

M/26. Scarisbrick Hall, Lancashire (Plate 331)
Oak. Flemish. 1440-45
Height of seat capping 123cm (4ft.½in.)
(For Scarisbrick Hall, see also pages 76-78, M/27 and M/28)
There are four matching stall standards, two made up into the seat of honour in the Great Hall (Plate 331) and two more on either side of the fireplace in the Oak Room. Although the seat standards are genuine, it is sometimes

hard to disentangle them from the 'Wardour Street' embellishments. Some of these are themselves ancient, such as the late 15th century North French tracery infills in the quadrants of the Great Hall standards (Plate 331).

These stall standards are stylistically quite close to, but somewhat later than, those at St Peter's, Leuven, of 1438-41, by the joiner Gort Gorys and the carver Claes de Bruyn (Plate 332 and (M/19).

PLATE 333. *Scarisbrick Hall, Lancashire. Fool with target and cudgel misericord. Low Countries, late 15th century. (M/27)*

M/27. Scarisbrick Hall, Lancashire (Plates 333 and 334)
Oak. Low Countries. Late 15th century
24cm x 25cm (approx.) (9½in. x 9¾in.)
(For Scarisbrick Hall, see also M/26 and M/28)

There are five misericords mounted, incongruously, above the frieze on the north side of the Great Hall. Positioned here as if they were corbels, and stained almost black, they are difficult to make out from floor level. The five figurative subjects are as follows:

1 and 2. A warrior with shield and club (Plate 333).
3 and 4. A fool holding up a buckled belt in both hands.
5. Man playing a bagpipe (Plate 334).

The misericords are triangular in shape and four of them have spikes at the bottom. This is an authentic feature, but the moulded plinth at the base of the bagpiper subject is probably a modern addition.

PLATE 334. *Scarisbrick Hall, Lancashire. Bagpipe player misericord. Low Countries, late 15th century. (M/27)*

M/28. Scarisbrick Hall, Lancashire (Plates 9a, 9b and 335-339)
Oak. Probably Brussels work. *c.*1520
Dimensions of inset upper panels 204cm x 49cm (6ft.8in. x 19¼in.)
Bought in June 1837 from Edward Hull for £22
(For Scarisbrick Hall, see also M/26 and M/27)

Two pairs of made-up doors, leading from the King's Room to the Dining Room (sometime the North Library) and the Red Drawing Room (sometime the South Library). In each case the zone above plinth level is filled with a carved panel consisting of prominent scrollwork interspersed with figurative and historiated scenes. In the Dining Room doors (Plates 9 and 335) the lower panels are compartmentalised at the bottom, those on one side comprising the figures of a bishop and a pope, and on the other, human figures, a mermaid and dragon with human head, sitting on arches overhanging castle gatehouses. On both sides of the door leading from the King's Room to the Red Drawing Room, the design conforms entirely to the scrollwork configuration, with historiated scenes at both levels (Plates 336 and 338). The narrative content, if any, of the panels on the Red Drawing Room side of this door, and on the Dining Room side of the other door (Plate 335), is hard to make out. In both cases the protagonists are facing away from the viewer. The recognisable scenes are on the King's Room side of both doors, which is appropriate as these would be the first sides to be taken in by a visitor (Plates 9, 10, 336 and 337).

Of the six intelligible scenes, four of them have been connected by Woods with the *Life of St Anthony*, according to Jerome's life of Paul the Hermit (Woods 1983). In the bottom left-hand corner of the Red Drawing Room door is *The meeting of St Anthony and St Paul* and the *Bread fetched by the Ravens before St Paul's Death* (Plates 336 and 337). Above this *St Anthony kneels in Front of the Dead Body of St Paul* and, the *Lions Dig St Paul's Grave*. To the right is the scene of *St Paul's Burial* and underneath, we see the *Bearing of the Relics*. The other St Anthony scene is in the upper left-hand area, on the King's Room side of the Dining Room (Plates 9 and 10). It shows *St Anthony being tempted by the Women*. On the other door leaf is the only non-Anthonine scene, that of *Pilate's wife urging him to abjure any part in Christ's Judgement*, whilst *Pilate washes his Hands*. Meanwhile *Christ is led away to be scourged* (Plate 339). Scarisbrick Hall is now a school and this explains why the rabble-rouser in the background has had his mouth filled with chewing-gum!

The main components of these doors seem to be eight high quality choir-stall ends. They must have been laminated together inside to inside, as it were, so as to avoid the seat side being exposed to view, which it is at Adare Manor, Limerick, but on the *verso* of the image in Plate 11. Iconographically and stylistically, the carvings are all of a piece. Moreover, when placed side by side they

PLATE 335. *Scarisbrick Hall, Lancashire. Door from Dining Room to King's Room. The panels probably Brussels work, c.1520. North side. (M/28)*

PLATE 337. *Scarisbrick, Lancashire. Red Drawing Room doors. King's Room side. The panels probably Brussels work, c.1520. 1. St Anthony kneels in front of the dead Body of St Paul and The Lions dig St Paul's Grave; 2. St Paul's Burial; 3. The Meeting of St Anthony and St Paul and The Bread fetched by the Ravens before St Paul's Death; 4. Bearing the Relics. (M/28)*

PLATE 336. *Scarisbrick Hall, Lancashire. Door from King's Room to Red Drawing Room. The panels probably Brussels work, c.1520. North side. (M/28)*

PLATE 338. *Scarisbrick Hall, Lancashire. Door from Red Drawing Room to King's Room. The panels probably Brussels work, c.1520. South side. (M/28)*

fit. This is additional evidence that they all came from the same suite of furniture. In the upper sections, around the scrolling foliage, the panels seem to have been pierced originally. During the 19th century transformation thin pieces of board were fitted, like the filling of a sandwich, between each of the panels, probably because the piercing would not have matched exactly each side. The total of eight stall ends required would have been twice the usual number for a choir and presupposes that the furniture came from a very grand church. The fact that the lower sections of the panels are in the solid, rather than being pierced, suggests that the reverse side would

have had a structural role. The sides of the doors, within the Dining Room and the Red Drawing Room, where the protagonists are looking in the opposite direction, must have originally been stall ends that were placed in inconspicuous positions and not intended to be often seen.

In the upper part of the panels, the straddling of the spaces across the scrolling tracery seems to be authentic. One has to imagine that on the reverse side the pierced intervals, and such details, are replicated exactly. Apart from any obvious repairs the only new work is the sculpture in the spandrels at the top, and the face and scrollwork at the top of the left-hand door in the Dining Room, and most probably the upper scroll on the other side. Some of this is a very careful copy of figures on the original work (Appendix 3, Dec. 1836, Feb. 1837, Feb. 1838, June 1839).

The figure style of the ancient work is a long way from the lingering Gothic conventions of the wooden sculpture on the stall ends at mid-15th century St Janskerk, s'Hertogenbosch (Plate 312), although rather closer in figure style to the work of Martin Borchmans at early 16th century St Peter, Oirschot, which are transitional between

PLATE 339. *Scarisbrick Hall, Lancashire. Door from King's Room to Red Drawing Room. The panels probably Brussels work, c.1520. North side. Panel showing* Pilate washing his hands *and* Christ led to the Scourging. *See also Plates 9 and 10. (M/28)*

PLATE 340. *Stonyhurst College, Lancashire. Section of choir-stalls. Flemish, early 18th century. (M/29)*

PLATE 341. *Stonyhurst College, Lancashire. Choir-stall standard. Flemish, early 18th century. Detail. (M/29)*

Gothic and Renaissance. In any case, if we can accept most of the bold squared-up succulent leaves at Scarisbrick as authentic, the date of the work must be somewhere in the first twenty years of the 16th century. The inhabited stall end with scrolling foliage has a long pedigree. It was probably invented in France in the 13th century, as is evidenced in the sketchbook of the architect Villard de Honnecourt from the period 1240-50. The motif is also to be seen on the 13th century stalls at Lausanne Cathedral (which Villard probably had a hand in designing), and gained popularity in the Rhineland and Switzerland during the 14th century. A couple of rare French examples from the later Middle Ages are the stalls at Villefranche-de-Rouerge, Aveyron, of 1462-70, and those at Chaise-Dieu, south-west of Lyons, of *c.*1500.

The style of the figure sculpture at Scarisbrick is most probably Brussels work of *c.*1520.

M/29. Stonyhurst College, Lancashire (Plates 340 and 341)
Oak. Flemish. Early 18th century
Centre to centre stall width 68.5cm (2ft.3in.); height of capping 115.5cm (3ft.9½in.), including plinth; depth of seat 37.75cm (14¾in.)
Probably by the same workshop as the choir-stalls at Oscott College (M/31) and Weare Giffard Hall (M/32)
There are two banks of five choir-stalls placed opposite each other in the house, in the 'front quadrangle'. There is only one end stall amongst them. In addition there is a bank of six stalls, and another four, in storage, making a total of twenty. These have not been examined, but photographs show that they are from the same set.

The seat standards have plain scrolls for elbows, with angel heads below the seat capping. These heads are usually turned one way or another, except for that on the terminal seat, which looks straight ahead. One of the angel heads has a cornucopia filled with flowers behind it, with flowers in its hair (Plate 341). There are plain moulded panels above and below the seats.

The stalls at Stonyhurst College are very close indeed to those at Oscott College (M/31) and Weare Giffard Hall (M/32). The mouldings of the seat capping, the panelling behind the seats, the profile of the seat standards and the style of the misericords are so close as to leave no doubt that they must have been made by the same workshop. Indeed, the treatment of the cherub heads under the seat capping at Oscott and Weare Giffard, with their characteristic head-dresses, is so similar as to allow one to assume that these two refugee amalgams must have formerly constituted part of the same set of choir-stalls. It is only the lack of head-dresses on the Stonyhurst College cherubs that suggests that those twenty stalls, although made by the same craftsmen, may not have been actually part of the same set of choir furniture.

The stalls were acquired for use in the College chapel in 1851 and were presumably expelled at some time during the 20th century.

M/30. Church of the Ascension, Southam, Gloucestershire (Plates 342 and 343)
Oak. Flemish. End 16th century
Centre to centre width of seats 73cm (2ft.4¾in.); height of capping 114cm (3ft.9in.)

These three seats must have been taken from a longer run of stalls as the seat capping is cut in two places. Both of the end seat standards were originally stall ends. The seats are embellished with strapwork on the sides of the dividers, with a pounced ground in the interstices (Plate 342). The seat capping is decorated with fluting at intervals along the front surface. There are term figures underneath the capping projections, and lions' heads with a ring in their mouths for the elbows. The fronts of the dividers are fluted and form claw feet at the base. The misericords depict the figures of Neptune, a winged lion and a crouching nude figure in strapwork (Plate 343).

The seating is reminiscent of that at Jeper, in Flanders of 1598 (Debergh 1982, pls. 44-54).

The church was reopened in 1862, having been restored by Lord Ellenborough, sometime Viceroy of India, in memory of his first wife, Countess Octavia (page 84).

PLATE 342. *Church of the Ascension, Southam, Gloucestershire. Choir-stalls. Flemish, end 16th century. Detail. (M/30)*

PLATE 343. *Church of the Ascension, Southam, Gloucestershire. Choir-stall misericord. Flemish, end 16th century. (M/30)*

PLATE 344. *St Mary's College, New Oscott, Sutton Coldfield, Warwickshire. View of choir-stalls on south side Flemish, early 18th century. (M/31)*

M/31. St Mary's College, New Oscott, Sutton Coldfield, Warwickshire (Colour Plate 18; Plates 344-346)
Oak. Flemish. Early 18th century
Centre to centre stall width 60cm (23½in.); height of capping 114cm (3ft.9in.), including plinth; depth of seat 37cm (14½in.)
Probably from the same set of choir-stalls as those at Weare Giffard Hall (M/32)
(For Oscott, see also B/13, J/12, J/13 and J/14)

There are ten stalls each side, but they are cut from a longer run of seats, and there are no original stall ends (Plate 344). The Gothic-style stall ends and backs, and most of the other stallwork in the chapel, are of the 1920s. The stalls, as originally set up, had no backing whatsoever. The seat standards are characterised by large and vigorously carved angel heads beneath the seat capping, with wings spreading on to the plain surface on either side (Plate 345). Some of the heads face in different directions and some are singing. The elbows are simple volutes with classical foliage in the spandrels. The plain foliage misericords, five of which on the south side are missing, have no supporters (Plate 346).

The stalls at Oscott College are very close indeed to those at Weare Giffard (M/32) and Stonyhurst College (M/29). The mouldings of the seat capping, the panelling behind the seats, the profile of the seat standards, and the style of the misericords are so close as to leave no doubt that they must have been made by the same workshop. The treatment of the cherub heads under the seat capping at Oscott and Weare Giffard, with their characteristic head-dresses, is so close as to allow one to assume that these two refugee amalgams must have formerly constituted part of the same set of choir-stalls. It is only the lack of head-dresses on the Stonyhurst College (M/29) cherubs that suggests that those twenty stalls may not have been part of this particular suite of furniture.

The stalls were placed in the new chapel shortly before 1837.

PLATE 345. *St Mary's College, New Oscott, Sutton Coldfield, Warwickshire. Choir-stalls. Flemish, early 18th century. Detail of south side. (M/31)*

PLATE 346. *St Mary's College, New Oscott, Sutton Coldfield, Warwickshire. Choir-stalls. Flemish, early 18th century. Misericord. (M/31)*

PLATE 347. *Weare Giffard Hall, Bideford, Devon. Choir-stalls. Flemish, early 18th century. General view. (M/32)*

M/32. Weare Giffard Hall, Devon (Plates 347 and 348)
Oak. Flemish. Early 18th century
Centre to centre seat width 68cm (2ft.2¾in.); height of seat capping 107cm (3ft.6in.); depth of seat 38cm (15in.)
Probably from the same set of choir-stalls as those at Oscott College (M/31)
This run of six stalls is complete, although the stall ends have been shaved back to fit into their position in the house (Plate 347). The lively and vigorously carved angel heads beneath the seat capping sometimes turn towards each other, and one of them is singing (Plate 348). The seats are otherwise plain and there are simple moulded panels behind them at both levels. The misericords are purely decorative but match the muscular Baroque scale of the rest of the work.

The stalls at Weare Giffard are very close indeed to those at Oscott College (M/31) and Stonyhurst College (M/29). The mouldings of the seat capping, the panelling behind the seats, the profile of the seat standards, and the style of the misericords are so close as to leave no doubt that they must have been made by the same workshop. The treatment of the cherub heads under the seat capping at Oscott and Weare Giffard, with their characteristic head-dresses, is so close as to allow one to assume that these two refugee amalgams, amounting to a total of twenty-six stalls, must formerly have constituted part of the same set of choir furniture. It is only the lack of head-dresses on the Stonyhurst College cherubs that suggests that those six stalls, although made by the same workshop, may not have been part of the same choir furniture.

PLATE 348. *Weare Giffard Hall, Bideford, Devon. Choir-stalls. Flemish, early 18th century. Detail. (M/32)*

Notes (*Introduction and Chapters I-V*)

Introduction (pages 11 to 16)
1. A. Arnould, 'Flemish books for English readers', from A. Arnould and J.M. Massing, *Splendours of Flanders. Late medieval art in Cambridge collections,* Exh. Cat. (Cambridge 1993), 113, *et al.* See also N. Rogers, 'Books of Hours produced in the Low Countries for the English market in the fifteenth century', M.Litt. dissertation, University of Cambridge (1982).
2. See the reference to the artist Harry Blankston in E. Auerbach, *Tudor Artists* (London 1954), 15-16; and the bibliography in Malcolm H. Jones, 'The Misericords of Beverley Minster: a Corpus of Folkloric Imagery and its Cultural Milieu, with special reference to the influence of Northern European iconography on Late Medieval and Early Modern English Woodwork', Ph.D. thesis submitted to the Council for National Academic Awards (1991), 214-227.
3. Jones has undertaken a useful round-up of the accumulated publications on mainly Flemish imports into Britain, and the work of alien Flemings and others. His own survey covers a broad spectrum of goods including books and woodcuts, wooden furniture and wainscoting, carved and painted altar tables, wall and paving tiles, pottery, musical instruments and painted cloths. See Jones, *Misericords of Beverley Minster.* In the past the literature on the subject has been rather sketchy, but the output has accelerated more recently. See in particular P. Eames, *Furniture in England, France and the Netherlands from the Twelfth to the Fifteenth Century* (London 1977); G. Kipling, *The Triumph of Honour – Burgundian Origins of the Elizabethan Renaissance* (Leiden 1977); P.G. Lindley, '"Una Grande Opera al mio Re": Gilt-Bronze effigies in England from the Middle Ages to the Renaissance', JBAA, 143 (1990), 112-130, and 'Two late medieval statues at Eton College', JBAA, 141 (1988), 169-178; H. Wayment, *King's College Chapel Cambridge, The Great Windows* (Cambridge 1982); and K.W. Woods, 'Netherlandish carved wooden altarpieces of the fifteenth and early sixteenth centuries in Britain', Ph.D. thesis, Courtauld Institute of Art, University of London (1989).
4. J.A. Fleming, *Flemish Influence in Britain,* 1 (Glasgow 1930), 233.
5. The Lullingstone rood screen was made on the orders of Sir John Peche between 1510 and 1522. The Lavenham chantry is dated by the will of Thomas Spring, *ob.* 1523.
6. S.L. Thrupp, 'The alien population in England in 1440', *Speculum,* 32 (1957), 262-72.
7. Fleming, *Flemish Influence,* 191.
8. 1 Ric.III.C.9, 10.
9. L. Stone, *Sculpture in Britain. The Middle Ages* (Harmondsworth 1955), 212.
10. J. Geddes, *Medieval Decorative Ironwork in England* (London 1999), 261-72.
11. The Timberhill candelabrum was attributed by Pevsner to Germany.
12. S. Simpson, 'The Choir-Stalls and Rood Screen', from J. Geddes, *King's College Chapel, Aberdeen, 1500-2000* (Aberdeen 2000), 74-97.
13. *Royal Commission on the Ancient Monuments of Scotland* (Edinburgh 1956), 2, 272; J. Curle, 'Some notes upon the Abbey of Melrose', *Berwickshire Naturalist's Club,* 29 (1935), 51-70.
14. The original document setting out the terms of the settlement is preserved in the Bruges town archives. It was transcribed by O. Delepierre, in *Archaeologia,* 31 (1846), 346-49.
15. W. Kelly, 'Carved Oak from St Nicholas Church Aberdeen', *Soc. Ant. Scot. Proc.,* 68 (1933-34), 355-66.
16. Simpson, *The Choir Stalls,* 93.
17. The section on Melrose and Kinloss relies heavily on Curle's article 'Some Notes…'. The choir-stalls at Dunblane are often supposed to be partly Flemish work. Although I have not seen them, they seem more likely to be wholly of local manufacture.
18. Bénézit, *Dictionnaire des Peintres, etc.,* 2 (1948), 448.
19. G. Hay, 'A Scottish altarpiece in Copenhagen', *Innes Review,* 7 (1956), 10.
20. R.K. Hannay (ed.), *Rentale Dunkeldense* (Edinburgh 1915), 2.
21. Hay, *Scottish Altarpiece,* 10.
22. D. McRoberts, 'Material destruction caused by the Scottish Reformation', *Innes Review,* 10/1 (1959), 92.
23. Now in the Scottish National Gallery.
24. D. McRoberts, 'Notes on Scoto-Flemish artistic contacts', *Innes Review,* 10/1 (1959), 92.
25. *Ibid.*
26. K.W. Woods, *Netherlandish Altarpieces* 49.
27. R. Didier, 'Les retables de Ternant', *Congrès Archéol. France,* 125 (1967), 258-76.
28. *Retabels, Openbaar Kinstbezit in Vlaanderen* xvii/i (Antwerp 1979).
29. J. de Borchgrave d'Altena, 'Les retables brabançons conservés en Suéde' (Brussels 1948).
30. D. Ewing, 'Marketing in Antwerp, 1460-1560. Our Lady's *Pand', Art Bulletin* (1990), 558-84.
31. L. Jacobs, *Early Netherlandish Carved Altarpieces 1380-1550* (Cambridge 1998).
32. Quoted in Ewing, 567.
33. G. Asaert, 'Documenten voor de geschiedenis van de beeldhouwkunst to Antwerpen in de xve eeuw', *Jaarboek van het Koninklijk Museum voor Schone Kunsten Antwerpen* (1972), 48.
34. C. Grössinger, *North-European Panel Paintings* (London 1992), 12.
35. A. Martindale, 'The Ashwellthorpe Triptych', D. Williams (ed.), *Proceedings of the 1987 Harlaxton Symposium* (Woodbridge 1989), 107-23. The work is now in the Norwich Castle Museum.
36. *Ibid,* 119.
37. Grössinger, *Panel Paintings,* Cat. 54.
38. *Borthwick Institute Probate Register,* f. 107r. These Hull references are discussed in P. Heath, 'Urban piety in the later middle ages: the evidence of Hull wills', in R.B. Dobson (ed,), *The church, politics and patronage in the 15th century* (Gloucester 1984), 209-29.
39. *Ibid.,* 9, f. 112v.
40. Woods, *Netherlandish Altarpieces,* 100.
41. Woods, *Netherlandish Altarpieces,* 92. Jones has pointed out that the record relates to London not King's Lynn as was stated.
42. *Ibid.*
43. *Ibid,* 94.
44. W.R. Childs (ed.), *The Customs Accounts of Hull, Yorkshire Archaeological Society, Record Series,* 144 (1984), where the term 'kyst' is referred to as a box containing sugar. Chests were imported in 'nests' or batches.
45. The sources used for the customs accounts were N.S.B. Gras, *The Early English customs system,* Cambridge, Mass. and London (1918); H.J. Smit, *Bronnen tot de geschiedenis van den handel met England, Schotland en Ierland 1150-1485,* 'S-Gravenhage, 2 vols (1928); and Childs, *Customs Accounts.*
46. C.J. Hart, 'Old Chests', *Birmingham and Midland Institute Trans,* 20 (1894), 20, 63.
47. T.S. Willan, *A Tudor Book of Rates (1582)* (London 1962).
48. P. Thornton, 'Two problems', *Furniture History,* 7 (1971), 67-68.
49. *Ibid.*
50. These wills and inventories are quoted from Hart, *Old Chests,* 65.
51. For a discussion of the specimen in the Victoria and Albert Museum, London, see C. Tracy, *English Medieval Furniture and Woodwork, Victoria and Albert Museum* (London 1988), Cat.301.
52. The Wath chest is said by tradition to have come from Jervaulx Priory. Hart suggested 'that it could be the one given by Christopher Best, the last priest of the chantry or chapel of St John the Baptist, bequeathed to the church. In his will, dated 23 April 1557, he directs: "I gyffe unto George Best xls. that he hath of mine remaining in his hande with all other stuff … excepe a Flanders kyste and yt ys within yt"'. See Hart, *Old Chests,* 83.
53. R. Didier, 'Sculptures, style et faux', from H. Krom and C. Theuerkauff (eds.), *Festschrift für Peter Bloch* (Mainz 1990), 356-360.
54. S. Jervis, 'Other Foreign Furniture', from T. Murdoch (ed.), *Boughton House, The English Versailles* (London 1992), 138-41.
55. Thornton, *Two problems.*
56. *Ibid.*
57. Act II, 1, 344-48.

Chapter I (pages 33 to 35)
1. The phenomenon has been well chronicled for the late 17th and 18th centuries. See, in particular, *The Quiet Conquest. The Huguenots 1685-1985, Museum of London,* Exh. Cat.(London 1985). B.M. Forman's helpful appendices of alièn craftsmen working and living in London lean on R.E.G. Kirk's volumes of city records, church registers, state papers

etc., published as Vol.10 of the *Publications of the Huguenot Society of London*. See also B.M. Forman, 'Continental Furniture Craftsmen in London: 1511-1625', *Furniture History*, 7 (1971), 94-120.

2. Kipling, *Triumph of Honour*.

3. Wayment, *The Great Windows*.

4. *Ibid*, 9.

5. Quoted in A.W. Moore, *Dutch and Flemish Painting in Norfolk* (London 1988), xi. The following passage is based on his useful analysis.

6. R.D. Gwynn, 'Patterns in the Study of Huguenot Refugees in Britain: Past, Present and Future', from I. Scouloudi (ed.), *Huguenots in Britain and their French Background, 1550-1800, Contributions to the Historical Conference of the Huguenot Society of London* (24-25 Sept., 1985), 218.

7. William White, *History, Gazetteer and Directory of Norfolk, and the City and County of Norwich* (Sheffield 1845).

8. *Ibid*, xiii.

9. A.M. Oakley, 'The Canterbury Walloon Congregation from Elizabeth I to Laud', from Scouloudi, *Huguenots in Britain*, 62.

10. A. Wells-Cole, *Art and Decoration in Elizabethan and Jacobean England* (New Haven and London 1997), 172.

11. *Ibid*, 199.

12. Forman, *Huguenot Society*, Appendix 1.

13. *Ibid.*, Appendix 3.

14. Forman, *Furniture History*.

15. A. Vallance, *Greater English Church Screens* (London 1947).

16. A. Wells-Cole, 'Oak Furniture in Norfolk, 1530-1640', *Regional Furniture*, 4 (1990), 36.

17. *Ibid.*, 40.

18. A few churches had altar rails since Elizabeth's reign. For an exposition of the Laudian Reformation, see G.W.O Addleshaw and F. Etchells, *The Architectural Setting of Anglican Worship* (London 1948), 120-47.

19. It was built by Bishop Wren and finished in about 1632. See Vallance, *Greater Screens*, 143.

20. *Ibid.* 160, 164, 166, and 159.

21. B/E, *London, 2: South* (1983), 344.

22. Illustrated in A. Tipping, *Grinling Gibbons and the Woodwork of his Age, (1648-1720)* (London 1914), fig.4.

23. B/E, *Hampshire* (1967), 750.

24. His drawing for the organ case is illustrated in K. Downes, *Sir Christopher Wren; the Design of St Paul's Cathedral* (London 1988), pl.185. The stalls in their original state are shown in A.F.E. Poley, *St Paul's Cathedral*, 2nd edn. (London 1984), pls.xxvi and xxvii. The most recent work on Gibbons is D. Esterly, *Grinling Gibbons and the art of carving*, Victoria and Albert Museum (London 1998).

25. Since destroyed. See R. Gunnis, *Dictionary of British Sculptors, 1660-1851*, revd. edn. (London 1951), 102.

26. *Ibid.*, 313.

27. B/E, *South and West Somerset* (1958), 109-10.

28. *Ibid.*

29. S. Jervis, *Woodwork of Winchester Cathedral* (Winchester 1976), 27-28.

30. G. Cobb, *English Cathedrals. The forgotten centuries* (London 1980), 143-44, and pls.244 and 246.

31. *Ibid.*, pl.13.

32. *Ibid.*, pls.95 and 96.

Chapter II (pages 36 to 38)

1. G. Reitlinger, *The economics of taste,: the rise and fall of objets d'art: prices since 1750*, ii (London 1963), 78-79.

2. *Ibid.*

3. C. Wainwright, *The Romantic Interior. The British Collector at Home. 1750-1850* (New Haven and London 1989), 84, and pls.60 and 65.

4. *Ibid.*, 93, and pls.72-74.

5. *Ibid.*, pl.77.

6. *A Description of the Villa of Mr Horace Walpole ... at Strawberry Hill* (1774), 113.

7. *Ibid.*, Appendix, 144-45.

8. Wainwright, *Romantic Interior*, 107 and pl.89.

9. Horace Walpole, *Anecdotes of Painting in England* (reprinted London 1871), 1, 229, n.3.

10. *The Yale Edition of Horace Walpole's Correspondence*, XX, (London and Oxford 1955-67), 371.

11. Walpole, *Anecdotes*, 1, 229, n.3.

12. J. Lafond, 'The traffic in old stained glass from abroad during the 18th and 19th centuries in England', *Journal of the British Society of Master Glass Painters*, 14, No.1 (1964), 10.

13. K. Woods, *Netherlandish Altarpieces*, 197-206.

14. T.D. Whitaker, *An History of the Original Parish of Whalley* (London 1818), 487.

Chapter III (pages 39 to 78)

1. G.F. Waagen, *Works of Art and Artists in England* (London 1838), 1, 50.

2. 105. For a discussion of England as the principal market for works of art during the period 1795-1815, see F. Haskell, *Rediscoveries in Art* (London 1976); and Reitlinger, *Economics of Taste*, 1 and 2 (London 1963-70).

3. 106. John Milner, *The History, civil and ecclesiastical, and survey of the antiquities of Winchester* (Winchester 1809), 230.

4. *Ibid.* For an up-to-date assessment of Milner, see M.N.L. Couve de Murville, *John Milner* (Birmingham 1986).

5. R. O'Donnell, 'Pugin at Oscott', J.F. Champ (ed.), *Oscott College 1838-1988* (1988).

6. Grössinger, *Panel Paintings*, 16.

7. From Pugin's First Lecture at Oscott. Quoted in A. Farrell, 'Pugin and Oscott', *The Oscotian*, 3rd Ser., 5 (1905), 107-114.

8. A.W.N. Pugin, *A Treatise on Chancel Screens and Rood Lofts* (London 1851).

9. L. Réau, *Les monuments détruits de l'art Français*, 2 vols, 1 (Paris 1959), 308.

10. *Ibid.*, 1, 322.

11. 114. *Ibid.*, 1, 327.

12. *Ibid.*, 1, 340.

13. *Ibid.*, 1, 346.

14. A. de Herdt, in 'Saint-Pierre, cathédrale de Genève', Exh. Cat., *Musée Rath* (Geneva 1982), Cat.138.

15. *Ibid*, 1, 339.

16. Taylor, Nodier and de Cailleux, *Voyages pittoresques et romantiques dans l'Ancienne France, Picardy*, 1 (Paris 1835), on sheet 32 of this unpaginated book.

17. M.B. Freeman, 'Late Gothic Woodcarvings from Normandy', *MMA Bull.*, 9, 10 (1951), 260-69. The plate in Taylor, *Voyages pittoresques*, showing the demolition of Les Andelys, is reproduced in Wainwright, *Romantic Interior*, pl.45. Baron Taylor's description of the château is given in *Réau, Monuments Détruits*, 2, 122-23.

18. Freeman, *Woodcarvings in Normandy*, 260.

19. *Ibid.*

20. J. Lafond, 'The traffic in old stained glass from abroad during the 18th and 19th centuries in England', *The Journal of the British Society of Master Glass Painters*, 14, No.1 (1964), 65.

21. Other windows from this church are now in the Burrell Collection, Glasgow and many other places. See H. Wayment, *King's College Chapel, Cambridge, The Side-Chapel Glass* (Cambridge 1988), catalogue of windows 41, n.1-3.

22. *Ibid.*, 23 and n.5.

23. *Ibid.*, 23 and n.6.

24. E. de la Quérière, *Description historique de Maisons de Rouen*, 2 (Rouen 1841), 248-49.

25. Now in the Fitzwilliam Museum, Cambridge.

26. These are transcribed in Bernard Rackham, 'English Importations of Foreign Stained Glass in the early Nineteenth Century', *The Journal of the British Society of Master Glass Painters*, ii (1927), 86-94. For a contemporary critique on Rackham's work, see Wayment, *King's College Chapel, Cambridge. Side-Chapel Glass*, 23-24.

27. A. Lenoir, *Musée des Monuments Français. Histoire de la Peinture sur Verre* (Paris 1803), 87. Quoted in Lafond, *Traffic in old stained glass*, 60.

28. E.H. Langlois, *Mémoire sur la Peinture sur Verre* (Rouen 1823), 42. Quoted in Lafond, *Traffic in old stained glass*, 27. The Chartreuse of Rouen windows were in Stevenson and Hampp's second catalogue. The museum to which Lenoir refers is his *Musée des Monuments Français*, in the cloister and gardens of the Petits Augustins at Paris. For Langlois' career see C. Wainwright, 'A.W.N. Pugin and France', from P. Atterbury (ed.), *A.W.N. Pugin. The Master of the Gothic Revival* (New York and London 1995), 69.

29. Lafond, *Traffic in old stained glass*, 60.

30. See D. Harford 'On the east window of St Stephen's Church, Norwich', *Norfolk Archaeology* (1904), 15, 335-48, where the written comments of the Rev. J.O. Müller in 1903, are quoted.

31. C. Avery, 'The Rood-Loft from Hertogenbosch', *Victoria and Albert Museum Yearbook*, 1 (London 1969), 110-36.

32. A. Macgregor (ed.), *Tradescant's Rarities* (Oxford 1983), cat.225, 80.

33. For the early history of French museums, see A. Erlande-Brandenberg, 'Alexandre Lenoir et le musée des monuments Français', from *Le Gothique Retrouvé avant Viollet-le-Duc, Hôtel de Sully* (Paris 1980), 75-84.

34. Album, 1st Ser., Chapter 12, pl.xvii.

35. Album, 1st Ser., Chapters 5 and 7, pl.xxviii.

36. Album, 1st Ser., Chapter 12, pl.xxxiii.

37. Album, 2nd Ser., Chapters 4 and 5, pl.xii.

38. Album, 2nd Ser., Chapter 12, pl.xxxv.

39. 142. Erlande-Brandenberg, *Alexandre Lenoir*, above, No. 227.

40. Wainwright, *Romantic Interior*, Chapter 3.

41. H. Shaw, *Specimens of Ancient Furniture drawn from existing authorities ... with descriptions by Sir Samuel Rush Meyrick ..., Prospectus* (1836).

42. Letter to Braikenridge, dated Oct. 17, 1827 (HB/C.38), Bristol record Office.

43. For instance, the canopy of the bishop's throne at St Chad's.

44. P.F. Anson, *Fashions in church furniture 1840-1940* (London 1960), 28.

45. H.N. Humphries, *Ten Centuries of art* (London 1852), 95. Quoted in Woods, *Netherlandish Altarpieces*.

46. For instance, Sir Walter Scott's Abbotsford, the Lucy's Charlecote Park, and Samuel Rush Meyrick's Goodrich Court, all three analysed in detail in Wainwright, *Romantic Interior*. Other houses of importance in this context are the Pryor'sbank, Fulham, London, see S. Jervis, 'The Pryor'sbank, Fulham. Residence of Thomas Baylis Esquire, F.S.A.', *Furniture History*, 10 (1974), 87-98; Ingress Abbey, Kent, see S. Jervis, 'Ingress Abbey', *Furniture History*, 9 (1973), 122-24 and pl.44a; Knebworth, Hertfordshire, see S. Jervis, 'Knebworth, Hertfordshire. The Re-birth of a Baronial Hall', unpublished article in the Department of Furniture and Woodwork archive, *Victoria and Albert Museum*; and Costessey Hall, Norfolk, see G. Birkbeck, *Old Norfolk Houses* (1908), 30.

47. B/E, *Bedfordshire and the County of Huntingdon and Peterborough* (1968), 130-31.

48. The pulpit was sold to Carlisle Cathedral in 1963.

49. In a letter from Simon Jervis to Miss F. Finch Dawson and Mrs Bouch, dated 24 July 1981. Quoted by permission.

50. Woods, *Netherlandish Altarpieces*, 211.

51. B/E, *Dorset* (1989), 140.

52. Woods, *Netherlandish Altarpieces*, 220-26.

53. S. Stoddard, *Mr Braikenridge's Brislington* (Bristol, 1981), pl.14. The rails were given to Braikenridge's son, the Rev. G.W. Braikenridge, in 1873, and their present whereabouts is unknown.

54. See *ibid.*, 49 for an account of Braikenridge's garden antiquarian embellishments.

55. S. Jervis, 'Gothic Rampant: Designs by L.N. Cottingham for Snelston Hall', *Victoria and Albert Museum Album*, 3 (1984), 322-331.

56. C. Tracy, *A Catalogue of English Gothic Furniture and Woodwork, Victoria a Albert Museum* (1988), xxi.

57. B. Ferry, *Recollections of A.N. Welby Pugin and his father* (1861), eds. C. and J. Wainwright (London 1978), xxiii.

58. *Ibid.*

59. W. Greaney, *The buildings, museum, pictures and library of St Mary's College, Oscott* (Birmingham 1899), 11.

60. 'A report on the opening of the college', *Catholic Magazine*, ii (1838), 693. Pugin's role as antiquary and collector is discussed in C. Wainwright, 'The Antiquary and Collector', from P. Atterbury and C. Wainwright (eds.), *Pugin. A Gothic Passion* (New Haven and London 1994), 63-77; and Wainwright, *Pugin and France*, 63-77.

61. Foster & Son, 'Catalogue of the Museum of Mediaeval Art collected by the late L.N. Cottingham, F.S.A., architect, which will be sold by auction 3 November 1851'.

62. 'Descriptive Memoir and Catalogue of the Museum of Mediaeval Art collected by the late L.N. Cottingham' (London 1850).

63. Foster & Son, *Museum of Mediaeval Art*.

64. Quoted in Paul Millar, 'The woodcarvings at Oscott', *The Oscotian*, 3rd Ser., 14 (1913), 140.

65. 167. W.J.A., 'The History of St Mary's College, Oscott', *The Oscotian*, n.s. 20 (1920), 184-89.

66. Quoted in *The opening of the college* (1838).

67. R. O'Donnell, 'Pugin as a Church Architect', from Atterbury and Wainwright, *Pugin. A Gothic Passion,* 79.

68. Pugin also designed the stone altar table, as well as the wooden altar frontal. Sadly the stone table has been destroyed but the frontal, which was rediscovered at Oscott by Williams, could be re-instated. See S. Williams, 'The Birth of Functionalism; Pugin's furniture designs for St Mary's College, Oscott', Dissertation submitted for History of Art Tripos, part 2, (Cambridge May 1991). I am grateful to the author for the loan of his thesis.

69. J.F. Champ, *Oscott, Archdiocese of Birmingham Historical Commission* (Birmingham 1987), 3-4.

70. M. Hodgetts, 'St Chad's Cathedral, Birmingham' (Birmingham 1987).

71. Originally intended for Oscott.

72. For an up-to-date summary of the donations, see Hodgetts, *St Chad's,* 5-6.

73. Greaney, *St Mary's College*, 10.

74. F. van Kalken, *Histoire de la Belgique* (Brussels, 1954).

75. This story is related in Greaney, *St Mary's College.*

76. Shaw, *Specimens of Ancient Furniture*, Pl. XIV.

77. O'Donnell, *Pugin as a Church Architect,* 101, pl.187.

78. Ferry, *Recollections* (1861), 63.

79. J.H. Powell, 'Pugin in his home' (1889) (unpublished typescript in National Library, *Victoria and Albert Museum*), 25. Pugin's intimate connections with, and many visits, to France are chronicled in Wainwright, *Pugin and France*. The most recent account of his activities can be found in A. Wedgwood, 'A.W. Pugin's Tours in Northern Europe' from J. de Meyer and L. Verpoest (eds.) *Gothic Revival. Religion, Architecture and Style in Western Europe 1815-1914* (Leuven 2000), 93-98.

80. A.Wedgwood, *A.W.N. Pugin and the Pugin Family, Catalogues of Architectural Drawings in the Victoria and Albert Museum* (London 1985).

81. 182. *Ibid.*, 83, n.81.

82. Edward Hull is discussed in C. Wainwright, 'The antiquarian interior in Britain 1780-1850', University of London, Ph.D. thesis (1986),

86-87; and Wainwright, *Romantic Interior,* 39-40 and 43-44.

83. R. Hasted, 'Scarisbrick Hall: a guide', *Lancashire County Council* (Preston 1987), 7 and 10.

84. Hasted observes that Scarisbrick's romantic antiquarianism must have been strongly influenced by Sir Walter Scott, of whose works he kept an 88 volume edition in the library at Scarisbrick. *Ibid.*, 11.

85. Lancashire Record Office: DDSc 78/4.

86. Hasted, *Scarisbrick Hall.*

87. Letters and accounts in Lancashire Record Office: DDSc 78/4.

88. There exists a bill from Hull to Scarisbrick, dated July 1834, mentioning a sum for 'Pugin's work'. See Hasted, *Scarisbrick Hall,* 11.

89. 190. Lancashire Record Office: DDSc 78/4.

90. *Ibid.*

91. *Ibid.*

92. NAL, L5156-1969; L5160-1969; L5163-1969.

93. NAL, L5171-1969.

94. NAL, S3/3; A. Wedgwood, *The Pugin family: catalogue of drawings of the collection of the RIBA* (London 1977), no. 64/147.

95. 196. NAL, L525-1965/3, letter 15 November 1840.

96. NAL, L5158-1969, Pugin's 1837 diary, 16 January, see Wedgwood, *Pugin Family.*

97. NAL, L525-1965/2.

98. O'Donnell points out that the payments to Webb and Hull correspond to receipts at Oscott, namely *Oscott Archives* Box 1537: No 851, 20 December 1837, Edward Hull for £600 from Pugin; No 853, 20 December 1837 John Bankes (for John Webb) for L [*sic*] 80 from Pugin. See O'Donnell, *Pugin at Oscott,* 62, n.34.

99. Wedgwood, *Pugin Family,* France, 3; A.W.N. Pugin, 107, 124 and 151.

100. Williams, *Birth of Functionalism.*

101. A. Farrell, 'Pugin and Oscott', *The Oscotian*, 3rd Ser., 5, (1905) 107-114. The pulpit succumbed to the major re-ordering of the chapel in the 1920s.

102. Woods, *Netherlandish Altarpieces,* 140. These conclusions are endorsed in Williams, *Birth of Functionalism.*

103. Greaney, *St Mary's College,* 14.

104. E.T. Joy, 'John Coleman Isaac. An early nineteenth century antique dealer', *The Connoisseur* 151 (1962), 241-42.

105. Edward Baldock (1777-1845) described himself as 'E.H. Baldock Antique Furniture & ornamental china dealer 7 Hanway Street, Oxford Street'. See Wainwright, *Romantic Interior,* 42-43.

106. For Swaby and Webb, see *Ibid,* 44-45 and 45-46.

107. A. Wedgwood (ed.), *A History of the Church and Parish of St Martin's Dorking* (Dorking 1990), 32.

108. Pl.3, fig.2.

109. Pl.3, fig.3.

110. S. Stoddard, 'George Weare Braikenridge 1775-1856, A Bristol Antiquarian and his Collections', University of Bristol thesis (1983), and Stoddard, *Mr Braikenbridge's Brislington.*

111. There are nine letters from Rodd to Braikenridge in the Bristol Record Office (HB/C)

112. The so-called 'Henry V's cradle' was supplied by Rodd. It is now in the Museum of London.
113. Bristol Record Office, HB/C/40.
114. Henry Rumsey Forster, *The Stowe Catalogue Priced and annotated* (London 1848), Lot 2477.
115. *Ibid.,* Lot 2482.
116. Woods, *Netherlandish Altarpieces,* 133.
117. National Library of Scotland MS 3887, f.72. Quoted in Wainwright, *Antiquarian Interior,* 47.
118. Essex Record Office, 'The Journal of the 3rd Lord Braybook', Acc. 6767. Quoted in Wainwright, *Antiquarian Interior,* 100.
119. M.W. Brockwell, *Catalogue of the Pictures and other works of art in the collection of Lord St Oswald at Nostell Priory* (London 1915), 52.
120. Nostell Priory MSS, Leeds District Archives, NP/A1/7 Part II.
121. There is an inscription and memorial by Chantrey to John Winn at Wragby Church.
122. He was appointed a canon on 4 January 1813.
123. In the 1880s, the Brownlows owned over 58,000 acres, and enjoyed a gross income of £86,000. See D. Cannadine, *The Decline and Fall of the British Aristocracy* (New Haven and London 1990), Appendix A.
124. *Alumni Cantabrienses,* pt 2, 2 (Cambridge 1944), 207.
125. *Ibid.*
126. Cannadine, *Decline and Fall,* 260. By 1900 it had fallen to nearly half this level. *Ibid.*
127. 'The Church of St John the Baptist, Cockayne Hatley, Bedfordshire', *Friends of Cockayne Hatley Church* (1987).
128. A. Tinniswood, 'Belton House, Lincolnshire', *The National Trust,* London, 1992.
129. Rushbrooke was born in 1779.
130. Letter from Robert Rushbrooke to Henry Cockayne Cust, June 13, 1826. See Appendix II.
131. R.N. Cust, *Some Account of Cockayne Hatley, Bedfordshire (*1851).
132. This is Cust's terminology in his journals.
133. R.N. Cust, *Some Account of Cockayne Hatley.*
134. Extracts from the diary of J.M. Neale, 1839-40 (Lambeth Palace Library: Ms. 3107).
135. Wainwright, *Antiquarian Interior,* 55.
136. *Ibid.,* 55.
137. See the pedigree of the Hibberts of Marple in J.P. Earwaker, *East Cheshire etc.,* ii, (London 1877), 55. It has been suggested that the 19th century Hibberts made their money out of West Indies sugar plantations, but it has not been possible to confirm this.
138. Ormerod, *History of Cheshire,* 3 (London 1819-82), 711.
139. R. Richards, *Old Cheshire Churches* (London 1947), 60-62, and pls. 62-66.
140. The inscriptions are recorded in *ibid.,* 62; the west screen is illustrated on pl.66.
141. See J. Vickers, 'A History of Christ's Church, Harwood. 1840-1990', Bolton, n.d.
142. Subsequently they have disappeared.
143. 'Christchurch, Eccleston', 1988.
144. 242. R. Freeman, *The Art and Architecture of Owen Browne Carter (1806-1859)*

(Winchester 1991), 7-8.
145. There is a measured architect's ground plan of the church in the Hampshire Record Office. The church was enlarged at Charlotte Yonge's expense by T.H. Wyatt in 1875. A north nave aisle was added, and the chancel was extended into a polygonal apse. See Freeman, *Owen Browne Carter,* 7. He points out that the unaltered church at Ampfield, also built for Keble and designed by the Yonge/Carter partnership between 1838-41, gives a good idea of the original form of Otterbourne Church without the transepts.
146. Freeman, *Owen Browne Carter,* above, 21.
147. C.M. Yonge, *John Keble's Parishes* (London 1898), 101.
148. This and the following information is based on Hasted, *Scarisbrick Hall.*
149. John Liddle, 'The Scarisbrick Estate', *Lancashire Record Office. Annual Report* (1977). Quoted in Hasted *Scarisbrick Hall.*
150. Quoted in F.H. Cheetham, 'Scarisbrick Hall, Lancashire', *Trans Lancs & Cheshire Antiq. Soc.,* 24 (1906), 76-104.
151. Hasted, *Scarisbrick Hall,* 8.
152. Appendix III. Note from Edward Hull, Jan 1833.
153. *Ibid.*
154. Wedgwood, *Pugin Family,* 81.
155. A watercolour of the interior of the chapel, painted by Sir Henry's daughter Mathilda probably in the 1840s, shows an altarpiece. See Woods, *Netherlandish Altarpieces,* Catalogue section: Oxburgh Hall, 230-31.
156. *Ibid.,* 230.
157. 'The English Convent' (at Bruges), n.d., 16, 17.
158. Anson, *Fashions,* 84.

Chapter IV (pages 79 to 87)
1. 259. G.W. Addleshaw and F. Etchells, *The Architectural Setting of Anglican Worship* (London 1948), 84.
2. Cannadine, *Decline and Fall,* 260.
3. Avery, Roodloft from Hertogenbosch, 110.
4. 262. The museum description of these items is: 'Ninety-six pieces of Gothic architectural decoration, chiefly of oak, consisting of panels, friezes, pilasters etc. English, Flemish etc. 15th and 16th centuries... Transferred to the South Kensington Museum from the Office of Works. 8129 to 8224'. See Wainwright, *The Antiquary and Collector,* 101-02, pls.191, 192.
5. C.E. Hardy, *John Bowes and the Bowes Museum,* privately published (Bishop Auckland 1970).
6. For the latter, see Woods, *Netherlandish Altarpieces,* 157-89.
7. *Ibid.,* 162.
8. 266. *Ibid.,* 143-44.
9. *Ibid.,* 144.
10. 268. *Ibid.,* 146.
11. Henry Russell Hitchcock, quoted in Anson, *Fashions,* 45.
12. The lectern is inscribed on a brass plate: 'An offering to Methley Church from David Leake. Easter Day 1869'.
13. G.F. Waagen, *Galleries and cabinets of art*

(London 1857), 189.
14. 272. Woods, *Netherlandish Altarpieces,* 144.
15. For articles on Parnham, see *Country Life,* 24 (1908), 288-97, and 320-31.
16. Quoted in Woods, *Netherlandish Altarpieces,* 296.
17. *Ibid.*
18. Tilmann Breuer, *Stadt un Landkreis Memmingen* (Munich 1959), 86.
19. B/E, *London except the Cities of London and Westminster* (1952), 372.
20. Letter to Miss Judith G. Scott from Mr S.W. Wolsey, 10 May, 1963, quoted by kind permission of the Council for the Care of Churches.
21. B/E, *Suffolk* (1974), 160. Interestingly, the main figures are in alabaster. As in the case of the reredos at Coveney, this panel is very overrestored.
22. B/E, *Cornwall* (1951), 91-92.
23. 281. DNB (1892), 224.
24. *Ibid,* 223.
25. H.J.M. Milne, 'Diaries of Thomas Needham Cust, 1842-1909', *British Museum Quarterly,* 14 (1940), 7-8.
26. H. Avray Tipping, 'Southam Delabere, Gloucestershire', *Country Life,* 22 (1907), 600.
27. B.H.C. Dickinson, 'The Parish Church of St. Peter, Lew Trenchard and The Rev. Sabine Baring-Gould', Third Impression (1972), 5.
28. 286. *Who Was Who,* 1916-28.
29. 287. W. Addison, *The English Country Parson,* (London 1947), 204-14. Referred to in Cannadine, *Decline and Fall.*
30. Dickinson, *Lew Trenchard,* 7.
31. The Misses Pinwell of Plymouth and Ermington. The work was supervised by F. Bligh Bond, cousin of Gould, and author, with B. Camm, of *English Church Screens and Roodlofts,* 2 vols (London 1909).
32. Dickinson, *Lew Trenchard,* 7. The chandelier was stolen in 1980.
33. *Ibid.,* 8.
34. Temple Moore's sentiments are quoted in C. Pullin and N. Frayling, 'A Short History of All Saints Tooting Graveney', from *A Royal Visit to All Saints Tooting Graveney* (1983).
35. Anson, *Fashions,* 318.

Chapter V (pages 88 to 91)
1. They were returned to Oscott in 1872. See Champ, *Oscott,* 9.
2. Information from the Revd. Prebendary G. Irvine, by letter.
3. Letter from Frederic de Sautoy, vicar of March, in the church, dated 1891.
4. Letter from the Provost, 16 June 1992.
5. Information from Warwick Rodwell; see also W. Rodwell and J. Bentley, *Our Christian Heritage (*London 1984).
6. B/E, *South Lancashire* (1969), 132.
7. 'Bedfordshire Churches in the 19th century', Part ii, 1998, *Bedfordshire Historical Record Society* (1998).
8. *Ibid.,* n.25, p.338.
9. B/E, *Shropshire* (1985), 293.10. B/E, *North-West and South Norfolk* (1962), 388.
10. B/E, *North-West and South Norfolk* (1962), 388.

Glossary of Terms

Aediculae The framing of a door, window, or other opening with two columns, piers or pilasters supporting a gable, lintel, plaque, or an entablature and pediment.

Back Stalls The back row of choir-stalls ranged along the choir arcade and sometimes returned against the pulpitum.

Boarded chest A chest made from four planks of wood jointed together.

Caryatid A carved female figure employed as a column to support an entablature or other similar architectural member. A male figure in the same role is an Atlas figure.

Crocket A carved decorative feature usually of foliage, projecting from the angles of spires, gables, pinnacles, canopies etc. in Gothic architecture.

Dexter In heraldry, of, on, or starting from the right side of a shield from the bearer's point of view and therefore on the spectator's left.

Hutch-type chest A chest with wide upright stiles at the corners with:
1) plain boarded sides or
2) sides made up from a simple grid of timbers with hidden joints behind, or a grid with visible dovetails, or sides fitted with rails only.

Imbrication Decoration of a flat surface with a repeating pattern resembling scales or overlapping tiles.

Lateral Stalls The stalls running along the axis of the choir.

Linenfold Late 15th century and early 16th century panelling ornamented with a depiction of a piece of linen laid in vertical folds. Arranged one piece for each panel.

Misericords A bracket underneath the hinged seat of a choir-stall, which, when lifted could support the occupant whilst standing during the long services.

Moresque, or Arabesque Surface decoration probably originating in Saracenic ornament, particularly found on objects made by Moslem craftsmen in Europe. Engraved designs of these were published from *c.*1530.

Paten Shallow dish usually made of silver or gold on which the bread is placed in the Eucharist.

Pallium Originally a woollen vestment worn by archbishops, usually shown as a narrow Y-shaped strip, with embroidered crosses, falling down the centre front and back.

Plinth Chest The plinth form is derived from the hutch chest (see above), which has four stiles at the corners which lift the chest off the ground. In this case the downwards projecting stiles are hidden by a plinth which fills in the space below. The chest was largely in contact with the floor and placed upon a tiled or wooden floor.

Pulpitum A stone screen in a greater church intended to shut off the choir from the nave. It could also be used as the backing for the return choir-stalls.

Prie-dieu A piece of furniture with a low surface for kneeling on and a narrow front surmounted by a rest for the elbow or for books, for use when praying.

Putto A representation of a small boy, a cherub or cupid, common particularly in Baroque art.

Quadrant The recessed quadrant-shaped portion on the inside of a stall standard, within which the tip-up seat can swivel.

Rayonnant A style of architecture typified by the greater French churches being constructed in the second half of the 13th century, when decoration became more important than structure. The rose windows at Notre-Dame, Paris encapsulate the style, which during the 14th century was to spread throughout Northern Europe.

Reredos A decorated wall or screen, usually of wood or stone, behind an altar.

Rochet A white surplice with tight sleeves, worn by bishops, abbots and certain other Church dignitaries.

Seat Capping Planks of 5-10cm. (2-4in.) thick, about 50cm. (20in.)wide and up to 2.5m. (8ft.) long, continuous on one side and cut away to form the top of choir-stall seating on the other. The capping projections carry the front supports of a superstructure, if any.

Seat Elbow Hand rest projecting from the arm of the stall, or standard, consisting of a knop of carved foliage, or animal and human forms, or plain.

Seat Standards The division between one choir-stall and another. Grooved each side to take the tip-up seats. The latter are secured into position, either by a pivot which is part of the seat, or by metal hinges attached to the back. Standards are sometimes called divisions or counters.

Sinister The opposite of dexter (see above).

Solomonic Columns A twisted column, so called because of its supposed use in King Solomon's temple.

Stall End This feature closes off a run of choir-stalls. Where there are substalls, it occurs frequently because the gangways break the seating up into short sections. Stall ends are usually thicker than normal seat divisions and, at the end of the back stalls, sometimes carry a side screen above seat capping level.

Strapwork Decoration originating in the Netherlands *c.*1540, using interlaced bands and forms similar to fret or cut-leather work.

Term A bust surmounting a tapering pedestal Also a pedestal that merges into a carved human or mythical head. A bracket with a term on it would be described as a terminal bracket.

Acknowledgements

Collins English Dictionary, London and Glasgow, 1979; P. Dirsztay, *Church Furnishings*, London 1978; P. Eames, *Medieval Furniture*, London, 1977; J. Fleming et al., *A Dictionary of Architecture*, Harmondsworth, 1977; J. Fleming and H. Honour, *The Penguin Dictionary of Decorative Arts*, Harmondsworth, 1977.

THE NATIONAL COLLECTION

Abbreviations and Select Bibliography

BOE	Buildings of England Series
BRO	Bristol Record Office
CWAAS	Cumberland and Westmorland Antiquarian andArchaeological Society
LA	Lincolnshire Archives
LRO	Lancashire Record Office
MRO	Middlesex Record Office
NAL	National Art Library (Victoria and Albert Museum)
RCHME	Royal Commission on the Historical Monuments of England
VCH	Victoria County History Series
WCRO	Warwickshire County Record Office
WWW	Who Was Who

UNPUBLISHED DOCUMENTARY SOURCES

Braikenridge Papers, HB/C (BRO).

Brownlow Papers, Personal Journals/Account Books of the Hon. & Revd Henry Cockayne Cust, 1812-59, 35 vols (LA).

Letters from Robert Rushbrooke Esquire to the Hon. & Revd Henry Cockayne Cust (LA).

Nostell Priory MSS, Leeds District Archives NP/A1/7 Part II.

Scarisbrick Papers, DDSc 78/4 (LRO).

PUBLISHED BOOKS AND ARTICLES

Addleshaw & Etchells 1948. G.W.O. Addleshaw & F. Etchells, *The Architectural Setting of Anglican Worship*, London.

Arnould & Massing, 1993. A. Arnould & J.M. Massing, *Splendours of Flanders. Late medieval art in Cambridge colleges*, Cambridge.

Ars Sacra 1962. Ars Sacra Antiqua, Stedelijk Museum, Leuven, 4 August-4 November.

L'Art du Moyen Âge 1998. *L'Art de la Fin du Moyen Âge (1380-1520) dans les diocèses de Coutances et d'Avranches, Exh. Cat., Saint-Lô,* 128-32.

Anon 1844. *The History and Antiquities of Dartford.*

Anson 1969. P.F. Anson, *Fashions in church furniture 1840-1940*, London.

Atterbury *et al.* 1995. P. Atterbury (ed.), A.W.N. Pugin, *The Master of the Gothic Revival*, New York and London.

Atterbury, Wainwright *et al.* 1994. P. Atterbury & C. Wainwright (eds.), *Pugin. A Gothic Passion*, New Haven and London.

Avray Tipping 1907. H.A. Tipping, 'Weare Giffard, Devonshire', *Country Life*, 22, 594-600.

van Balen 1677. *Beschryvinge van Dordrecht*, Dordrecht.

Bangs 1997. J.D. Bangs, *Church Art and Architecture in the Low Countries before 1566*, vol. xxxvii, *Sixteenth Century Essays & Studies*, Kirksville.

Bartsch 1980. *The Illustrated Bartsch* (ed. J.C. Hutchinson), New York.

Billings 1840. R.W. Billings, *Architectural Illustrations, History and Description of Carlisle Cathedral*, London.

Billings 1842. R.W. Billings, *Illustrations of Geometric Tracery from the panelling belonging to Carlisle Cathedral*, London.

Billings 1845. R.W. Billings, *The Geometric Tracery of Brancepeth Church in the County of Durham*, London.

Bond 1902. F. Bligh Bond, Devonshire Screens and Rood Lofts, *Devonshire Association for the Advancement of Science, Literature and Art*, 34.

Bossaglia 1978. R. Bossaglia (ed.), *I Fantoni*, Vicenza

Boussel 1979. P. Boussel, *Les Grands Styles: Les styles du Moyen Âge à Louis xiv*, Paris.

Braconnier n.d. E. Braconnier, 'Notice sur Ragnies, son château et son église'.

Brears 1972. P. Brears, 'The Renaissance Furniture from Bretton', *Leeds Art Calendar*, 70, 13-17.

Bridge 1916. A. Bridge, 'Worth Church, Sussex', London

Brockwell 1915. M.W. Brockwell, *Catalogue of the Pictures and other works of art in the collection of Lord St Oswald at Nostell Priory*, London.

Bromley-Davenport 1974. L. Bromley-Davenport, 'The History of Capesthorne, Cheshire', revd. edn.

Bulman 1955. C.G. Bulman, 'The Gondebour and Salkeld screens in Carlisle Cathedral', CWAAS, NS 56, 104-27.

Chaperon 1985. H. Chaperon, *Le Bénitier de Chevet*, Paris.

Coppens 1948. M. Coppens, *Koorbanken in Nederland. Gothiek I*, Amsterdam and Brussels.

Coppens 1949. M. Coppens, *Koorbanken in Nederland. Gothiek II*, Amsterdam and Brussels.

Coppens 1954. M. Coppens, *Koorbanken in Nederland. Barok*, Amsterdam and Brussels.

Cornforth 1981. J. Cornforth, 'Wroxton Abbey, Oxfordshire', *Country Life*, 160, 4385, 770-775; 4386, 854-857; 4388, 1010-1013.

Crallan 1896. F.A. Crallan, *Details of Gothic Woodcarving etc.*, London.

Crollalanza 1886. G.B. di Crollalanza, *Dizionario Storico-Blasonico delle famiglie nobili e notabili Italiane*, Pisa.

Crook 2000. J. Crook, *The Architectural Setting of the Cult of Saints in the Early Christian West, c. 300-1200*, Oxford.

Cumps 1978. J.A. Cumps, 'De Koorbanken van de Onze Lieve Vrouwkerk te Aarschot', *Brjdrage tot de geschiedenis van het Land van Aarschot*, 209-11.

Cust 1851. R.N. Cust, *Some Account of Cockayne Hatley, Bedfordshire*.

Dalton 1985. C. Dalton, 'All Saints Holdenby, Northants', Redundant Churches Fund.

Damiani 1669. D. Damiani, *La gloria de S.Corrado … patrono della nobile ed antica città di Molfetta*, Naples.

Danmarks Kirker. Udgivet af Nationalmseet, Copenhagen.

Debergh 1982. N. Debergh, Koorgestoelten in West-Vlaanderen, Tielt en Bussum.

Von W. Deutsch 1964. Von W. Deutsch, *Die Constanzer Bildschnitzer der Spätgotik und ihr Verhältnis zu Niklaus Gerhaert*, Constance.

Doggan & Vanderbroucke n.d. A. Doggan & E. Vanderbroucke, *St Andrieskerk to Antwerpen*, Antwerp.

van Duinen 1997. H.A. van Duinen, *De Koorbanken van de Grote- of Onze Lieve Vrouwekerk te Dordrecht*, Leiden.

Eames 1977. P. Eames, *Furniture in England, France and the Netherlands from the Twelfth to the Fifteenth Century*, London.

Elias 1944. J.S. Witsen Elias, *Koorbanken Koorhekken en Kansels*, Amsterdam.

Ferry 1861. B. Ferry, *Recollections of A.N. Welby Pugin and his father*, C. & J. Wainwright (eds.), London, 1978.

Fichefet 1977. J. Fichefet, *Histoire du prieuré de l'eglise Saint-Nicolas et du béguinage d'Oignies*, Administration Communale d'Aiseau.

Gilbert 1978. C. Gilbert, *Furniture at Temple Newsam House and Lotherton Hall*, 2 vols., Leeds.

Greaney 1899. W. Greaney, *The buildings, museum, pictures and library of St Mary's College, Oscott*, Birmingham.

Gonzalez-Palacius 1969. A. Gonzalez-Palacius, *Il mobile nei secoli*, 1, Milan, 1969.

Goovaerts 1978. B. Goovaerts, 'Sint-Andriskerk to Antwerpen', Antwerp.

Grössinger 1992. C. Grössinger, *North-European Panel Paintings*, London.

Harding 1853. W. Harding, 'The Church of Colebrooke', *Exeter Diocesan Architectural Society Trans*, v, Pt 1, 9-21.

Hasted 1987. R. Hasted, 'Scarisbrick Hall: a guide', *Lancashire County Council*, Preston.

Hind 1938. A.M. Hind, *Early Italian Engraving*, New York and London.

Hodder 1984. J. Hodder, 'S. Peter ad Vincula, Coveney'.

Hodgetts 1987. M. Hodgetts, 'St Chad's Cathedral, Birmingham', Birmingham.

Howard & Crossley 1917. F.E. Howard & F. Crossley, *English Church Woodwork*, London.

Husenbeth 1882. F.C. Husenbeth, *Emblems of Saints*, 3rd edn., Norwich,

Jervis 1974. S. Jervis, *Printed Furniture Designs before 1650*, Furniture History Society, London.

Jervis 1992. S. Jervis, 'Other foreign furniture', from T. Murdoch (ed.), *Boughton House, The English Versailles*, London, 138-41.

Jopek 2002. N. Jopek, *German Sculpture, 1430-1540, A Catalogue of the Collection in the Victoria and Albert Museum*, London.

van Kalken 1954. F. van Kalken, *Histoire de Belgique*, Brussels.

Kavaler 1994. E.M. Kavaler, 'The Jubé of Mons and the Renaissance in the Netherlands', *Netherlands Kunsthistorisch Jaarbock*, 349-82.

Koldeweij et al. 1991. A.M. Koldewij, *De Koorbanken in de St-Janskathedraal te 's-Hertogenbosch*, 's-Hertogenbosch.

Laat-gotische 1990. *Laat-gotische beeldsnijkinst uit Limburg en Greensland*, St Truiden.

Lamey 1941. H. Lamey, 'Une competition de sculpteurs pour l'éxecution de la statue de saint Norbert à Saint-Pierre à Rome (1738-67), *Revue Belge Arch.*, xi, 71-77.

Lehrs 1921. M. Lehrs, *Geschichte und Kritische Katalog des Deutschen, Niederländischen und Französischen Kupfersticks in xv. Jahrhundert*, 9 vols., Vienna.

Mallé 1965. L. Mallé, *Museo Civico di Torino. Le Sculpture de Museo d'Arte Antico*, Turin.

Martin 1992. G. Martin, *The Opera Companion*, London.

Meurer 1970. H. Meurer, *Das Klever Chorgestühl und Arnt Beeldesnider*, Düsseldorf.

Musée d'Art Ancien 1977. *La Sculpture au siécle de Rubens*, Exh. Cat., Brussels.

Oswald 1949. A. Oswald, *Andrew Doket and his Architect*, Cambridge Antiquarian Society Procs, xlii.

Pickford 1995. C. Pickford, 'The stalls in Cockayne Hatley Church', *Bedfordshire Magazine*, 25, No.193.

Pickford 1998. C. Pickford, 'Bedfordshire Churches in the 19th century', ii, *Bedfordshire Historical Record Society*, 77.

Pirenne 1950. H. Pirenne, *Histoire de Belgique*, ii, 3rd edn., Brussels.

Pont 1915. J.W. Pont, Het doophek uit de Kerk der Evangelisch-Luthersche gemeente van Alkmaar, in London', *Jaarboek der vereeniging voor Nederlandsch - Luthersche Kerkeschiedenis*, Amsterdam.

Powell 1889. J.H. Powell, 'Pugin in his home' (unpublished typescript in *National Art Library*).

Richards 1973. R. Richards, *Old Cheshire Churches*, 2nd edn., Manchester.

Rodwell & Bentley 1984. W. Rodwell & J. Bentley, *Our Christian Heritage*, London.

Roe 1905. F. Roe, *Old Oak Furniture*, London.

RSA 1929. *An Exhibition of Catholic Art and Antiquities, Royal Society of Arts,* Birmingham.

Royal Visit 1983. C. Pullin & N. Frayling, 'A Short History of All Saints Tooting Graveney', from *A Royal Visit to All Saints Tooting Graveney.*

Saumery 1738-44. O.L. de Saumery, *Les Délices du Pais de Liège,* Liège (reprinted 1970).

Schiller 1972. G. Schiller, *Iconography of Christian Art,* London.

Simpson 2000. S. Simpson, 'The Choir Stalls and Rood Screen', from *J. Geddes (ed.), King's College Chapel, Aberdeen, 1500-2000,* Aberdeen.

Stone 1955. L. Stone, *Sculpture in Britain. The Middle Ages,* Harmondsworth.

Strange 1927. E.F. Strange, 'The Henry VIII Room at Bretton Park', *Old Furniture,* November 1927, 96-100.

van Swigchem *et al.* 1984. C.A. van Swigchem, T. Brouwer & W. van Os, *Een huis voor het Woord. Het Protestantse kerkinterieur in Nederland tot 1900,* 's-Gravenhage.

Thirion 1998. J. Thirion, *Le Mobilier du Moyen Âge et de la Renaissance en France,* Dijon.

Tinniswood 1992. A. Tinniswood, 'Belton House, Lincolnshire', The National Trust, London.

Tracy 1988. C. Tracy, *A Catalogue of English Gothic Furniture and Woodwork,* Victoria and Albert Museum, London.

Tracy 1990. C. Tracy, *English Gothic choir-stalls, 1400-1540,* Woodbridge.

Vanhoof 1987. F. Vanhoof, 'Het koorgestoelte van het klooster Sint-Nilkaasberg te Aarschot', *het oude land aarshcot,* xxii, No. 2, June 1987.

Vallance 1947. A. Vallance, *Greater English Church Screens,* London.

Verspaandonk 1986. J.A.J.M. Verspaandonk, 'Laatgotische Zuidnederlandse misericorden in het Victoria & Albert Museum te Londen', *Antiek,* June/July, 1986, 12-21.

Vlieghe 1998. H. Vlieghe, *Flemish Art and Architecture, 1585-1700,* New Haven and London.

de Vries 1630. *Verscheyden Schrynwerck.*

Wainwright 1976. C. Wainwright, 'Oxburgh Hall', Notes deposited in the library of the Department of Furniture and Woodwork, V & A Museum.

Wainwright 1986. C. Wainwright, 'The antiquarian interior in Britain 1780-1850', University of London, Ph.D. thesis.

Wainwright 1989. C. Wainwright, *The Romantic Interior. The British Collector at Home, 1750-1850,* New Haven and London.

Wedgwood 1977. A. Wedgwood, *The Pugin family: catalogue of the drawings of the collection of the RIBA,* London.

Wedgwood 1985. A. Wedgwood, *A.W.N. Pugin and the Pugin Family. Catalogues of Architectural Drawings in the Victoria and Albert Museum,* London.

de Werd 1978. G. de Werd, 'Enn Antwerps retabel van omstreeks 1525 in de St Walbürgeskerk te Netterden (Gld.)', in *Antiek,* Feb. 1978, 555-567.

Williams 1959. R.H. Isaac Williams, 'A short History of Elham and its Parish Church'.

Williamson 2002. P. Williamson, *Netherlandish Sculpture. 1450-1550,* Victoria and Albert Museum, London.

Willis & Clarke 1886. R. Willis & J.W. Clarke, *The Architectural History of the University of Cambridge,* 1, Cambridge.

Woodman 1981. F. Woodman, *The Architectural History of King's College, Cambridge,* Cambridge.

Woods 1983. K.W. Woods, 'Scarisbrick Hall', Manuscript copy deposited in the archives of the Department of Furniture and Woodwork, Victoria & Albert Museum, London.

Woods 1989. K.W. Woods, 'Netherlandish carved wooden altarpieces of the fifteenth and early sixteenth centuries in Britain', Ph.D. thesis, Courtauld Institute of Art, University of London.

Woods 1999. K.W. Woods, 'Some sixteenth-century Antwerp carved wooden altarpieces in England', *Burlington Magazine,* March 1999, no. 1152, vol. cxli, 144-55.

Yorke 1989. J. Yorke, 'Engraved Decoration on early Fifteenth-Century Italian Furniture', *Apollo,* June 1989, 389-92, 445.

Zajadacz-Hastenrath 1970. S. Zajadacz-Hastenrath, *Das Beichenstuhl der Antwerpen St. Pauluskirche,* Brussels.

Appendix 1

Brownlow Papers. Personal journals/account books of the Honourable and Revd Henry Cockayne Cust, 1812-1859, 35 volumes (Lincolnshire Archives)

		£
1823		
w/c Sept. 22	Hill for Altar Piece for Hatley Church	100- 0- 0
	Wilson painter & gilder for ditto	16- 9- 0
	...for carriage of Altar Piece	8- 9- 9
Annual Consolidated Account		
	Altar piece for Hatley church	124-18- 9
1824		
Journal missing		
1825		
	No woodwork purchased for church	
	Excursion to Holland, Belgium and France	96- 8- 0
1826		
Jan 1	Custom House duties on Woodwork from Ghent	28- 5- 4
w/c 22 May	R. Rushbrooke Esq. for Wood Work for Church	174- 0- 0
	Customs House Duties & Freight	51- 2- 6
	Custom House Duties Freight on Pulpit	37-15- 6
May 30	Moved the pulpit brought from Antwerp into Cockayne Hatley Church	
June 18	Hatley Church not being in a fit state for Divine Service in consequence of the new Pewing	
June 25	Morning Service at Cockayne Hatley preached for the first time from the new Pulpit etc.	
w/c June 19	*[Approximately £40 laid out on wages to workmen, including a bricklayer]*	
	No foreign excursion	
Annual consolidated account		
	Woodwork for Church	174-17- 6
	Customs House Duties etc.	131- 3- 8
1827		
w/c April 16	Woodwork, altar rail etc for Hatley church	22- 0- 0
	Customs House duties & freight over woodwork	15-15- 0
	Rhine excursion	110- 0- 0
Annual Consolidated Account		
July 2 –		
August 5	Woodwork for Hatley Church	96-10- 0
1828		
w/c March 3	Bill for Wood & Work etc. Hatley Church	74- 0- 0
w/c July 14	Swabey for Wood Work for Cockayne Hatley Church	11-10- 0
	No foreign excursion	
Annual Consolidated Account		
	Woodwork for Hatley Church	102- 4- 3
	Bells for Hatley church	30- 4- 3

APPENDIX 1

1829
	Woodwork for Cockayne Hatley	39- 5- 0
	Woodwork for church	25- 0- 0
	No foreign excursion	

Annual Consolidated Account
| | Wood Work for Hatley Church | 64- 5- 0 |

1830

12 March   'walked with Peregrine to ye Customs House'
            [diary entry]

	Webb – woodwork for Hatley church [diary entry]	5- 3-10
w/c May 26	Organ pipes for Hatley	5- 0- 0
	Willement for painting and gilding organ pipes	5- 0- 0
	Willement's bill for sundries on account of church	15- 1- 4
	Willement painted window for Cockayne Hatley church	100- 0- 0
	Willement's bill for putting up window for Cockayne Hatley church	14- 9- 0
	East window for Hatley church	114- 9- 0
w/c August 9	Fairs [Thomas] for Painting Roof of Hatley Church	62-18- 7
	Fairs for painting, papering [illeg.]	208- 2- 6
	Armstrong Plaisterer for work	16- 3-11

Annual Consolidated Account
	Furniture for C Hatley	66-11- 3
	Painting for Hatley Church	62-18- 7
	Old Woodwork & Organ Pipes for CH church	45- 2-10
	East window for CH church	114- 9- 0

August 28 -
October 25   Foreign excursion to Germany, Switzerland and Paris

1831
Jan 1   New western window of painted glass in the tower
         of church – complete and opened Cockayne Hatley

1832
         No relevant entries

1833
w/c Feb. 4   Barrel Organ for Hatley Church   36-17- 0

1840
| | Window and altar rails at do | 19- 9- 8 |
| | chancel windows in CH | 143- 9- 0 |

Annual Consolidated Account
| | Excursion to Paris [July] | 165- 6- 2 |
| | Chancel windows in CH | 43- 9- 0 |

No diaries survive for 1841-43, 1846 or 1851

Appendix 2

Letters from Robert Rushbrooke Esquire to
The Honourable and Reverend Henry Cockayne Cust
Brownlow Papers (Lincolnshire Record Office)

Incomplete letter. Dated JUNE 13 1826. Posted in Liverpool.

do the stalls re-echo their Abbots' Hexameter in its most comprehensive senses, the *honest* pulpit is without the pale, Till pickaxes and spades for such a guest most meet, conduct it to its *recantation*. Plague on the Primrose proportions what trouble they give you! I must continue if steal one day for Cockayne Hatley to see you and yours how you *enjoy* all these concerns with my naked, not my mind's Eye – but with that I am *for present satisfied* since I find my Commission has given *such complete satisfaction*. I cannot fail being amused with your *heathenish* compliment to Self & Joe – 'not to speak profanely' – an *odd* thought came into my mind for a moment *coupled with our Service to the Church* which carried me to Lystra – verb. sat –. By the by, not to detract from Joe's merits, I must announce that my Grocer's son, from Antwerp, has all the merits of the pulpit's safety – when it *is* set up, your choice of spot will be the most effective – it having no sounding board, of course no panel at your back will be required – so that those behind you will hear well. I am glad you are not alarmed at all the cost. By adding to that already incurred...................
I made a very pleasant tour in Holland etc about a fortnight since. ... With the pictures at Hague and Amsterdam, I was enchanted, and the trip to Brock and Laardam [? S]. The *organ* at Haarlem was in *full blow* – not so the *Hyancinths* and *Tulips,* they were nipped by the frost. Our journey was chiefly by water, i.e. from Antwerp to Rotterdam by steam, passing all the objects of interest, so made our various xions xxxxxx, attended with mixed adoration of pride and regret. The succession of Truhtschusts [?] conveyed us thence as far as Utrecht on the banks of whose Canal are some villas which are really, in taste of planting, Twickenham-esque. We returned thence to Antwerp in hired vehicle particular [?]. I took Dilly back to Bruxelles. The House in the wood is a bad affair, save for the over-powering room in the Centre. The walk thither from Hague delightfully varied by the new lakes & winding paths. We were at the H [Hague] during the fair which rivals Bury in Munchery & Monkeyism. The sameness of style in the Dutch towns gives a surfeit ere you reach the Capital. The doggedness of the natives & the dearness [?] of their charges, are great drawbacks to this tour ....

16 JANUARY 1827

Written from Brussels

My dear Henry,

Lest you should think me *dead* (at least to your interests) I will no longer delay acknowledging *your* amiability & my idleness which has been *incurable* since August last. In my hurried trip to the Customs House I begged the worthy Commissioner to assure you of my xxxxx xxxx to the – *fille de quartier* in placing the abbey of Anne in *Commendation* in your hands, tho at the same time raising false papers of a Mitre [?]. Day after day has *Josephine* offered me fresh *Chapters.* But none of the works sufficiently ample for your purpose. N.B. You have sent me more than once the width (viz 13ft) but the height I have been obliged "to put x" up to this time. – Let that be *given* in xxx next & *most speedily,* that I may be able to calculate the Q[uantit]y required [gives diagram of a window with letters relating to different parts] – Let me have the dimensions of the *lancet* abcdefgh [gives diagram of a window with letters relating to different paints on the window head] – so as to have the curvature correctly in case we can fit it, bearing in mind the application of an organ case when occasion serve.

I am on the scent both here and Gand & hope in a week or ten days to hear of my *Hammock* Joe. & in the mean time to have your Ms for my Guide. I must make my usual excuses for scrawlery, having had much use for my pen this post, as well as little arrangements in my composition. It was with great practice of forbearance that I eschewed the *Land of Cockayne* in my last flight to Britain. But I had to trespass on a day or two of the Boy's Vacation, and it was, for business sake & their desire of Reunion was too ardent to admit of it. Joseph [Heminius], enquired how far from London was the *revived abbey,* & literally will *some* day pay you a visit of respect & curiosity. As to the little Balance against me, let it rest. I pray, until it be *swollen* by the *gateway.* You are so prudent a personage. No one will accuse you, or fear that you are

"Keeping a more *swelling post*
"Than what your means may grant continuance"

For myself, on that head what with feelings of the present & fears for the future, I have resolved to extend my stay herein one twelvemonth more that at first intended. So that if you have more *Abbeys* to endow & to decorate, you may be assured of my *Agency* until September 1828. Unless unforeseen accidents or good fortune accelerate my return. Bye the Bye in the collection of *Candlesticks* from Gand, have you been so thoughtful as to reserve me a *pair?* I hope I sent as liberal a supply as to be able to put in a *Claim* for twain of these for *my* Altar piece, but do not spoil any of your plans if they be requisite for the -one more word on the title History of the Abbey d'Anne – Mons. Paquot-Syphorien learned from a Monk that a Proverb arose out the "Porta patens" line, which caused the Author's ejection from the Monastery – it was this "Faute d'un *point* Martin perdit son Ane". Your delight with these well applied materials which my researches have procured so happily gives me an equal enthusiasm with yourself and fancy for my reward, I shall say, as the Poet to his mistress. "You are pleased & *your'e* my pleasure" – and it shall go hard but I will assist in its completion, by following the Skreening materials to xxxx distinction if times and dates allow – I am proud to find my example, or even my offer, taken at Bury St Edmunds. Some years ago I volunteered the inspection & arrangements so as to reduce all the payments of xxx at St James's Court with xxx "Swizzling xxx tax al et unum" – which I doubt not but Hazzitt junior – *(no* degenerate Youth) has executed much better than I should have done. Let us have spending but of your family varieties – be *friend of the interior.*

JUNE 9 1829.

Says he hopes that Cust will come to London ...

'And we must carry Swabey in our eye to fit at Hatley vice [*sic*] seeing what is wanted at Hatley to be supplied by S'.

Appendix 3

Bills from Edward Hull, 109 Wardour Street, Soho to Charles Scarisbrick
Esquire, and summaries of accounts.
Scarisbrick Papers, DDSc 78/4 (LRO, Preston)

*The entries have been amalgamated in chronological order. Only items in the summaries
which clearly duplicate invoiced goods have been omitted. Even so, the entries for the double
doors leading from the King's Room ('Ante Room') remain ambiguous (cf. August 1840
and December 1840).*

(Charles Scarisbrick's annotations in plain brackets)

	£	
Dec 1836		
Very fine pieces of Gothic for Doors	30	-
5 Feb 1837		
Richly carved Oak Gothic Eagle Desk with figures under canopies	40	-
The Large Gothic Oak Doorway including the new Carvings and		
two Gothic figures on top (for library)	94	10
Feb 1838		
Library.		
The very fine Gothic chimney piece	300	-
Middle Library.		
The large oak Doorway including the new carvings on top of frieze	94	10
June 1839		
Gothic shrine in pieces	2	10
Gothic shrine in pieces (Blue)	60	-
Gothic Pillars for the [centre of] Large Doors library	4	10
The Gothic chandilier – Gothic stall		
Two Gothic canopies and 2 open panels	85	-
August 1839		
Lot of Stall Seats ends etc	33	-
Small Shrine St Hubert	8	-
Fine carved Oak Pulpit staircase & c.	100	-
Jan 16 1840		
Gothic Shrine	60	-
Gothic Shrine for Chimney Piece	25	-
August 1840		
Ante Room to Libraries		
Canopies bought at sale	100	-
The two double doors carved on both sides making out of my old		
materials £165 & £94.10	259	10
South Library		
Chimney piece made out of my own carvings	30	-
Dec 1840		
Making pair of large Gothic Doors for Library	94	10
Making Gothic Chimney Piece for small room	58	--
The very fine Screen and Panelling Doors etc – for end of the Hall	1000	--

Jan 7 1841
From sale at Deacons
3 Carved Friezes	2	15
Gothic Groups	4	4
Fine [very early] Oak Gothic Door in subjects	4	10
Gothic figure St Catherine	4	4
2 Gothic little open work/Cornices	6	10
8 Ditto panels	3	3
Fine Gothic figure	4	8

May 21st 1841
Panelling from Strawberry Hill and Commission	105	1

July 19th 1841
Large Hall Screen	12	15

14 August 1841
Lot of fine canopy work and Groups [now in Scarisbrick anteroom]	100	--

August 31 1841
513 Gothic Panel (in two pieces)	4	4
510 Small Shrine	1	2
504 3 Gothic figures for small chimney piece	14	-
459 8 Panels and 2 large ditto	2	2
238 10 Open Panels [Gothic]	2	14
230 12 Panels	1	12
229 8 Ditto	2	-
223 Gothic Chest front	1	14
219 15 x pattern Panels	3	5
216 Gothic fragments 140 pieces	4	-

October 1841
The large Gothic Shrine in Cases	100	-
Making pair of Large Gothic Doors for Library (1st pair sent down)	94	10
The very fine Screen and Panelling Doors etc, etc. for end of the Hall	1000	-

December 10 1841
4 Carved figures/curled leaves over head/ [Italian]	6	-
7 Richly Carved Panels inc Subjects	20	-

May 23 1842
Pair of Very Richly Carved Doors in small Subjects	18	-

From Charles Scarisbrick's summary of Edward Hull's and Baylis's bills

Dec 1836
4 Very fine Pieces of Gothic for doors	30	-

June 1837
3 Large Gothic doors and one fine Gothic ditto carved on both sides	22	-

October 1839
Lot of stalls seats & ends etc	33	-

May 1840
3 Pair of Large Carved Oak Doors	18	-

Feb 1841
Gothic Screen or Gates   23   -
Pannels & Pillars to make into Doors taken out of a large screen   50   -

Oct 1844
Lot of very fine Gothic Work to be used for the Lanthorn over
Staircase & window frame   150   -

Charles Scarisbrick's Notes Miscellaneous

June 1837
3 Large Gothic Doors and one finer Gothic door carved both sides   22   -

May 1840
3 Pair of Large Carved Oak Doors   18   -

Feb 1841
Gothic screen or gates   23   -
Pannels & Pillars &/or 2 Doors Confessional   50   -

March 1846
2 Large Pannels in subjects   20   -

He notes that he made his last purchase from Edward Hull September 1848.

Note from Edward Hull

One hundred Pounds shall be paid for Pulpit with all its accessories
and then delivered restored and complete
On the back CS notes (Frieze – Communion Rail)
Account for the pulpit rendered Jan 1833

Notes from Charles Scarisbrick [n.d.]

Spanish Carvings   98   -
Two pillars Spanish   22   10

1846 Articles not settled for [CS's hand]

April 25 Two Gothic Crosses   24   -
Gothic shrine for chimney   25   -
Large Gothic shrine in cases, this with Pulpit stem is at Bird's Ship Ya 22rd 100   -

Gazetteer

This is a list of wooden fragments, including related works of sculpture outside the scope of the main study, mostly not inspected or discussed in the main text. For all its shortcomings, such a list is at least an attempt at inclusivity, although it will fail sometimes in accuracy, and in comprehensiveness. The descriptions are excerpted from the *Buildings of England* series, where indicated, by kind permission of the publishers. In the BOE volumes it has not always been possible to be certain that some of the reliefs referred to are unquestionably in wood. Other entries are from the *Royal Commission on the Historical Monuments of England* volumes, church guides and the author's own observations. The Victoria and Albert Museum entries are based on the catalogues in the Furniture and Woodwork Department. Organ cases are omitted.

BEDFORDSHIRE

Apsley Guise. Pulpit: a made-up piece with Netherlandish 17th c. panels and English late 17th c. decoration (BOE, *Bedfordshire, Huntingdonshire and Peterborough*, 1968).

Cockayne Hatley. Door: of Cust family pew on north side of nave. Said to be from St Bavo, Ghent, but a mixture of different periods; Lectern: made up from different 17th and 18th c. ingredients. Incorporates in the front a prophet figure, said to be the St Andrew from the back board of the pulpit (K/4), now at Carlisle Cathedral; Low screenwork: two pieces now at the west end. Deeply moulded auricular panels divided by buttresses with cabochons. Inside the panels are cartouches of best Dutch mid-17th c. quality.

Old Warden. Box pews: throughout the church, all made up with applied decoration of Continental origin. Thirteen of the fifteen Dutch and Flemish 15th/16th c. applied panels have been stolen. The many panels with AC on the altar and elsewhere are said to come from the House of Anne of Cleves at Bruges, but they look to be French 18th c. In the panelling behind the altar young caryatids.

BUCKINGHAMSHIRE

Burnham. Wall panelling: possibly 17th c. Flemish; Loose panels: on the walls of south transept, formerly part of the 'Dropmore Pew'.

Chalfont St Giles. Communion rail: with opulent openwork acanthus foliage in the panels. Probably *c*.1700, and perhaps foreign (BOE, *Buckinghamshire*, 1994).

Dropmore. Pulpit: with Early Renaissance panels with heads in roundels. Probably Flemish (BOE, *Buckinghamshire*, 1994, and author).

CAMBRIDGESHIRE

Abington Pigotts. Pulpit: two-decker with various 17th c. panels stuck on. The sculpture may be Flemish (BOE, *Cambridgeshire*, 1977).

Bourn. Sculpture: two wood-carved panels of *c*.1540, probably Flemish, one with the Virgin, the other looks like a Lucretia (BOE, *Cambridgeshire*, 1977).

Buckden. Reader's desks: with eight later 16th c. Flemish reliefs of scenes from the *Passion* (BOE, *Bedfordshire, Huntingdonshire and Peterborough*, 1968).

Coveney. Supposedly a German reredos of *c*.1500, with painted and carved scenes of the Passion. Too heavily restored to retain much authenticity.

Croxton. Door: to the north aisle. 17th c. In the tympanum some carved fragments, 18th c., apparently Flemish or French (BOE, *Cambridgeshire*, 1977).

Doddington. Relief: small wooden relief of *Christ and the Woman of Samaria*. ? Dutch 18th c. (BOE, *Cambridgeshire*, 1977).

Wisbech St Mary. Chairs: in the chancel three gilt chairs from Culford Hall, Suffolk. Italian and of *c*.1730. The settee to go with them is at Peckover House, Wisbech. Also some late medieval and Baroque panels, brackets and wooden sculpture.

CHESHIRE

Barthomley. Sculpture: five medallions of saints, Baroque, probably Flemish or French (BOE, *Cheshire*, 1978).

Birtles. Choir-stall backing: seventeen bays at the west end, in the north chapel and three more at the base of the pulpit, with canons' names inscribed above each (Richards 1973). Pulpit: At the top there is a cresting on the wall with the bust of a woman and several unrelated pieces with it. Below a series of historiated panels, dated 1686. At the base a frieze dated 1655.

Tarvin. Reredos: with reliefs, four saints and four narrative scenes (*Christ's Baptism, Crucifixion, Resurrection and Ascension*). They are *c*.1500, and probably Flemish. The saint panels are in the transitional Gothic Renaissance style, *c*.mid.-16th c. The narrative panels, under arches with cabochons, etc., are 17th c., and possibly English. All eight panels in a 19th c. mount.

CORNWALL

Antony, Plymouth. Pulpit: with four carved panels of the Evangelists, *c*.1500, not English, perhaps Spanish (BOE, *Cornwall*, 1951).

Feock, Truro. Pulpit: with four late 16th c. Flemish panels with religious scenes (BOE, *Cornwall*, 1951).

CUMBERLAND AND WESTMORLAND

Brougham, St Wilfrid's Chapel. Benching: arranged college-wise, incorporating panels of ecclesiastical origin with Flamboyant tracery, IHS symbols, the initials M.A. and secular coats of arms, said to be French. Some of these could have come from chests. The framing is modern. A few of the panels have been made up into wainscoting on the side walls, with initials M.A. and fleur-de-lis; Stallwork: almost entirely 19th c. work. Four early 16th c. stalls on the south side, west of the entrance door, and another single standard. This last is freely copied elsewhere. Probably two ancient figural poppy-heads on south side at west end, let into modern work; Reredos: A made-up piece, only the posts each side, traceried and sculptured panels being old. The four figurative panels are South German early 16th c. They depict *Mary and Joseph at the Manger,* the *Crucifixion, Adoration of the Shepherds* and *Entry into Jerusalem;* Miscellaneous panels: at the back of the altar, dado panels, c.1500, gilded and painted probably in the 19th c. Also four panels with saints in high relief (? 19th c.); Forming a partition at west end of church – imported carved panels of the early life of Christ, David and Goliath, Cain and Abel, etc. frieze of 17th c. panels carved with cherub-heads and swags; Eight low-relief Continental narrative panels in seats at the far west end (one stolen); Pulpit: in the middle of the south wall, but formerly in the centre to the west of the altar. Modern, but incorporating geometrical panels, imported figure-subjects of the Virgin and Child, the *Assumption,* a *Pietà* and probably God the Father (BOE, *Cumberland and Westmorland,* 1980); RCHME, *Westmorland,* 1936; and author).

Carlisle Cathedral. Altarpiece: Netherlandish, formerly at St Wilfrid's, Brougham, Cumbria; Miniature Flemish twisted Solomonic columns: a pair, with twisted columns, Corinthian capitals and lavishly decorated with vine-trail, birds and putti. Similar to those at Madley, Herefordshire.

Corby Castle. In the chapel. Altar-reredos: said to be from Rome and to have been once the property of Lord Stafford, who was executed in 1680 (BOE, *Cumberland and Westmorland,* 1980).

Wigton St Mary. Retable: of the north aisle altar, made up of 16th c. and 17th c. North German woodwork. Said to come from Cleves. The panels with religious scenes (BOE, *Cumberland and Westmorland,* 1980).

DERBYSHIRE

Chatsworth House. Oak Room. Wall panelling made up from the backs of 17th c., supposedly South German or Austrian, choir-stalls. But are they Flemish? Twelve sculptured busts of prelates, with turned columns either side on balusters. The cupboards below have carved pilasters with figures, seraphim etc. on scroll brackets. Are these part of the original ensemble? Probably not, although they are Continental, but slightly earlier in style. The busts include representations of a pope, cardinal, bishop, St Dominic with star on his forehead, and monks. The room ceiling is supported by four giant Solomonic columns. Probably Flemish.

Derby Cathedral. Cupboard: at W end of N aisle, with cupboard section in the centre, and drawer underneath. Oak. In the centre a carved panel with *Christ at Gethsemane.* A made-up piece using 18th c. Flemish material (BOE, *Derbyshire,* 1953, and author).

Pleasely. Reading desk: a 19th c. framework incorporates an 18th c. Italian carving of a scribe in his study.

DEVON

Newton St Cyres. Two carved panels (Flemish ?), incorporated in lectern and aumbry (BOE, *Devon,* 1989).

Offwell. Reader's desk: made up in 1935 incorporating a richly carved Flemish panel of the *Last Supper* (BOE, *Devon,* 1989).

Plymstock. Chest: made up with early 16th c. carved panels (German ?) formerly part of a font cover (BOE, *Devon,* 1989).

Uffculme. Pulpit. An early 17th c. Flemish sculptured panel of the *Resurrection* has been grafted on to one of the faces of this English 18th c. object.

Weare Giffard Hall. Much imported Flemish woodwork, incorporated into wainscot, screens, etc. (BOE, *Devon,* 1989).

Widdicombe-on-the-Moor. Continental tracery, built into modern panelling (Hugh Harrison).

DORSET

Brownsea Island. Parchemin panelling: in the chancel. English or Netherlandish. Also some sculpture (BOE, *Dorset,* 1972).

Charborough. Stalls: with dates 1626 and 1651 and with pieces both English and Continental; Pulpit: with scenes and decorative figures from 16th c. to 18th c. Two decker. Scenes Mannerist work probably from the Netherlands; Altarpiece: pediment only from probably Netherlandish Baroque example with *Last Judgement* low relief sculpture (BOE, *Dorset,* 1972 and author).

Whitchurch Canonicorum. Choir benches: the arabesque panels at the top and the mostly traceried panels at the ends are said to be French 16th c. (BOE, *Dorset,* 1972).

COUNTY DURHAM

Bowes Museum. Six carved chestnut panels: framed, one with a trophy of religious symbols, five with saints with wreaths. French 18th c. These must have formed part of a scheme of panelling. One carries a London shipper's label, dated 1869; Carved and pierced oak balustrade: from a pulpit staircase. French, early 18th c. (FW312); Predella panel: painted and carved limewood, showing a scene of the *Last Supper.* South German, early 16th c. (W129); Oak stall standard with cherub's head as elbow: probably French, 18th c.

Ryton. Continental work given by the Rev. Charles Thorp in 1826. Altar rails: restored and fragmentary. Sculpture: Two seated Apostles on the communion rail, with modern bases, look as if they might be from the Lower Rhine, c.1500-10 (BOE, *County Durham,* 1983 and author).

Stanhope. Sculpture: two oval wood panels with Adam and Eve and Christ and St Peter. Baroque, probably Flemish (BOE, *County Durham,* 1983).

ESSEX

Castle Hedingham. Sculpture: small wooden relief of the *Magdalene washing Christ's feet* probably Flemish, early 16th c. East end of south aisle (BOE, *Essex,* 1954).

Newport. Communion table: with three Flemish early 17th c. reliefs (BOE, *Essex,* 1954).

Orsett. Sculpture: five Italian 18th c. panels; *Annunciation, Holy Family, Mourning of the Dead Christ, Ascension, Pentecost* (BOE, *Essex,* 1954).

Rayne. Woodwork: *c.*1500. Tracery panels and also a later 16th c. figure relief, said to be Flemish (BOE, *Essex,* 1954).

White Colne. Pulpit: hexagonal, with, at the angles, term pilasters with ornament in Jacobean style. But on three of the panels, in relief, well carved figures of the Virgin, St James the Great, and St Augustine of Hippo. The style is not English. Can it be Flemish? (BOE, *Essex,* 1954.

Witham. Sculpture: small wooden relief of the Nativity (south chapel). Mannerist, not English (BOE, *Essex,* 1954).

GLOUCESTERSHIRE

Berkeley Castle Chapel. Altar: made up from four-bayed arcading with Biblical scenes interspersed with terminal figures. There are other similar panels in a bedroom in the castle. 16th c.

Wyck Rissington. Carvings: in the chancel are twelve 16th c. carved wooden plaques, thought to be Flemish. Discovered *c.*1890 at Wyck Hill House and show scenes from the *Life of Christ* (BOE, *Gloucestershire: The Cotswolds,* 1970).

HAMPSHIRE

Binstead (I.O.W.). Sculpture: Flemish. Various historiated panels. Late 16th c. to early 17th c. (BOE, *Hampshire,* 1967).

Chapel of Our Lady of the Rosary, Bursledon. Panelling: round the apse beside the altar, with very delicate carved representations of biblical scenes in medallions; Sculpture: pair of Solomonic columns decorated with vine leaves and Corinthian capitals above. Heavy 19th c. lintel above embellished with 17th c. carved fragments (BOE, *Hampshire,* 1967 and author).

Otterbourne. Sculpture: the 19th c. pulpit incorporates five 15th c. German panels, and two copies in the same style in cast iron. They consist of standing figures under traceried canopies, some with inscriptions underneath. The three in oak represent St Jerome, St Augustine, the Virgin, a pope and a bishop. The cast figures are also bishops.

Romsey Abbey. French chest with all-over tracery decoration. A shield in the centre with chevrons and a crown on top. The only ecclesiastical allusion is the figure of God the Father with orb, on the lock hasp.

Sherfield English. Pulpit: incorporates Mannerist panels (Netherlandish?) cf. Temperance, Justice, and Charity, set in much strapwork (BOE, *Hampshire,* 1967).

Sparsholt. Sculpture: three Netherlandish panels of the second quarter 16th c. (BOE, *Hampshire,* 1967).

Winchester Cathedral. Against the north and south screens of the choir sanctuary, two sections of Flemish choir-stalls of *c.*1725. Each section incorporates four stalls divided by boldly scrolled arm-rests and supported by twisted columns. The ends have panels of Baroque strapwork, and the seats are supplied with vestigial scrolled misericords. The only old woodwork is the top part of the standards and the misericord. The dividers at each end are possibly wholly authentic. The end panels and the twisted columns under the seat standards are 19th c.

Woodcott. Pulpit and reading desk: they incorporate angle-posts with angels and 18th c. oval medallions with St Peter and St Paul with ribbons. Probably Netherlandish or French (BOE, *Hampshire,* 1967).

HEREFORDSHIRE

Ewyas Harold. Reredos: with bits of imported carvings, including two Netherlandish, very Mannerist figures of *c.*1530 (cf. Kinnersley below), and two scenes from the *Passion*, North German, mid-17th c. (BOE, *Herefordshire,* 1982).

Hereford Cathedral. Audley Chapel. Relief: Tuscan, 15th c. Virgin and Child, in an original frame (BOE, *Herefordshire,* 1982).

Kinnersley. Pulpit: of divers pieces. They include four Mannerist allegorical figures. Flemish, *c.*1530, and similar to the free-standing figurines of King's College Chapel, Cambridge, choir-stalls. Compare also the Ewyas Harold (above) and the loose and incorporated panels at Harwood, Lancashire (M/12) (BOE, *Herefordshire,* 1982).

Madley. Woodwork: three high-quality 17th c. carved oak panels from Flanders, which were until recently displayed in the south choir aisle in the form of an altar reredos, but have now been ousted and given temporary accommodation under the west tower. Three rectangular panels, all in later frames, are carved in high relief. Two are a pair, whilst the third and larger one, which is stylistically different, is an important refugee Flemish altar frontal (A/4). Sculpture: Also there are four miniature Solomonic twisted columns, which are decorated with lavish vine leaves and grapes.

Wormbridge. Woodwork: bits under the tower and in three big composite panels in the nave. They were given to the church in 1870 and came from Newnham Paddox near Lutterworth, Leicestershire. Some Netherlandish Mannerist (the caryatids in strapwork fetters). (BOE, *Herefordshire,* 1982.)

Yatton. Lectern: stem is foreign late 17th c. work made for a different purpose. Sculpture: Flemish early 16th c. relief of *Christ before Pilate*. Another of the Resurrection, also 16th c., but later, and also Continental (BOE, *Herefordshire,* 1982).

HERTFORDSHIRE

Knebworth. Pulpit: with carved panels of Flemish origin, one of them dated 1567 (BOE, *Hertfordshire,* 1978).

KENT

Davington. Pulpit: incorporating crude 17th c. panels of the Resurrection and four Evangelists. ? Foreign (BOE, *North-East Kent and East Kent,* 1969).

Hadlow. Chair: said to have come from Exeter Cathedral and to be associated with Coverdale. But a close look shows that it was made up in the 19th c. from old bits: Late 16th c. panels of allegorical figures low down at the side, and a relief of the *Expulsion,* which is probably 17th c. Flemish (BOE, *West Kent and The Weald,* 1969).

Hever Castle. Chair: in walnut, with high back, open sides but panelled base (Plate 5). Said to be French, *c.*1500. It has the carved figure of a bishop, holding a pastoral staff in his right hand and the model of a church in the other, on the back. There are two Corinthian columns on either side. Below is another panel with the prostrate figure of a woman. On the front base panel are two cherubs holding a cartouche. The mouldings throughout are finely fluted. The crowning entablature is modern, including the figure of God the Father inside. The right-hand side panel is also of relatively new manufacture, and probably much else besides, particularly the mouldings. Much of the decorative carving, particularly the mouldings, is genuine and probably of late 16th c. date. It is a spectacular piece, but it was probably put together at the end of the 18th c.

Leigh. Lectern: incorporating a 17th c. Flemish relief in wood of the *Journey to Emmaus* (BOE, *West Kent and The Weald,* 1969).

North Cray. Choir benches: incorporate Düreresque reliefs of the *Adoration of the Shepherds* (South) and the *Visitation* and *Circumcision* (North); Behind the stalls on the north side, a 15th c. relief of the *Seven Acts of Mercy*. The end panels, with Renaissance shell-hoods, must be later. Reredos: large panels in very high relief of the *Adoration of the Magi* and the *Flight into Egypt* (BOE, *West Kent and The Weald,* 1969).

Plaxtol. Reredos: A frame for the little wooden reliefs of Passion scenes. The reliefs must be 15th c. Flemish. The voluminous, crinkly draperies very characteristic. Note too the stylized rocks. Another carved panel (17th c.?), of the *Crossing of the Red Sea,* as a reredos in the south transept; Pulpit: 17th c. Not English? The relief figures obviously don't belong (BOE, *West Kent and The Weald,* 1969).

Sidcup, St John. Reredos: flanked by twisted columns, with a flat projecting top which has a modillion cornice. Both these components are mostly ancient, and probably Flemish, 17th c.

Swanscombe. 'Litany desk': supposed to have been made up from a 'tabernacle' bought in Seville in 1911, and given to Galley Hill church nearby. The authentic parts are the three painted panels with *Christ displaying his Wound* (in the centre), St Peter (angled left) and St Paul (angled right). Panels of Renaissance design above each painting. The piece functions as a cupboard, with the central panel fitted with hinges and a lock.

LANCASHIRE

Harwood. 'Credence' table: a made-up piece of Flemish 17th c. components; Altar/Vestment Cupboard: another made-up object with Flemish components, with two historiated panels dated 1561; Woodwork: a set of fine Mannerist figured panels, four of them incorporated into the choir-stalls (cf. Ewyas Harold and Kinnersley, Herefordshire). Are they French or Netherlandish?

Huyton. 'Credence' table: made up of two panels of different dates. Probably brought from the Netherlands by the Earl of Derby, 1850-60.

Knowsley. Desk: 19th c. structure incorporating 18th c. Flemish sculptured panel of *Christ carrying the Cross*.

Scarisbrick Hall. Miscellaneous: major public rooms and spaces furnished with fragments of structural woodwork, e.g. the screen at the east end of the Great Hall, and many items of loose panelling and sculpture, in the Oak Room, King's Room, Dining Room, Red Drawing Room and elsewhere. In the Red Drawing Room there are two Netherlandish carved oak panels built in on either side of the mantelpiece by Edward Hull (Appendix 3, August 1840), showing 1. ? the *Death of the Virgin,* and 2. the death of a bishop. Were they originally desk ends ?

Worsley. Made-up 19th c. pulpit, incorporating three, probably, 17th c. Dutch Christological panels, and three Continental Evangelist carvings. Organ case with early 16th c. French panels incorporated. The Belgian stair panelling may be 19th c.

LEICESTERSHIRE

Coleorton. Woodwork: screening off the last bay of the north aisle a large number of Flemish and English 17th c. bits, including several scenic reliefs (BOE, *Leicestershire and Rutland,* 1984).

LINCOLNSHIRE

Appleby. Pulpit: with many small Flemish 16th c. reliefs (BOE, *Lincolnshire,* 1989).

Revesby. Pulpit: incorporated in it three small Flemish reliefs of the late 16th c. (BOE, *Lincolnshire,* 1989).

LONDON

East Bedfont. Relief: of the Crucifixion of *c.*1530. Flemish (BOE, *London 3: North West,* 1991).

St Dunstan's, Fleet Street. Reredos: covers the width of the chancel. A domed canopy in each corner (19th c.) and a projecting four-bay tester above the altar (there is more of this canopywork in the vestry). The central pendent boss of the tester is in the form of two angels holding a chalice. Three tiers of panelling below, with traceried and crocketed arches at top and bottom and linenfold in the centre. At each end of the dado zone three panels with the figures of saints. The whole ensemble is made up from bits and pieces, united under a dark varnish. The Gothic fragments, the saint panels and the linenfold work are early 16th c. Flemish work.

This Gothic Revival church was completed in 1833, but there was a re-ordering of the chancel in 1887.

St Mark, Clapham Road, Kennington. Reredos: in the south aisle chapel, incorporating late medieval carved panels (? Flemish). Given in 1935 (BOE, *London 2: South*, 1983).

Victoria and Albert Museum

Carved oak panel. perforated. With *David and Bathsheba*. German or Flemish, *c*.1500 (Acq. No. 43-1852.

Stall end. Scroll-type elbow with floral volute in centre and terminations. German. 14th c. (Acq. No. 4240-1857).

Carved panel. Walnut, carved with a shield of arms surmounted by a cardinal's hat. The arms are those of Alonso de Santa Maria, Bishop of Valencia (1480-99), and were probably from the Colegio de San Gregorio, Valladolid (Acq. No. 246-1864).

Marquetry panel. Representing in low relief *Christ after the Scourging*, with female figure possibly the Virgin, looking on. Eger, Bohemia. Dated 1661 (Acq. No. 41-1869)

Panel, decorated with intarsia, representing a cupboard or cabinet with open doors and shelf, containing a chalice, pyx, and missal above, and a clock and crucifix below. Probably the work of Fra Raffaelle da Brescia for the choir of S. Michele in Bosco, near Bologna. The choir-stalls are datable to 1513-37. See M.J. Thornton, 'Three unrecorded panels by Fra Raffaelle da Brescia', *The Connoisseur*, April, 1978 (Acq. No. 150-1878).

Wood panel, painted and gilt. In the centre is a medallion with the name of the Virgin surrounded by rays. Prayers to the Virgin form the border. Estofado work. 16th c. (Acq. No. 202-1879).

Oak panel. Carved in high relief with *St Eligius exhorting King Dagobert*. Flemish 17th c. (Acq. No. 603-1883).

Walnut panel, inlaid with two curved olive branches interlacing at the bottom, and forming a compartment occupied by a censer hanging by chains from branches. Beneath is a nef. Another with stem of lilies symmetrically arranged and bound together at the bottom by a ribbon. They enclose a compartment occupied by a holy water vessel with sprinkler and inscription 'Asperges Me'. Italian (Florentine). 16th c. (Acq. No. 86 and 87-1892).

Fragment of an oak stall. With carving of a friar preaching, the pulpit is carved with three round-headed niches, enclosing figures, and rests on a pedestal. Above is a canopy carved with Gothic tracery and two grotesque masks. Northern French. Late 15th c. (Acq. No. 492-1895).

Panel, covered with gilt gesso. In the centre is a circular medallion with beaded outline, containing a representation of the Annunciation in relief, enriched with colours. Baluster-shaped columns on either side. Italian. Late 15th c. (Acq. No. 512-1895).

Four buttresses of oak, carved in relief in Gothic niches. Northern French. Early 16th c. (Acq. Nos 690 and 691-1895).

Portion of an oak pulpit, in the shape of a half octagon, consisting of a framework enclosing eight panels arranged in two rows. The panels in the upper row are carved with Gothic tracery. Below are four with specific decorative motifs, including a crowned fleur-de-lis and a shield bearing the arms of Brittany dimidiating the royal arms of France. Brittany. Late 15th c. (Acq. No. 647-1895).

Portion of an oak pulpit, in the shape of a half-octagon, consisting of a framework enclosing eight panels in two rows of four; the panels are carved as follows (left to right): 1. and 4. A shield of arms surmounted by a leafy branch and the head of a pastoral staff; 2. A tree with berries; 3. An angel supporting a shield of arms and the head of a pastoral staff. In the lower row: 1. A male head in profile facing to the left; 2. An oak tree; 3. An oak tree and a grotesque animal with a human head; 4. A tree with leaves and fruit in the branches of which is a monkey. Brittany. Early 16th c. (Acq. No. 701-1895).

Portions of an oak retable. Carved in high relief with ten figures of male and female saints. French. 16th c. (Acq. Nos 704 to 704e-1895).

Pilaster of oak, carved with a figure of Adam (the face missing) standing on a tall pedestal within a Gothic niche which is surmounted by a pinnacle. Northern French. 15th c. (Acq. No. 718-1895).

Oak panel, carved with Gothic tracery. In the centre a shield bearing a merchant's mark. From the Abbey of Cluny. Another with sacred monogram and circular framework of quatrefoils. French. Early 16th c. (Acq. Nos 743 and 771-1895).

Another panel, as above, with shield bearing a portion of a crowned letter (Acq. No. 772-1895).

Fragments of an oak screen, pierced with ogee-shaped arches, the spandrels of which are carved partly with floral ornament and partly with the following subjects: On the left of the largest fragment is *Satan tempting Christ to turn the Stones into Bread*, and on the right, *Satan tempting him to throw himself down from the Pinnacle of the Temple*. On another fragment, St John is baptising Christ and, on the third fragment, is the *Massacre of the Innocents*. French. 15th c. (Acq. Nos 776 to 776d-1895).

Portion of an oak-fronted singing gallery. Consisting of one large and five smaller panels, carved in openwork with floral scrolls, strapwork, cartouches, masks and other ornaments. At the top is a projecting rail with plain mouldings, and at the bottom are two rails similarly treated and separated from one another by three gadrooned panels and four brackets carved with acanthus leaves. French, second half 16th c. (Acq. N0.761-1895).

Walnut panel, carved *with a shield, bearing a fleur-de-lys within a border of four crosses fleury*. Above the shield is a prelate's hat, and below is Gothic tracery. Spanish. 15th c. (Acq. No. 804-1895).

Portion of an oak panel. Carved with a representation of *St Mary Magdalene meeting Christ in the Garden after the Resurrection*. The figures are beneath the canopy of a tent inscribed NOLI ME TANGERE DIXI (John xxii, 17), while above the canopy are four angels, two of which hold up the front of the tent. On either side there is a pilaster decorated with interlacing bands. Below is a panel containing two interlacing branches bearing leaves and flowers, surmounted by a band of leaf ornament and between two pilasters decorated with 'money' ornament. Northern French. Early 16th c. (Acq. No. 812-1895).

Oak stall end. Arranged in two tiers each having a pilaster carved with floral ornament on either side. The upper section contains a group of the Virgin and Child (the latter gone), and the lower a figure of St Sebastian. French. 16th c. (Acq. No. 839-1895).

Portion of oak stall standard, with kneeling female figure at elbow. French. 15th c. Ex Peyre Collection (Acq. No. 699-1897).

Portion of an oak stall terminal standard, with kneeling female figure at elbow. French. 15th c. Ex Peyre Collection (Acq. No. 699-1897).

Part of an oak stall standard. The elbow is a kneeling figure (headless). The spandrels contain foliage and vine ornament. French. 15th c. (Acq. No. 700-1897)

Part of oak stall standard, the lower part of which is carved with acanthus leaves, volutes, and a rosette from which issues a wavy stem bearing acanthus and laurel leaves. At the top is a bird's head terminating in acanthus leaves and holding in its beak a festoon of drapery, from which are suspended bundles of flowers and laurel leaves. French. 18th c. (Acq. No. 79-1898)

Oak panel, carved in the centre with the *Crucifixion* with the Virgin and St John the Evangelist. Inscription at base in German. mid-18th c. (Acq. No. 768-1899).

Lectern, a 16th c. reading desk of walnut, inlaid with wood and enriched with carving and gilding. Inscribed ASPERAMONTIS MIRANDVLE: FECIT. On the base are the arms of the Bartolini (?) family. The head consists of two sloping sides surmounted by a scrolled pediment and a book-rest below with shaped and grooved edges. One side is inlaid with the inscription surrounded by a geometrical border. The head rotates on a baluster-shaped column decorated with acanthus foliage, rosettes, imbrication and other ornament. The whole rests on a triangular base consisting of enriched voluted scrolls supported by three pawed feet. Between each pair of volutes there is a cartouche, bearing the arms, two of which have been defaced.

Two panels of carved walnut, from the choir-stalls in the cathedral of St Claude, Jura, France, carved by Jean de Vitry 1449-1465 (Acq. Nos W.176 and 177-1910). See P. Lacroix and A. Renon, *Les stalles de Jehan de Vitry*, Lyon, 1984; & C. Graham, 'Two fifteenth-century stall backs from the Jura in the Victoria and Albert Museum', *The Burlington Magazine*, May 1989, 342-45. C. Charles, *Stalles sculptés du XVe Siècle. Genève et le Duché de Savoie* (Paris 1999).

Fragment of an oak pinnacle, with the remains of gilding. Triangular in plan, the lower part has three buttresses one ending in a pinnacle, between which are two crocketed gables, and, above, a gallery of open tracery. The upper part, which is recessed, has three buttresses with pinnacles and two

traceried openings with crocketed gables. From the screen of Remagen Cathedral, Westphalia (Acq. No. W.16-1915).

Cupboard door in oak, carved with the IHS monogram enclosed by arabesque foliage. Lock missing. Flemish. Early 16th c. (Acq. No. W.498-1921).

Cedar wood panel, carved with *The Judgement of Solomon*. Italian. Early 16th c. (Acq. No. W.89-1929).

Panel of church screen in pine, with decoration carved in openwork relief, covered with paint over gesso, and partly gilt. South Italian. Late 17th c. (Acq. No. W.3-1936).

Panel in marquetry of various woods and inlay of composition and pewter, depicting the *Conversion of St Paul*. German. Early 17th c. (Acq. No. W.41-1938).

Panel in marquetry of various woods, carved in relief with a representation of the *Death of Absolom*. German (Eger), c.1660 (Acq. No. W.61-1938).

Pulpit in carved oak, consisting of console base, two sides, and a door forming a third side. The pulpit was originally attached to a pier, which formed the fourth side. Sounding board missing. The whole pulpit is carved with fleshy Rococo scrolls except for the front panel, the centre of which displays the Sacred Monogram surrounded by a sunburst within a cartouche. About one third of the base is missing, many of the scroll terminals are damaged or missing. The top of the back is missing. Flemish. Mid-18th c. (Acq. No. W.6-1962).

NORFOLK

Aslacton. Sculpture: the lectern of the pulpit is supported by a shaft with victorious David, and David and Goliath small below. Probably Flemish, 16th c. (BOE, *Norfolk 2: North-West and South*, 1999).

Crownthorpe. Pulpit: incorporates three Flemish panels of 18th c.: *Sermon on the Mount, Noli me tangere,* and the *Ascension* (BOE, *North-West and South Norfolk*, 1962. Not mentioned in the 1999 edition).

Happisburgh. Cross: on the altar, wood faced with mother-of-pearl. Probably Spanish and 17th c. (BOE, *North-East Norfolk and Norwich*, 1962. Not mentioned in the 1999 edition).

Heydon. Pulpit: Perp., on a re-used stone with fleurons. The back panel probably Flemish 18th c. (BOE, *Norfolk 1: Norwich and North-East*, 1997).

Norwich, St George Tombland. Sculpture: wood relief of St George, N. German or Flemish, c.1530 (BOE, *Norfolk 1: Norwich and North-East*, 1997).

Rushall. Prie-dieu: seems to have been made up from Spanish/Moorish screen panels, with Renaissance-type foliage decoration elsewhere.

West Acre. Sculpture: in the reredos small wooden panels with religious scenes or single figures. Mannerist pieces, no doubt from the Netherlands (BOE, *Norfolk 2: North-West and South*, 1999).

NORTHAMPTONSHIRE

Cranford St Andrew. Pulpit: with late 16th c. Flemish

panels with biblical stories. cf. Cranford St John (BOE, *Northamptonshire*, 1973).

Cranford St John. Pulpit: with two Flemish 16th c. panels with religious stories. cf. Cranford St Andrew (BOE, *Northamptonshire*, 1973).

Harlestone. Pulpit: incorporates fine Flemish panels of *c*.1500 (BOE, *Northamptonshire*, 1973).

Kelmarsh. Screen: in the tower arch. With late 16th c. or early 17th c. panels of Netherlandish *(Story of Esther)* and German origin (BOE, *Northamptonshire*, 1973).

NORTHUMBERLAND

Berwick-upon-Tweed. Late 19th c, chest in south aisle, made up from five French early 16th c. panels of *Cardinal and Theological Virtues*.

NOTTINGHAMSHIRE

Bole. Pulpit: given by a noted local Ecclesiologist, Sir H.J. Anderson. Set in it Flemish late 16th c. panels with the story of *Esther and Ahasuerus* (BOE, *Nottinghamshire*, 1979).

Stapleford. Relief: wood-carving, *Last Supper, c*.18th c. Flemish (?) (BOE, *Nottinghamshire*, 1979).

OXFORDSHIRE

Drayton. Pulpit: Victorian, but incorporating four 17th c. panels, probably Flemish, carved with biblical scenes (BOE, *Oxfordshire*, 1974).

Ducklington. Reredos: three 17th c. Flemish carved wooden panels set in a Victorian frame (BOE, *Oxfordshire*, 1974).

Holwell. Pulpit: incorporates Flemish 17th c. carved panels (BOE, *Oxfordshire*, 1974).

Oxford, St Mary Magdalen. Sculpture: female saint 17th c., perhaps German. Two reliquaries: Baroque, Continental. May be Italian (BOE, *Oxfordshire*, 1974).

Wroxton Abbey, chapel. Elaborate woodwork introduced in the 19th c. It is all 16th c. and 17th c., probably Flemish and Italian, and includes Biblical scenes around the altar and small standing figures along the gallery which runs around three sides of the chapel (BOE, *Oxfordshire*, 1974).

Wroxton. Wainscoting: in the chancel, elaborately carved with figures of saints and narrative scenes in relief. Communion rails: have 17th c. panels carved with geometrical patterns. Pulpit: made up from Continental 16th c. and 17th c. woodwork given to the church in the late 19th c. by Colonel North (BOE, *Oxfordshire*, 1974).

SHROPSHIRE

Atcham. Two Stations of the Cross reliefs. Flemish 16th c.

Oteley Park. Flemish caryatid figures incorporated into a chimney piece.

Petton. Sculpture: a Dutch panel of the *Resurrection of Christ* (Christ opsta) (BOE, *Shropshire*, 1958).

SOMERSET

Clevedon, St Andrew. Pulpit: at the back four Dutch later 16th c. panels of the *Annunciation, Nativity, Purification*

and *Circumcision* (BOE, *South and West Somerset*, 1958).

Wiveliscombe. Altar rails: with heavy balusters, said to be Flemish and 18th c. (BOE, *South and West Somerset*, 1958).

SUFFOLK

Barham. Communion rail: Italian, it seems, and dated 1700. With putti and dolphins. Another part of the same rail is used in the Middleton Chapel. Probably not originally communion rails because they seem to have been made from a cut-down full size screen. (BOE, *Suffolk*, 1974 and observation by Hugh Harrison.)

Barking. Pulpit: incorporating one Flemish late 16th c. or early 17th c. relief (BOE, *Suffolk*, 1974).

Cavendish. Sculpture: south chapel altar: Flemish 16th c. relief of the *Crucifixion*. From private chapel of Athelstan Riley's house in London. Unfortunately it has been horribly overpainted. It is none the less of great interest because much of it is in alabaster. (BOE, *Suffolk*, 1974 and author.)

Falkenham. Reredos: this incorporates some fine tracery panels, supposed to come from a Flemish chest (BOE, *Suffolk*, 1974).

Stowlangtoft. Left and right of the reredos nine Flemish early 16th c. reliefs.

Wangford, near Southwold. Pulpit and reader's desk: made up of 17th c. woodwork from Henham Hall, supposedly Flemish. Much fine marquetry (BOE, *Suffolk*, 1974).

Seckford Hall, near Woodbridge. Two late 17th c. Flemish cherub heads with wings, on scrolls. In dining room.

SURREY

Cranleigh. Lectern: late 16th c., a twisted column with vine fruit and foliage for a stem and a strapwork base. The desk is 19th c., but there is evidence for an earlier one at the top of the stem. The stylistic dissimilarity between the stem and the base suggests that the components are disparate, and may have been brought together in the 19th c.

Dorking. Pulpit: said to have been brought from Holland in about 1837 for the former church. In fact, the carcase is 19th c. work, but it incorporates a panel with *St Martin and the Beggar*, probably 17th c., and figures of apostles and busts of angels, which appear to be late Gothic (BOE, *Surrey*, 1971).

Gatton. Doors: from Rouen in the south transept, carved in linenfold pattern. The framework is 19th c. Chancel panelling: completely surrounding a 13th c. piscina from the original church. From Burgundy; Pulpit: suspended at first-floor level as part of the south transept gallery front. The carved scenes of *c*.1530 formed part of the same composition as the carvings now made up into the altar table. They have been attributed to Dürer, but they are probably Flemish (BOE, *Surrey*, 1971).

Littleton. Rood screen: the heavily-restored screenwork of this made-up ensemble is Flemish, early 16th c.

Mickleham. Pulpit: Belgian, of about 1600, with ornately carved scenes on the panels and saints under crockets on the corners. Altered in restoration. (BOE, *Surrey*, 1971.)

SUSSEX

Brede. Chest: dated 1633, with religious scenes on front, sides, and top. Scandinavian. An enterprising 19th c. conflation. (Stolen.)

Slaugham. Wood panels: early 16th c. Next to the pulpit, four with linenfold, two with small standing saints, perhaps from the lower Rhine or Holland. A yet smaller panel of the same style in the vestry (BOE, *Sussex*, 1965).

Ticehurst. North chapel. Four small Netherlandish Mannerist panels (BOE, *Sussex*, 1965).

Turner's Hill. Reredos: said to have been brought from St Mary Poultry when that City church by Wren was pulled down in 1872. A composite piece, the caryatids mostly from one source, the upper reliefs – German or Netherlandish 17th c.? – from another, and the principal relief probably from yet another. Two of the caryatids must be Victorian (BOE, *Sussex*, 1965).

Twineham. Reredos: some probably French or Italian panels with Flamboyant tracery (BOE, *Sussex*, 1965).

West Grinstead, St George. Panelling: in the chapel. Renaissance, undoubtedly. But whose Renaissance and where from? Religious scenes above, profile heads underneath (BOE, *Sussex*, 1965).

WARWICKSHIRE

Oscott College, Sutton Coldfield. Confessional: A confection of A.W.N. Pugin's, with an arcade supported by 17th c. caryatid figures. Massive cornice above crowned by a broken arch with cartouche in the centre. All of this top section and the whole carcase is 19th c.

Shotteswell. Sculpture: behind the altar religious scenes, Flemish, early 17th c. (BOE, *Warwickshire*, 1966).

Wasperton. Pulpit: with Flemish carved scenes of *c.*1600 (BOE, *Warwickshire*, 1966).

WILTSHIRE

Bishopstone. In the chancel, made-up choir benches with 16th c. panelled backs.

Brixton Deverill. Sculpture: four Flemish panels with scenes from *Genesis*.

Grittleton. Screen: with oval, probably French 18th c. panels.

Kingston Deverill. Pulpit: with Flemish panels of Flamboyant tracery (BOE, *Wiltshire*, 1975).

Wilton. Reading desk: with Flemish, possibly Spanish Baroque reliefs; Doors: modern but with old panels: Flemish 16th c. (north aisle), Flemish 16th c., and others, west doors (BOE, *Wiltshire*, 1975).

WORCESTERSHIRE

Broadway, St Eadburga. Sculpture: wood panel with eight small saints. It looks Flemish and may be the front of a chest (BOE, *Worcestershire*, 1968).

Ipsley. Sculpture: *Sacrifice of Isaac;* small Netherlandish wood relief, probably early 17th c. (BOE, *Worcestershire*, 1968).

YORKSHIRE

Bradfield (West Riding). Reredos: including medieval panels from Caen (bought in 1887) (BOE, *Yorkshire: The West Riding*, 1986).

Ecclesfield (West Riding). Pulpit: 1880s, incorporating four historiated panels, including scenes of *Christ Calming the Storm* and *Christ Disputing with the Elders*. Said to be Antwerp work. Reredos: Four more Continental panels in this Victorian ensemble, including a scene of *Christ at Emmaus* and *Moses Striking the Rock*.

Kilnwick Percy (East Riding). Woodwork: A surprising array of largely 17th and 18th c. woodwork which was collected by Robert Denison in London and on the Continent in the early 19th c. (cf. the altarpiece at Pocklington). It is of mixed quality but some is superb, much of it Flemish. Carved figures, biblical reliefs and decorative friezes and panels have been fixed to the pulpit, reading desk, communion rail and the box pews in the chancel. One of the panels fixed to the front of the nave pews is dated 1633. Where more was needed, e.g. for two figures along the communion rail and the frieze around the nave, it is reproduced in cast iron, c.f. some of the pulpit panels at Otterbourne, Hampshire (BOE, *Yorkshire: York and the East Riding*, 1995, and author).

Methley (West Riding). Lectern: incorporating three carved early 16th c. German figures. Hexagonal base and eagle 19th c. (BOE, *Yorkshire: The West Riding*, 1986, and author).

Rosedale (North Riding). Lectern: said to come from Holland. An angel holds it up on his wings. He grows out of a term pillar. Foot with putto heads. Foliage decoration too. The date may be the late 17th c. This is a made-up piece, with a modern base. (BOE, *Yorkshire: The North Riding*, 1966, and author.)

Welburn Hall (North Riding). Two winged seraph-like figures, supporting a mantelpiece, one holding a sword, the other a key. Flemish, late 17th c.

Well (North Riding). This 'reredos' incorporates five historiated panels, from left to right portraying: *Adam and Eve; The Sacrifice of Isaac; The Annunciation; The Adoration of the Shepherds;* and *Christ rising from the Tomb* (stolen). Above is an inscription in Dutch from John, 3, 16. This object was formerly in the chapel of nearby Snape Castle. It is not thought to have been a reredos but part of some secular furniture.

West Tanfield (North Riding). Two 17th c. Flemish oval plaques showing: 1. St Nicholas and 2. *Simeon blessing Christ.*

Wragby (West Riding). Pulpit: 19th c. structure but incorporates four Venetian panels from the *Life of Christ* in Turkish boxwood; Lectern: 19th c. structure, but incorporates 18th c. Flemish figure of a saint.

Index (*Introduction and Chapters I-V*)

References in italic type indicate plates